INTERPERSONAL COMMUNICATION

Second Edition

AN OVERVIEW OF BASIC PRINCIPLES AND CONTEXTS

endall Hunt
blishing company

DITORS:

dd Lee Goen, Brianna Lane, Linda D. Manning, and Alice E. Veksler

www.kendallhunt.com
Send all inquiries to:
4050 Westmark Drive
Dubuque, IA 52004-1840

Contents

chapter **3**   Nonverbal Communication: It's Not *What* You Said;
It's *How* You Said It   45

chapter **4**   Understanding Self   71

chapter **9**   Terminating Relationships: Knowing When to
Throw in the Towel   235

chapter **13**   Health Communication   347

Interpersonal Communication:
Significance and Explanation of Key Concepts

OBJECTIVES

- Identify three mistakes prospective employees often make in job interview situations.
- Cite three to four examples of research that emphasize the importance of effective interpersonal communication.
- Define the term communication competence and describe the three components of Spitzberg and Cupach's component model of communication competence.
- Define interpersonal communication and distinguish it from other types of communication (e.g., intrapersonal, small group, organizational).
- Explain the four different approaches to defining interpersonal communication.
- Describe the pivotal research and historical events that contributed to the development of the field of interpersonal communication.
- Define the term theory and explain the four goals of a theory.

SCENARIO: SOUND FAMILIAR?

Emma is a business major who is required to enroll in an interpersonal communication (IPC) class at her university. As she walks to her first class, she thinks to herself, "Why do I need an interpersonal communication course? I have at least a thousand followers on Twitter and Instagram and two thousand Facebook friends." Because she exchanges hundreds of text messages regularly with her friends, family members, and boyfriend, she certainly does not need a class on how to communicate!

KEY TERMS

Attribution theory	Interpersonal	Mass communication
Communication	communication	Message-centered
competence	(IPC)	approach
Connected individuals	Intrapersonal	Motivation
Content component	communication	Metacommunication
Context	Kinesics	Organizational
Developmental	Knowledge	communication
approach	Maslow's hierarchy of	Process
Interactional approach	needs	Proxemics

Relational component	Skill	Theory
Roles	Small group	Verbal and nonverbal
Rules	communication	component
Shared meaning	Symbolic	
Situational approach	interactionism	

OVERVIEW

This scenario illustrates a phenomenon that has dramatically changed the way we establish and maintain connections with others. In Sherry Turkle's (2012) *New York Times* article, "The Flight from Conversation," she argues that many people have sacrificed meaningful face-to-face conversations for mere *connection* through different forms of technology. Turkle describes how we connect to others through technologies such as cell phones and computers and simultaneously customize our lives by controlling the images and messages we share with others. These technologies are often used strategically to manage our self-images. For example, we may post only certain pictures on Facebook or Instagram and edit tweets or text messages to be certain that we are depicted in a favorable light.

Despite all of our seemingly widespread social *connections*, Turkle notes that we often find ourselves "alone together" and, as a result of this, our interpersonal communication skills are starting to deteriorate. In the past it was important to hold eye contact while speaking with someone; today, an essential "skill" is being able to maintain eye contact with someone while sending text messages (Turkle, 2012). This example illustrates one of the many challenges we face as we attempt to learn more about what it means to be a competent communicator. Helping students become more competent communicators and establish healthy interpersonal relationships are the primary objectives of this textbook. In the next sections we examine two broad reasons to study interpersonal communication: improving our communication in professional and personal relationships.

WHY STUDY INTERPERSONAL COMMUNICATION?

Significance of Interpersonal Communication (IPC) in Establishing Professional Relationships

One probable reason for taking this course is to improve your ability to communicate in the workplace. Virtually all job applications list "strong interpersonal communication skills" as a job requirement. Prospective employees are expected to understand what it means to possess "strong interpersonal communication skills" when they apply and interview for positions. Can you identify several examples of strong interpersonal communication skills? Not surprisingly, many interviewees do not know what this entails and often fail to display appropriate interpersonal skills in the interview process. As a result of this, they are not hired.

Here are some research conclusions that highlight the importance of communication skills in the workplace:

- Personnel interviewers indicate that strong communication skills are essential for success in corporate settings; however, only 60 percent feel that applicants exhibit effective communication skills during job interviews. The five most frequently identified verbal and nonverbal communication skill inadequacies exhibited during interview situations include: topic relevance, response organization, response clarity, grammar, and response feedback (Peterson, 1997, p. 289).
- A recent Forbes.com article identified active listening skills as one of the top four skills needed to gain employment in 2013 (Casserly, 2012). If job applicants do not actively listen during interviews, they are more likely to provide responses that are irrelevant, disorganized, or inaccurate.
- Even job candidates for prestigious positions such as presidents, provosts, and deans make numerous communication mistakes. Dennis Barden (2013), a search firm executive in higher education, notes that prospective job candidates make mistakes such as dressing inappropriately for the position, telling the search committee what they think they want to hear, and talking too much during interviews.

What interpersonal skills are important to exhibit during a job interview?

Once you get the job, it is important to communicate effectively to keep your job, establish strong work relationships, and move up in your organization. Regardless of the profession you enter, it is very likely that effective communication skills will be required for your success.

A number of studies point out the importance of communication skills in maintaining employment and succeeding in your chosen profession. Consider the following research:

- Health care professionals who participate in interpersonal skills training improve their ability to treat patients (Rath et al., 1998).
- Health care providers who communicate effectively (i.e., are clear, immediate, humorous, etc.) have more satisfied patients (Wanzer, Booth-Butterfield, & Gruber, 2004).
- A study published in the *Harvard Business Review* found most people would rather work with "loveable fools" than "competent jerks." Being perceived as likeable may help individuals establish relationships and succeed in the workplace, even when task competence is lacking (Casciaro & Lobo, 2005).

Inaccurate Depiction of Communication in the Corporate World: Use of the Term "Soft Skills"

Developing strong interpersonal skills is more necessary than ever to negotiate in today's "bigger is better" business environment (Myers & Tucker, 2005). Organizations have undergone radical changes resulting in a

Regardless of the profession you enter, it is very likely that effective communication skills will be required for your success.

Individuals who are able to communicate effectively are not only happier and more satisfied with their relationships, but they are also healthier.

more diverse workforce, a greater ability to obtain and process information through the Internet, and an expanding global marketplace, which makes doing business with people from other cultures easier than ever before.

According to management professors Laura Myers and Mary Tucker, as these changes occur, more emphasis is being placed on "people skills" in business programs across the nation and the specific "soft skills" that distinguish effective from ineffective managers. Your textbook authors dislike the term "soft skills" because this label seems to imply that communication is easy, effortless, and unimportant. Communicating effectively is difficult! Instead of using the term "soft skills" to describe interpersonal communication skills, we recommend using the term "essential skills." This term illustrates the significance of IPC skills in workplace and relationship success. Because language influences thought, we need to change the words we use to describe communication to influence the way people think about communication. Using more powerful language to describe interpersonal communication (i.e., "essential skills" versus "soft skills") may alter the way people perceive and approach communication.

Effective managers must be able to deliver constructive criticism, manage conflicts between employees, persuade and influence individuals at all levels, provide support and guidance, and exhibit appropriate leadership behaviors. There is nothing "soft" or easy about executing those skills in the workplace!

A number of chapters in this textbook are intended to help you to become a more effective interviewee and employee, particularly the chapters on verbal and nonverbal communication, perception and listening, relationship maintenance and conflict, and organizational communication.

Significance of IPC in Establishing Personal Relationships

Throughout your lives you will use interpersonal communication skills to establish and maintain a number of important relationships that exist outside of the workplace setting. While establishing and maintaining healthy relationships with family members, friends, relationship partners, and members of the community takes a great deal of time and effort, it is well worth the work! The interpersonal communication concepts, models, theories, and skills you will learn about in this textbook will assist you in the process of managing these different types of relationships. Individuals who are able to communicate effectively are not only happier and more satisfied with their relationships, but they are also healthier.

IPC and Health Social science researchers have had a longstanding interest in the relationship between communication practices and health. Not surprisingly, people who have the ability to communicate effectively (i.e., express emotions, listen effectively, manage conflict) often lead healthier lives. Conversely, those who are unable to communicate effectively often experience health problems. The inability to communicate effectively and establish meaningful relationships can have deleterious effects on your mental and physical health. Several studies highlight the association between satisfying relationships and mental and physical health:

- Effective communication and rewarding relationships with others are closely connected to both mental and physical health (Burleson & MacGeorge, 2002; Omarzu, Whalen, & Harvey, 2001).
- People who report high levels of social isolation and loneliness often lack the skills needed to establish and maintain healthy relationships. Research indicates that socially isolated and lonely individuals are less likely to exercise regularly and more likely to smoke and to experience other significant health problems (Shankar, McMunn, Banks, & Steptoe, 2011).
- A meta-analysis of 32 studies (involving more than 6.5 million people) found a significant increase in risk for premature death among separated/divorced individuals over married individuals (Sbarra, Law, & Portley, 2011).
- Knowing that others will "be there" for us during stressful or traumatic times in our lives offers us a sense of perceived social support, which correlates to mental well-being (Burleson & MacGeorge, 2002).
- Daniel Goleman (2006) argues that our social brains are biologically "wired to connect" with those around us. According to Goleman (2006) "our social interactions even play a role in reshaping our brain, through 'neuroplasticity,' which means that repeated experiences sculpt the shape, size, and number of neurons and their synaptic connections" (p. 11).
- The ongoing relationships we establish can shape the intricate "wiring" or neural circuitry of our brain. To further emphasize the link between our relationships and our health, Goleman describes unhealthy or abusive relationships as "toxic" to our social brains and healthy relationships as "vitamins." Thus, when we are around individuals who love and support us, this experience is analogous to taking vitamins that assist in the functioning of our social brains (Goleman, 2006).

Many interpersonal communication scholars agree that effective communication is essential to achieving healthy relationships. When communication between individuals deteriorates or ceases to exist, relationships are often doomed to failure. A significant body of research focuses on the relationship between specific communication patterns or practices, such as emotional communication, and relationship satisfaction and longevity (see, for example, Burleson & MacGeorge, 2002; Burleson & Samter, 1996; Metts & Planalp, 2002; Noller & Feeney, 1994; Roloff & Soule, 2002).

Interpersonal communication researchers have studied nearly all aspects of romantic and platonic relationships, including how people come together to form meaningful relationships (Knapp & Vangelisti, 2000), how they maintain these relationships (Canary & Stafford, 2001), the factors individuals consider when deciding to terminate a relationship, and the methods used to disengage these relationships (Baxter, 1982; Cody, 1982). Learning about effective communication practices can assist individuals throughout every stage of relationship development, from the beginning stages when individuals are uncertain about how to proceed, to the relational maintenance stage, or to the end of a romantic relationship. In this textbook we provide you with several chapters that focus on the stages of relationship development as well as the communication practices that both contribute to and detract from a relationship's reported "health."

The following sections of this chapter highlight the broad learning objectives to be addressed throughout this textbook. While there are specific learning objectives and key terms for each chapter, the following three primary objectives are the overall purpose of this textbook.

The first objective of this textbook:

1. Students will learn about a wide range of communication concepts and theories that are central to the process of interpersonal communication.

In this chapter we define interpersonal communication and distinguish it from other forms of communication. Also, in an effort to better understand the "roots" of interpersonal communication, we discuss its history, with an emphasis on classic research and on the historical events that stimulated interest in this topic. Throughout the entire textbook you will see numerous bold-faced terms, concepts, and theories that we consider central to understanding the process of interpersonal communication. Our hope is that you will be able to define these terms and concepts and relate them to your own experiences.

The second objective of our textbook:

2. Students will become more competent communicators.

Communication competence the ability to send messages that are perceived as appropriate and effective by receivers.

Knowledge component of the communication competence model that refers to understanding what reaction or action is best suited for a particular situation.

Skill component of the communication competence model that addresses the ability to utilize the appropriate behaviors in a situation.

Motivation component of the communication competence model that refers to the desire to achieve results in a competent manner.

Many of you are probably taking this course to improve your ability to send and receive messages from others, also known as communication competence. Communication competence is defined as the ability to send messages that are perceived as appropriate and effective by receivers (Spitzberg & Cupach, 1984). The model most often used to describe communication competence is the Components Model advanced by Spitzberg and Cupach. This model highlights three key components of communication competence: knowledge, skill, and motivation.

The knowledge component of this model refers to understanding what reaction or action is best suited for a particular situation. Taking a class in interpersonal communication is the first step in acquiring knowledge and information about the process of forming relationships with others. The skill component of this model addresses the ability to utilize the appropriate behaviors in a situation. It is important to remember that there is a difference between *knowing* how to do something (e.g., knowledge of interpersonal models, theories, and concepts) and actually *being able* to do it. For example, a person may understand the principles and concepts associated with managing conflict in relationships. However, when the time comes to put that knowledge to use, it may be difficult to engage in the appropriate behaviors. The final component of the model, motivation, refers to the desire to achieve results in a competent manner. It is not enough to have knowledge and skills. You must also have a desire to achieve communication competence. To assess your current level of communication competence, we suggest you complete the Communication Competence Scale found in the final pages of this chapter at the beginning of the course, and then again at the end of the semester.

It is not enough to have knowledge and skills. You must also have a desire to achieve communication competence.

While we can address the knowledge and skill aspects of communication competence, it is up to you to become more motivated and make attempts to achieve your interpersonal goals. Many of the chapters in this textbook offer valuable information about the communication process and emphasize specific communication behaviors linked to interpersonal communication competence. For example, our chapter on perception and listening highlights specific communication behaviors associated with effective communication. We often forget to focus on the process of message reception, which is why listening is often referred to as the "forgotten" communication skill. Also, in Chapters 2 and 3 we focus on the highly complex process of sending and receiving verbal and nonverbal messages. By calling attention to certain important aspects of nonverbal messages such as dress, body movements, gestures, or eye contact, we hope students will hone in on the specific skills needed to communicate more effectively.

The third and final objective of the textbook:

3. Students will achieve rewarding personal and professional relationships.

People communicate and ultimately establish different types of relationships to satisfy three universal human needs: control, inclusion, and affection (Schutz, 1966). We communicate with others and establish relationships to control or manage our surroundings, to be part of a group, and to fulfill the need to feel liked. Virtually every chapter in this textbook explains interpersonal communication concepts and theories that will help you understand how relationships work. By teaching you the important communication concepts that are central to understanding the process of interpersonal communication, and by helping you acquire the skills needed to communicate more effectively, we are certain that our third and final goal will be met. And so we begin our journey by clarifying what we mean when we use the term *interpersonal communication*.

WHAT EXACTLY IS INTER-PERSONAL COMMUNICATION?

Communication researchers continue to study many forms of communication, including:

- Mass or mediated communication
- Organizational communication
- Small group communication
- Intrapersonal communication
- Interpersonal communication

Mass or Mediated Communication   The study of mediated communication involves communicators who are typically separated by both space and time and who send and receive messages indirectly. Mass communication typically occurs when a small number of people send messages to a large, diverse and geographically widespread population (Cathcart & Gumpert, 1983; Kreps & Thorton, 1992).

Mass communication involves communicators who are typically separated in both space and time and who send and receive messages indirectly; typically occurs when a small number of people send messages to a large, diverse, and geographically widespread population.

Often people in small groups are working to achieve a set goal.

Organizational communication communication that occurs within businesses or organizations; takes place between organization members within a clear hierarchical structure; individuals are typically encouraged to adhere to roles and rules established within this structure.

Small group communication interaction among a small group of people who share a common purpose or goal, who feel a sense of belonging to the group, and who exert influence on one another.

Intrapersonal communication takes place inside your head and is silent and repetitive.

Interpersonal communication (IPC) a complex process that occurs in a specific context and involves an exchange of verbal or nonverbal messages between two connected individuals with the intent to achieve shared meaning.

Situational approach focuses on the specific features or aspects of the communication context in defining the type of communication taking place.

Organizational Communication Communication scholars also study organizational communication, which is recognized as communication that occurs within businesses or organizations. Organizational communication takes place between organization members within a clear hierarchical structure; individuals are typically encouraged to adhere to roles and rules established within this structure. In this text, we examine the role of interpersonal communication in organizations, and different types of relationships in this context will be discussed.

Small Group Communication Small group communication, another area frequently studied by communication scholars, is defined as "interaction among a small group of people who share a common purpose or goal, who feel a sense of belonging to the group, and who exert influence on one another" (Beebe & Masterson, 1997, p. 6). Small group communication is complex and often occurs between three or more people who are interdependent and working to achieve commonly recognized goals or objectives.

Intrapersonal Communication Intrapersonal communication, the most basic level of communication, takes place inside your head and is silent and repetitive (Kreps & Thorton, 1992). Many of us talk to ourselves, which often affects our interpersonal communication decisions. Think about a time when you rehearsed what you were going to say before engaging in a conversation with someone. Perhaps it was a situation where you were building up the courage to ask someone on a date, or maybe you planned out a conversation with a colleague regarding a project at work. These examples would fall under intrapersonal communication. This type of communication is often repetitive and can be motivational. Think about a time when you were running the last few yards of a race and you told yourself, "Keep going" or "You can do it!"

Interpersonal Communication Interpersonal communication, sometimes referred to as *dyadic* communication or IPC, is often loosely described as communication that occurs between two individuals. While most agree that interpersonal communication typically involves at least two people (Knapp, Daly, Albada, & Miller, 2002), there is great disparity in the actual definitions advanced by interpersonal communication researchers.

There are four distinct approaches to defining IPC: situational, developmental, interactional, and message-centered (Burleson, 2010). All four definitions are important and help us understand what it means to engage in interpersonal communication.

Situational definitions of interpersonal communication were the first to emerge in the field (Miller, 1990). These definitions focus on the specific features or aspects of the communication context in defining the type of communication taking place. In offering a situational definition of interpersonal communication, the most important features are the number of interactants and the exchange of messages (Burleson, 2010). An example of a situational definition is "two people exchanging messages with each other." A criticism of situational definitions of IPC is that they seem to focus more on the number of interactants and contextual factors and less on the quality of the relationship and the specific messages exchanged (Miller, 1978).

Instead of emphasizing the number of interactants involved and the context, developmental definitions focus more on qualitative aspects of the relationship and information exchanged when defining IPC. According to this approach, IPC occurs only when individuals develop a reciprocal relationship and relate to each other as unique individuals (Burleson, 2010). DeVito's (2001) definition of interpersonal communication, "communication that takes place between two persons who have an established relationship; the people are in some way connected," emphasizes the qualitative aspect of the relationship and falls under the developmental definitions.

The third type of definition, interactional, "treats most, if not all, cases of social interaction as instances of interpersonal communication" (Burleson, 2010, p. 150). Cappella (1987) describes interpersonal communication as one person influencing another person's behavior, above and beyond that explained by "normal baselines of action" (p. 228). We agree with Burleson and other scholars who argue that, while these approaches address the importance of interaction in IPC, they appear to neglect or underemphasize the role that verbal and nonverbal messages play in creating meaning.

> Interpersonal communication, sometimes referred to as *dyadic communication*, is often loosely described as communication that occurs between two individuals.

The message-centered approach to defining IPC advanced by Burleson (2010) addresses limitations in the other approaches and argues that definitions should emphasize processes involved in producing and interpreting messages. For example, Burleson's (2010) definition of IPC focuses on the importance of a communicative relationship between social interactants as well as the significance of both expressive and interpretive intent. According to Burleson (2010), IPC "is a complex, situational social process in which people who have established a communicative relationship exchange messages in an effort to generate shared meanings and accomplish social goals" (p. 151). This definition emphasizes the importance of exchanging messages (verbal and nonverbal) to reach goals or objectives during interaction and agree on what messages mean.

Working from a message-centered approach to defining IPC, we define interpersonal communication *as a complex process that occurs in a specific context and involves an exchange of verbal or nonverbal messages between two connected individuals with the intent to achieve shared meaning.* While there is a wide range of definitions available, we chose one that emphasizes the importance of communication as a complicated process that consists of the intentional exchange of both verbal and nonverbal messages and results in shared understandings between connected interactants. Similar to the views expressed by Burleson in the message-centered approach, our definition addresses the following key elements of interpersonal communication:

- Process—The process is complex and includes message production, message reception, and message interpretation. All of these processes are related and must be coordinated. Communication is also described as a process because it is continuous, or ongoing (Berlo, 1960).
- Context—All communication occurs in a context or situation. People assume different roles (parts that people play) and adhere to different

Developmental approach focuses more on qualitative aspects of the relationship and information exchanged when defining IPC.

Interactional approach treats most, if not all, cases of social interaction as instances of interpersonal communication.

Message-centered approach addresses limitations in the other approaches and argues that definitions should emphasize processes involved in producing and interpreting messages.

Process includes message production, message reception, and message interpretation.

Context the situation in which communication takes place.

Roles parts that people play.

Rules guidelines for social interaction.

Verbal and nonverbal component IPC consists of both verbal (words/symbols) and nonverbal (everything else other than the words exchanged) messages.

Connected individuals When two or more people come together to communicate, they are connected by a common social goal, which is to create meaning.

Shared meaning the source and receiver agree on the meaning of the verbal and nonverbal messages exchanged; primary goal of interpersonal communication.

rules (guidelines for social interaction) depending on the communication situation; hence, where the communication occurs often helps us determine our roles and rules in the situation.

- Verbal messages—Communication involves the use of words or symbols (additional information in Chapter 2).
- Nonverbal messages—Communication also involves the use of nonverbal messages, which are defined as everything else other than the words exchanged (i.e., eye contact, facial expressions, gestures, clothing, artifacts, etc.) (additional information in Chapter 3).
- Connected individuals—When two or more people come together to communicate, they are connected by a common social goal, which is to create meaning.
- Shared meaning—The primary goal of interpersonal communication is to achieve shared meaning; that is, the source and receiver agree on the meaning of the verbal and nonverbal messages exchanged.

| Figure 1.1 | **Key elements of IPC** |

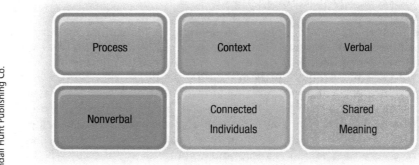

© Kendall Hunt Publishing Co.

BASIC PRINCIPLES OF INTERPERSONAL COMMUNICATION

Now that you understand what interpersonal communication is, as well as the key elements of interpersonal communication, it is important to understand more about the nature of IPC. In the next section we highlight basic principles of interpersonal communication. These basic principles have been endorsed by numerous communication scholars and are related to a number of IPC theories, concepts, and models. As you begin your journey to becoming a more competent communicator and establishing rewarding relationships, it is important to understand these four principles as they relate to IPC:

1. Interpersonal communication is irreversible.
2. Interpersonal communication can be intentional or unintentional.
3. Interpersonal communication is dynamic.
4. Interpersonal communication is composed of content and relational components.

PRINCIPLE 1: Interpersonal communication is irreversible. First, interpersonal communication is irreversible. This means that once you say something, you cannot take it back. It is permanent. You cannot remediate or replace remarks by saying, "Oh, forget I said that." Do you remember the last time someone asked you, "How do I look?" The slightest pause or facial expression on your part cannot be taken back once it is detected by the receiver. Once we communicate something, verbally or nonverbally, it cannot be undone.

It is important to note that each interpersonal communication exchange we have affects future interactions. For example, Joe is at a party and tells a sexist joke to Kayla, who is someone he just met for the first time. Joe can't undo this interaction with Kayla and the next time Kayla sees Joe she will remember him as the guy who told the inappropriate dumb blonde joke. Since Joe can't erase his comments and the impression he made, what can he do to fix the situation and alter Kayla's impression?

If you thought that Joe should apologize to Kayla for the dumb blonde joke, you are correct. Darby and Schlenker (1982) define apologies as "admissions of blameworthiness and regret for an undesirable event" (p. 743). In order to manage your impression effectively, it is important to deliver an apology that is sincere. An effective apology typically includes the following elements: (1) admitting fault, (2) admitting damage, (3) expressing remorse, (4) asking for pardon, and (5) offering compensation (Darby & Schlenker, 1982; Schlenker & Darby, 1981).

Based on this information Joe might say to Kayla, "The joke I told you the last time we met was offensive, and I probably hurt your feelings. I feel horrible about what I said to you and I hope you will forgive me. Maybe I can buy you coffee sometime?"

PRINCIPLE 2: Interpersonal communication can be intentional or unintentional. Communication scholars often assert that "one cannot not communicate" (Watzlawick et al., 1967, p. 51) because during interpersonal encounters it is likely people will attach meaning to everything you say and do. Intentional messages are often perceived when sources exhibit nonverbal behaviors such as eye contact, gestures and body movements, facial expressions, and touch. It is often the case that receivers perceive these nonverbal behaviors exhibited by sources as intentional nonverbal communication. Remember Joe from the last scenario? Let's say his apology to Kayla was effective and they started dating. Joe decides to drop in and visit Kayla after class. When he enters her apartment, he sees Kayla slouched on the couch with a dazed look on her

© g-stockstudio/Shutterstock.com

© Pressmaster/Shutterstock.com

© conejota/Shutterstock.com

Just by looking at their expressions and gestures, can you tell what these individuals are feeling?

> Once we communicate something, verbally or nonverbally, it cannot be undone.

face and her arms hanging limply at her sides. Joe asks Kayla, "Why are you so upset?" He perceived the dazed facial expression and slouched body position as the message "I am upset" when, in actuality, Kayla was just tired and thinking about whether she passed her philosophy exam.

PRINCIPLE 3: **Interpersonal communication is dynamic.** Since communication in interpersonal relationships is a process and is constantly evolving, each time we speak with someone, we are building on previous messages. We are developing a history with this person and, therefore, our communication reflects this change. Think about the conversations you have with your closest friends. Because you have probably spent countless hours discussing family, friends, career goals, and other topics of mutual interest, it is not necessary to revisit these conversations in detail each time you see each other. Instead, you may make quick references to previously discussed events in your conversations.

Joe and Kayla have been dating for almost a year. Their communication, like their relationship, has changed dramatically and they now know a great deal about each other. Kayla teases Joe about their first meeting and asks, "Remember the joke you told me when we first met? Nice!" Joe does not answer this question because he knows this is an inside joke they often share with each other. Joe smiles and laughs at this comment and then asks Kayla a series of questions about her day. Joe asks about Kayla's classes, work schedule, and plans for the week. Asking these types of questions illustrates how conversations and relationships evolve over time.

Content component
informational component of a message; the verbal message you send or the specific words you choose.

Relational component
composed of information that indicates how people feel about their relationship.

PRINCIPLE 4: **Interpersonal communication is composed of relational and content components.** Each message exchanged between interactants is made up of two types of meaning: content and relational (Bateson, 1951). The content, or informational component of a message, is the verbal message you send or the specific words you choose. The relational component of a message is composed of information that indicates how people feel about their relationship. These signals might include nonverbal messages such as eye contact, gestures, facial expressions, and vocal inflection. The relational component of the message tells the receiver how you would like the message to be interpreted as well as how you view your relationship (i.e., intimate, platonic, impersonal, etc.). Consider the following situation.

Joe: I just got us tickets to see the Sabres play the Penguins next Friday!

Kayla: Shut up!

Joe: I know, I really can't believe I was able to get these tickets!

Kayla: Shut up! You really are the best!

Accurately interpreting this conversation requires us to focus on both the *content* and the *relational* information in the message. By examining both the parts of the message we should be able to determine the type of relationship Joe and Kayla have with each other, their level of intimacy, and power distribution.

After Joe tells Kayla he purchased Sabres tickets, she tells him to "Shut up!" If we just examined the content or words in this exchange, we might think Kayla is more powerful, doesn't want Joe to talk anymore, and is being rude. A closer examination of this exchange requires us to also consider the relational components of this message. The relational information may be conveyed through idiosyncratic verbal (i.e., "Shut up!") and nonverbal messages (i.e. smiling, facial expressions, emphasis) that signal the type of relationship that exists between Joe and Kayla. When Kayla smiles and lightly taps Joe on the arm when she says, "Shut up!" this indicates how she feels about the message and her relationship with Joe. By examining both the content and relational information in this conversation, we might conclude that Joe and Kayla are in a close relationship where they are able to joke around with each other.

> More often than not, people engage in metacommunication to clarify relational information to better understand message content.

Metacommunication an important tool that is often used during social interaction to increase our shared meaning and to reduce uncertainty about the status of our relationships; "communicating about communication."

Relational information is important because it affects how people interpret message content. A friend might say to her roommate, "What did you mean when you said 'I am fine' in that tone of voice?" Or a man might ask his significant other, "I think we need to talk about why you've been so quiet lately." Often people engage in what Gregory Bateson (1972) conceptualized as metacommunication, "communicating about communication," when they want to clarify a message's meaning. More often than not, people engage in metacommunication to clarify relational information to better understand message content. Metacommunication is an important tool that is often used during social interaction to increase our shared meaning and to reduce uncertainty about the status of our relationships.

How important is it to engage in metacommunication? If we Google "relationship talk," this search results in millions of sources or "hits" emphasizing the importance of talking about the communication that occurs between parents and children, relationship partners, friends, coworkers, health care providers and patients, etc. Not surprisingly, the inability to communicate effectively about communication (i.e., "What did you mean when you said…?") can cause problems for both sources and receivers. This book will explore the importance of effective relationship communication in depth.

© Advertising Group/Shutterstock.com

How important is it for children to feel comfortable talking with their parents?

HISTORY OF INTERPERSONAL COMMUNICATION

In order to completely understand an academic area, you must start at its roots. In the *Handbook of Interpersonal Communication*, Knapp, Daly, Albada, and Miller (2002) provide an overview of the historical foundations of the field of interpersonal communication. The introductory chapter of the *Handbook* is dedicated to providing a framework for tracing the development of the field. Readers are presented with a timeline highlighting the accomplishments of scholars who have made prominent contributions to the understanding of relational communication.

According to Knapp and his colleagues (2002), one of the most influential studies for providing a framework for both interpersonal and organizational communication was the result of research conducted by Elton Mayo from 1927 until 1932 at the Western Electric Hawthorne Works in Chicago. Mayo, a professor at the Harvard Business School, originally designed the study to examine the impact of fatigue and monotony on work production. But while the study was designed to focus on one aspect of the work process, an interesting thing happened. Mayo discovered that social relationships and, more specifically, positive interactions between coworkers and supervisors, resulted in higher productivity. The Mayo study is an excellent example of how researchers sometimes stumble upon unexpected results that change the way we view phenomena.

During the 1930s, a series of research studies was conducted by scholars in other disciplines. These would provide the groundwork for the field of interpersonal communication. Researchers had begun to systematically study children's interactions to learn more about patterns of social interaction and role-taking behavior (see, for example, Piaget, 1926). Also during this time period, George Herbert Mead, a philosophy professor from the University of Chicago, studied the relationship between the meanings that result from our interactions with others and our sense of self. Mead is often credited with the theory that came to be known as symbolic interactionism.

Symbolic interactionism a theory based on the premise that people form meanings based on the symbols used in interactions.

Herbert Blumer, a colleague from the University of California-Berkeley, actually coined the term symbolic interactionism and described this concept as a "label for a relatively distinctive approach to the study of human group life and human conduct" (Blumer, 1969, p. 1). One of the first premises of this theory is that people form meanings based on the symbols used in interactions. These symbols include words or messages, roles that people play, gestures, and even rules that exist for interactions. The theory of symbolic interaction is significant because it recognizes the importance of our responses to symbols or words and the impact this has on the development of self. Consider your current role as a college student. It is likely that you gained the self-confidence to pursue a college degree as a result of the encouragement you received from parents and teachers, as well as the expectations that you and your family members have for your future education. Perhaps when you were in high school, someone asked you which college you planned to attend. All of these symbols helped shape your perception of self.

Maslow's hierarchy of needs a model that depicts our basic human needs.

Also during this period, Abraham Maslow, a psychology professor at Brooklyn College, strove to understand the forces that cause humans to engage in certain behaviors. Beginning in 1939, he conducted research that specifically focused on human needs, resulting in the pyramid that has become widely known as Maslow's hierarchy of needs (See Figure 1.2). Many of these needs have been identified as forces that motivate people to form interpersonal relationships with one another. Once the basic physiological and safety needs have been fulfilled, humans seek to fulfill the love and belonging needs by interacting with other individuals. As a result of our interactions with others, self-esteem needs, the fourth level of Maslow's hierarchy, are addressed. Messages received from others are influential in forming self-esteem and tackling issues of identity (Maslow, 1943). The fifth and final need in Maslow's hierarchy of needs is self-actualization. Self-actualization is the most complicated human need to be fulfilled. When you self-actualize, you realize what you are capable of becoming—understanding your true self.

Figure 1.2 Maslow's Hierarchy of Needs

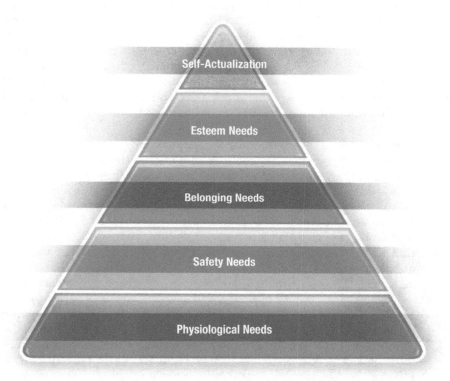

© Kendall Hunt Publishing Co.

Progressing into the 1950s and '60s, new scholars produced significant research that began shaping and defining the field of interpersonal communication as it evolved into its own discipline. In the 1950s, anthropologist Ray Birdwhistell (1952) created the term kinesics to refer to the use of body movements and gestures as forms of communication. In the late 1950s and early '60s, anthropologist Edward T. Hall focused on the role of space, or proxemics, in shaping and influencing our interactions with others (1959). While the study of nonverbal behaviors has evolved as an intriguing aspect of interpersonal interactions, additional studies during this time contributed to our understanding of the role of self and others in relationships.

In 1959, while he was at the University of California, Berkeley, sociologist Erving Goffman published *The Presentation of Self in Everyday Life*. His work has served as the foundation for communications scholars' understanding of the role that impression management plays in our interactions with others. Goffman's work has been influential in shaping many subsequent theories of self-versus-other perceptions in interpersonal relationships.

During the late 1950s, Fritz Heider, a psychologist who taught at the University of Kansas, published work that addressed how attributions shape

Kinesics refers to the use of body movements and gestures as forms of communication.

Proxemics refers to the role of space in IPC.

Attribution theory a theory that explains our tendency to attribute causes or explanations to people's behaviors.

our interactions with others (Heider, 1958). Attribution theory has been influential in interpersonal studies because it addresses the judgments that we make when we communicate with others. Research on relationship initiation has drawn from Heider's work to explain the evolving process of attributions as we make decisions to pursue interactions.

While these prominent scholars provided a solid foundation for our current approaches to investigating interpersonal relationships, you may have noticed that they are not communication researchers. Scholars often cross boundaries and build on ideas initiated by researchers in other fields. Recognizing the contributions that scholars in the fields of psychology, sociology, and anthropology have made to the communication discipline is critical to understanding the interdisciplinary nature of our work. It is fascinating to explore human relationships from such a variety of perspectives! In fact, as you take classes in other disciplines, you may learn about some of the same theories and concepts that were presented in your communication classes.

While the study of communication has existed for decades, it was not until the late 1960s and into the '70s and '80s that interpersonal communication scholars began to carve out their own niche in the study of human communication and to clearly define the study of interactions in relationships. Increasing political and social unrest in the late 1960s and early 1970s caused scholars to direct their attention to individuals and their relationships. Significant historical events like the civil rights movement and the Vietnam War stimulated research activity in such areas as group dynamics, decision making, and conflict resolution.

In 1967, *Pragmatics of Human Communication* was published (Watzlawick, Beavin, & Jackson) and was one of the first books to adopt an interactional approach to communication. In the first chapter of the book, the authors acknowledge that each communication situation involves a "frame of reference." Two key concepts that have become central to the study of interpersonal communication are addressed in this initial chapter: the relationship between communication partners, and the function of the communication interaction. As a result of this groundbreaking text, colleges and universities added courses focusing specifically on the dynamics of interpersonal communication. Other textbooks soon followed (Keltner, 1970; McCroskey, Larson, & Knapp, 1971; Giffin & Patton, 1971).

As the level of interest in interpersonal communication mushroomed, scholars in the discipline turned their attention to research studies designed to explain the dynamics of relationships. Professional associations at the international, national, and regional levels formed interest groups and divisions devoted to interpersonal topics. By the late 1970s, interpersonal communication had become firmly established as a prominent field of study. During the early 1980s, it was difficult to open an issue of any leading communication journal and not find an article pertaining to research

© NSC Photography/Shutterstock.com

© PathDoc/Shutterstock.com

on interpersonal communication. Scholars began directing their attention to developing and testing theories directly related to interpersonal interactions.

Recognizing the contributions that scholars in the fields of psychology, sociology, and anthropology have made to the communication discipline is critical to understanding the interdisciplinary nature of our work.

INTERPERSONAL COMMUNICATION THEORY

Many significant theoretical contributions are provided in the historical foundations of interpersonal communication. While you may experience a heightened sense of anxiety when your instructor mentions "theory," the concepts are actually quite simple and very useful. A theory is nothing more than a set of statements about the way things work. Julia Wood (2000) recognizes theories as "human constructions—symbolic ways we represent phenomena" (p. 33) and notes that we use theories to achieve one of four basic goals. The four widely recognized goals of a theory are: (1) to describe phenomena; (2) to explain how something works; (3) to understand, predict, and control occurrences; and (4) to make social change (Wood, 2000). As students of communication, you will find theories to be useful tools for explaining interactions or categorizing behaviors.

Theory a set of statements about the way things work.

Over the past 30 years, interpersonal communication scholars have truly made their mark as a core focus in the field of communication studies. While the seeds for many of today's prominent interpersonal theories may have been planted by experts in the fields of psychology, sociology, and anthropology, the discipline has grown into an area that interpersonal researchers have defined as their own. In fact, scholars who study communication in other contexts (i.e., instructional communication, organizational communication, intercultural communication) are now applying interpersonal theories as the foundation for studying interactions in other areas.

Many different theories will be discussed throughout this text as we explore key components of interpersonal communication in a variety of contexts. Here is an overview of some of the prominent theories:

- Attribution Theory
- Symbolic Interaction Theory
- Attachment Theory
- Objective Self-Awareness Theory
- Behavioral Confirmation/Self-Fulfilling Prophecy
- Information Processing Theory
- Constructivist Theory
- Social Identity Theory
- Script Theory
- Communication Accommodation Theory
- Fundamental Attribution Error
- Self-Serving Bias
- Equity Theory
- Family Communication Patterns Theory
- Interpersonal Deception Theory
- Leader-Member Exchange Theory

- Nonverbal Expectancy Violation Theory
- Social Comparison Theory
- Social Exchange Theory
- Social Penetration Theory
- Systems Theory
- Uncertainty Reduction Theory
- Predicted Outcome Value Theory

SUMMARY

This chapter provided a framework for the interpersonal communication discipline. We defined interpersonal communication and distinguished it from other types of communication. We identified key interpersonal communication concepts and principles. Finally, we provided an overview of the history of interpersonal communication to help you understand the roots of this discipline and the contributions from scholars in other fields. Now it is time to embark on your interpersonal journey.

DISCUSSION QUESTIONS

1. Why should college students take a course on interpersonal communication?
2. Based on your interactions with your peers, what specific communication skills do most college students lack?
3. What theories do you have about how and why people use communication to establish relationships with others?

REFERENCES

Barden, D. M. (2013). Not dressing the part, and other interview markers. *Chronicle of Higher Education, 59*, 38–39.

Bateson, G. (1951). Information and codification: A philosophical approach. In J. Ruesch and G. Bateson (Eds.), *Communication: The social matrix of psychiatry.* New York: Wiley and Sons.

Bateson, G. (1972). *Steps to an ecology of mind.* New York: Ballantine Books.

Baxter, L. (1982). Strategies for ending relationships: Two studies. *The Western Journal of Speech Communication, 46*, 223–241.

Beebe, S. A., & Masterson, J. T. (1997). *Communicating in small groups* (5th ed.). New York: Addison-Wesley Longman.

Berlo, D. K. (1960). *The process of communication.* San Francisco: Rinehart.

Birdwhistell, R. L. (1952). *Introduction to kinesics: An annotation system for analysis of body motion and gesture.* Washington, DC: U.S. Department of State, Foreign Service Institute.

Blumer, H. (1969). *Symbolic interactionism: Perspective and method.* Englewood Cliffs, NJ: Prentice-Hall.

Burleson, B. R. (2010). The nature of interpersonal communication: A message-centered approach. In C.R. Burger, M.E. Roloff, & D.R. Roskos-Ewoldsen (Eds.), *Handbook of communication science* (2nd ed.) (pp. 145–163). Thousand Oaks, CA: Sage.

Burleson, B. R., & MacGeorge, E. L. (2002). Supportive communication. In M. L. Knapp & J. A. Daly (Eds.), *Handbook of interpersonal communication* (pp. 374–424). Thousand Oaks, CA: Sage.

Burleson, B. R., & Samter, W. (1996). Similarity in the communication skills of young adults: Foundations of attraction, friendship, and relationship satisfaction. *Communication Reports, 9,* 127–139.

Canary, D. J., & Stafford, L. (2001). Equity in the preservation of personal relationships. In J. H. Harvey & A. Wenzel (Eds.), *Close romantic relationships: Maintenance and enhancement* (pp. 133–151). Mahwah, NJ: Lawrence Erlbaum.

Cappella, J. N. (1987). Interpersonal communication: Definitions and fundamental questions. In C. R. Berger & S. H. Chaffee (Eds.), *Handbook of communication science.* Newbury Park, CA: Sage.

Casciaro, T., & Lobo, M. S. (2005). Fool vs. jerk: Whom would you hire? *HBS Working Knowledge.* N.p., 25 July 2005. Web. 10 July 2013.

Casserly, M. (2012). The student loan debt crisis is a women's issue: Here's why. *Forbes.* Forbes Magazine, 19 Nov. 2012. Web. 24 Oct. 2013.

Cathcart, R., & Gumpert, G. (1983). Mediated interpersonal communication: Toward a new typology. *Quarterly Journal of Speech, 69,* 267–277.

Cody, M. (1982). A typology of disengagement strategies and an examination of the role intimacy, reactions to inequity, and relational problems play in strategy selection. *Communication Monographs, 49,* 148–170.

Darby, B. W., & Schlenker, B. R. (1982). Children's reactions to apologies. *Journal of Personality and Social Psychology, 43,* 742–753.

DeVito, J. (2001). *The interpersonal communication book* (9th ed.). New York: Addison Wesley Longman Inc.

Giffin, K., & Patton, B. R. (1971). *Fundamentals of interpersonal communication.* New York, NY: Harper & Row.

Goffman, E. (1959). *The presentation of self in everyday life.* Garden City, NY: Doubleday.

Goleman, D. (2006). *Social intelligence: The new science of human relationships.* New York, NY: Bantam Dell.

Hall, E. T. (1959). *The silent language.* Garden City, NY: Doubleday.

Heider, F. (1958). *The psychology of interpersonal relations.* New York, NY: Wiley.

Keltner, J. W. (1970). *Interpersonal speech-communication: Elements and structures.* Belmont, CA: Wadsworth.

Knapp, M. L., & Vangelisti, A. (2000). *Interpersonal communication and human relationships.* Boston: Allyn & Bacon.

Knapp, M. L., Daly, J. A., Albada, K. F., & Miller, G. R. (2002). Background and current trends in the study of interpersonal communication. In M. L. Knapp & J. A. Daly (Eds.), *Handbook of interpersonal communication* (pp. 3–20). Thousand Oaks, CA: Sage.

Kreps, G. L., & Thorton, B. C. (1992). *Health communication: Theory & practice.* Prospect Heights, IL: Waveland Press.

Maslow, A. H. (1943). A theory of human motivation. *Psychological Review, 50,* 370–396.

McCroskey, J. C., Larson, C., & Knapp, M. L. (1971). *An introduction to interpersonal communication.* Englewood Cliffs, NJ: Prentice-Hall.

Metts, S., & Planap, S. (2002). Emotional communication. In M. L. Knapp & J. A. Daly (Eds.), *Handbook of interpersonal communication* (pp. 339–373). Thousand Oaks, CA: Sage.

Miller, G. R. (1978). The current status of theory and research in interpersonal communication. *Human Communication Research, 4,* 164–178.

Miller, G. R. (1990). Interpersonal communication. In G. L. Dahnke & G. W. Clatterbuck (Eds.), *Human communication: Theory and research* (pp. 91-122). Belmont, CA: Wadsworth.

Myers, L. L., & Tucker, M. L. (2005). Increasing awareness of emotional intelligence in a business curriculum. *Business Communication Quarterly, 68,* 44–51.

Noller, P., & Feeney, J. A. (1994). Relationship satisfaction, attachment and nonverbal accuracy in early marriage. *Journal of Nonverbal Behavior, 18,* 199–222.

Omarzu, J., Whalen, J., & Harvey, J. H. (2001). How well do you mind your relationship? A preliminary scale to test the minding theory of relating. In Harvey, J. & A. Wenzel. (Eds.), *Close romantic relationships: Maintenance and enhancement* (pp. 345–356). Mahwah, NJ: Lawrence Erlbaum.

Peterson, M. S. (1997). Personnel interviewers' perceptions of the importance and adequacy of applicants' communication skills. *Communication Education, 46,* 287–291.

Piaget, J. (1926). *The language and thought of the child.* New York: Harcourt Brace.

Rath, D., Poldre, P., Fisher, B. J., Laidlaw, J. C., Cowan, D. H., & Bakker, D. (1998). Commitment of a cancer organization to a program for training in communication skills. *Journal of Cancer Education: The Official Journal of the American Association for Cancer Education, 13,* 203–206.

Roloff, M. E., & Soule, K. P. (2002). Interpersonal conflict: A review. In M. L. Knapp & J. A. Daly (Eds.), *Handbook of interpersonal communication* (pp. 475–528). Thousand Oaks, CA: Sage.

Sbarra, D. A., Law, R. W., & Portley, R. M. (2011). *Divorce and death: A meta-analysis and research agenda for clinical, social, and health psychology.* Thousand Oaks, CA: Sage.

Schlenker, B. R., & Darby, B. R. (1981). The use of apologies in social predicaments. *Social Psychology Quarterly, 44,* 271–278.

Schutz, W. (1966). *The interpersonal underworld* (pp. 13–20). Palo Alto, CA: Science and Behavior Books.

Shankar, A., McMunn, A., Banks, J., & Steptoe, A. (2011). Loneliness, social isolation, and behavioral and biological health indicators in older adults. *NCBI.* U.S. National Library of Medicine, 30 July 2011. Web.

Spitzberg, B. H., & Cupach, W. R. (1984). *Interpersonal communication competence.* Beverly Hills, CA: Sage.

Turkle, S. (2012). The flight from conversation." *The New York Times.* N.p., 21 Apr. 2012. Web. 2 July 2012.

Wanzer, M. B., Booth-Butterfield, M., & Gruber, K. (2004). Perceptions of health care providers' communication: Relationships between patient-centered communication and satisfaction. *Health Communication, 16,* 363–384.

Watzlawick, P., Beavin, J., & Jackson, D. D. (1967). *Pragmatics of human communication.* New York: Norton.

Wood, J. T. (2000). *Communication theories in action.* Wadsworth: Belmont, CA.

Verbal Communication:
Words of Wisdom

OBJECTIVES

- Define verbal communication and understand the characteristics of verbal communication.
- Distinguish between connotative and denotative meaning.
- Differentiate between relational and content levels of meaning.
- Explain the difference between constitutive and regulative rules.
- Describe the four functions of verbal communication.
- Explain the Sapir-Whorf hypothesis.
- Explore how uncertainty reduction is associated with verbal communication.
- Discuss the difference between direct and indirect verbal communication styles.

SCENARIO: SOUND FAMILIAR?

Lauren has been living with her partner for over a year now but they cannot seem to agree on simple household chores. Her frustration grew this morning when she stumbled over her partner's shoes and noticed the garbage was piled up by the doorway. She left their apartment in a hurry and yelled, "You are such a slob!" An hour later, she was feeling bad about what she said and called to apologize for her choice of words.

KEY TERMS

Abstract Symbols	Concrete Symbols	Direct communication style
Appropriateness	Concreteness	
Character	Confirming Messages	Disconfirming Messages
Clarity	Connotative meaning	
Cognitive Function	Constitutive rules	Equivocation
Communication accommodation theory	Content level of meaning	Expressing affection
	Context	Formal communication style
Communication Predicament of Aging	Convergence	Goodwill
	Credibility	Group Identification
Competence	Denotative meaning	Hate Speech

Immediacy	Powerful language	Semantics
Indirect communication style	Powerless language	Sexist Language
	Rapport talk	Social Change
Informal communication style	Regulative rules	Social Reality
	Relationship level of meaning	Status
KISS		Subjective
Linguistic determinism	Report talk	Symbol
Linguistic Relativity	Rules	Uncertainty reduction theory
Metacommunication	Sapir-Whorf hypothesis	
Organizational Jargon		Verbal communication
Overaccommodation	Self-disclosure	Verbal Immediacy

OVERVIEW

In this scenario, we can relate to Lauren's verbal reaction, which often occurs when we are frustrated. When we are not mindful of our actions and the effect they have on others, it is sometimes referred to as being on "autopilot." Being on autopilot suggests we are just reacting to situations and not thinking of how our word choice may impact others. Depending on our goals, verbal communication can be used to enhance our relationships or to destroy them. We have the power to make others feel competent, attractive, and strong. On the other hand, our words can also upset and annoy others, and our messages can cause them to feel weak. This chapter discusses how the words we use impact our interpersonal relationships.

We begin by defining verbal communication and examining several of its distinct features and functions. Next, we will examine factors that impact our verbal communication and how it is perceived by others.

DEFINING VERBAL COMMUNICATION

Verbal communication refers to the words we use during the communication process.

Verbal communication refers to the words we use during the communication process. We use words strategically to relate to the outside world and to create meaning. Have you ever tried to communicate with someone who did not speak your language? Have you ever attempted to convey a message to others without using words or played a game of charades? These two examples illustrate how difficult it can be to express ourselves without verbal communication. The words we use have a strong impact on our interpersonal relationships. What we say initially often determines whether we will have future interactions with others. There are four key characteristics of verbal communication that explain how and why we use words to create meaning: rules, symbols, subjectivity, and context.

Rules

Rules guidelines for social interaction; agreed upon guidelines that provide a structure for what is social acceptable communication in our culture

It is important to realize that there are certain rules we must follow when using language. Rules are agreed-upon guidelines that provide a structure for what is socially acceptable communication in our culture. You follow certain rules when talking with your friends that are quite different than when you talk with your grandparents. There are two basic types of rules that relate to verbal communication: constitutive and regulative (Cronen, Pearce, & Snavely, 1979; Pearce, Cronen, & Conklin, 1979). Constitutive rules help guide our communication by identifying appropriate language and interpreting word meanings. In essence, constitutive rules address word meanings. It would probably be easy for you to come up with words to illustrate support, trustworthiness, anger, and/or respect. According to dictionary.com, the word "respect" is defined as *a certain esteem for or a sense of the worth or excellence of a person.* How do we use words to communicate respect in a classroom? Addressing your professors formally, using Dr., Mr., or Mrs., is an example of complying with constitutive rules. Constitutive rules are also in effect when students avoid using slang or swear words in classroom settings. Failure to understand word meanings and make appropriate choices in selecting words can be detrimental to a student's success as an appropriate and effective interpersonal communicator.

What constitutive rules do parents and children have for communicating mutual respect?

Regulative rules guide our communication by identifying when, how, where, and with whom we communicate in certain situations. Regulative rules can include aspects of communication such as grammar, syntax, and age-appropriate language. Seale (1995) suggests that these regulative rules are like traffic laws because they help to create a sense of communication order. These rules help us answer questions such as: Who are we supposed to talk with and how should we speak to this person? What topics are acceptable? For how long should we talk? Think about the regulative rules in the classroom that are not explicitly stated but tell you how to interact with your classmates and professors. Students greet one another when they enter the classroom, they do not interrupt the professor, and they take turns speaking. These rules are context-bound and will change depending on the audience and context.

What regulative rules do you practice in the classroom?

Our verbal communication is governed by constitutive and regulative rules and through language structure.

Our verbal communication is governed by constitutive and regulative rules and through language structure. This makes it possible for us to create shared meaning and have a common understanding of appropriateness across contexts. Therefore, it is critical for all of us to observe, listen, research, and ask questions to understand more clearly the appropriate rules in new situations.

Symbols

A second feature of verbal communication is that it is symbolic. Symbols are socially agreed-upon representations of an event, action, person, object, or phenomenon. Symbols can range from concrete to abstract. The more a symbol resembles what it represents, the more concrete that symbol is. If we were sitting in a room with a chair, a photo of a chair, and a piece of paper with the word "chair" typed on it, this would illustrate how we move from concrete to abstract symbols. Concrete symbols are more likely to resemble what they represent. Therefore the chair itself is the most concrete symbol. We use the chair to sit on, and this is how it is represented. Abstract symbols are arbitrary and nonrepresentational. Therefore, the printed word "chair" is abstract and arbitrary. The more concrete (and therefore less abstract) a

Constitutive rules rules that help define communication by identifying appropriate word use and interpreting word meanings.

Regulative rules rules that control our communication by managing or guiding interaction by identifying when, how, where, and with whom we communicate in certain situations.

Symbol socially agreed-upon representations of an event, action, person, object, or phenomenon.

Concrete symbols a type of symbol that is more likely to resemble what they represent.

Abstract symbols a type of symbol that is arbitrary and nonrepresentational.

symbol is, the more it is associated with its meaning. Verbal communication is made up of abstract, arbitrary, and agreed-upon concrete symbols or words.

semantics the study of meaning we attribute to each word

It is difficult to discuss symbols without discussing semantics, or the study of meanings we attribute to each word. When people interpret words, they focus on both the denotative and connotative meanings. The denotative meaning refers to the universal meaning of the word, or the definition you would find in the dictionary. The denotative meaning of the word "fireplace" is *any open structure, usually of masonry, for keeping a fire, as at a campsite* (dictionary.com). The connotative meaning refers to the personal meaning that the source has with that word. For example, the word "fireplace" connotes hospitality and warmth. Connotative meanings are often quite difficult to explain because they can be different for everyone. This leads us to the third characteristic of verbal communication, subjectivity.

denotative meaning refers to the universal meaning of the word, or the definition you would find in the dictionary.

connotative meaning refers to the personal meaning that the source has with that word.

Subjectivity

Because everyone has a unique worldview, the way we use and interpret verbal communication is strongly influenced by individual biases. Verbal communication is subjective because we interpret the world through our own experiences, historical perspective, cultural upbringing, our physical environment, and the socio-emotional nature of relationships. Our perceptions are distinct and limited to our personal field of experience and developed schema.

subjective interpreting meaning through one's own experiences, historical perspective, and cultural upbringing and/or our physical environment

The subjective meanings we place on our verbal communication have different levels of meaning. Recall our description of these two concepts from Chapter 1. The relational level of meaning is highly sensitive to the people involved in the conversation and indicates how people feel about the relationship, whereas the content level of meaning is the informational component and relies on the specific words you use. Consider the following conversation:

> When people interpret words, they focus on both the denotative and connotative meanings.

Samantha: Do you want to come to my mom's birthday party?

Edgar: Well, it's in an hour, and I'm in the middle of working on the house.

Samantha: So, you don't want to come?

Edgar: Well, the contractor is coming tomorrow, so I have to get this done.

Samantha: You missed my sister's birthday party, also. I'm starting to think you just don't want to spend time with my family.

Edgar: That is not true. I just have to get this work done.

Samantha: I cannot believe you are going to miss my mom's birthday party!

Edgar: Do you want me to drop everything and come?

Samantha: I shouldn't have to tell you what to do; you should know what the right thing to do is!

Edgar: I'm sorry, but I have to finish this project before the contractor comes.

The conversation above illustrates a common problem in interpersonal relationships: one individual is focused on the content level of meaning, and the other is interested in the relationship level of meaning. Edgar is focused on the content or the information in the message, while Samantha is concerned with how the communication process is affecting the relationship. Edgar is determined to finish working on the house and cannot understand why Samantha would be upset. Samantha feels Edgar is not really listening to what she is saying and does not understand. The content level of meaning is found in the words we use, and the relationship level of meaning is often interpreted through our nonverbal behaviors, through *how* something is said. Because of Edgar's past behavior and concern for the house, Samantha perceived his nonverbal behavior as insincere. Edgar, however, heard Samantha complaining about not going to the birthday party and offered a valid reason for not attending.

When one individual is focusing on the content level of meaning and the other is focused on the relationship level of meaning, conflict may often result. Verbal communication is widely subjective and is a function of our personal associations and the meanings we place on words, situations, and experiences. In order to improve our communication with others, it is important to do the following: (1) seek clarification of ambiguous messages, (2) identify areas of miscommunication, and (3) talk about ways to improve communication. Metacommunication is when we "communicate about our communication" and we can use it to help clarify a message's meaning. The role of metacommunication in verbal communication is a helpful strategy for relationship partners as they continuously work to improve understanding of messages.

relationship level of meaning the level of meaning in verbal communication that is highly sensitive to the people involved in the conversation and the process of communicating; found in the words we use.

content level of meaning the level of meaning in verbal communication that is primarily related to the topic at hand; often interpreted through our nonverbal behaviors (through how something is said).

Metacommunication an important tool that is often used during social interaction to increase our shared meaning and to reduce uncertainty about the status of our relationships; "communicating about communication."

Context

The final feature of verbal communication is the contextual framework. The context refers to the environment, situation, or setting in which we use verbal communication. The context may influence the interpretation, meaning, and appropriateness of the communication. For example, we may use a particular greeting with our roommates such as, "What's up?", while we may choose alternative words when we are greeting our grandparents, such as "Good morning, Grandfather!" The interpretation of our words changes when we consider the context in which they are used. In the last section of this textbook, we review five general contexts in which interpersonal communication occurs. These are: intercultural communication, family communication, organizational communication, health communication, and mediated communication.

In the next section, we will discuss two specific examples of contextually bound verbal communication: organizational jargon and expressing affection.

context a particular setting or environment in which the communication takes place.

© Matej Kastelic/Shutterstock.com

A person who doesn't work in the lab would have a difficult time understanding the scientists' jargon.

Organizational Jargon Organizational jargon is defined as a specialized vocabulary that is socially constructed and regularly used by members of a particular trade, profession, or organization. Jargon will differ greatly in different organizations and workplaces. Jargon is often used in technical and scientific fields to refer to concepts and terms in a universal manner. One category of

Organizational jargon a specialized vocabulary that is socially constructed and regularly used by members of a particular trade, profession, or organization.

jargon is the development of acronyms/abbreviations. Members of the military may use jargon such as MREs, PCDs, MEO, and CDC when communicating with each other. What is the purpose or function of jargon? These verbal shortcuts can enhance communication by increasing precision and speed during social interaction (Hirst, 2003). However, this specialized language may be abused when individuals use it with receivers who are not familiar with the vocabulary, and the speaker may be perceived as being pretentious (Nash, 1993). For example, most of us prefer our health-care providers to communicate clearly with us, and this means they avoid the use of jargon and technical language. Organizational jargon or "shop talk" is contextually bound and may be considered rude when communicating with individuals outside of the organization.

expressing affection
exchanging messages of liking

Expressing Affection

Another example of contextually bound verbal communication is expressing affection. Many of us reserve special terms for our most intimate relationships. Consider the last time you told someone "I love you." You may have contemplated these three little words for quite a while before actually saying them. That is because these few words have large implications. These expressions of affection often initiate or accelerate relational development (Floyd, 1997). We often save particular words or phrases for special individuals who impact or influence us. Communicating affection is risky. When the receiver is not on the same page as the sender, the communicative attempt may have a negative outcome. It is important that the sender consider the trust level, reciprocity, and future interactions, as well as the length of the relationship before conveying these types of messages. If the receiver does not feel the same way, they may feel manipulated or perceive the sender as imposing confusing relational boundaries (Ebert & Floyd, 2004). Once again, our verbal messages are interpreted based on the context or type of relationship we are in.

Now that we have defined verbal communication and provided its features, we can discuss the specific functions verbal messages serve in interpersonal communication.

FUNCTIONS OF VERBAL COMMUNICATION

There are four functions that help explain how we use our verbal communication. They are: cognitive function, social reality function, group identity function, and social change function. Each is discussed below.

Cognitive Function

cognitive function
a function of verbal communication that explains how we use language to acquire knowledge, to reason, and to make sense of the world

The cognitive function of verbal communication can be defined as how we use language to acquire knowledge, to reason, and to make sense of the world. The cognitive function of verbal communication maintains a strong connection with culture. Our culture greatly influences our language choices. Growing up in a small town versus a large city, being a member of a quiet family versus a loud family, or growing up in the South versus the North all result in distinct language differences.

Once again, we use the cognitive function of verbal communication to acquire information. One way to do this is through the process of uncertainty reduction. Berger proposed that the main purpose of verbal communication is to "make sense" out of our interpersonal world (as cited in Griffin, 2003).

Berger's uncertainty reduction theory suggests that human communication is used to gain knowledge and create understanding by reducing uncertainty and, therefore, increasing predictability. The more we ask questions and learn about someone new, the more we reduce our uncertainty about them. For example, when we are first introduced to someone we typically experience high levels of uncertainty. We may ask ourselves: "Who is this person?" "Where are they from?" "Are they like me?" Consider the last time you met someone new. Chances are the conversation went something like the one below.

uncertainty reduction theory suggests that human communication is used to gain knowledge and create understanding by reducing uncertainty and, therefore, increasing predictability.

> **James:** Hi, I'm James. What's your name?
>
> **Erica:** My name's Erica. Where are you from?
>
> **James:** I'm from New York, and you?
>
> **Erica:** I'm from Florida, but I'm here studying communication.
>
> **James:** That's my major also. Are you interested in broadcasting?
>
> **Erica:** No, I'm studying communication studies. I'm interested in going to law school.

This example demonstrates how we use verbal communication to acquire knowledge through uncertainty reduction. Through the process of self-disclosure, or purposefully revealing personal information about ourselves, we are able to decrease the ambiguity of a situation. When we do this we increase our ability to predict future interactions. This is an example of how our verbal communication serves the cognitive function of acquiring knowledge and making sense out of the world.

self-disclosure purposefully revealing personal information about ourselves.

We will examine the concept of uncertainty and self-disclosure and their roles in relationship initiation more closely in Chapter 7.

> ... what appears to be real in society is socially agreed upon through our communication with others.

Social Reality Function

"The language used in everyday life continuously provides me with the necessary objectifications and posits the order within which these make sense and within which everyday life has meaning for me. I live in a place that is geographically designated; I employ tools from can openers to sports cars which are designated in the technical vocabulary of my society; I live within a web of human relationships from my chess club to the United States of America which are also ordered by means of vocabulary. In this manner, language marks the co-ordinates of my life in society and fills that life with meaningful objects." (Peter L. Berger and Thomas Luckman, *The Social Construction of Reality*, New York: Doubleday, 1966, p. 22).

In this quote from *The Social Construction of Reality*, the authors suggest that reality is socially constructed through language and vocabulary. In other words, *what appears to be real in society is socially agreed upon through our communication with others*. Consider the words that have evolved in the U.S. culture across previous decades. Throughout the 1970s and 1980's the terms "Watergate," "test-tube baby," and "Rubik's cube" became words that were widely understood in the United States because of events or products that had been introduced during that time period. Similarly, the words "AIDS"

social reality   a function of verbal communication that explains how individuals socially construct or agree upon language that influences how we see and interact in the world.

linguistic determinism   a concept that suggests language determines thought or that there is a relationship between language and cognition.

and "compact disc" were added to dictionaries in the 1980s. And words such as "selfie," "phablet," and "fauxhawk" were added in 2013. As the reality of the culture evolved, new words were created to explain and describe our changing society. Thus, our verbal communication serves to create our social reality.

Two American linguists, Edward Sapir and Benjamin Lee Whorf, were interested in how we used language as a tool to make sense of the world. They developed the concept of linguistic determinism, which suggests that "language *determines* thought" (Whorf, 1956; Sapir, 1956). Most agree that there is a relationship between language and cognitions. You may agree that if we use certain words, it will influence what people think about. This helps us understand why particular groups are passionate about making adjustments in our language. Take, for example, the movement to more gender- neutral titles of occupations, including mail carrier (mailman); police officer (policeman); chairperson (chairman); and salesperson (salesman). If we change our language, we can start to change the way people think about these occupations. Can you think of additional examples of how changing our words can influence our cognitions?

linguistic relativity   concept that suggests distinctions encoded in one language are unique to that language

Sapir and Whorf also conceptualized linguistic relativity, which proposes that distinctions encoded in one language are unique to that language alone, and that "there is no limit to the structural diversity of languages" (Whorf, 1956; Sapir, 1956). By comparing the vocabulary of Inuit and Aztec peoples they found that the Inuit have many different words for "snow." There are different words for falling snow, powdery snow, slushy snow, packing snow, and icy snow. On the other hand, in Aztec there is only one word for snow, one word for cold, and one word for ice. In addition, Sapir and Whorf were fascinated by the fact that the Hopi language did not distinguish between past, present, and future tense. Time is not considered multidimensional in their culture, whereas time is a fundamentally critical concept in Western society. Think about how we use time in such fields as physics and engineering. Also, our culture is embedded with daily planners, calendars, and appointments that rely heavily on our shared meaning of time.

Sapir-Whorf hypothesis   suggests that the language we learn, as well as the culture we are exposed to, is used to shape our entire reality.

The Sapir-Whorf hypothesis suggests that the language we learn, as well as the culture we are exposed to, is used to shape our entire reality.

LANGUAGE, GENDER AND THE MEDIA

A 2008 study examined language and gender during the prime-time coverage of the Beijing Olympic Games on NBC (Angelini & Billings, 2010). This study used agenda-setting and framing theories to explore differences in commentators' explanations of athletes' success and failure. The researchers found that 90 percent of the prime-time coverage was devoted to only five sports (gymnastics, diving, swimming, track and field, and beach volleyball) out of a possible 31. In addition, they identified significant gender differences in the way commentators discussed the athletes' performances. For example, male beach volleyball athletes succeeded because of their "overall intelligence" and "athletic ability" while female beach volleyball athletes succeeded because of "luck" and "level of experience." Do you think the way commentators frame athletes' accomplishments during broadcasts influences our perceptions of these athletes?

Group Identity Function

Another function of verbal communication is to serve as a symbol of group solidarity. Because we have similarities in language at work, in our family, and throughout our interpersonal relationships, verbal communication fulfills an identity function. Consider the cliques that are formed in high school. Distinctions are often drawn between band members, athletes, theatrical or drama students, and student council members. Students in your school may have used labels such as "preps," "skaters," "hipsters," "emo kids," or "mean girls." Students often describe and define themselves based on their affiliations, actions/behaviors, or social groups.

Were you a part of a clique in high school? How did you treat your peers?

Within the different groups, shared "codes" develop that only members of the group might understand. These codes may be in the form of inside jokes, nicknames, abbreviations, or other specialized vocabulary. Their purpose is to form a sense of group identification. In other words, this function of verbal communication serves to distinguish one group from another and to provide a sense of similarity and cohesiveness for its members. This makes sense with our earlier discussion of organizational jargon. It may increase group identity with organizational members, but it may isolate individuals who do not belong or understand this language.

group identification a function of verbal communication that serves to distinguish one group from another and to provide a sense of similarity and cohesiveness for its members.

Families can also be considered a type of group. Think about your family. Are there inside jokes that get repeated over and over? You may hear something like, "Remember the time that Mom made Julie walk across the kitchen to get an apple, because she did not believe she had a broken leg? Or the time Shawn lied to Mom and Dad about that 'hit and run' so he could get a new bike?" We choose to let others "in" on the joke when we allow new members to enter into the group. From outside the group, nonmembers may interpret the stories, jokes, and nicknames as inappropriate, inconsiderate, and not humorous. However, group members who use verbal communication to fulfill this function feel a sense of belonging. Verbal communication used to establish group identity helps maintain the group's rituals and celebrate the history of the group.

Social Change Function

Language can "imprison us" or it can "set us free." This is how Ting-Toomey and Chung (2005) describe the social change function of language. In other words, language can inhibit our abilities to perceive the world in unique ways, or it can dynamically change habits and prejudices. We often try to avoid offending others by using politically correct language. Political correctness stems from the convergence of several factors, three of which are the Sapir-Whorf hypothesis, the civil rights movement, and language reform. In addition, the feminist and racial equality movements altered our language system by attempting to eliminate gender-based and racial-based terms from our vocabulary. It is suggested that a more sensitive language will reflect a more caring society.

social change a function of verbal communication that explains how language can inhibit or encourage change in society

Now that we have explored the cognitive, social reality, group identity, and social change functions of verbal communication, we turn our attention to the different types of verbal communication styles.

RESEARCH IN REAL LIFE: TOP TEN WORDS OF 2013

The Global Language Monitor (GLM) is a San Diego-based company that tracks and analyzes trends in the English language. The GLM staff monitors the evolution and demise of language, word usage, word choices, and their impact on the various aspects of culture. GLM suggests that the September 11 attacks on America have changed forever the way we speak and interpret various words. Currently, they suggest, the numbers "9/11" are the official shorthand for the 2001 terrorist attacks, and "ground zero" stirs up thoughts of a sacred burial ground where the twin towers once stood. Also since the attacks, the word "hero" includes police, firefighters, EMTs, and any type of first responders who place their lives on the line for the public good.

Consider the Top Words of 2013 identified by GLM:

1. 404—The near-universal numeric code for failure on the global Internet.

2. Fail—The single word fail, often used as a complete sentence ("Fail!") to signify failure of an effort, project, or endeavor.

3. Hashtag—The "number sign" and "pound sign" reborn as the all-powerful Twitter hashtag.

4. @Pontifex—The handle of the ever-more popular Pope Franciscus (Francis).

5. The Optic—The "optic" is threatening to overtake "the narrative" as the narrative overtook rational discourse. Does not bode well for an informed political discussion.

6. Surveillance—The revelation of the unprecedented extent of spying by the NSA into lives of ordinary citizens to the leaders of the closest allies of the United States.

7. Drones—Unmanned aerial vehicles (UAV) that are piloted remotely or by onboard computers used for killing scores or even hundreds of those considered to be enemy combatants of the United States.

8. Deficit—Looks like deficit-spending will plague Western democracies for at least the next decade. Note to economists of all stripes: reducing the rate of increase of deficit spending still increases the deficit.

9. Sequestration—Middle English sequestren, from Old French, from Latin sequestrare: to hide away or isolate or to give up for safekeeping.

10. Emancipate — Grows in importance as worldwide more women and children are enslaved in various forms of involuntary servitude.

VERBAL COMMUNICATION STYLES

Everyone has his or her own unique style of communicating and each comes with benefits and drawbacks. In this section we will explore four common verbal communication styles: direct–indirect, informal–formal, clarity–equivocality, and powerful–powerless. There are a number of different strengths and weaknesses associated with each of these verbal communication styles. These individual differences exist on a continuum and are not to be viewed as dichotomous. In other words, you will not necessarily be "one or the other" but you may be closer to one end of the spectrum than the other. While some people may consider themselves to be at the midpoint between the two extremes of the spectrum, you may be more likely to describe yourself as using a particular verbal style more consistently.

Direct/Indirect

Direct communication style explicitly verbalizes inquiries and comments in a straightforward manner, while the indirect communication style relies on a more roundabout or subtle method of communicating. Individuals who rely on indirect communication often use nonverbal communication, such as facial expressions and eye contact, more often than verbal communication to convey a message. Indirect language may use ambiguous words and phrases, and the intended meaning may not be accurately interpreted by the receiver. For example, you overhear someone at work say, "This generation is lazy." Was this message intended for you?

Baxter (1984) refers to the extent to which individuals are direct and indirect in her theory of relationship dissolution. She suggests individuals have differ-

> Individuals who rely on indirect communication often use nonverbal communication, such as facial expressions and eye contact, more often than verbal communication to convey a message.

ent styles when it comes to ending relationships. Withdrawing, being annoying or hurtful, or suggesting "being friends" are all examples of indirect strategies used to terminate relationships. Individuals may also rely on direct strategies to end a relationship. A simple statement that "It is over" or a fight where each partner blames the other would be examples of direct strategies. Baxter (1984) suggests that apprehensive people are more likely to use indirect strategies. It is important to point out that individuals will often intentionally choose a more indirect communication style over a direct style to save face for the receiver. Picture yourself at a boring party. Instead of telling the host you are bored and are ready to leave, you may engage in a more subtle approach. Perhaps you start to yawn and hint that you did not get much sleep last night. Engaging in an indirect communication style is sometimes more considerate than directly expressing your true feelings.

Informal/Formal

The formality of a communicated message refers to the extent to which it is "official" and "proper." A formal communication style involves an *organized* and managed message and is typically used when you are communicating with someone of higher power, such as a parent, grandparent, teacher, boss, or health professional. Formal communication uses proper words and pronunciation for the particular context and is often planned. It can be used to show respect and professionalism.

An informal communication style uses relaxed, casual, and familiar language. This is typically used with your peers and coworkers. In the workplace, it is best to be formal until the relationship is clearly defined. When a receiver expects a formal style and does not receive it, it significantly impacts his or

Direct communication style   a communication style that explicitly verbalizes inquiries and comments in a straightforward manner.

indirect communication style   a communication style that relies on a more roundabout or subtle method of communicating.

formal communication style   a communication style that involves an organized and managed message; is typically used when you are communicating with someone of higher power.

© wavebreakmedia/Shutterstock.com

What strategy do you think he is using to end this relationship?

informal communication style   using a relaxed, casual, and familiar verbal communication style.

her impressions of the communicator. This includes messages sent over email. Consider the research below that examines students informal email messages to instructors.

> ## RESEARCH IN REAL LIFE: STUDENTS INFORMAL EMAIL MESSAGES
>
> Researchers found that instructors are bothered by students' overly casual email messages (Stephens, Houser, & Cowan, 2009) and prefer more formalized communication to demonstrate respect and professionalism. Students in the study suggested that technology was the reason behind their informality (for example, using "RU" instead of "are you"). However, there are serious implications to sending such casual emails. Findings suggested that instructors liked students who sent informal emails less and were less likely to comply with their requests when compared to students who sent more formal emails.

Informal communication styles are most used when speaking with peers and co-workers.

© gosphotodesign/Shutterstock.com

Choosing between informal and formal communicative styles can be tricky, particularly in intercultural situations. People who live in the United States, Canada, Australia, and Scandinavia tend to be more informal in their communication styles, whereas people of Asian and African cultures tend to be more formal. Adler and Rodman (2006) suggest there are different degrees of formality for speaking with old friends, acquaintances, and strangers. The ability to use language that acknowledges these differences is the mark of a learned person in countries like South Korea. Whenever you are uncertain about a situation, it is better to be formal than informal, since most cultures value formality. Adopting a more formal communication style will demonstrate respect on your part.

Clarity/Equivocation

clarity refers to the simplistic, down-to-earth, and understandable nature of the communication.

equivocation involves communicating by choosing words that may not demonstrate the whole truth.

Another aspect of verbal communication involves the extent to which you express yourself clearly. While clarity refers to the simplistic, down-to-earth, and understandable nature of the communication, Bavelas and his colleagues (1990) define equivocation as "nonstraightforward communication . . . [that] appears ambiguous, contradictory, tangential, obscure, or even evasive" (p. 28). In other words, equivocation involves communicating by intentionally choosing words to conceal elements of the whole truth. Equivocation may be used for different reasons. For example, equivocation allows an individual the possibility to deny events after the fact. Former President Bill Clinton denied having "sexual relations" with Monica Lewinsky. Later, Clinton stated he interpreted the agreed-upon definition of sexual relations to exclude oral sex. This example demonstrates how individuals use equivocation to protect themselves by intentionally not revealing the entire truth. However, like indirect communication, individuals may choose to act in an equivocal manner to protect someone else's feelings. For example, you may tell your date, "This lunch was very thoughtful," even though you have no intention of going on another date with this person. Be aware that sending mixed messages may lead to confusion and awkward discussions in the future.

Communicating with clarity obviously has many benefits. For example, in the classroom, researchers found that students taught by teachers with a clear communication style learned more than those taught by teachers with an ambiguous communication style. Students reported less receiver apprehension, less fear of misinterpreting, and less fear of inadequately processing information when teachers communicated clearly (Cheseboro, 2003). Finally, students indicated that they liked clear teachers and their course material more than those who were not clear (Cheseboro, 2003).

Powerful/Powerless Language

The final verbal communication style we will discuss is the extent to which your language is powerful or powerless. In our society, powerful language is associated with positive attributes such as assertiveness and importance, and it can be influential, commanding, and authoritative. Powerful language combines the use of proper English, clear thoughts, organized ideas, and a persuasive structure. Powerless language, on the other hand, is associated with

> **powerful language** associated with positive attributes such as assertiveness and importance; it can be influential, commanding, and authoritative.

> Research has shown that we need to hear only ten to fifteen seconds of an individual's speech to form initial perceptions.

negative attributes such as shyness, introversion, timidity, nervousness, lack of confidence, and apprehension. Avoiding linguistic features that suggest powerless language may positively impact the way we are perceived by others. Types of powerless speech include hesitations, hedges, tag questions, polite forms, intensifiers, and disclaimers. See Table 2.1 for examples of each of these.

> **Powerless language** associated with negative attributes such as shyness, introversion, timidity, nervousness, lack of confidence, and apprehension.

An interesting study examined the use of powerless language in health magazines (Fandrich & Beck 2012). They found that female authors and health magazines use more powerless language compared to male authors or generic types of magazines. Overall the researchers concluded that powerless language was used more often with female audiences. Can you offer any explanations for why powerless language was used more often with female audiences?

The use of powerful language has also been studied in the classroom. Haleta (1996) examined students' perceptions of teachers' use of powerful versus powerless language. Findings suggest that students' initial perceptions of powerful teachers were significantly higher in perceptions of dynamism, status,

Table 2.1	**Powerless Language, Interpretation, and Examples**	
Powerless Language	**Interpreted as**	**Example**
Hesitation	Uncertain, nervous, timid	*"I think . . . well, yeah . . . I saw someone take, er, your notebook."*
Hedges	Less absolute, qualifying phrases	*"I guess that would be a good idea."*
Tag questions	Weak assertion, less absolute	*"That was a good idea, wasn't it?"*
Polite forms	Subordinate	*"Please pick up your dishes."*
Intensifiers	Unsuccessful attempt to make words sound stronger	*"It's really, really easy."*
Disclaimers	Diversion of responsibility, fault, truth	*"Remember, this is just what I heard . . ."*

and credibility than those teachers who used powerless language. Students' level of uncertainty was significantly higher with those teachers who used powerless language. This study reminds us that it is important to be mindful of how we use language in the classroom and its impact on learning.

PERCEPTIONS AND VERBAL COMMUNICATION

Credibility believability; has three dimensions: competence, character, and goodwill.

Competence the knowledge or expertise of a source.

character dimension of competence that evaluates the extent to which a source is perceived as being trustworthy.

goodwill dimension of credibility that refers to perceptions of one's ability to demonstrate concern for others.

Status refers to the level of position an individual has when compared with others; this may be social, socio-economic, and/or organizational status.

One study found that we need to hear only ten to fifteen seconds of an individual's speech to form initial perceptions (Entwisle, 1970). Often perceptions remain stable over time. The next section is designed to give you some insight on some typical perceptions of verbal communication. First, we explore how language choices can impact perceptions of credibility and status. We then discuss types of communication considered biased. Afterwards we explore the concept of verbal immediacy as it relates to confirming and disconfirming messages.

Credibility and Status

We can demonstrate credibility in our interpersonal relationships through our verbal communication messages. Credibility or believability can be defined as having three dimensions: competence, character, and goodwill (McCroskey & Young, 1981; McCroskey & Teven, 1999). Competence refers to your knowledge or expertise, while character is the extent to which you are trustworthy. The third dimension, goodwill, refers to your ability to care or feel concerned.

Typically, we base our perceptions of credibility on the perceived status of an individual. Status refers to the level of position an individual has when compared with others. This may be social, socio-economic, and/or organizational status. In addition to nonverbal behavior, we can gain an understanding of credibility through an individual's verbal comments. The degree of formality, vocabulary, accent, rate of speech, fluency of language, and articulation all play a role in our perceptions of credibility and status. Recall our earlier example of instructors perceptions of informal email messages from students. In this example, the instructor is of higher status in the educational system than students. Therefore instructors were bothered by casual emails because it did not communicate respect and professionalism. As a result, future communication with the student was negatively impacted. Our perceptions also affect our ability to listen. We tend to listen more attentively to persons of high status than to someone we perceive as having low status. Do you think you may listen to secretaries differently than you do medical doctors? Being mindful of your own communication practices can help improve your interpersonal relationships. When we are mindful we give attention to our reactions to communication interactions. By paying attention we may be open to other types of reactions that may be more aligned with our relational goals.

How might verbal perception impact this person's credibility?

© VGstockstudio/Shutterstock.com

Biased Communication and Language

In the beginning of this chapter, we said that the words we choose can be used to strengthen relationships or to destroy them. When we use biased, sexist, racist, and offensive language, we are choosing to cause harm to others.

Recall the following riddle:

A doctor and a boy are fishing. The boy was the doctor's son, but the doctor was not the boy's father. Who was the doctor?

The answer is: The doctor is the boy's mother. The punch line of this riddle is relying on the fact that we would initially assume that the doctor was male. Researchers have agreed that sexist language ultimately reinforces a sexist community. Sexist language refers to any speech that is degrading to males or females. Most of the research examines how females are subordinate figures in our male-geared vocabulary, with words like *chairman* and *fireman* illustrating the masculine focus of our language structure. To avoid sexist language, researchers suggest using gender-neutral words. The National Council of Teachers of English (NCTE) suggests several guidelines (see Table 2.2).

Verbally attacking individuals on the basis of their race, ethnic background, religion, gender, or sexual orientation is considered hate speech (Pember, 2003). As with sexist language, hate speech is used to degrade others. Hate speech includes racist language or words that dehumanize individuals from a particular ethnicity. Anthony Hudson (2003) argues, "The use of language to achieve and/or perpetuate the subordination of a group of people is well documented. Whether it be Jews in Nazi Germany, African Americans in the U.S., or slaves in Mauritania, language has been and continues to be a vital tool in the oppression and abuse of minority groups" (p. 46). Do you recall the Paula Deen controversy in 2013? Certainly you may be able to recall other media figures who have received negative press when they utilized certain words to express themselves.

Sexist language refers to any speech that is degrading to males or females

hate speech a the act of verbally attacking individuals on the basis of their race, ethnic background, religion, gender, or sexual orientation

Table 2.2   Suggestions for Avoiding Sexist Language

National Council of Teachers of English Guidelines

Examples	Alternatives
mankind	humanity, people, human beings
man's achievements	human achievements
manmade	synthetic, manufactured, machine-made
the common man	the average person, ordinary people
man the stockroom	staff the stockroom
nine man-hours	nine staff-hours
chairman	coordinator, moderator, presiding officer, head
businessman	business executive
fireman	firefighter
mailman	mail carrier
steward and stewardess	flight attendant
policeman/woman	police officer
congressman	congressional representative

EXAMPLE: Give each student his paper as soon as he is finished.
ALTERNATIVE: Give students their papers as soon as they are finished.
EXAMPLE: The average student is worried about his grade.
ALTERNATIVE: The average student is worried about grades.

Adapted from http://owl.english.purdue.edu/handouts/general/gl_nonsex.html.

It is important to be aware that we have choices in deciding our verbal communication and our words may have powerful implications.

VERBAL IMMEDIACY

It makes sense to say that we approach things we like and avoid things we do not. Albert Mehrabian and his colleagues used this approach-avoidance theory as a basis for the concept of immediacy in the late 1960s. Mehrabian describes immediacy as the process of using communication behaviors purposefully to reduce psychological and physical distance (1969). Researchers have found many benefits to engaging in immediacy behaviors, including increased perceptions of liking and attraction. Immediacy may be enacted verbally and nonverbally, but we will focus on the verbal features in this chapter.

Verbal immediacy refers to using specific word choices and syntactic structures to increase perceptions of psychological closeness. Something as simple as using words such as "we" and "our" is considered more immediate than "I" and "yours." Consider this the next time you confront your roommate about the apartment being cluttered. You might say, "We should clean this apartment before dinner. Our stuff is everywhere," instead of "You should clean the apartment. I cleaned last time."

Gorham (1988) examined verbal immediacy in the classroom. She suggests that instructors can gain a psychological closeness with their students by engaging in a variety of verbal immediacy behaviors such as using humor, self-disclosing, utilizing students' names and viewpoints throughout the lecture, incorporating student suggestions into the course, and showing a willingness to work with students outside of the classroom. Teachers' use of verbally immediate messages was correlated with perceived cognitive and affective learning outcomes. Utilizing verbally immediate messages with friends, family members, and coworkers can also increase perceptions of liking and attraction.

One way to portray verbal immediacy is through confirming messages. Research suggests we discover and establish our identity through confirming messages in interpersonal relationships (Buber, 1957). Confirming messages can help others feel recognized, acknowledged, valued, and respected. (Laing, 1961). Conversely, disconfirming messages communicate a sense of insignificance and worthlessness and act to invalidate the source (Watzlawick, Beavin, & Jackson, 1967). Research in this area has found that our self-esteem is impacted by these confirming and disconfirming messages (Cissna & Keating, 1979).

There are four functions of confirming messages: (1) to express recognition of the other's existence, (2) to acknowledge a relationship of affiliation with the other, (3) to express awareness of the significance or worth of the other, and (4) to accept or endorse the other's self-experience (Cissna & Sieburg, 1981).

In Table 2.3 we list the four functions of confirming messages, state what is being intrinsically expressed to the other person for each function, provide examples of how to verbalize the confirming messages in interpersonal relationships, and describe possible outcomes of communicating in this manner.

Conversely, there are three groupings of disconfirming messages: indifference, imperviousness, and disqualification of the message or speaker. Are you aware of the extent to which you may rely on these behaviors? They may be the

---

immediacy the process of using communication behaviors purposefully to reduce psychological and physical distance.

Verbal immediacy refers to using specific word choices and syntactic structures to increase perceptions of psychological closeness.

Confirming messages messages that communicate feelings of recognition, acknowledgement, value and respect

disconfirming messages messages that communicate a sense of insignificance and worthlessness.

cause of unsatisfying relationships and ineffective communicative patterns. In Table 2.4 we list three disconfirming messages, with specific types and examples. The Confirming/Disconfirming Scale located at the end of this chapter will enable you to evaluate how your own instructor uses confirming and disconfirming messages in the classroom.

Table 2.3   Confirming Messages

Function of Confirming Message	Expresses	Example of Confirming Message	Outcome
To express recognition of the other's existence	*"To me, you exist."*	*"Certainly, that is upsetting."*	This recognizes and validates the speaker's feelings
To acknowledge a relationship of affiliation with the other	*"We are relating."*	*"Wow! That happened to me, too."*	This recognizes that you can relate to the speaker
To express awareness of the significance or worth of the other	*"To me, you are significant."*	*"What happened to you is terrible!"*	This suggests you are attentive to their situation
To accept or endorse the other's self-experience	*"Your way of interpreting the world is valid."*	*"Sure, I can see how you thought that."*	You are increasing perceptions of value and respect

Table 2.4   Types of Disconfirming Messages

Disconfirming Message	Type	Example
Indifference response	Denying the presence of the other	Being silent when a response is expected, looking away, withdrawing, engaging in unrelated activities
	Denying the relation or involvement of the other	Using impersonal language by avoiding using the first person, avoiding feeling statements or disclosures, using nonverbal "distancing," avoiding eye contact and touch
	Rejecting the communication of the other	Talking "over" another, interjecting irrelevant comments
Imperviousness or lack of accurate awareness of others' perceptions	Denial or distortion of others' self-expression	*"You don't really mean that,"* or *"You are only saying that because . . ."*
	Pseudo-confirmation	*"Stop crying, there is nothing wrong with you,"* or *"Don't be silly, of course you are not scared."*
	Mystification	*"No matter what you say, I know you still love me,"* or *"You may think you feel that way now . . ."*
	Selective responses	Rewarding speaker with attention and relevant responses only when he communicates in an approved fashion, while becoming silent or indifferent when the communication does not meet the responder's approval
Disqualification	Messages that disqualify the other person by direct disparagement	Insult, name-calling, or indirect disparagement (verbal or nonverbal)
	Messages that disqualify another message by transactional disqualification or tangential response	Using the speaker's remark as a starting point for a shift to a new topic to accomplish your own agenda
	Messages that are self-disqualifying	Being unclear, incomplete, ambiguous, or sending incongruent verbal–nonverbal messages

FACTORS AFFECTING VERBAL COMMUNICATION

Factors such as age, sex, and context influence the words that we choose to use when communicating as well as how we interpret verbal messages from others. One factor that influences how we choose to verbally communicate and how others interpret messages is age. This includes how our communication changes and is interpreted over time or life span.

Life Span

From perceptions of control in mother-daughter relationships (Morgan & Hummert, 2000) to the meaning of friendships (Patterson, Bettini, & Nussbaum, 1993), our communicative patterns differ over our lifetime. Jon Nussbaum and his colleagues have conducted a considerable amount of research on the relationship between life-span factors and communication behaviors (see Williams and Nussbaum, 2001 for a more recent review). In the next section, we offer three examples of how our verbal communication with different age groups has an impact on our lives.

How parents *respond to their children* may impact how they view themselves. For example, those parents who are controlling and critical may threaten a child's self-esteem. Self-esteem is the value we place on ourselves. Some research indicates that having high self-esteem has been associated with several positive attributes such as competence, assertiveness, and tenacity. Many parents struggle to establish environments where children have the opportunity to develop a heightened view of themselves through achieving goals and task completion. Some research has shown that children with low or unstable self-esteem levels reported significantly more instances of critical and psychologically controlling parent-child communication than children with high self-esteem (Kernis, Brown, & Brody, 2000). When parents are less likely to acknowledge their children's positive behaviors or show approval in value-affirming ways, children are more likely to develop low self-esteem. To improve children's perceptions of self, parents should attempt to occasionally use confirming messages and avoid disconfirming messages. Confirming messages will express recognition of the child's existence and the worth of the child. These findings suggest that parent-child verbal communication effectiveness can impact a child's level of self-esteem.

© Golden Pixels LLC/Shutterstock.com   © bokan/Shutterstock.com

How do confirming messages function for parents and children?

What *parents choose to talk about with their teens* and what they choose to ignore may have a serious impact on their teen's behavior. Research on parent-child communication indicates that the extent to which parents communicate with their teens about sex, birth control, and sexually transmitted diseases will directly impact the teen's sexual behavior. Specifically, research by Whitaker and Miller (2000) found that parents who spoke to adolescents about sex reduced the associations the adolescents made about their own behavior with perceptions of their peers' sexual behavior. Whitaker and Miller also found that communicating to teens about condom use correlated with adolescents' safer sexual behavior.

Finally, how some *young people communicate with the elderly* may be considered patronizing and inappropriate. Consider the following scenario.

> Patrick goes to the nursing home to visit his only living grandmother. He typically goes with his mother, but since he was leaving for college the next day, he thought he would stop in to say goodbye before he left town. Patrick walks in the room and yells, "HELLO, GRANDMA!" His grandmother acknowledges his greeting by shaking her head and smiling. "How are you feeling today?" he asks slowly. She replies jokingly, "I would be feeling better if I could get some decent food." Patrick notices his grandmother has not eaten much from the lunch tray lying over her lap. "Grandma, you really should eat . . . it's good for you," he asserts. He proceeds to pick up her fork. "Here . . . let me help you." She pushes his hand away, and snaps, "I am fine, stop talking to me like a baby!"

It appears that Patrick is going too far to accommodate his grandmother. Why does Patrick treat his grandmother like this? According to communication accommodation theory (Giles & Wiemann, 1987):

1. During social interaction people will accommodate their speech based on the receiver.
2. People adjust their speech to gain approval and maintain positive impressions.

In most circumstances, individuals have good intentions to shift their speech patterns to more closely resemble their receiver—this is called convergence. This may mean they hide or emphasize a particular accent or choose slang words for particular groups of people. When individuals overdo convergence, it may backfire and end up insulting or patronizing their receiver. This is called overaccommodation. In this situation, it appears that Patrick is exhibiting overaccommodation. Overaccommodating can make the receiver feel degraded and underestimated. As a result, Patrick was interacting with his grandmother as if she were a baby.

The communication predicament of aging model (Coupland, Coupland, & Giles, 1991; Ryan, Giles, Bartolucci, & Henwood, 1986; Ryan, Hummert, & Boich, 1995) suggests that when young people communicate with the elderly, they often rely on negative stereotypes. These negative stereotypes imply that the elderly have declined in cognitive, perceptual, and emotional competence. As a result of these faulty perceptions, young people overcompensate by engaging in "patronizing communication" with the elderly. These patronizing communicative behaviors include: (1) speaking in short sentences, (2) using simple words, (3) using a high volume, (4) speaking at a slow rate, and

communication accommodation theory suggests that people accommodate their speech to their receivers in order to help gain approval and maintain positive impressions.

convergence a process referred to in communication accommodation theory that refers to shifting speech patterns to more closely resemble their receiver.

overaccommodation a negative results referred to in communication accommodation theory when individuals shift speech patterns so severely that it insults or makes the receiver feel degraded or underestimated.

communication predicament of aging a model that suggests that when young people communicate with the elderly, they often rely on negative stereotypes; these negative stereotypes imply that the elderly have declined in cognitive, perceptual, and emotional competence.

How can intergenerational interactions be improved?

(5) exaggerating articulation. This patronizing talk may contribute to unsatisfactory intergenerational interactions.

Although it is important to be able to communicate across age groups, it is often difficult because of the lack of homophily, or similarity. These three examples offer some insight into the problematic symptoms and implications of verbally communicating outside of your age group.

Sex Differences in Verbal Communication

When it comes to communicating, are men really from Mars and women from Venus? Maltz and Borker (1982) theorize that the way in which girls and boys play at a young age impacts their speech later in life. Let us look at the type of games young children play.

> ... no one approach or style of communication is better than the other, just different.

Girls often enjoy games that rely on cooperative play, such as house, Barbie dolls, or school. In these types of play there needs to be a negotiation of rules. Questions like who will be Barbie and who will be the teacher need to be answered. After all, it would be difficult to play school if everyone wanted to be the teacher and no one wanted to be the students. During these childhood games, girls focus on their own and others' feelings, attitudes, and emotions. In addition, girls often discuss taking turns and decide on imaginary scenes. Therefore, girls encourage talk that emphasizes collaboration and sharing. Their conversations emphasize cooperativeness and discourage aggressiveness.

Boys, on the other hand, tend to be more competitive in their childhood games. Cops and robbers, war, sports, video games, and "king of the hill," are just a few examples of boys' games. Typically in these games, there are set rules, so there is less negotiation and, therefore, less talk. Discussions are usually driven by reiterating the rules or reinforcing them. Boys value competitiveness and aggressiveness because their games center on clear winners and losers. They value assertiveness, direct communication, and having a clear purpose.

rapport talk talking for the sake of talking.

report talk talking to accomplish goals.

Additionally, you may recall our discussion of rapport talk and report talk from an earlier chapter. Deborah Tannen, a professor at Georgetown University and the author of several best-selling books, including *You Just Don't Understand: Women and Men in Conversations*, proposes that women engage in "rapport talk," or talking for the sake of talking. In other words, women talk for pleasure and to establish connections with others. In contrast, men engage in "report talk," or talking to accomplish goals. Males talk to solve problems and are more instrumental in their approach to communication. Over the last 20 years, Tannen has identified a number of differences in male and female perspectives in regard to communication and relationships. She emphasizes that no one approach or style of communication is better than the other, just different. To improve male-female communication, it is important to understand the differences in perspective as well as the reasons they exist.

How does rapport talk differ from report talk?

This section provides some insight into how men and women may be socialized to communicate differently. This is not to say that throughout your experiences, you have not met males who engage in rapport talk and females who engage in report talk. We acknowledge that these are research generalizations, and they certainly do not apply to everyone.

Contextual Differences

In addition to age and gender, the context of the verbal communication will impact the outcome of the message. We identified context as a characteristic of verbal communication in the beginning of this chapter. We believe this is a key feature when determining appropriate verbal communication. Therefore we have provided a more in-depth examination into how to communicate effectively within specific contexts, including within intercultural relationships (Chapter 11) and our families (Chapter 12), and health-care professionals (Chapter 13). Furthermore, we will discuss how appropriate communication is used when our relationships are initiating (Chapter 7), sustaining (Chapter 8), growing dark (Chapter 10), and terminating (Chapter 9).

BEST PRACTICES: AVOID VERBAL PITFALLS

Utilizing appropriate words that are clear and direct are our best chances of reaching shared meaning in our interpersonal communication. This section will offer three strategies that will help you avoid verbal pitfalls such as misinterpretations in your interpersonal relationships.

Clarity

When you are composing a message, keep in mind the KISS acronym: Keep It Short and Simple. Be clear and succinct. Often we think that using large words will make us sound intelligent, but this is a risky strategy. We may confuse our audience. Direct and clear language will increase your chances of reaching *shared meaning*—your ultimate goal.

KISS the "keep it short and simple" principle

Appropriateness

Appropriateness refers to the ability to send messages that uphold the expectations for a given situation. When we send appropriate messages we are considering the contextual and personal attributes of the communication environment. Ask yourself, "What is the best way to send this message to this particular receiver?" This question will help you become more empathetic, compassionate, and sensitive over time. In order to send appropriate messages, we must try to understand the contextual and personal attributes that exist within our communication environments. One way to get better is to try different approaches and see how they work. Look for nonverbal and verbal feedback. Most people will appreciate your genuine effort to "reach" them.

Appropriateness refers to the ability to send messages that uphold the expectations for a given situation and that are aligned with the contextual and personal attributes of the communication environment.

Concreteness

Concreteness refers to
being able to communicate
thoughts and ideas
specifically; utilizing symbols
that are likely to resemble
what they represent

Concreteness refers to being able to communicate thoughts and ideas specifically. In other words, choose your words wisely. Avoid jargon and superfluous words that are unnecessary. This will keep the receiver of your message "on track." Intentionally choosing words your receiver will relate to can increase your chances of being understood. Be specific and illustrative. For example, when an employer asks you to describe yourself, you might say that you are a "good leader"—but do not stop there. Offer a specific example of how you demonstrated leadership in a past role.

SUMMARY

Research on verbal communication dates back to Aristotle and continues to this day. We are fascinated with how individuals learn and use words because their impact is so powerful and significant. Catastrophes such as 9/11, Hurricane Katrina, and the Sandy Hook Elementary School shooting affect our language and change it forever. We start to think differently when we hear words like "terrorist," "gun control," and "evacuee" after such events. Television and movies also introduce new words and phrases, such as "Vote for Pedro" (*Napoleon Dynamite*), "Bazinga" (*The Big Bang Theory*), "That's what she said" (*The Office*), and "May the odds be ever in your favor," (*The Hunger Games*) into our vocabulary. In this chapter we presented definitions, features, functions, and perceptions of verbal communication. The goal of this chapter was to increase your understanding of verbal communication and how certain verbal styles are perceived by others. Heightening awareness of our own verbal communication as well as the verbal communication used by others will ultimately improve our understanding of interpersonal relationships.

DISCUSSION QUESTIONS

1. Recall the scenario in the beginning of the chapter. How could you redesign the verbal communication Lauren used to her partner to express her thoughts?
2. Are there gender differences in regulative and constitutive rules? Do men and women follow different rules? When is it socially acceptable for a male to violate a rule? What about females?
3. What is your position on the role that politically correct language plays in our interactions with others? Are we too sensitive?
4. Recall an example of a situation in which your own words (or the words of others) affected your perceptions. What strategies did/could you use to ensure that there was shared understanding of the message?

REFERENCES

Adler, R. B., & Rodman, G. (2006). *Understanding human communication*. New York: Oxford University Press.

Angelini, J. R., & Billings, A. (2010). An agenda that sets the frames: Gender, language, and NBC's Americanized Olympic telecast. *Journal of Language and Social Psychology, 29*, 363–385.

Bavelas, J. B., Black, A., Chovil, N., & Mullett, J. (1990). *Equivocal communication.* Newbury Park, CA: Sage.

Baxter, L. (1984). Trajectories of relationship disengagement. *Journal of Social and Personal Relationships, 1,* 29–48.

Berger, P. L., & Luckmann, T. (1966). *The social construction of reality: A treatise in the sociology of knowledge.* Garden City, New York: Anchor Books.

Buber, M. (1957). Distance and relation. *Psychiatry, 20,* 97–104.

Cheseboro, J. L. (2003). Effects of teacher clarity and nonverbal immediacy on student learning, receiver apprehension and affect. *Communication Education, 52,* 135–147.

Cissna, K. N., & Keating, S. (1979). Speech communication antecedents of perceived confirmation. *The Western Journal of Speech Communication, 43,* 48–60.

Cissna, K. N., & Sieburg, E. (1981). Patterns of interactional confirmation and disconfirmation. In C. Wilder-Mott & J. H. Weakland (Eds.), *Rigor and imagination: Essays from the legacy of Gregory Bateson* (pp. 253–282). New York: Praeger.

Coupland, N., Coupland, J., & Giles, H. (1991). *Language, society and the elderly.* Oxford: Basil Blackwell.

Cronen, V. E., Pearce, W. B., & Snavely, L. (1979). A theory of rule structure and forms of episodes, and a study of unwanted repetitive patterns. In D. Nimmo (Ed.), *Communication Yearbook III, New Brunswich, NJ: Transaction Press.*

Ebert, L., & Floyd, K. (2004). Affection expressions as face threatening acts: Receiver assessments. *Communication Studies, 55,* 254–270.

Edwards, A., & Shepherd, G. J. (2004). Theories of communication, human nature, and the world: Associations and implications. *Communication Studies, 55,* 197–208.

Entwisle, D. R. (1970). Semantic systems of children: Some assessments of social class and ethnic differences. In F. Williams (Ed.), *Language and poverty,* New York: Sage.

Fandrich, A. M., Beck, S. J. (2012). Powerless language in health media: The influence of biological sex and magazine type on health language. *Communication Studies, 63,* 36–53.

Floyd, K. (1997). Communicating affection in dyadic relationships: An assessment of behavior and expectations. *Communication Quarterly, 45,* 68–80.

Giles, H., & Wiemann, J. M. (1987). Language, social comparison and power. In C.R. Berger & S. H. Chaffee (Eds.), *Handbook of communication science* (pp. 350–384). Newbury Park, CA: Sage.

Gorham, J. (1988). The relationship between verbal teacher immediacy and student learning. *Communication Education, 37,* 40–53.

Griffin, E. (2003). *A first look at communication theory.* Boston: McGraw-Hill.

Haleta, L. (1996). Students' perceptions of teachers' use of language: The effects of powerful and powerless language on impression formation and uncertainty. *Communication Teacher, 45,* 16–28.

Hirst, R. (2003). Scientific jargon: Good and bad. *Journal of Technical Writing and Communication, 33,* 201–229.

Hudson, A. (2003). Fighting words. *Index on Censorship, 32,* 45–52.

Kernis, M. H., Brown, A. C., & Brody, G. H. (2000). Fragile self-esteem in children and its associations with perceived patterns of parent-child communication. *Journal of Personality, 68,* 225–252.

Laing, R. D. (1961). *The self and others.* New York: Pantheon.

Maltz, D., & Borker, R. (1982). *A cultural approach to male-female miscommunication.* In J. Gumperz (Ed.), *Language and social identity,* Cambridge: Cambridge University Press (pp. 196–216).

McCroskey, J. C., & Teven, J. J. (1999). Goodwill: A reexamination of the construct and its measurement. *Communication Monographs, 66,* 90–103.

McCroskey, J. C., & Young, T. J. (1981). Ethos and credibility: The construct and its measurement after three decades. *Central States Speech Journal, 32,* 24–34.

Mehrabian, A. (1969). Some referents and measures of nonverbal behavior. *Behavioral Research Methods and Instrumentation, 1*, 213–217.

Morgan, M., & Hummert, M. L. (2000). Perceptions of communicative control strategies in mother-daughter dyads across the life span. *Journal of Communication, 50*, 49–64.

Nash, W. (1993). *Jargon: Its uses and abuses.* Oxford: Blackwell Publishers.

Patterson, B., Bettini, L., & Nussbaum, J. F. (1993). The meaning of friendship across the life-span: Two studies. *Communication Quarterly, 41*, 145–161.

Pearce, W. B., Cronen, V. E., & Conklin, R. F. (1979). On what to look at when studying communication: A hierarchical model of actors' meanings. *Communication, 4*, 195–220.

Pember, D. (2003). *Mass media law.* Boston: McGraw-Hill.

Persing, B. (1977). Sticks and stones and words: Women in the language. *Journal of Business Communication, 14*, 11–19.

Rickford, J. (1999). *African American Vernacular English.* Malden, MA: Blackwell Publishers.

Rickford, J., & R. Rickford. (2000). *Spoken soul: The story of black English.* Hoboken, NJ: John Wiley.

Ryan, E. B., Giles, H., Bartolucci, G., & Henwood, K. (1986). Psycholinguistic and social psychological components of communication by and with the elderly. *Language and Communication, 6*, 1–24.

Ryan, E. B., Hummert, M. L., & Boich, L. H. (1995). Communication predicaments of aging: Patronising behavior towards older adults. *Journal of Language and Social Psychology 14*, 144–166.

Sapir, E. (1949). *Selected writings of Edward Sapir in language, culture, and personality.* D. G. Mandelbaum (Ed.). Los Angeles: University of California- Berkeley.

Seale, J. (1995). *The construction of social reality.* New York: The Free Press.

Stephens, K. K., Houser, M. L., & Cowan, R. L. (2009). R U able to meat me: The impact of students' overly casual email messages to instructors. *Communication Education, 58*, 303–326.

Ting-Toomey, S., & Chung, L. C. (2005). *Understanding intercultural communication.* Los Angeles, CA: Roxbury.

Watzlawick, P., Beavin, J. H., & Jackson, D. D. (1967). *Pragmatics of human communication: A study of interactional patterns, pathologies, and paradoxes.* New York: W. W. Norton & Company.

Whitaker, D. J., & Miller, K. S. (2000). Parent-adolescent discussions about sex and condoms: Impact on peer influences of sexual risk behavior. *Journal of Adolescent Research, 15*, 251–273.

Whorf, B. L. (1956). *Language, thought, and reality: The collected papers of Benjamin Lee Whorf.* J. B. Carroll (Ed.). Cambridge, MA: MIT Press.

Williams, A., & Nussbaum, J. F. (2001). *Intergenerational communication across the life span.* Mahwah, NJ: Lawrence Erlbaum.

Nonverbal Communication:
It's Not *What* You Said; It's *How* You Said It

OBJECTIVES

- Define nonverbal communication and its distinct characteristics.
- Explain nonverbal expectancy violation theory.
- Recall the four functions of nonverbal messages.
- Describe three functions of facial communication.
- Explain and provide examples of the five categories of kinesics and the four types of space.
- Distinguish between the five categories of touch.
- Discuss how we use nonverbal communication to regulate our conversations.

SCENARIO: SOUND FAMILIAR?

David woke up and thought he and his partner were on the same page about saving money for an upcoming trip. His partner repeatedly said, "Sounds fine" and "Everything is good." However, their limited conversation over breakfast and the way his partner rushed out of the house suggested the conversation was anything but "fine."

KEY TERMS

Accenting
Acronyms
Adaptors
Affect displays
Artifacts
Back-channeling cues
Believable
Chronemics
Cognitive arousal
Complementing
Continuous
Contradicting
Culturally bound
Decoding
Ectomorph
Electronic
  paralanguage

Emblems
Emoticons
Encoding
Endomorph
Environmental
  adornment
Environmental factors
Facial communication
Flaming
Friendship-warmth
Functional-
  professional
Haptics
Homophily
Illustrator
Immediacy
Kinesics

Love-intimacy
Markers
Mesomorph
Monochromic
Multi-channeled
Nonverbal
  communication
Nonverbal expectancy
  violation theory
Oculesics
Paralanguage
Personal adornment
Physical appearance
Physical arousal
Polychromic
Proactive attribution
Proxemics

Contradicting when we say one thing and behave in a way that is inconsistent with our verbal message

Polychromic time is perceived as circular

Regulate	Sexual-arousal	Turn-maintaining
Regulator	Social-polite	Turn-requesting
Repetition	Social referencing	Turn-yielding
Retroactive attribution	Turn-denying	

OVERVIEW

This familiar scenario reminds us that our verbal communication and nonverbal communication are not always in sync. However, when *what* we are saying contradicts *how* we are saying it, we know that individuals tend to believe the nonverbal cues over what has been said. Therefore understanding nonverbal communication is critically important in initiating and maintaining healthy and effective interpersonal relationships. This chapter identifies and defines characteristics of nonverbal communication and reviews eight types of nonverbal behavior. The theories, research, and applications of nonverbal communication throughout this chapter will help you apply appropriate and effective communication with others. Furthermore, you will gain an enhanced understanding of how nonverbal communication functions and be able to consider how nonverbal communication influences our everyday interactions.

DEFINING NONVERBAL COMMUNICATION

There has been a vast amount of research done in the area of nonverbal communication. Scholars have examined everything from the importance of physical attractiveness in the job interview (Watkins & Johnston, 2000) to the implications of creating positive impressions in the physician-patient interaction (Street & Buller, 1987). From something as obvious as our physical appearance to a subtle pause during a conversation, we are captivated by the meanings created by others' nonverbal behaviors. While it is impossible to put a numerical value on the amount of meaning created through nonverbal and verbal communication, we know that the majority of meaning is generated through nonverbal communication. This makes sense if you think about the amount of time you spend communicating nonverbally versus verbally. Even when we are not speaking, we are constantly sending nonverbal messages to others. Consider all of the nonverbal messages you sent to your instructor today while you were sitting in class listening to the lecture. Have you thought about how online students also send nonverbal messages to their instructors?

What nonverbal messages are communicated in this picture?

© wavebreakmedia /Shutterstock.com

nonverbal communication refers to all aspects of communication other than the words we use

The popular phrases "It's not *what* you said, it's *how* you said it," or "Actions speak louder than words," are examples of the emphasis our culture places on the nonverbal portion of communicating. While verbal communication refers to the words we use to express ourselves, nonverbal communication refers to all aspects of communication other than the words we use, including but not limited to: facial expressions, body movements and gestures, physical appearance, and voice. As explained in Chapter 1, each message we send has two components: the content level of meaning and the relationship level of meaning. While the content level of meaning is usually conveyed through the words we use, the relationship level of meaning is often created through *how* we say those words. Therefore, understanding nonverbal communication will play a critical role in understanding the relationship level of meaning in our messages.

Throughout the remaining sections of this chapter, we isolate specific types of nonverbal communication and discuss relevant research findings. However, before we do this, it is first necessary to distinguish nonverbal communication from verbal communication.

DISTINCT CHARACTERISTICS OF NONVERBAL MESSAGES

The first characteristic that is unique to nonverbal communication is that it is continuous. While there is a clear distinction between when we begin verbally communicating and when we stop, nonverbal communication continues beyond our words. Some say, "*You cannot not communicate.*" This suggests we are continuously sending nonverbal messages that are being perceived by others. Even in the absence of others, we are sending nonverbal messages. For example, think about a high school friend you have not spoken to in a long time. She may perceive your silence and distance in several ways. Perhaps she thinks you are extremely busy or maybe she thinks that you are upset with her. What else might she think?

> **continuous** refers to the fact that there is no clear distinction between when we start and stop nonverbal communication; it continues beyond our words

Our nonverbal messages may conflict with our verbal messages. We may say one thing, but behave inconsistently with our verbal message. For example, you might tell Aunty Lucy you liked the knit scarf she made for you. However, your facial expressions might tell another story as you pull the purple-and-red polka dot creation out of the package. When our nonverbal and verbal messages contradict each other, research has shown that we tend to believe the nonverbal messages. Therefore, a second unique feature of nonverbal communication is that nonverbal is more believable than verbal communication. Although our nonverbal communication often supplements our verbal communication, such as raising our eyebrows to help stress or emphasize certain words, we tend to believe the nonverbal more than the verbal when there is a discrepancy between the two. While Aunt Lucy heard you say you liked the scarf, she will probably interpret your facial grimace as a stronger indicator of whether it will actually become a part of your wardrobe.

> When our nonverbal and verbal messages contradict each other, research has shown that we tend to believe the nonverbal messages.

> **believable** refers to the fact that when our nonverbal and verbal messages contradict each other, research has shown that we tend to believe the nonverbal messages

While verbal communication relies solely on the words we exchange with others, nonverbal communication has many different outlets. Therefore, a third distinct feature of nonverbal messages is they are multi-channeled. We can use several channels to communicate something nonverbally. Doctors dress professionally, maintain eye contact, listen attentively, and hang their diplomas on the wall in an attempt to establish credibility with their patients. Likewise, day spas manipulate lighting, music, and aroma to communicate a relaxing and calm atmosphere. Because we use multiple cues to send the same message, it makes sense that we will have a higher chance of nonverbal effectiveness. Although it may seem that nonverbal and verbal messages are quite different, they do have similar characteristics. Let us discuss three similarities between verbal and nonverbal communication.

> **multi-channeled** refers to the fact that we can use several senses to communicate something nonverbally

NONVERBAL FEATURES THAT ARE SIMILAR TO VERBAL MESSAGES

Just like verbal messages, nonverbal messages are rule-guided. As mentioned in Chapter 2, there are certain rules we must follow to be socially appropriate, and these rules are culturally defined. In regard to nonverbal communication, *constitutive rules* refer to the behaviors we enact to help define the appropriateness of our communication. For example, if we asked you to generate a list of nonverbal behaviors that would communicate respect in a job interview, could you do this? We can demonstrate respect and professionalism in a job interview through our choice of clothing and use of certain gestures and facial expressions. Also, we adhere to specific rules when it comes to regulating or monitoring our communication with others. Recall from Chapter 2 that we use *regulative rules* to control and/or manage our interaction. In the same way that we use words to start, maintain, or end our conversations with others, we also use nonverbal communication to control or regulate our conversations. Eye contact (or lack thereof), specific hand gestures, paralanguage, and nods are all examples of nonverbal signals that we use to indicate turn-taking cues in conversation. We can use humor to help demonstrate these concepts. In order for a joke to be funny, we must properly apply both constitutive and regulative rules. When applying constitutive rules to telling jokes, we have to ask ourselves: Is it appropriate for this environment and audience? Is it age-appropriate? When considering regulative rules, we can identify good joke tellers versus bad joke tellers based on how they utilize regulative rules. For example, to tell a good story or joke, you must be able to take a dramatic pause before the punch line. Also, effective use of inflection, facial expressions, and eye contact are necessary to pull off a good joke.

Burgoon (1978) developed nonverbal expectancy violation theory to help understand rule-guided behavior. The theory suggests that individuals hold expectancies for nonverbal behavior and, when these expectations are violated (or the rules are not abided by), there are two common reactions, physical arousal and cognitive arousal. Physical arousal refers to the physical response a person has to nonverbal expectancies being violated. The cognitive arousal is the mental response a person has to nonverbal expectancies being violated.

Many of our behaviors are rule-guided. These rules are culturally created and maintained. Recall the last time you entered an elevator, you probably adhered to rule-guided behavior in this situation. If you are in an elevator alone and the door opens and a stranger enters, the nonverbal expectancy is that he or she will stand as far away from you as possible (in order to maximize each other's personal space). If this stranger stood directly next to you, this would be a violation of a space rule. In response to this space violation, you probably would consider stepping away (physical arousal) and also might consider the person odd (cognitive arousal) for not abiding by the "elevator rules." Nonverbal expectancy violation theory has helped shed light on our societal rules and responses to violations of these rules. Can you think of more examples of behaviors that are guided by rules? What would happen if these rules were violated?

Another similarity between nonverbal and verbal messages is that they are culturally bound. The rules we follow during social interaction are socially constructed and are restricted to a specific culture. Nonverbal gestures in the United States that imply certain meanings are not universally understood. In the United States, when we touch our forefinger to our thumb to create a circle and splay the other three fingers upward, we are signaling to others "OK" (see Figure 3.1) In France, this same gesture means "zero." In Japan it signals "money," and in Germany it is considered an obscene gesture.

nonverbal expectancy violation theory suggests that individuals hold expectancies for nonverbal behavior and when these expectations are violated (or the rules are not abided by) there are two common reactions, physical arousal and cognitive arousal

Physical arousal the physical response a person has to nonverbal expectancies being violated

cognitive arousal the cognitive or mental response a person has to nonverbal expectancies being violated

culturally bound characteristic of both verbal and nonverbal communication; states that the rules we follow during social interaction are socially constructed and are restricted to a specific culture

Figure 3.1 **Nonverbal symbols like this one are culturally bound.**

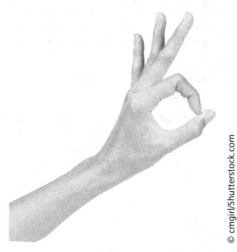

© cmgirl/Shutterstock.com

As with our verbal language, nonverbal messages are culturally bound and do not necessarily translate to other cultures. Even within the United States, there are several subcultures that attribute their own distinct meanings to particular nonverbal behaviors. Consider gang members and their particular signs of inclusion, or social groups such as fraternities that have specific handshakes. Nonverbal communication can be unclear and confusing and may lead to many misinterpretations. Therefore, it is important to be aware of how we enact these behaviors and to be sure to confirm their meaning by asking questions when messages are perceived as ambiguous.

Finally, both verbal and nonverbal messages are contextually restricted. As we previously mentioned, we must consider the situation, environment, and setting

> Depending on the context of the nonverbal communication, it may influence the interpretation, meaning, and appropriateness of the communication.

we are in when deciding on appropriateness. Depending on the context of the nonverbal communication, it may influence the interpretation, meaning, and appropriateness of the communication. When we are pitching a new idea to our boss, we tend to dress more formally and manipulate our posture to appear more professional. However, can you imagine how surprised your friends would be if you continued this behavior while you were relaxing at home? Just like the words we use, our nonverbal behaviors should be modified to fit the situation. To gain a better understanding of these specific nonverbal behaviors, we will discuss eight types of nonverbal communication.

EIGHT TYPES OF NONVERBAL COMMUNICATION

We have grouped nonverbal communication into eight broad categories: facial communication, kinesics, haptics, proxemics, paralanguage, physical appearance, artifacts, and chronemics. In this section we will explain each type and provide insight on how the particular nonverbal behavior influences meaning during social interaction.

Facial Communication

Facial communication includes any expression on the face that sends messages. Think about the thousands of different expressions you can make with your face by raising or lowering your eyebrows, shutting or opening your eyes, wrinkling your nose, and protruding your lips. Three functions of facial communication are:

- to display emotion;
- to supplement verbal communication; and
- to reinforce verbal communication.

To begin, our face is the primary channel for expressing emotions. The most basic emotions displayed through our facial expressions are often referred to by the acronym SADFISH, which stands for sadness, anger, disgust, fear, interest, surprise, and happiness. Can you determine each of these emotions in the pictures displayed in Figure 3.2?

Figure 3.2 **Can you identify the emotions in these images?**

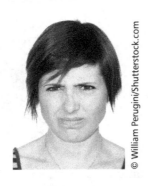
© William Perugini/Shutterstock.com

© ArtFamily/Shutterstock.com

© Ollyy/Shutterstock.com

© Pius Lee/Shutterstock.com

© djile/Shutterstock.com

© PathDoc/Shutterstock.com

© Jeanette Dietl/Shutterstock.com

The second function of facial expressions is to supplement or take the place of something it is missing, such as the verbal communication. Individuals reveal their attitudes through their facial expressions in this way. Think about how we analyze facial expressions when someone opens a gift from us. We can typically tell if they like the gift by the type of facial expression revealed. Researchers Ekman and Friesen (1969) were very interested in these types of behaviors and referred to them as nonverbal leakage or deception clues. The television series *Lie to Me* (2009–2011, on FOX) was based on Ekman's decades of research. See http://www.paulekman.com/lie-to-me/. During each episode, Dr. Cal Lightman (played by Tim Roth) would assist law enforcement by investigating whether individuals were telling the truth by analyzing microexpressions and body language.

In addition, we use facial communication to reinforce, or go along with, our verbal message. For example, when we want to emphasize a word, we tend to raise our eyebrows and open our eyes wide. This type of facial display matches the verbal portion of the message and reinforces the message. Overall, our facial movements communicate emotions, attitudes, and motivation.

One type of facial communication that has received a great deal of attention in the literature is oculesics. Oculesics is the study of eye behavior. Researchers are fascinated by oculesics and how it influences meaning. Eye behavior in the United States is very particular and is often perceived as an important means of showing attention, interest, and respect to others. We often encourage students to engage in eye contact during interviews for internships or jobs. However, if someone provides too much direct eye contact, it can be interpreted as disturbing and frightening. Eye contact is a perfect example of a nonverbal behavior that is culturally defined. Direct eye contact in Asian cultures is considered rude, disrespectful, and intimidating, while in the United States, eye contact during conversation is expected.

Oculesics the study of eye behavior

Kinesics

Another type of nonverbal communication often associated with facial expressions is kinesics, or body movements. Ekman and Friesen (1969) classify kinesics into five categories:

1. Emblems
2. Illustrators
3. Affect displays
4. Regulators
5. Adaptors

kinesics body movements; includes emblems, illustrators, affect displays, regulators, and adaptors

Emblems specific nonverbal gestures that have a particular translation

Let us examine each of these. Emblems are specific nonverbal gestures that have a particular translation. For example, extending your forefinger over your lips

> Eye behavior in the United States is very particular and is often perceived as an important means of showing attention, interest, and respect to others.

means to be quiet. Or if you wanted to signal to someone to "come here," you would wave your hand toward your body. Because these emblems are context-bound, they are often misinterpreted when communicating with individuals from other cultures. Kitao and Kitao (1988) explain that the emblem for "OK" in the United States is the emblem used for "money" in Japan. They write, "An American and a Japanese man wanted to meet some friends. The American called from a pay phone and signaled to the Japanese man the American emblem for 'okay,' indicating that the friends would be able to meet them. The Japanese man interpreted the emblem as meaning that more coins were needed for the pay phone and rushed over to put in more money" (p. 89). Although this is a lighthearted example, you can imagine how misinterpretations during business exchanges might not be humorous and may even be costly.

© PathDoc/Shutterstock.com

What is this emblem conveying?

Illustrator when you use your body to help describe or visually depict something

Indicating something with a body gesture is an illustrator.

Regulator any type of body movements that are used in conversation to control the communication flow

Affect displays overt physical responses to our emotions that can be either positive or negative

Positive affect displays are constructive and encouraging.

Social referencing the process by which individuals rely on those around them to determine how to respond to unfamiliar stimuli

Adaptors body movements that are enacted at a low level of awareness and usually indicate nervousness, anxiety, or boredom

Do you have any nervous habits that you do unconsciously?

Illustrator is the label used to indicate when you use your body to help describe or visually depict something. You have probably heard someone say, "I caught a fish this big!" while indicating the size of the fish with his or her hands. This is an example of an illustrator. We use illustrators to visually demonstrate how big our nephew is or to point someone in the right direction when he is lost. Illustrators are more universal and less ambiguous than emblems.

Regulators are any type of body movements that are used in conversation to control the communication flow. Sometimes one person is monopolizing the conversation and you want to signal to him that you have something to say.

What would you do? You have many options such as leaning forward, opening your mouth, nodding, eye rolling, eyebrow raising, and/or using your hand to gesture.

We can demonstrate our emotions nonverbally through affect displays. **Affect displays** are overt physical responses to our emotions that can be either positive or negative. Positive affect displays are constructive and encouraging. Patting or rubbing a close friend on the back when he is sad is an example of an affect display. Hugging and kissing are additional ways to display positive affect toward another. What about negative affect displays? Recall the last time someone asked you why you were angry. Perhaps it was because you were clenching your teeth or glaring with your eyes. In what ways have you physically manifested feelings of boredom, frustration, or sadness?

It is amazing how quickly infants and young children pick up on these displays. These learned behaviors are typically modeled by the infant's parent or caregiver through a process called social referencing. **Social referencing** refers to the process by which individuals rely on those around them to determine how to respond to unfamiliar stimuli (Campos & Stenberg, 1988). For example, when infants are introduced to someone or something new, they look to the parent for reassurance. When the parent responds with a positive affect display, like a smile, she sends a message to the infant that this new stimuli is comforting and not threatening. It is not long before the child displays more complex emotions through nonverbal affect displays. He may roll his eyes because he is annoyed or stomp his feet and cross his arms in disgust.

Adaptors are body movements that are enacted at a low level of awareness and usually indicate nervousness, anxiety, or boredom. Individuals may display these types of behaviors in situations that evoke anxiety such as public speaking classes or other types of public performances. Sometimes students are not aware that while they are giving a speech they are also engaging in behaviors such as tapping a pen on the podium, cracking their knuckles, and fixing their hair. When they watch themselves on videotape later, they are surprised. Outside of the classroom, individuals who work in human resources departments are often trained to look for adaptors during interviews and screening processes. Interviewee behaviors such as fidgeting hands, playing with paper, and postural changes are examples of adaptors that are often exhibited during interviews and considered signs of nervousness or weakness.

Haptics

An additional type of nonverbal communication is haptics, or touch. The amount of touch in interpersonal relationships is related to liking and status. Anderson and Sull (1985) suggest that individuals who like each other will touch each other more often than those who do not. In fact, if individuals are not fond of each other, they will actively avoid touching. Individuals with higher status, such as your boss or professor, typically choose whether to initiate touch into the relationship. They also may use touch to maintain control. For example, a middle school teacher may lead a student by physically directing him toward the corner of the room while saying, "Let's move over here." This type of touch is considered role-bound because the teacher and student are working within specific positions. Thayer (1988) offers categories of touch based on people's roles and relationships.

Functional-professional are touches that occur while accomplishing a specific task, which is performed by those working within a specific role. For example, a barber, doctor, or nail technician will perform tasks that involve touch as part of their occupation. Functional touch also includes any touch that is done while trying to accomplish a goal. Helping a player off the ice when you are playing hockey or assisting an elderly woman across the street would both be situations employing functional touch. Social-polite are touches that occur between business partners, acquaintances, and strangers. These include greetings and salutations, such as a handshake. Friendship-warmth are touches that occur between extended family members, close business associates, and friendly neighbors. This type of touch signals caring, concern, and interest between interactants. A hug and a pat on the back are examples of this type of touch. There are some gray areas between this type of touch and the "love-intimacy" category, which may be a cause of great misinterpretation. Love-intimacy are touches that occur between family members and friends where there is affection and a deep level of caring. Extended hugs and holding hands are often examples of this type of touch. Sexual-arousal are touches that occur within sexual/erotic contexts. Kissing is an example of this type of touch. Sometimes we use touch to initiate permission to enter into a "deeper" relationship with someone. If there is a discrepancy between the level of touch and your interpretation of the level of the relationship, it is important to be assertive and direct in your communication about this discrepancy with your relationship partner. Touch is the most intimate type of nonverbal communication and is also the most ambiguous. We interpret touch differently depending on the context. In a crowded club, party, elevator, or subway, touch is not interpreted as intrusive. However, within different contexts, when people intentionally enter our space, we may view it as a violation. Now, let us discuss how our use of personal space contributes to nonverbal communication.

haptics nonverbally communicating through touch

functional-professional touches that occur while accomplishing a specific task that is performed by those working within a specific role

Social-polite touches that occur between business partners, acquaintances, and strangers

Friendship-warmth touches that occur between extended family members, close business associates, and friendly neighbors

Love-intimacy touches that occur between family members and friends where there is affection and a deep level of caring

Sexual-arousal touches that occur within a sexual/erotic context

© wavebreakmedia /Shutterstock.com

Love-intimacy touches occur between family members and friends where there is affection and a deep level of caring.

Proxemics

The fourth type of nonverbal communication is space, or proxemics, which refers to the invisible bubble we place around our bodies. Often this space is considered our "comfort zone." Americans are highly conscious of our space

proxemics space; refers to the invisible bubble we place around our bodies and our territory. We allow certain individuals into our space, depending on the context of the situation. Hall (1966) defined four categories of space zones as listed on the next page (See Table 3.1).

Although this chart provides us with a general idea of how individuals use space, perceptions of appropriate personal space differ among individuals. In the United States, we are generally very concerned with others infringing on what we consider to be "our space" and are very protective of it.

markers physical objects that we place between ourselves and others

We may even go so far as to place physical objects, or markers, between ourselves and others. Similar to the ways in which animals mark their territory, we may claim the territory around us by using markers to show others that this is our space. Think about all of the different ways that you may protect space that you consider yours. Have you ever spread out your books, bag, and articles of clothing in the library to purposefully take up more space? Have you ever spread out your belongings at the lunch table to discourage others from sitting next to you? Finally, have you ever had someone invade your space while conversing? A popular *Seinfeld* episode referred to this type of individual as a "close talker." They are often considered annoying and inappropriate. These are all examples of how our use of space influences our perceptions of messages and the meanings we assign to them. (See Table 3.1)

How do you react when you feel like you do not have enough space?

© wavebreakmedia /Shutterstock.com

Table 3.1	**Space, Context, and Nonverbal Communication**	
Type of Space	**Distance**	**Individuals/Groups**
Intimate	0 to 18 inches	Reserved for those that are closest to us (e.g., boyfriend, girlfriend, spouse)
Personal	18 inches to 4 feet	Reserved for family members and close friends
Social	4 to 10 feet	The distance that we feel comfortable conducting everyday social situations with strangers, acquaintances, and business partners
Public	10 feet and farther	The distance reserved for large audiences

Paralanguage

paralanguage everything beyond the words in the verbally communicated message

A fifth category of nonverbal behavior is paralanguage, which focuses on everything beyond the words in the verbally communicated message. Paralanguage, or vocalic components of messages, includes:

- Pitch (high—low)
- Rate (fast—slow)
- Volume (high—low)
- Pronunciation (clear—unclear)
- Inflection (high—low)
- Tempo (fast—slow)

- Accents (slight—thick)
- Vocal fillers ("ahh," "ummm")
- Hesitations (grunts, screams, laughs, gasps, sighs, and even silence) (Hickson, Stacks, & Moore, 2004, p. 258).

Have you ever thought about the ways you use silence? You may use silence to show disgust, to keep a secret, to reveal a secret, or to enhance the importance of your message. Knapp and Hall (2002) identified five primary functions of silence:

1. To punctuate or emphasize certain words or ideas
2. To evaluate or provide judgment of another's behavior (showing favor or disfavor, agreement, disagreement, attacking)
3. To hide or to reveal information
4. To express emotions: the silence of disgust, sadness, fear, anger, or love
5. To engage in mental activity: show thoughtfulness, reflection, or ignorance (Bruneau, 1973; Jaworski, 1993; Jensen, 1973)

Because silence serves several functions, it is important to understand that it is often misunderstood. Can you recall a time when your silence was misconstrued?

> Because silence serves several functions, it is important to understand that it is often misunderstood.

Physical Appearance

A sixth category of nonverbal communication is physical appearance, which includes our body, clothing, makeup, height, size, and hair. Much of the literature on physical appearance examines the attractiveness of individuals. The literature (see, for example, McCroskey 1992) on this topic recognizes three different types of attraction: 1) physical attraction (how visibly pleasing someone is), 2) task attraction (how pleasing someone is to work with), and 3) social attraction (how pleasing someone is to interact with). We will focus primarily on physical attraction in this section. A more comprehensive discussion of all three types of attraction is provided in Chapter 7.

physical appearance includes our body, clothing, makeup, height, size, and hair

What is perceived as attractive in the United States may be quite different from what is considered attractive in Thailand or Egypt. Likewise, what you might find attractive, your neighbor may find repulsive. However, we know that individuals are more attracted to physically attractive people than to physically unattractive people (Sprecher, 1989). But perhaps this has more to do with homophily, or how similar we consider the target to be to ourselves. Although we cannot develop a global list of physically attractive attributes, we do know that there are benefits to being attractive. However, an interesting study found that when screening job applicants, attractiveness had no impact when the quality of the application was high. But attractiveness was a significant advantage when the application was mediocre (Watkins & Johnston, 2000).

homophily how similar we consider another person to be to ourselves

Body size is one aspect of physical appearance that has been studied by researchers and is linked to how we form impressions of others. Body size is the relationship between an individual's height, weight, and muscular build, and it has received a considerable amount of attention in the nonverbal communication literature. In 1942, Sheldon and Stevens theorized that there was a link between a person's physical attributes and personality traits. After collecting data on male body types and temperament, they distinguished between three primary body types: endomorphs, mesomorphs, and ectomorphs.

endomorph a short, round, and soft body type

The endomorph body type is described as being short, round, and soft. Researchers have associated the endomorph body type with being lazy, better-natured, more old- fashioned, less good-looking, more agreeable, and more dependent on others compared to the other body types. One interesting study found that self-perceived endomorphs had significantly stronger intentions to smoke cigarettes compared to the other body types (Tucker, 1983). But are all individuals with this body type lazy? Certainly former NBA player Charles Barkley, who was at one time referred to as "The Round Mound of Rebound," is not described as lazy, dependent, or even overly agreeable. It is important to be aware of our tendency to inaccurately stereotype individuals based on their appearance.

Mesomorph a physically fit, muscular, average height and weight, and athletic body type

Mesomorphs are described as being physically fit, muscular, average height and weight, and athletic. Researchers have associated this body type with being stronger, better looking, more adventurous, younger, taller, and more mature compared to the other body types (Sheldon, Hartl, & McDermott, 1949). The mesomorphic body type was perceived by college students as an ideal body type for both males and females (Butler & Ryckman, 1993). Even professional clinicians have been found to stereotype based on body type. Fletcher and Diekhoff (1998) found that therapists judged more muscular males, or male mesomorphs, as more mentally healthy than endomorphs and ectomorphs.

ectomorph a tall, thin, and frail body type

The ectomorph body type is described as being tall, thin, and frail. Characteristics associated with this body type include being tenser, nervous, quieter, taller, younger, introverted, more afraid of people, lacking confidence, and being less social when compared with the other body types (Sheldon, Hartl, & McDermott, 1949). Not all perceptions of this body type are negative. For example, our culture certainly seems to value a thin or ectomorphic body shape, especially in women. The media has been criticized for disproportionally displaying images of thin women and contributing to the problem of eating disorders in young women. More recently, you may recall that the modeling industry has adopted healthier standards for their models' body weight. As we consume media messages with models that are more representative of our culture in respect to body shape, pay attention to how you react to these messages.

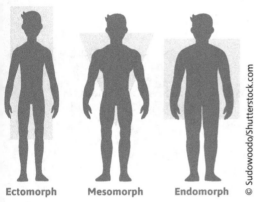

Ectomorph   Mesomorph   Endomorph

© Sudowoodo/Shutterstock.com

The three primary body types.

In addition to body type, height has also been examined as a physical characteristic that influences meaning. Are taller people perceived as

Our subjective view of time is contingent on our personal/ psychological orientation and our cultural influences.

more competent? To date, Judge and Cable (2004) have designed the most comprehensive analysis between physical height and work success. Their meta-analysis found that while controlling for sex, age, and weight, there were significant positive relationships between height and social esteem, leader emergence, performance, and income. Therefore, not only are taller people perceived as more competent, they actually get paid more. How much more? Their findings suggest that someone who is six feet tall earns, on average, nearly $166,000 more during a thirty-year career than someone who is five feet, five inches.

Artifacts the physical objects and environmental attributes that communicate directly, define the communication context, or guide social behavior in some way

Artifacts

The seventh type of nonverbal communication is artifacts. Artifacts are defined as "the physical objects and environmental attributes that communicate directly, define the communication context, or guide social behavior in some way" (Burgoon, Buller, & Woodall 1994, p. 123). We can think about artifacts in terms of personal adornment and environmental adornment. Personal adornment refers to how we use artifacts on our bodies. Tattoos, jewelry, branding, scarring, painting, makeup, glasses, and body piercing are all examples of artifacts that can be considered personal adornment. Two popular personal adornment artifacts addressed in the literature are tattoos and body piercing.

Although tattoos and body piercings are becoming more mainstream, negative perceptions are still sometimes associated with these artifacts. Some of these perceptions may be founded, since Carroll, Riffenburgh, Roberts, and Myhre (2002) noted that study participants with tattoos and body piercings were more likely to engage in high risk-taking behaviors such as disordered eating behavior, gateway drug use, hard drug use, sexual activity, suicide, and violence. Forbes (2001) also found that tattoos and piercings in college students are associated with more risk-taking behavior, greater use of alcohol and marijuana, and less social conformity. Another study found individuals with body modifications (tattoos or body piercings other than earlobes) reported more symptoms of depression and trait anxiety than individuals without body modifications (Roberti & Storch, 2005).

Environmental adornment refers to artifacts that we use in our environment to identify ourselves. Consider how much you can learn about someone just by walking through his or her bedroom. Think about the artwork on the wall, the cleanliness, the type of objects on the dresser, and the clothes hanging in the closet. The MTV show *Room Raiders* capitalized on this phenomenon. Contestants decided who to go out with based solely on the contents of the bedrooms of the prospective dates. In addition to our bedrooms, we often use artifacts in our cars, offices, and other personal spaces to reflect our identity. Try to identify the environmental adornment artifacts the next time you are in your professors' offices. Do they have any artwork? Do they have photos of their dog or children? Can you identify their alma mater?

Closely related to those artifacts are additional environmental factors, such as the context, room layout, lighting, and/or color. Environmental factors will influence how we interpret meaning. Consider the environmental factors inside a McDonald's. Think about the lighting, seating, and colors— do they encourage you to eat fast? Fast-food restaurants are interested in high turnover and do not typically want you to become too comfortable while eating your burger and fries. In contrast, high-end restaurants are more concerned with having their patrons relax, order more food and drinks, and stay for a long time in their establishments. These types of restaurants will often use candlelight, comfortable seating, and soft music to create an environment that says "stay awhile." Around the holidays, department stores often play specific music and try to create a certain mood to encourage shoppers to spend more money. Be aware of the setting and environment around you. Do you respond to certain colors? Is there a reason why most classrooms have white walls and very little artwork? Does certain music put you in a certain mood? What types of smells make you hungry? What scents make you calm? Being more mindful and heightening your awareness of the impact of environmental factors is critical to your success as a competent communicator.

Personal adornment refers to how we use artifacts on our bodies

Environmental adornment artifacts that we use in our environment to identify ourselves

environmental factors include the context, room layout, lighting, and/or color of a particular environment

Chronemics

chronemics   how we use
and perceive time

The final type of nonverbal communication is referred to as chronemics, or how we use and perceive time. Our subjective view of time is contingent on our personal/psychological orientation and our cultural influences. Hall (1976) suggests that each culture operates on a continuum from a monochronic orientation to a polychronic orientation to time. In general, Americans tend to be more monochronic because time is considered to be "linear" in nature. It spans across a "time line" and we can schedule appointments one after another in an orderly fashion. Think about how your daily planner is set up. (Or the fact that you *have* a daily planner.) You can segment time and schedule classes, appointments, and social events for each week, each day, and within each hour. Being punctual, scheduling appointments, and having strict adherence to starting times and ending times are all valued behaviors in the United States. During one of the authors' first day of graduate school, faculty stressed to the students, "Being on time is being late; being early is synonymous with being on time." This example reinforces the monochronic orientation that is valued in our culture. Being early in our culture is perceived as being organized, professional, prepared, and productive. Being late in our culture is perceived as being lazy, disorganized, uninterested, and unprofessional.

monochromic   time is
considered to be "linear" in
nature

In contrast to a monochronic time orientation, polychronic cultures perceive time as circular. This time orientation suggests that several things can be done at the same time. Polychronic cultures do not rely as heavily on the clock as monochromic cultures do. Meetings are viewed as time to cultivate relationships, and it is more important to finish the conversation than to be "on time" for the next appointment. Time and activities are more fluid and things will "get done when they get done." Work time and personal time typically overlap in these cultures. Within the United States, this orientation has negative perceptions, such as being "nonambitious and a waste of precious time" (Hickson, Stacks, & Moore, 2004, p. 316).

In addition to our cultural norms, we must also consider individual orientations. Consider how monochronic or polychronic your parents are. Did you grow up with a curfew? Did you have daily chores? Did you eat dinner at the same time each evening? Answering these types of questions, can give us more clarity on how we interpret and react to chronemics across our interpersonal relationships.

FOUR FUNCTIONS OF NONVERBAL MESSAGES

Now that we have discussed the eight types of nonverbal communication, we will review four ways in which we use nonverbal behavior. Four primary functions of nonverbal messages are:

1. to facilitate our cognitive meaning;
2. to encode and decode emotions;
3. to express affection and support; and
4. to aid in impression formation and/or identity management.

Facilitate Cognitive Meaning

One primary function of nonverbal messages is to aid in cognitive meaning. We can use our nonverbal behavior in several ways to help create meaning. Ekman and Friesen (1969) specify five ways we aid our cognitive meaning:

1. repetition;
2. contradiction;
3. complementation;
4. accent; and
5. regulation.

First, repetition refers to both verbal and nonverbal expressions made simultaneously to reinforce each other. The nonverbal message repeats the verbal message in order to increase the accuracy of the message. For example, when a police officer is directing traffic, she may extend her hand and yell, "Stop!" In this example, the cognitive meaning of the verbal message is repeated with the nonverbal emblem. We can use this function when we want to clarify or increase the accuracy of the messages we send.

repetition both verbal and nonverbal expressions made simultaneously to reinforce each other

On the other hand, our nonverbal and verbal expressions may be contradictory. Oftentimes we say one thing and behave in a way that is inconsistent with our verbal message. When our nonverbal and verbal messages contradict each other, research has shown that we tend to believe the nonverbal messages. Once again, we refer to the heuristic, "It is not what you said, but *how* you said it." If someone says, "I really like your new car," you will determine the sincerity of the message by dissecting the nonverbal cues. Was it said sarcastically? What do their facial expressions reveal? After scrutinizing the nonverbal and verbal messages, we will determine whether the verbal portion of the message was genuine. If there are any discrepancies between the two messages, we will rely on the nonverbal portion of the message.

Third, complementing is a process by which our nonverbal communication is used in conjunction with the verbal portion of the message. We can determine the attitudes people hold when we examine the extent to which the verbal and nonverbal messages are complementing each other. If you want to make sure that your relationship partner knows that you are angry with her, you may glare at her and say, "I am so angry with you!"

complementing a process by which our nonverbal communication is used in conjunction with the verbal portion of the message

The fourth way we aid our cognitive meaning, according to Ekman and Friesen (1969), is through accenting. Accenting is used when we want to stress or emphasize a particular word or phrase in our verbal message. If a friend says, "Please, do not be *late* to the party" and stresses the word "late," her use of accenting implies that it is important to her that you are on time for the party. Accenting can change the meaning of the original message, as well as the emotion conveyed (Anderson, 1999). Consider how the meaning and the emotion of the same sentence changes slightly when we accent different words in the following statements:

Accenting used when we want to stress or emphasize a particular word or phrase in our verbal message

George, will you pick up fat-free milk from the store today?
George, will you pick up *fat-free* milk from the store today?
George, will you pick up fat-free milk from the store *today?*

The final way to aid our cognitive meaning is to regulate conversations. Researchers have introduced several ways we use nonverbal communication to regulate or negotiate our conversations:

- Turn-yielding (Duncan, 1972)
- Turn-maintaining (Duncan, 1972)
- Back-channeling (Duncan, 1972)
- Turn-requesting (Wiemann & Knapp, 1975)
- Turn-denying (Burgoon, Hunsaker, & Dawson, 1994)

First, we engage in turn-yielding behaviors, which signal to the listener that we are going to stop talking. Some examples of these signals include placing a drawl on the final syllable, placing emphasis on a final word, saying, "do you know what I *mean*?", displaying an open and direct body position, and leaning forward. Second, we can also engage in suppressing signals or turn-maintaining, which suggests to the listener that we want to continue talking. These behaviors include talking more quickly and/or more loudly, using hand gestures that suggest "wait a minute" or "one last point," and filling more pauses. Back-channeling cues are used by listeners to signal that they are motivated to listen to us and that they are not interested in "taking over the floor." Some nonverbal behaviors they may engage in include nodding their heads, and saying "I agree" or "uh-huh." They are confirming interest in our message, but they are not interested in speaking themselves. Turn-requesting behaviors are utilized when listeners use buffers, short words or phrases such as, "But uhhh . . ." or "You know . . ." to signal to the speaker that they are interested in speaking (Wiemann & Knapp, 1975). These buffers may be used while the speaker is talking or during a pause in conversation. If they are used properly, the speaker should finish his thought and relinquish the floor to them. Burgoon, Hunsaker, and Dawson (1994) identified an additional turn-taking cue referred to as turn-denying. Listeners use this cue when they are not interested in "taking over the floor." They may signal that they are not interested by increasing space between themselves and the speaker and/or avoiding direct eye contact with the speaker.

Encoding and Decoding Emotions

A second function of nonverbal communication is to display and interpret emotions. In chapter 3 we described emotions as subjective feelings such as happiness, anger, shame, fear, guilt, sadness, and excitement that produce positive or negative reactions that are physical, psychological, and physiological. We often weigh the appropriateness of our outward emotional reaction and judge whether it is desirable and/or acceptable (see Anderson, 1999). Emotion is primarily communicated through nonverbal means.

Encoding emotions refers to an individual's ability to display feelings. Scholars have suggested that as we get older, we are better able to encode emotions such as happiness, anger, sadness, and fear (Mayo & LaFrance, 1978). Furthermore, a seminal study found that regardless of gender, young children seem to express emotions quite similarly. However, as girls become older they are more accurate in detecting affective states in others. They also are more expressive. Boys, on the other hand, are less accurate in detecting affective states in others and are less expressive encoders (Buck, 1975). Another study revealed that women were more effective in encoding emotions than men (Wagner, MacDonald, & Manstead, 1986). This research makes sense because it is more socially acceptable for women to express their emotions in the U.S. culture. U.S. men are more likely to suppress their feelings. In 1994, Kring, Smith, and Neale developed the Emotional Expressivity Scale (EES) to measure the extent to which individuals outwardly display their emotions. You can complete the scale at the end of the chapter to determine your own emotional expressivity.

Decoding emotions refers to the ability to accurately read and interpret the emotional states of others. Most scholars agree that individuals who are skilled encoders are also skilled decoders (see Burgoon, Buller, & Woodall, 1994). Therefore, women tend to be better decoders than men (Wagner, MacDonald, & Manstead, 1986). However, research has shown that men tend to improve their sensitivity to facial expressions with individuals over time (Zuckerman, Lipets, Koivumaki, & Rosenthanl, 1975). As you can imagine, being able to appropriately encode and decode emotions can enhance our ability to connect and relate to others. This emotional skill set allows us to react with more compassion and understanding within our interpersonal relationships.

What are these facial expressions saying?

Decoding refers to the ability to accurately read and interpret the emotional states of others

Table 3.2	**Nonverbal Communication: Comforting Strategies**
Comforting Strategy	**Examples**
Attentiveness (Showing you care)	Activing listening behaviors and head nodding
Eye contact	Maintaining direct eye contact with the person
Crying	Referencing crying or weeping, either the other person's or the comforter's
Vocalics	Using one's voice to show concern, references to tone of voice, intensity, and speaking softly
Instrumental activity (Doing something for the other person which may or may not be directly related to the distress)	Making dinner or running errands for the other person to show support
Facial expression (Showing emotional reaction through one's face)	Adapting facial features to show empathy or simply looking concerned or sad
Proxemics	Using proxemics to close up the space without touching
Gesturing	Using hand and arm movements to show empathy, anger, and/or agitation about what the person is saying
Hugs	Directly hugging the person, either a whole or half hug
Pats	Touching arm or shoulder
Increased miscellaneous touch	Any type of increase in touching that does not fall into hugging or patting category
Emotional distancing (Comforting avoidance response)	Behaviors that are self-oriented and avoidant, intended to keep distance or to remain uninvolved

Express Affection and Support

A third function of nonverbal communication is to provide affection and support. Oftentimes we will display nonverbal comforting strategies in our interpersonal relationship when someone is going through a difficult or stressful time. Researchers identified 12 nonverbal comforting strategies that college students employ to lend support to others (Dolin & Booth-Butterfield, 1993).

Their study revealed that females reported more nonverbal comforting strategies and more diverse comforting responses than males. This means that females not only use nonverbal comforting strategies more frequently, but they also use several different types of strategies. Males were more likely to use emotional-distancing behaviors than females. See Table 3.2 for a complete list of comforting strategies and messages.

Aid in Impression Formation/Identity Management

proactive attribution
formation of first impressions through the use of nonverbal cues.

retroactive attribution
process of using nonverbal cues to help explain the behaviors of others in hindsight or after-the-fact.

Another significant function of nonverbal communication is creating first impressions. Typically, our initial perception of someone is based on observing nonverbal behavior such as physical appearance, eye contact, and facial expressions. The information gathered through these first impressions is used to predict attitudes and opinions not yet revealed. This is referred to as proactive attribution. This information is also used for retroactive attribution, or to help explain the behavior of others in hindsight (Berger, 1975). Although we gather this information quickly, it tends to remain stable over time—making these initial perceptions critical for future interactions. For example, research suggests that roommates whose initial impressions were positive had more satisfying subsequent interactions and used more productive strategies to solve conflict (Marek, Knapp, & Wanzer, 2004). However, how often do you think our first impressions are inaccurate? We do not often provide second chances, as we do not communicate long enough to find out if our first impressions were accurate.

In 2007, Houser, Horan, and Furler examined heterosexual speed daters and their impressions after 30 seconds. Their results suggest:

- Both males and females identified positive communication behaviors (example: good communication skills, acting nice, being nonverbally responsive) as being important in date prospects.
- Males identified physical attraction in simple terms, such as "cute" and "pretty," while females used more specific terms, such as "stylish clothes," "nice eyes," and "neatly groomed."
- Friendliness was identified as being an important characteristic that was displayed nonverbally, mostly through smiling. Females used descriptors such as, "great smile," "cute smile," "friendly smile," and "warm, accepting smile."
- Both males and females identified lack of attraction or negative physical qualities as primary negative judgments.
- Females reported approximately three times the negative evaluations, compared to males.

This study reminds us how quickly first impressions are formed and how detailed the interpretation of nonverbal behavior can be when we are establishing relationships.

BEST PRACTICES: AVOID COMMON NONVERBAL COMMUNICATION MISTAKES

To increase how effectively and appropriately you receive and display nonverbal communication in your interpersonal relationships, we offer suggestions in four areas. This section provides suggestions on how to monitor and adapt your nonverbal messages to your audience and context.

Common Areas of Miscommunication

First, nonverbal messages are often perceived as ambiguous and open for misinterpretation. The cultural barriers attached to many nonverbal behaviors can inhibit our interpretation of the meaning. Additionally, we do not usually have an extended period of time to create first impressions, which may have lasting results. Therefore, it is important to reinforce that nonverbal communication is not clear and is often misinterpreted. The more time we spend with others, the more accurately we can interpret their nonverbal behavior. Remember, nonverbal communication is multi-channeled and we can increase our chances of accurately interpreting others' behavior if we take all of the cues into consideration. Similarly, if we want to become more successful at getting our messages across to others, we will employ a number of different nonverbal behaviors that reinforce or clarify our verbal message. These strategies will help reduce miscommunication that often occurs within the nonverbal communication arena.

Nonverbal Messages and Social Influence

Have you ever caused someone to change a behavior or attitude without intending to do so? Can you recall a specific time when you unintentionally influenced another person's attitudes or actions by displaying certain nonverbal behaviors? The two examples below illustrate how we can unintentionally influence others through our nonverbal behaviors.

1. Perhaps you broke eye contact with your sibling while she was telling you about something that happened to her at school. As a result of this behavior, your sister stopped talking and walked away from you. When you asked her later why she walked away from you, she told you that she could tell that you were not interested in her story.
2. Several years ago a famous supermodel cut her long hair quite short and, as a result of this choice, many other women did the same. In an interview the model stated that she certainly did not intend to influence others to cut their hair short.

These examples illustrate how we may influence others' attitudes or behaviors through our nonverbal messages without intending to do so. Thus, it is important to monitor our nonverbal behaviors closely and consider how our actions may influence others. Be aware that we may unintentionally influence someone else's behavior or attitude through our nonverbal behaviors.

Of course there are also many times when we intend to influence others by exhibiting certain nonverbal behaviors. For example, each time you dress professionally for a job interview, you attempt to influence the interviewer's perceptions of you as a viable job candidate. Communication researchers have had a longstanding interest in learning more about how certain verbal and nonverbal behaviors influence those around us. Much of the research in this area suggests that you can influence individuals by displaying nonverbal behaviors associated with power and authority or kindness and liking, or both. Individuals can give the impression of authority and expertise through nonverbal cues such as wearing uniforms (e.g., military), nametags that include titles (e.g., manager), and personal artifacts. Military personnel, police officers, doctors, or managers in a retail store all have control over certain resources, and have power to reward or punish. We are more likely to obey a police officer's suggestion to move our car than the suggestion made by a stranger on the street because the officer wearing the uniform has the power to give us a ticket. Other nonverbal messages that project an image of authority and power are eye contact, touch, voice, and space. We often can tell who has the most power in an organization by the size of his or her office. Other persuasive tactics involve liking and kindness. We can persuade others by our charismatic tone, physical attractiveness, and smile. Nonverbal immediacy behaviors have also been shown to be associated with social influence.

Immediacy refers to the psychological and physical closeness we have with one another

Immediacy refers to the psychological and physical closeness we have with one another. Mehrabian (1971) developed this principle that suggests we are drawn to people and things that we like, prefer, and value highly. Nonverbal immediacy behaviors can indicate inclusion, approachability, involvement, warmth, and positive affect. Some examples of nonverbal immediacy behaviors that individuals might use during social interaction include: eye contact, decreasing distance, appropriate touch, positive facial expressions, open body positions, varying pitch and tempo, and spending time with another person. In general, nonverbal immediacy behaviors produce direct, positive effects on other people (Mehrabian, 1971, p. 207). This direct-effects model suggests that individuals who engage in immediacy behaviors are more likely to be perceived as warmer, friendlier, more intimate, and more attractive (Anderson, 1999). Although immediacy behaviors seem to be ultimately a good thing, can you think of a circumstance where enacting nonverbal immediacy behaviors may be detrimental to your interpersonal relationships? In other words, can you think of a time when you might want to increase the psychological space between yourself and a relational partner? Anderson (1999) suggests that in less positive relationships, immediacy behaviors can be perceived as suffocating and threatening. At the end of the chapter, you can measure your own nonverbal immediacy behaviors by taking a self report measure.

> Remember, nonverbal communication is multi-channeled and we can increase our chances of accurately interpreting others' behavior if we take all of the cues into consideration.

RESEARCH IN REAL LIFE: NONVERBAL IMMEDIACY IN THE CLASSROOM

Research on nonverbal immediacy has exploded in the last 25 years. McCroskey and his colleagues have specifically explored nonverbal immediacy in the educational context. They have found that a teacher's use of nonverbal immediacy behavior is highly related to positive student affect for the teacher (McCroskey & Richmond, 1992; McCroskey, Richmond, Sallinen, Fayer, & Barraclough, 1995), greater student affective learning (McCroskey, Fayer, Richmond, Sallinen, & Barraclough, 1996), greater student cognitive learning (McCroskey, Sallinen, Fayer, Richmond, & Barraclough, 1996), and enhanced student motivation toward studying (Christophel, 1990; Richmond, 1990). Therefore, it appears that teachers who enact nonverbal immediacy behaviors provide many benefits to their students.

Practice Sending and Receiving Nonverbal Messages

As mentioned previously, it is often quite difficult to interpret the nonverbal behavior of others. Therefore, we need to supplement our observations with questions. We can clarify our perceptions of others' nonverbal messages simply by asking questions such as: "Are you upset?", "Were you being sarcastic?", and "Are you serious?" Remember that not all nonverbal communication is intentional. Typically, the intentional nonverbal signals are emphasized. Subtle nonverbal behaviors may not be intentional. To accurately interpret others' nonverbal messages it is important to pay attention to all of the behaviors exhibited and seek clarification when verbal and nonverbal messages are contradictory.

Are you aware of the potential impact of the nonverbal messages you send to others? Because the assumption is that all nonverbal messages are intentional, we must be aware of the nonverbal messages we send. How do others interpret your facial expressions, use of space, and touch? We may never find an answer to this question unless we ask others for feedback.

Recognize Differences in Nonverbal Communication Perceptions

Sometimes individual differences can influence an individual's nonverbal behavior. One example of this is the extent to which individuals have communication apprehension. Recall our discussion of communication apprehension (CA) in Chapter 3. CA refers to the level of fear or anxiety an individual has that is associated with real or anticipated communication with another person (McCroskey, 1977). McCroskey (1976) proposes that high CAs avoid communication situations and actively try to decrease communication attempts. Therefore, he predicts that high CAs are more likely than low CAs to have increased space, to avoid eye contact, to be averse to being touched, to have less vocal variety, to have fewer kinesic movements, and to have longer pause times in conversation. The degree of CA an individual has can determine the nonverbal impact on their interpersonal communication situations.

Age is another factor that may impact how we interpret nonverbal behavior. Life span refers to how our communication changes over time. Just as our verbal communication changes over time, so does our nonverbal behavior. Because we learn most of our nonverbal communication through cultural exposure, it is common for children to lack knowledge in what is considered socially appropriate nonverbal expression. As adults, we have a good time laughing at young people when they make mistakes like making a disgusted face when they taste Grandma's signature soup. We do not expect them to have mature social skills, since those skills are acquired over time, although research has shown that throughout our life span we tend to express emotions such as SADFISH similarly. In other words, the way a child would act surprised is similar to how a 90-year-old woman would—by opening her eyes, raising her eyebrows, and dropping her jaw. While initially we may have similar ways of expressing emotions, as we grow older we tend to engage in more self-monitoring techniques, become more aware of the rules regarding nonverbal behavior, and modify our behavior to fit these socially appropriate rules.

To send and receive nonverbal messages effectively, it is important to take into consideration the ambiguous nature of nonverbal messages. To make sure that the intended message is effectively communicated to your receiver, be sure that the verbal message is accompanied by multiple nonverbal behaviors that are consistent with the verbal message. Also, be aware of the fact that you can influence others both intentionally and unintentionally by exhibiting nonverbal messages. When you are confused about the nonverbal messages someone is sending, ask questions to clarify the message's meaning. Finally, when interpreting others' nonverbal messages, always consider the impact of individual differences such as personality, age, and culture on message delivery.

FUTURE DIRECTION FOR NONVERBAL COMMUNICATION: ELECTRONIC PARALANGUAGE

A direction for future research in nonverbal communication may be how we employ nonverbal messages in the mediated environment. Current research has explored how we compensate for the lack of nonverbal cues during mediated communication. Nonverbal communication researchers know it is difficult to express emotions verbally. This is why in face-to-face situations we rely on a certain glance, smile, wink, or even tears to express our emotions. During mediated communication, we do not have the luxury of traditional nonverbal cues. Therefore we rely on electronic paralanguage to express emotions and regulate our conversations.

Electronic paralanguage includes emoticons, acronyms, abbreviations, and flaming. Emoticons (short for "emotion icons") are symbols made up of combinations of keyboard keys that convey emotions. For example, :) refers to a smiley face, while :(refers to a frowning face, and ;) refers to someone winking. In addition, text messages and instant messages may insert actual artwork or emojis such as ☺ or ☹.

Researchers have examined the use of emoticons in chat rooms (Constantin et al., 2002) and email (Yoo, 2007). They have found that, in general, those individuals who utilize "smiley emoticons" have positive relational outcomes including increased perceptions of liking by the receiver. However, Walther and D'Daddario (2001) warn us that the overuse of these emoticons can cause them to lose their effectiveness. In other words, their "cuteness" factor does fade over time. We suggest individuals consider the task of the message and the relationship with the receiver before considering the use of emoticons. Emoticons can be misinterpreted and should be used cautiously.

One difference between face-to-face nonverbal communication and engaging in electronic paralanguage is that emoticons are more deliberate and voluntary (Walther & D'Addario, 2001). In traditional face-to-face situations, our nonverbal behavior is often unintentional. However, it is impossible to insert these emoticons without intent. Research has found that emoticons may serve the function of complementing the "written" statements, but they do not necessarily enhance them (Walther & D'Addario, 2001).

© 4zevar/Shutterstock.com

Electronic paralanguage includes emoticons, acronyms, abbreviations, and flaming

Emoticons short for "emotion icons"; symbols made up of combinations of keyboard keys that convey emotions

Acronyms or text messaging shorthand are used to express a variety of nonverbal cues. Three functions include:

1. to express emotions;
2. to regulate conversations; and
3. to provide feedback.

Acronyms text messaging shorthand; used to express a variety of nonverbal cues

Table 3.3	**Nonverbal Communication: Electronic Paralanguage**

Purpose	Text Messaging Shorthand
To express emotions	LOL, laugh out loud WYWH, Wish you were here
To regulate conversations	TTYL, talk to you later BRB, be right back L8R, later PMFJI, Pardon me for jumping in OMPL, one moment please GGFN, gotta go for now
To provide feedback	IGTP, I get the point J/K, just kidding ISWYM, I see what you mean

Communicating electronically is risky because of the lack of traditional nonverbal cues. Not all electronic communication is pro-social. Flaming refers to antisocial electronic behavior, such as swearing, firing insults, or shouting. Shouting or expressing anger in mediated communication is usually indicated by typing in all capital letters (Krohn, 2004). All in all, it will be interesting to examine how we continue to compensate or replace traditional nonverbal messages in the mediated environment.

Flaming refers to antisocial electronic behavior, such as swearing, firing insults, or shouting

SUMMARY

In this chapter we have introduced nonverbal communication and highlighted the importance of nonverbal communication in our everyday lives. We identified similarities to verbal communication and characterized the unique features of nonverbal behavior. Our hope is that you will heighten your awareness of how you use and interpret the eight types of nonverbal communication and understand how they function in your interpersonal relationships. By increasing your understanding of nonverbal communication, we hope you will avoid the communication problems that often accompany our nonverbal behavior. Remember that individuals are more likely to believe our nonverbal messages, regardless of intent. Therefore it is critical we understand the messages we are sending to others and how we interpret the nonverbal communication behaviors of others.

DISCUSSION QUESTIONS

1. In what circumstances has someone violated your nonverbal expectancies? How did you respond? Under what circumstances would violating someone's expectations be considered beneficial? Could there be benefits of violating someone's expectations?
2. While our primary emotions may be inherited, our social response to these emotions have been tied to cultural upbringing. Often our response is learned through our experiences. Discuss an example of how your response to a particular emotion was different than that of a close friend or family member.
3. Do you think instant messaging, text messages, email, and other computer-mediated methods of communication contribute to a polychronic culture? Why or why not?
4. Develop a list of regulative and constitutive rules for communicating online. How do you determine turn-taking? Is there such a thing as "interrupting" online? How do you demonstrate liking, professionalism, support, and/or anger?

REFERENCES

Anderson, P. A. (1999). *Nonverbal communication: Forms and functions.* Mountain View, CA: Mayfield Publishing.

Anderson, P. A., & Sull, K. K. (1985). Out of touch, out of reach: Tactile predispositions as predictors of interpersonal distance. *Western Journal of Speech Communication, 49,* 57–72.

Berger, C. R. (1975). Proactive and retroactive attribution processes. *Human Communication Research, 2,* 33–50.

Bruneau, T. J. (1973). Communicative silences: Forms and functions. *Journal of Communication, 23,* 17–46.

Buck, R. (1975). Nonverbal communication of affect in children. *Journal of Personality and Social Psychology, 31,* 644–653.

Burgoon, J. K. (1978). A communication model of personal space violation: Explication and an initial test. *Human Communication Research, 4,* 129–142.

Burgoon, J. K., Buller, D. B., & Woodall, W. G. (1994). *Nonverbal communication: The unspoken dialogue.* Columbus, OH: Greyden Press.

Burgoon, J., Hunsaker, F. G., & Dawson, E. J. (1994). *Human communication* (3rd ed.). Thousand Oaks, CA: Sage.

Butler, J. C., & Ryckman, R. M. (1993). Perceived and ideal physiques in male and female university students. *Journal of Social Psychology, 133,* 751–752.

Campos, J. J., & Stenberg, C. (1988). Perceptions, appraisals, and emotion: The onset of social referencing. In M. E. Lamb and L. R. Sherrod (Eds.), *Infant social cognition: Empirical and theoretical considerations.* Hillsdale, NJ: Erlbaum.

Carroll, S. T., Riffenburgh, R. H., Roberts, T. A., & Myhre, E. B. (2002). Tattoos and body piercings as indicators of adolescent risk-taking behaviors. *Pediatrics, 109,* 1021–1027.

Constantin, C., Kalyanaraman, S., Stavrositu, C., & Wagoner, N. (2002, August). To be or not to be emotional; Impression formation effects of emoticons in moderated chatrooms. Paper presented to the Communication Technology and Policy Division at the 85th annual convention of the Association for Education in Journalism and Mass Communication (AEJMC), Miami Beach, FL.

Christophel, D. M. (1990). The relationship between teacher immediacy behaviors, student motivation, and learning. *Communication Education, 39,* 323–340.

Darwin, C. (1965). *The expression of emotions in man and animals.* Chicago: University of Chicago Press. (Original work published 1872.)

Dolin, D., & Booth-Butterfield, M. (1993). Reach out and touch someone: Analysis of nonverbal comforting responses. *Communication Quarterly, 41,* 383–393.

Duncan Jr., S. D. (1972). Some signals and rules for taking speaking turns in conversations. *Journal of Personality and Social Psychology, 23,* 283–292.

Ekman, P. (1993). Facial expression and emotion. *American Psychologist, 48,* 384–392.

Ekman, P., & Friesen, W. V. (1969). The repertoire of non-verbal behaviour: categories, origins, usage and codings. *Semiotics 1,* 49–98.

Fletcher, C., & Diekhoff, G. M. (1998). Body-type stereotyping in therapeutic judgments. *Perceptual and Motor Skills, 86,* 842.

Forbes, G. B. (2001). College students with tattoos and piercings: Motives, family experiences, personality factors, and perception by others. *Psychological Reports, 89,* 774–786.

Hall, E. T. (1966). *The hidden dimension.* NY: Doubleday.

Hall, E. T. (1976). *Beyond culture.* New York: Doubleday.

Hickson III, M., Stacks, D. W., & Moore, N. (2004). *Nonverbal communication* (4th ed.). Los Angeles, CA: Roxbury.

Houser, M. L., Horan, S. M., & Furler, L. A. (2007). Predicting relational outcomes: An investigation of thin slice judgments in speed dating. *Human Communication, 10,* 69–81.

Izard, C. E. (1992). Basic emotions, relations among emotions, and emotion-cognition relations. *Psychological Review, 99,* 561–565.

Jaworski, A. (1993). *The power of silence: Social and pragmatic perspectives.* Newbury Park, CA: Sage.

Jensen, J. V. (1973). Communicative functions of silence. *ETC, 30,* 249–257.

Judge, T. A., & Cable, D. M. (2004). The effect of physical height on workplace success and income: Preliminary test of a theoretical model. *Journal of Applied Psychology, 89,* 428–441.

Kitao, S. K., & Kitao, K. (1988). Differences in the kinesic codes of Americans and Japanese. *World Communication, 17,* 83–103.

Kleinke, C. L., & Staneski, R. A. (1980). First impressions of female bust size. *Journal of Social Psychology, 110,* 123–134.

Knapp, M. L., & Hall, J. A. (2002). *Nonverbal communication in human interaction.* United States: Wadsworth.

Kring, A. M., Smith, D. A., & Neale, J. M. (1994). Individual differences in dispositional expressiveness: The development and validation of the emotional expressivity scale. *Journal of Personality and Social Psychology, 66,* 934–949.

Krohn, F. B. (2004). A generational approach to using emoticons as nonverbal communication. *Journal of Technical Writing and Communication, 34,* 321–328.

Marek, C. I, Knapp, J. L., & Wanzer, M. B. (2004). An exploratory investigation of the relationship between roommates' first impressions and subsequent communication patterns. *Communication Research Reports, 21,* 210–220.

Mayo, C., & LaFrance, M. (1978). On the acquisition of nonverbal communication: A review. *Merrill-Palmer Quarterly, 24,* 213–228.

McCroskey, J. C. (1976). The effects of communication apprehension on nonverbal behavior. *Communication Quarterly, 24,* 39–44.

McCroskey, J. C. (1977). Classroom consequences of communication apprehension. *Communication Education, 26,* 27–33.

McCroskey, J. C. (1992). *An introduction to communication in the classroom.* Edina, MI: Burgess Publishing Division.

McCroskey, J. C., Fayer, J. M., Richmond, V. P., Sallinen, A., & Barraclough, R. A. (1996). A multi-cultural examination of the relationship between nonverbal immediacy and affective learning. *Communication Quarterly, 44,* 297–307.

McCroskey, J. C., & Richmond, V. P. (1992). Increasing teacher influence through immediacy. In V. P. Richmond and J. C. McCroskey, (Eds.), *Power in the classroom: Communication, control and concern* (pp. 101–119). Hillsdale, NJ: Lawrence Erlbaum Associates.

McCroskey, J. C., Richmond, V. P., Sallinen, A., Fayer, J. M., & Barraclough, R. A. (1995). A cross-cultural and multi-behavioral analysis of the relationships between nonverbal immediacy and teacher evaluation. *Communication Education, 44,* 281–291.

McCroskey, J. C., Sallinen, A., Fayer, J. M., Richmond, V. P., & Barraclough, R. A. (1996). Nonverbal immediacy and cognitive learning: A cross-cultural investigation. *Communication Education, 45,* 200–211.

Mehrabian, A. (1971). *Silent messages.* Belmont, CA: Wadsworth.

Roberti, J. W., & Storch, E. A. (2005). Psychosocial adjustment of college students with tattoos and piercings. *Journal of College Counseling, 8,* 14–19.

Sheldon, W. H., & Stevens, S. S. (1942). *The varieties of temperament; a psychology of constitutional differences.* Oxford, England: Harper.

Sheldon, W. H., Hartl, E. M., & McDermott, E. (1949). *The variety of delinquent youth.* Oxford, England: Harper.

Sprecher, S. (1989). Premarital sexual standards for different categories of individuals. *Journal of Sex Research, 26,* 232–248.

Street, R. L., & Buller, D. B. (1987). Nonverbal response patterns in physician-patient interactions: A functional analysis. *Journal of Nonverbal Behavior, 11,* 234–253.

Thayer, S. (1988). Close encounters. *Psychology Today, 22,* 30–36.

Tucker, L. A. (1983). Cigarette smoking intentions and obesity among high school males. *Psychological Reports, 52,* 530.

Wagner, H. L., MacDonald, C. J., & Manstead, A. S. R. (1986). Communication of individual emotions by spontaneous facial expressions. *Journal of Personality and Social Psychology, 50,* 737–743.

Walther, J. B., & D'Addario, K. P. (2001). The impacts of emoticons on message interpretation in computer-mediated communication. *Social Science Computer Review, 19,* 324–347.

Watkins, L. M., & Johnston, L. (2000). Screening job applicants: The impact of physical attractiveness and application quality. *International Journal of Selection and Assessment, 8,* 76.

Wiemann, J., & Knapp, M. (1975). Turn-taking in conversation. *Journal of Communication, 25,* 75–92.

Yoo, J. (2007) To smile or not to smile : Defining the effects of emoticons in relational outcomes. International Communication Association annual meeting, San Francisco, CA.

Zuckerman, M., Lipets, M. S., Koivumaki, J. H., & Rosenthanl, R. (1975). Encoding and decoding nonverbal cues of emotion. *Journal of Personality and Social Psychology, 32,* 1068–1076.

Understanding Self

Interpersonal communication is a process of two people sharing themselves with each other. This process begins with you. Who are you? Try answering some of the following questions:

- How do I define myself?
- What do I believe in?
- What abilities and competencies do I possess?
- Do I value my abilities and myself?
- Am I pleased with the person I am becoming?
- How do I describe my personality and am I aware of how it affects my behavior?
- Am I aware of how I communicate and interact with other people?

If you can answer these questions easily, then chances are you understand yourself. Most people, however, struggle with these questions. Their answers are influenced by a variety of factors, including how their parents raised them, the media they watch and interact with, how their friends treat them, and how they compare themselves to others.

The purpose of this chapter is to help you answer these questions, give you new ways to think about who you are as a person, and help you

> If one is estranged from oneself, then one is estranged from others too. If one is out of touch with oneself, then one cannot touch others.
>
> —Anne Morrow Lindbergh

better understand others. The first part of the chapter focuses on understanding the self, paying particular attention to self-concept, self-esteem, developmental influences, and their impact on our communication. The second part allows you to self-assess two communication traits that are associated with your personality and provides you with some strategies for developing these communication personality traits. The third section of the chapter introduces you to identity management, including characteristics, influences, and strategies.

Learning Outcome 1

You will be able to differentiate self-concept from self-esteem.

UNDERSTANDING THE SELF

Understanding the self begins with knowing the difference between your self-concept and self-esteem. Both of these concepts impact your interpersonal communication in important ways, which will be discussed in greater detail in the next section of the chapter.

Self-concept is the sum total of a person's knowledge and understanding of his or herself. It is one's mental and conceptual understanding of who one is as a person. According to psychologist and philosopher William James, the individual has many different selves. Some people's self-concept is influenced by their material possessions. They are what they own. "I drive a Lexus and wear designer clothes." Some people self-identify by their friends, social networks, and careers. When interacting with them, you might hear them talking about a group they belong to, or you might hear them define themselves by their jobs or careers. "I belong to Kappa Kappa Kappa, and I am a fashion designer." Other people's self-concepts are heavily influenced by their spiritual selves, which are their internal thoughts and introspections about their values and moral standards. "I am a devout Buddhist." For most people, their self-concept is a combination of these various aspects and dimensions of a person's life.

Self-esteem reflects a person's overall self-appraisal of his or her worth. According to psychologist Morris Rosenberg, self-esteem is a feeling of self-worth and fundamental respect for oneself. Rosenberg characterized low self-esteem as a lack of respect for oneself and feelings of unworthiness, inadequacies, and deflciencies. "I'll never measure up enough to get a better job." Whereas your self-concept is descriptive (i.e., it's how you describe yourself), your self-esteem is evaluative (i.e., it's how much you value yourself). When you describe yourself as being a single mother of two who works part-time as a cashier at Barnes and Noble and is working on a degree in communication at the university, you're describing your self-concept. When you say that you feel that you're a good mother who is making a difference in the lives of her children by also being a competent employee and successful student, you're revealing your self-esteem, which is an evaluation of your self-concept.

Self-Concept

Your sense of who you are as a person is learned and is always developing and evolving from birth. You learn about who you are as a person through your self-perceptions, social comparison, peer group influence, and reflected appraisals. **Self-perceptions** include your own assessments of your abilities and talents. Psychologist Albert Bandura defined individuals' **self-efficacy** as their personal assessments of their ability to perform in a certain manner and their ability to reach their goals. When you say, "I can do this," when confronted with a challenging task, you have a high degree of self-efficacy, meaning that you believe you can do what it takes to accomplish the task. When you say, "There's no way I can do this," then your self-efficacy is low. How you think about your ability to accomplish goals shapes your conceptions of self.

Social comparisons occur when you compare yourself to others. For example, young children who are short don't recognize their height until taller children surround them. This type of social comparison is an important source of self-knowledge. At times, we consider ourselves to be successful or unsuccessful in terms of how we compare with others who are similar to us.

We use others, especially those we identify with in terms of age, education level, ethnicity, race, sex, and socioeconomic status, as benchmarks. If you have a friend who has reached a number of personal and professional goals, you might compare your accomplishments to this person's accomplishments. The research suggests that we interact with people we consider superior others when we need motivation to excel, and with people we consider inferior when we need to feel good about ourselves. How you compare to others influences your self-concept development.

Peer group influence involves the impact that your friends have on your self-concept development. Your peer group is a collection of people of approximately the same age, social status, and interests as yours. Put simply, your peer group is your potential friendship network. Psychologists Judith Harris and Steven Pinker's research confirmed what all parents feared: Their children's friends have more influence on their children's self-concept and behavior than they do as parents. Most parents intuitively understood this conclusion before it was published. This is why your parents are usually quite concerned about the company you keep and the friends you hang around with. These relationships play a role in the development of your self-concept.

Reflected appraisals are assessments you make about yourself based on how you believe others see and behave toward you. Sociologist Charles Cooley used the metaphor of a mirror to illustrate the self-concept as a reflected appraisal. If you see others reacting positively to you and wanting to be with you, then your self-concept as a potential friend slowly begins to develop. One of your authors clearly remembers his first professional position upon graduating from college as a trainer for an international airline. During a meeting with a group of airline executives, his colleagues treated him like a professional even when he didn't see himself in this new role. Over time, he started identifying as a professional because others perceived him in this manner and treated him as a professional.

Self-Esteem

Your self-esteem, or your overall self-appraisal of your worth and value, is a multidimensional psychological concept that influences your interpersonal communication in meaningful ways. New research also suggests that biology, in addition to your environment, plays a significant role in the development of your self-esteem.

Self-esteem is multidimensional.   Some researchers suggest that three major dimensions of self-esteem affect how people communicate and interact in their relationships. **Cognitive self-esteem** is your self-evaluation regarding your ability to learn, process, and use information and knowledge. **Social self-esteem** is your self-evaluation regarding your ability to interact and relate to others as well as your ability to develop and maintain friends. **Physical self-esteem** is your self-evaluation regarding your body image and attractiveness.

Another way in which researchers study the multidimensionality of self-esteem is by researching it as a state or a trait. When your self-esteem fluctuates from situation to situation, you have *state* self-esteem. The situation affects how much you value yourself. You may have high self-esteem when interacting with your friends but low self-esteem when interacting with your colleagues at work. There is something about the situation or the types of relationships that causes you to value yourself differently. When your self-esteem remains constant or consistent regardless of the situation, you have trait self-esteem. This type of self-esteem is unchanging and is not affected by the situation or types of relationships.

Researchers wonder whether there are differences between men's and women's levels of self-esteem. Communication researchers Mike Allen, Erin Sahlstein, and their research colleagues conducted a meta-analysis of the effects of sex (male and female) on self-esteem. This research method allows researchers to identify trends across a number of different studies. After collapsing the findings of 103 studies that examined sex differences in self-esteem into a single study, Allen and his colleagues found the following:

- In examining self-esteem, the data suggest that overall, women have slightly higher self-esteem than men do.
- In examining *cognitive* self-esteem, women have slightly higher self-esteem than men do.
- In examining *social* self-esteem, men have slightly higher self-esteem than women do.
- In examining *physical* self-esteem, men have slightly higher self-esteem than women do.

According to Allen and Sahlstein, the data suggest that there are only small differences between men's and women's levels of self-esteem. However, even minimal differences may have important implications for the mental, physical, and relational health of individuals and couples.

Self-esteem is affected by nature and nurture factors.   Researchers have found that your biology, that is, your genes, is partially responsible for your level of self-esteem. In fact, researchers have found that about 52% of your self-esteem is based on the genes you inherited from your parents and grand-parents. According to this group of researchers, 48% of your self-esteem is learned, while 52% of your self-esteem is genetically inherited. If you struggle with low self-esteem, chances are others in your family have also struggled with low self-esteem. Another way to recognize the power of your self-esteem genes occurs when you work hard to enhance your self-esteem and nothing seems to work. For example, you lose weight, excel in your studies, and help your team win the championship, and you still experience low self-esteem. What you're feeling at this moment is the 52% of your self-esteem genes that are stubborn and resistant to change. The good news is that a large portion of your self-esteem can be enhanced through your environment or your nurturing.

Your environment, including the relationships you have with your parents, friends, and teachers as well as your exposure to certain forms of media also influences your self-esteem development. Researchers have found that negative self-esteem develops when children are neglected by their parents, grow up with parents who struggle with depression or are exposed to negative parenting practices. Lowered self-esteem is also the result of negative interpersonal experiences with friends, such as when your friends provide negative feedback about your competence, physical appearance, and family.

Researchers have found that teachers play a significant role in the development of students' self-esteem, but they disagree on whether males or females benefit more from the attention that teachers give to students.

Educational researchers Myra and David Sadker argue that the educational system disadvantages girls. Their data suggest that instructors teach male and female students differently. For example, teachers pay more attention to male students, call on male students more often, and allow male students to interrupt female students more often. Because of differences in teaching styles, male and female students leave the classrooms with differing levels of self-esteem.

By contrast, psychologist Leonard Sax argues that the educational system disadvantages male students, in particular young boys. He argues that teachers and their teaching practices are ineffective with boys and young men. According to Sax and other researchers, young men are being left behind in the educational system, resulting in fewer men attending college. Regardless of which sex's self-esteem benefits more because of the attention teachers pay to students, teachers play a role in the development of their students' self-esteem.

Learning Outcome 1

You will be able to differentiate self-concept from self-esteem.

Which statement best describes the differences between self-concept and self-esteem?

A. Self concept is a person's overall self-evaluation of his or her own worth; Self-esteem is the sum total of a person's knowledge and understanding of his or herself.
B. When a person introduces himself as being an excellent athlete he is revealing his self-esteem. When he shares with others that being an athlete is a big part of his identity, he is revealing his self-concept.
C. Research suggests that men and women differ in terms of self-concept.
D. Researchers have found that your biology, that is your genes or nature, is partially responsible for your self-concept.

Answer key in back of chapter.

Learning Outcome 2

You will understand how self-concept and self-esteem impact communication.

Self-Concept and Self-Esteem Impact Your Communication

Now that you have an understanding of self-concept and self-esteem and how they develop, let's consider how self-concept and esteem affect communication.

Impact your motivation to communicate.   Your sense of who you are and your self-esteem influence your motivation or desire to communicate. Communication researchers have found that what motivates people to communicate is not so much their "real" or "actual" communication abilities, but how they perceive their abilities. A friend was recently surprised to receive so many compliments on a toast he gave at a wedding where he served as best man. He went into the wedding dreading this part of the ceremony because he perceived himself not be a competent public speaker. Based on the reactions of the wedding guests to his heartfelt toast, he was actually quite competent.

Researchers have found that some individuals who perceive themselves as competent communicate too much. The amount of talk is influenced by how one perceives the self.

Impact yourself and other expectations.

Your sense of who you are and your self-esteem influence the expectations you have for yourself and others. **Self-expectations** are the goals you set for yourself or how you believe you ought to behave and what you ought to accomplish. Self-esteem has an important effect on the prophecies people make. A **prophecy** is a prediction about a future event. Sociologist Robert Merton is credited with the expression "**self-fulfilling prophecy**," which is the idea that what you believe about yourself often comes true because you expect it to come true. Have you ever expected that your first date with someone was going to go well…and it did. What about a job interview? Have you ever had the expectation that you're not going to do well in a job interview and then performed incredibly poorly during the interview?

People with lower self-esteem are more likely to develop prophecies that include rejection and failure. For example, researchers found that when people expect rejection, they are more likely to behave in ways that lead others to reject them. You begin communicating in more negative ways, and you start believing your own words. You become the person you talk about in your own communication.

On the other hand, people with higher self-esteem are more likely to develop positive prophecies or predictions that include success. For example, researchers found that individuals with high self-esteem were more likely to be engaged in their studies and to experience success as a result of their motivation and engagement. They communicate in more empowering ways and believe the feedback they receive from their own voices.

Your self-esteem also influences **other-expectations**, which are the standards you set for others or how you believe others should behave in certain situations. On the basis of these expectations, you communicate and interact with people in a manner that tends to make these expectations come true. The teacher-student relationship is a unique relationship that has been studied extensively in terms of other-expectations. Here are a few research findings that reveal how the teacher-student relationship is different depending on the expectations teachers have for their students:

- Teachers respond to low-expectation students' incorrect answers by giving the student the answer or calling on another student to answer the question.
- Teachers respond to high-expectation students' incorrect answers by giving the student additional time, repeating the question, providing a clue, or asking a new question.
- Teachers criticize low-expectation students more frequently.
- Teachers are less likely to praise low-expectation students when these students provide a correct answer.
- Teachers are less nonverbally responsive (less eye contact, less smiling) to low-expectation students.

Impact how your messages are interpreted.

Your sense of who you are and your self-esteem influence how you interpret other people's messages. For example, people with lower levels of self-esteem don't interpret constructive feedback well. Regardless of how well the constructive feedback was discussed with them, they interpret the feedback in a very personal manner. Therefore, they experience feelings of hurt, stress, and sometimes embarrassment. In many interpersonal relationships, this can be a source of conflict that, if not managed well, can affect the quality of the relationship.

Another way in which your conceptions of yourself affect how you interpret messages is in your ability to be influenced and persuaded. Are you easily persuaded? Communication researchers have been able to determine that people with high and low levels of self-esteem are not persuaded as easily as are people who have moderate levels of self-esteem. People with high self-esteem are confident in their ability to critically listen and interpret information in order to make a decision that's right for them. People with low self-esteem are less confident in their ability to critically process and interpret information and are too concerned about what others think. Therefore, they have a tendency to avoid or ignore persuasive messages.

Finally, your sense of who you are and your self-esteem influence how you interpret situations. Table 4.1 illustrates how two different people interpret their relational success and failure differently depending on their level of self-esteem.

Table 4.1 The Effect of Self-Esteem on Relationships: Success or Failure

	High Self-Esteem	Low Self-Esteem
Cory: Relational Success	"I'm deserving of this relationship!"	"I got lucky with this relationship; it will probably not last."
Seth: Relational Failure	"There's always another relationship."	"I wasn't deserving of the relationship."

Relational success could be anything from your asking someone out on a date and this person accepting your invitation to your having a good relationship with your supervisor at work.

A Cory with high self-esteem interprets his relational success to his being a good person and deserving of the relationship. A Cory with low self-esteem interprets his relational success quite differently. Rather than believing that he is worthy and deserving of relational success, he interprets his relational success to his being lucky. He even questions whether the relationship will last.

A Seth with high self-esteem interprets his relational failure by shrugging it off and moving on to the next relationship. In fact, he is not devastated or

---

Learning Outcome 2

You will understand how self-concept and self-esteem impact communication.

Which statement most accurately describes how self-concept and self-esteem impact communication?

A. Communication researchers have found that what motivates people to communicate is their "real" or "actual" communication abilities rather than their "perceived" abilities.
B. Self-esteem does not impact the expectations we set for others. Self-concept does impact the expectations we set for others.
C. High self-esteem people interpret messages similarly to low-self esteem individuals.
D. High and low self-esteem individuals are not persuaded as easily as people who have moderate levels of self-esteem.

Answer key in back of chapter.

upset by the relational failure. A Seth with low self-esteem, by contrast, blames the relational failure on his not being worthy or deserving of the relationship in the first place. You might hear someone with low self-esteem saying, "It was too good to be true, and I didn't think it would ever work in the first place."

Enhancing Your Self-Concept and Self-Esteem

Because your self-concept and self-esteem affect your communication, it's best to continually find ways to enhance and develop your self-concept and self-esteem. Here are some strategies that you might find helpful.

Learning Outcome 3

You will be able to explain how one of the listed strategies can enhance your self-concept and self-esteem.

It's not the quantity of friends you have but the quality of your friendships that influences self-concept and self-esteem. Perhaps it's time you took inventory of your friendships.

© Rawpixel.com/Shutterstock.com

Develop supportive relationships.   Since the company you keep influences your self-concept and how you feel about yourself, it's important that you initiate, develop, and manage constructive relationships with others who can support you. Enhancing a positive self-concept begins by surrounding yourself with people who are interested in taking the time to understand you. They are more likely to become interested in understanding you if you're equally interested in understanding them. This mutual desire to understand each other lays the foundation for supportive relationships.

It's also important to get yourself out of destructive relationships. Unsupportive relationships harm self-concept and self-esteem and, over time, can have a devastating effect. Although it is not always an easy thing to do, it is healthy to end these relationships. You will see an enhanced self-esteem emerge simply by ridding yourself of unsupportive relationships that prevent you from reaching your goals.

Develop realistic expectations.   Developing realistic expectations begins by understanding the difference between the "real" self and the "ideal" self. The **real self** is your honest assessment of your current abilities. The **ideal self** is what you strive to become. Having expectations for yourself is important; however, it is important to set realistic expectations. For example, Javier has set expectations for himself that are outside of his abilities. He is an overachiever. Regardless of how hard he works, his goals are probably unreachable. Alexander, on the other hand, is an underachiever. His expectations for himself are too low; he can reach his goal with minimal effort. Unfortunately, both Javier and Alexander have unrealistic expectations that are likely to negatively influence their self-concept and self-esteem. Jillian has established expectations that are within her reach. She understands her abilities, skills, and talents and has some goals that are challenging but attainable.

Develop new competencies. Learning and self-esteem are related. As was discussed earlier, your belief that you can learn and influence your own thoughts and behaviors is referred to as self-efficacy. For example, many college students who successfully complete a semester of college leave with a level of self-confidence that they did not possess when they started the semester. Students leave with an "I can do it" attitude, which enhances their self-concept and self-esteem. Their sense of self-efficacy increases, as does their confidence in their ability to influence and take control of their lives.

Becoming proficient at a new skill allows you to feel productive. When you feel that you have something to offer others, your life is enriched. For example, many colleges and universities are becoming more accessible to community members by offering evening, weekend, and summer courses in cooking, various languages (e.g., Sign, French, Spanish, Japanese, Russian), public speaking, accounting, and massage therapy, to name a few. These courses allow people from the community to learn new skill sets or to fine-tune or polish their skills making them more proficient.

By developing a new skill, you can enrich your life.

Develop rational beliefs. You can enhance your self-concept and self-esteem by thinking differently. A number of people with low self-esteem and self-concept live with illogical, irrational beliefs; these thoughts are often exaggerated and extreme. You can begin by evaluating your own beliefs. Would you consider them irrational or rational? To get you started, consider some of the irrational beliefs showcased in Table 4.2. Do you see how replacing these irrational beliefs with rational beliefs could enhance your self-concept and self-esteem?

Table 4.2 Examining Differences Between Irrational And Rational Beliefs

Irrational Beliefs	Rational Beliefs
I must be loved or approved by everyone I consider significant.	I want to be loved and approved by most people, and I will try to act in a respectful manner so that they will love and approve of me. However, I must be respectful of those who don't love or approve of me. My self-esteem cannot depend on the whims of others.
I must be competent and perfect in all that I do.	I will strive to do my best rather than to be the best. I can enjoy doing things even if I'm not particularly good at them. I'm not afraid to try things in which I might fail. Taking risks is courageous and is necessary if I am to grow.
I must live in fear of the unknown and always be prepared for the worst to happen.	It is probably in my best interest to face the unknown and render it less dangerous, and if that is impossible, I will stop obsessing about it and being fearful. Worry will not stop it from occurring. Even if it does occur, I can manage and cope with it.
I must avoid life's difficulties and responsibilities.	I'll do those necessary things no matter how much I dislike them. Avoiding difficulties prevents me from living my life to the fullest. Difficulties and responsibilities are a major part of life.

Source: Adapted from Schiraldi, G. R. (2001). The *self-esteem workbook*. Oakland, CA: New Harbinger Publications.

Cognitive restructuring is the process that one goes through when one replaces debilitating irrational beliefs with empowering rational beliefs. There are a number of self-help books in the marketplace that can help you with this restructuring process. Although some people can learn how to replace their irrational beliefs with rational ones on their own, others have a more difficult time in changing their belief systems and might need some professional assistance.

For many people, their lowered self-concept and self-esteem are the culmination of many years living with their own irrational beliefs or with others who have irrational beliefs about them. For example, your parents might believe that you're the perfect child and that you will one day achieve great success because of your moral values and intelligence, and no other future seems possible or acceptable. Over time, you internalize these irrational beliefs of perfectionism. Striving to become perfect becomes your reality.

Develop Plan B. It's important that you prepare for setbacks when you are organizing and planning your life. A **setback** is something that reverses or delays your progress in reaching your goal. Setbacks are a part of life. They can paralyze people with low self-esteem and cause it to plummet further into an abyss. It's important that you learn how to cope and manage setbacks. You do this by developing an alternative plan, or a plan B. Although disappointing at first, some setbacks have a silver lining, meaning that in time, you will be glad they occurred. Other times, however, these setbacks are unfortunate, frustrating, and very disappointing. A part of enhancing your self-esteem and self-concept is learning how to anticipate, cope with, and learn from your setbacks. Here are a few guidelines for processing setbacks.

- *Anticipate setbacks*. Setbacks are a constant in life. Don't obsess about them, but realize that they could occur. There is always more than one way to achieve your goals. Expand your options.
- *Take responsibility*. Admit your role in the setback. Identify the behaviors or lack of behaviors that resulted in the setback.
- *Refocus*. Rather than focusing and obsessing on the setback, which is in the past, refocus on the future. Develop ways to repair the setback, or develop alternative plans.
- *Learn from your setbacks*. Take a few minutes to ask yourself the following questions, which will allow you to learn from the setback: Did certain things go well? What are the advantages of not getting what I want right now? What coping skills could I learn from this setback? Were there signs of an impending setback that I did not see? If a similar event occurred again, what could I do differently?

Learning Outcome 3

You will be able to explain how one of the listed strategies can enhance your self-concept and self-esteem

Which strategy would probably not lead to enhanced self-concept and self-esteem?

- A. Developing supportive relationships enhance self-concept and self-esteem through your experiencing others "having your back" during challenging times.
- B. Developing realistic expectations enhance self-concept and self-esteem by challenging you to reach "doable" expectations and the sense of fulfillment when accomplished.
- C. Developing new competencies enhance self-concept and self-esteem through the self-confidence one achieves from learning something new.
- D. Developing rational beliefs enhances self-concept and self-esteem by replacing rational behaviors with irrational behaviors through a cognitive restructuring process.

Answer key in back of chapter.

UNDERSTANDING COMMUNICATION TRAITS

Similar to personality traits, we also have **communication traits**, which are enduring consistencies and differences in message-sending and message-receiving behaviors among individuals. Some people are very talkative, whereas other people are quiet and prefer not to talk. Like our personality traits, our communication traits tend to be consistent ways of behaving. Communication researchers have identified a number of communication traits that influence how we relate and interact with others and our relationships. Two of these traits that are particularly important to understanding self are communication apprehension and socio-communicative orientation.

> ### Learning Outcome 4
>
> You will be able to identify the ways high levels of communication apprehension affect your communication with others.

Communication Apprehension

If you have ever experienced a bit of stage fright, then you've experienced **communication apprehension**, which is "an individual's level of fear or anxiety associated with either real or anticipated communication with another person or persons." Before you read any further, we want you to become aware of your level of communication apprehension when communicating with others. Please take a few minutes to complete the communication apprehension measure in the following self-assessment box.

Assess Your Communication Personality

MCCROSKEY'S PERSONAL REPORT OF COMMUNICATION APPREHENSION (PRCA-24)

Assess your communication apprehension by completing the assessment below. Also, encourage your relational partner (a friend, co-worker, family member, or romantic partner) to do the same. This way, you can compare and contrast your scores and begin to understand better how your communication traits may influence your interpersonal communication.

Directions:

This instrument, the PRCA-24, is composed of 24 statements concerning your feelings about communication with other people. Please indicate in the space provided the degree to which each statement applies to you by marking whether you (1) *strongly agree*, (2) *agree*, (3) *are undecided*, (4) *disagree*, or (5) *strongly disagree* with each statement. There are no right or wrong answers. Many of the statements are similar to other statements. Do not be concerned about this. Just work quickly, and record your first impression.

__2__   1. I dislike participating in group discussions.

__3__   2. Generally, I am comfortable while participating in a group discussion.

_4_ 3. I am tense and nervous while participating in group discussions.

_3_ 4. I like to get involved in group discussions.

_2_ 5. Engaging in a group discussion with new people makes me tense and nervous.

_3_ 6. I am calm and relaxed while participating in group discussions.

_3_ 7. Generally, I am nervous when I have to participate in a meeting.

_2_ 8. Usually, I am calm and relaxed while participating in meetings.

_4_ 9. I am very calm and relaxed when I am called upon to express an opinion at a meeting.

_2_ 10. I am afraid to express myself at meetings.

_3_ 11. Communicating at meetings usually makes me uncomfortable.

_4_ 12. I am very relaxed when answering questions at a meeting.

_2_ 13. While participating in a conversation with a new acquaintance, I feel very nervous.

_2_ 14. I have no fear of speaking up in conversations.

_4_ 15. Ordinarily, I am very tense and nervous in conversations.

_2_ 16. Ordinarily, I am very calm and relaxed in conversations.

_4_ 17. While conversing with a new acquaintance, I feel very relaxed.

_3_ 18. I'm afraid to speak up in conversations.

_5_ 19. I have no fear of giving a speech.

_3_ 20. Certain parts of my body feel very tense and rigid while I am giving a speech.

_5_ 21. I feel relaxed while I am giving a speech.

_2_ 22. My thoughts become confused and jumbled when I am giving a speech.

_4_ 23. I face the prospect of giving a speech with confidence.

_1_ 24. While giving a speech, I get so nervous that I forget facts I really know.

Scoring instructions:

The PRCA-24 permits computation of one total score and four subscores. The subscores are related to communication apprehension in each of four common communication contexts: group discussions, meetings, interpersonal conversations, and public speaking. To compute your scores, merely add or subtract the scores for each item as indicated below.

Subscore Desired		Scoring Formula
Group discussion	19	18 + scores for items 2, 4, 6; - scores for items 1, 3, 5
Meetings	20	18 + scores for items 8, 9, 12; - scores for items 7, 10, 11

Interpersonal conversations	17	18 + scores for items 14, 16, 17; - scores for items 13, 15, 18
Public speaking	26	18 + scores for items 19, 21, 23; - scores for items 20, 22, 24

To obtain your total score for the PRCA-24, simply add your four subscores together. Your score should range between 24 and 120. If your score is below 24 or above 120, you have made a mistake in computing the score.

Scores on the four contexts (groups, meetings, interpersonal conversations, and public speaking) can range from a low of 6 to a high of 30. Any score above 18 indicates some degree of apprehension. If your score is above 18 for the public speaking context, you are like the overwhelming majority of Americans.

Norms for PRCA-24		Average
For total score:	82	65.6
Group:	19	15.4
Meeting:	20	16.4
Dyad (interpersonal)	17	14.5
Public:	26	19.3

Courtesy of Dr. James C. McCroskey, Department of Communications Studies, University of Alabama-Birmingham

Understanding your communication apprehension. Research suggests that one in five Americans experience an abnormally high level of communication apprehension. You might have seen television commercials advertising social anxiety medication. Communication apprehension is a form of social anxiety. People who are high in the communication apprehension trait experience fear when communicating with others in a variety of contexts, including meetings, small groups, public presentations, and relationships. People who are low in the communication apprehension trait rarely experience fear when communicating with others. Research suggests that a high level of communication apprehension has a tendency to negatively affect all types of important interpersonal relationships, including parent–child, teacher–student, doctor–patient, workplace, and our intimate and sexual relationships.

To help you understand how your communication is affected by your communication apprehension, consider the following questions.

- *Do you avoid communicating with others?* Rather than informally socializing with others, do you make excuses for not attending social events?
- *Do you withdraw from communication?* Rather than getting more involved in conversations with friends or colleagues, do you have a tendency to pull away from these conversations and social opportunities?
- *Do you experience communication disruptions?* Rather than talking in a clear manner, do you have a tendency to mispronounce words and use too many vocal disfluencies or interrupters, such as "uhh," "ahh," "um," and "like"?
- *Do you overcommunicate?* Rather than having a discussion in which there is give and take in the conversation, do you have a tendency to dominate the conversation?

Nature/Nurture Intersections

Does your brain make you shy?

Did you know that a part of shyness has been linked to brain activity? Dr. Carl Schwartz of Harvard Medical School found that shyness has roots in an almond-shaped brain region call the amygdala, which is known to control emotions such as fear (see Figure 4.1).

The study used a tool called functional magnetic resonance imaging to look for differences in how the brains of introverts and extraverts reacted to pictures of unfamiliar faces. Schwartz and his team of researchers examined subjects who had been classified as shy or outgoing 20 years earlier when they were toddlers. Adults who had been classified as shy as children had a higher level of blood flow in the amygdala than the level of those who had been labeled as outgoing. "We found that individual differences in temperament (personality) are associated with persistent differences in the responsivity of the amygdala after more than 20 years of development and life experience," Schwartz says. Put simply, a part of shyness is linked to brain activity. Even after 20 years of experience interacting and relating to people, individuals continue to experience shyness in a consistent manner. Schwartz commented that this study demonstrated a relationship between brain activity and shyness; however, the study did not prove a direct cause-and-effect relationship.

Figure 4.1 **The Amygdala: The Portion of the Brain That Controls Emotions Such as Fear**

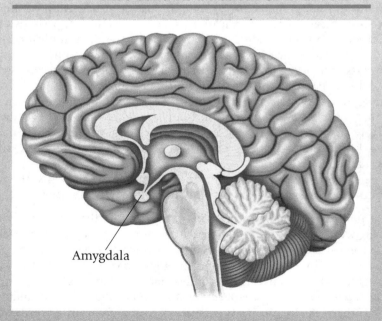

Amygdala

The more questions you answered yes to, the more likely you are to experience high levels of communication apprehension. Communication researchers agree that a person's level of communication apprehension is the result of both nature and nurture influences. Researchers have linked communication apprehension to one's biology and the genetics (nature) that have been passed down through the generations. Researchers have also been able to demonstrate how communication apprehension is learned (nature) through one's negative experiences in communicating with others, which is often due to underdeveloped communication skills.

The following section provides you with some ways to manage your apprehension when it comes to communicating with others.

WHAT CAN I DO NOW?

If you scored 18 or higher on any of the subscores of the PRCA-24:

- *You could avoid the triggers that activate your communication apprehension*. Try reducing the number of unfamiliar or formal situations. Also, try limiting situations in which people pay excessive attention to you or in which you are evaluated.
- *You could make sure that your personality, communication, and environment are in sync*. In other words, don't put yourself into situations that require excessive amounts of communication if you have a choice.
- *You could get skills training in communication*. You're already taking the first step in reducing your communication apprehension by reading this book and taking communication courses.
- *You could remember to visualize success*. Although it might seem a bit too simple, studies have found that if you take the time to imagine yourself being successful, the brain has a way of making you feel more confident and less anxious.
- *You could seek out professional assistance*. A variety of professional therapies and treatments have been shown to reduce communication apprehension. Your medical doctor can even prescribe social anxiety medication (e.g., Prozac, Zoloft , Paxil) if you have an extremely high level of communication apprehension.

Learning Outcome 4

You will be able to identify the ways high levels of communication apprehension affect your communication with others.

Which statement best describes how high levels of communication apprehension affect your communication with others?

- A. High levels of communication apprehension causes people to avoid communication, experience communication disruptions, and overcommunicate in some situations.
- B. High levels of communication apprehension causes people to avoid communication, withdraw from communication, experience communication disruptions, and undercommunicate in some situations.
- C. High levels of communication apprehension causes people to avoid communication, withdraw from communication, and engage in high assertive and low responsive communication behaviors.

D. High levels of communication apprehension causes people to avoid communication, withdraw from communication, and engage in low assertive and high responsive communication behaviors.

Answer key in back of chapter.

Learning Outcome 5

You will be able to differentiate the four social styles that comprise your socio-communicative orientation: amiables, analytical, drivers, and expressives.

Socio-Communicative Orientation

Your **socio-communicative orientation (SCO)** is how you perceive your levels of responsiveness and assertiveness when communicating with others. It's similar to your handwritten signature in that it is unique; no one has a signature that's exactly like yours. Your socio-communicative orientation is also unique; no one has a SCO that's exactly like yours. What is your social signature? To find out, take a few minutes to assess your socio-communicative orientation.

Understanding your socio-communicative orientation. Your social style is a composite of two communication factors: assertiveness and responsiveness. **Assertiveness** is the capacity to make requests; to actively disagree; to express positive or negative personal rights and feelings; to initiate, maintain, or disengage from conversations; and to stand up for one's self without attacking another. Put simply, it is your ability to express your needs, wants, and desires in a firm, but polite manner. **Responsiveness** is the capacity to be sensitive to the communication of others, to be seen as a good listener, to make others comfortable in communicating, and to recognize the needs and desires of others. When these two factors are combined, four distinct social styles emerge. The following list will help you to interpret your scores and describe some of the characteristics of these four social styles.

Analytical

© Daniel M Ernst/Shutterstock.com

Amiable

© ProStockStudio/Shutterstock.com

Driver

Expressive

© Rustle/Shutterstock.com

© Aaron Amat/Shutterstock.com

What is your social style? How does it influence how you communicate with others and how they communicate with you?

- *Amiables*. The **amiables** are considered relationship specialists and are high on responsiveness and low on assertiveness. The adjectives that are used to describe amiables are *conforming, unsure, pliable, dependent, awkward, supportive, respectful, willing, dependable*, and *agreeable*. Amiables seem to be most comfortable working in environments in which they can provide services and be supportive and helpful in their relationships with others. We often find these people in careers such as teaching, human resources, social work, psychology, and other helping professions.
- *Analyticals*. The **analyticals** are considered technical specialists and are low on responsiveness and low on assertiveness. The adjectives that are used to describe analyticals are *critical, indecisive, stuffy, picky, moralistic, industrious, persistent, serious, exacting*, and *orderly*. Professions such as science, engineering, construction work, accounting, and certain aspects of law often have a high proportion of people who have this style. Some research suggests that analyticals are more likely to be apprehensive about communication and, as a result, be more withdrawn and quiet. Thus, analyticals may be less effective communicators than people who have the other styles and more resistant to attempts to interact with them.
- *Driver*. The **drivers** are considered control specialists and are low on responsiveness and high on assertiveness. The adjectives that are used to describe drivers are *pushy, severe, tough, dominating, harsh, strong-willed, independent, practical, decisive*, and *efficient*. These people might be in careers such as small-business ownership, top management, production management, administrative personnel, politics, and other decision-making management positions. Because of their ability to take responsibility and direct others, top management often puts these individuals into positions of control.
- *Expressive*. The **expressives** are considered social specialists and are high on responsiveness and high on assertiveness. The adjectives that are used to describe expressives are *competent, excitable, versatile, reacting, ambitious, stimulating, enthusiastic, dramatic*, and *friendly*. People with expressive behavior are often found in sales, entertainment, advertising, art, music, and writing. These people know how to use their communication skills to gain recognition and attention, and they like being seen and noticed by others.

Assess Your Communication Personality

RICHMOND AND MCCROSKEY'S SOCIO-COMMUNICATIVE ORIENTATION ASSESSMENT

Assess your socio-communicative orientation by completing the assessment at http://www.jamescmccroskey.com/measures/sco.htm. Also, encourage your relational partner (a friend, co-worker, family member, or romantic partner) to do the same. This way, you can compare and contrast your scores and begin to understand better how your communication traits may influence your interpersonal communication.

Scores above 34 indicate high assertiveness or responsiveness. Scores below 26 indicate low assertiveness or responsiveness. Scores between 26 and 34 indicate moderate levels of assertiveness or responsiveness.

To identify the quadrant that most accurately reflects your socio-communicative orientation, map your assertiveness and responsiveness scores using the matrix in Figure 4.2. First, place an X on the vertical axis that reflects your assertiveness score. Second, place an X on the horizontal axis that reflects your responsiveness score. Now connect the two scores. For example, if you scored a 35 on assertiveness and a 46 on responsiveness, you would fall within the "Expressive" quadrant.

Figure 4.2   Assertiveness/Responsiveness Matrix

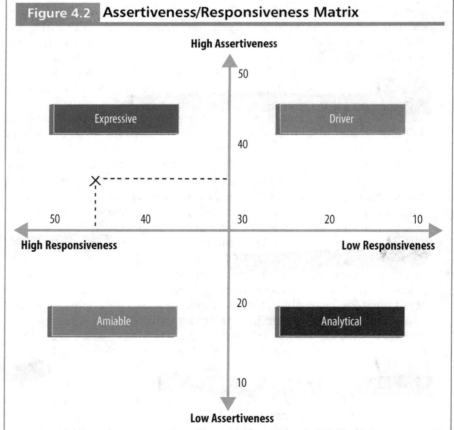

Source: Richmond, V. P., & McCroskey, J. C. (1990). Reliability and separation of factors on the assertiveness and responsiveness scales. *Psychological Reports, 67*, 449–450.

WHAT CAN I DO NOW?

If you're an amiable, you could...

- Let others know what you need and desire.
- Make requests, such as "When time permits, would you please do this...," rather than not asking for help.
- Learn to say no, and be careful that people do not take advantage of your willingness to help others.

When you're relating to an amiable, you could...

- Refrain from taking advantage of the person's willingness to help others.
- Talk about positive, people-oriented issues.
- Use responsive behaviors, such as vocal assurances (e.g., yes, okay, I hear what you're saying) and forward body leans to show your interest in the conversation.

If you're an analytical, you could...

- Let others know what you need and desire, making requests rather than demands.
- Increase your responsive behaviors by letting others know that you're listening and interested in what they're saying.
- Allow others to get to know you as a person by sharing more of yourself with them.

When you're relating to an analytical, you could...

- Talk about documented facts.
- Provide deadlines.
- Be patient, organized, and logical.
- Use task rather than relational communication, and focus on work rather than personal life.

If you're a driver, you could...

- Listen more and talk less.
- Paraphrase what you hear other people saying; for instance, you could say "Here's what I hear you saying.... Is my understanding correct?"
- Pay attention to other people's feelings and emotions, and acknowledge how others are feeling. Observe facial expressions, and listen to tone of voice. Usually, the face and the tone of voice reveal how the other person is feeling.

When you're relating to a driver, you could...

- Talk about task-related items, such as goals and objectives, in a direct manner.
- Encourage immediate action, and proceed rapidly with a degree of urgency.
- Behave in a professional and business-like manner, especially remaining time conscious.

If you're an expressive, you could...

Continue using assertive (making a request of others to make sure your needs are met) and responsive (actively listening to others and confirming them) behaviors.

- Monitor others' behaviors to make sure you're not "too much" for some people. If others are using avoidant behaviors, such as looking away, sighing, or using a closed body orientation, they might want you to tone down your communication style.

When you're relating to an expressive, you could...

- Use animated gestures and an open body position.
- Use an expressive voice by altering the rate (speed) and volume (loudness) of your voice.
- Talk about people and opinions while being stimulating, flexible, and open.

There are a number of reasons as to why some people are more or less assertive and responsive than others thus influencing their amiable, analytical, driver, or expressive social style. Some of the reasons are due to nature, while others are due to nurture influences. Again, some people are wired in a particular way meaning that the genes they inherited from birth influence how they communicate and interact with others. This is the nature perspective. Other reasons are due to the environment in which one learns and develops. This is the nurture perspective. Research suggests that both assertiveness and responsiveness are significantly related to genetic variables suggesting that nature may play a significant role in one's assertiveness and responsiveness (and corresponding amiable, analytical, driver, or expressive social styles) more so than the learning environment.

Learning Outcome 5

You will be able to differentiate the four social styles that comprise your socio-communicative orientation: amiables, analytical, drivers, and expressives.

Which item accurately describes the social styles?

A. Amiables are low on asssertiveness and high on responsiveness whereas analyticals are high on assertiveness and low on responsiveness.
B. Analyticals are excitable, versatile, reacting, ambitious, stimulating, enthusiastic, dramatic, and friendly whereas drivers are critical, indecisive, stuffy, picky, moralistic, industrious, persistent, serious, exacting, and orderly.
C. Drivers are high on assertiveness and low on responsiveness whereas expressives are high on assertiveness and high on responsiveness.
D. Expressives seem to be most comfortable working in environments in which they can provide services and be supportive and helpful in their relationships with others whereas amiables know how to use their communication skills to gain recognition and attention, and they like being seen and noticed by others.

Answer key in back of chapter.

Learning Outcome 6

Be able to identify and use strategies to manage your identity.

MANAGING YOUR IDENTITY

Your **identity** is a set of characteristics that you recognize as belonging uniquely to you and no one else. Some of these characteristics include the concepts that you have been learning about in this chapter: self-concept, self-esteem, and communication traits, to name a few. Most people invest considerable time in managing their identities. If you're on Facebook or LinkedIn, how much time did you spend creating your profile, making sure you had the right picture and profile description? **Identity management**, also known as impression management, refers to the ways in which people try to control the impressions others have of them. What parts of your self-concept and personality do you share with others? Are you successful in managing your identity? Answers to these questions will be addressed in the following three sections that examine identity management characteristics, influences, and strategies.

Identity Management Characteristics

The first characteristic of identity management is that most people construct and use both public and private identities in their interactions with others. When talking to your close friends, you use your **private identity**, the person you believe yourself to be in moments of honest self-examination. When talking to a potential employer, you use your **public identity**, the way you want others to view you; it's your public image. How accurate is your Facebook or Twitter profile? Does it reflect your private or your public identity?

Sociologist Erving Goffman considered people's social interactions to be similar to a theatrical performance in which people use verbal and nonverbal messages to manage the roles they're playing in a particular context in order to make an impression. Like an actor in a repertory company who plays different roles on different nights, you have different audiences for whom you perform throughout your day. Because of your different audiences, you have different identities. One way to illustrate how you use different identities for different audiences is to observe cell phone behavior. Someone talking to a friend on a cell phone quickly switches identity when accepting a call on the other line from a potential employer who wants to arrange a job interview. You see and hear a different person emerge from the conversation. The verbal and nonverbal messages you use with your close friends might not be the messages you use with a potential employer.

The second characteristic of identity management is that people have different beliefs about their identities that influence how they manage their identities. Some people endorse a pragmatic conception of self and identity management; others endorse a principled conception of self. People who endorse a **pragmatic self** believe identity to be flexible and adaptive. They consider managing one's identity to be a practical way to reach their goals in an appropriate manner without violating norms or standards that others consider to be important. For example, if you're meeting your dating partner's parents for the first time and you endorse a pragmatic self, you will manage your identity in such a manner that you will not offend the parents. Your goal is to earn the parents' approval.

People who endorse a **principled self** believe that identity should not be altered or adapted to fit situations. They value consistency between their actions in social situations and relevant underlying attitudes, feelings, and beliefs. Being principled in terms of identity management means that one's identity is a reflection of how one feels and what one believes. Being authentic and true to one's self takes priority over the impressions that others might have of one. If you endorse this view and were meeting your dating partner's parents for the first time, rather than managing your identity for the parents, you would present yourself as who are with the hope that they would not find your authentic self to be offensive or inappropriate.

Identity Management Nature/Nurture Influences

How you manage your identity is impacted by both nurture and nature influences. Most people learn (nurture) to carefully manage their identities when interviewing for a position. In fact, research suggests that interviewees who manage their impressions by engaging in appropriate waiting room behavior, dressing appropriately, managing communication apprehension, using technology strategically, and making a professional introduction are perceived as socially skilled and desirable by interviewers. You want to manage your identity well when there is a lot at stake—for example, when meeting and interacting with your significant other's parents and family members, your new neighbors, important clients at work, even teachers.

Second, there are personality factors that influence identity management. Psychologist Marc Snyder identified an individual difference in people that he referred to as **self-monitoring**, which is an internal process of being aware of yourself and how you are coming across to others. Research suggests that the genes we inherited from our parents are partially responsible for our self-monitoring. Put simply, self-monitoring is both learned and inherited, thus a nurture/nature influence. According to Snyder, "the self-monitoring individual is one who, out of a concern for social appropriateness, is particularly sensitive to the expression and self-presentation of others in social situations and uses these cues as guidelines for monitoring his own self-presentation." Put simply, some people are high self-monitors, and others are low self-monitors.

High and low self-monitors differ in a variety of ways. High self-monitors pay attention to others' behaviors and use these behaviors as a guide for their own communication and other behaviors. For example, high self-monitors might notice how others are constantly talking about sports, and regardless of whether they are sports fans, they quickly learn the language of sports and use it with fluency. High self-monitors are very observant and socially flexible.

High self-monitors are also very sensitive to social norms and make the necessary adjustments to present themselves in the best way possible. For example, high self-monitors notice the formality or informality of others' communication and then quickly adapt their own communication accordingly. It doesn't matter where they are, they fit in, and they feel comfortable in the various situations in which they find themselves. From the boardroom in the executive tower to working out in the field alongside volunteers rebuilding after an earthquake, high self-monitors adapt and make themselves similar to others in a particular situation.

Low self-monitors tend to pay more attention to their inner psychological states (i.e., feelings, attitudes, beliefs, personality traits) and use these states as guides for their communication and other behaviors. For example, low self-monitors who find themselves in a social function with hundreds of people quickly find a way out. Rather than mingling, socializing, and getting to know a lot of other people, low self-monitors are likely to single out a few people who are similar to them and then find a quiet corner where they can engage in a more intimate conversation. They're not necessarily shy; they just don't like spending a lot of time in an environment where they cannot be themselves.

Low self-monitors are consistent in their behavior. You know you're interacting with a low self-monitor when you see someone not adapting to a situation in a manner that you would consider normal. You might hear a friend of the low self-monitoring person saying, "That's just the way he is." Table 4.3 describes some of the research findings that differentiate high and low self-monitors.

Table 4.3	Differences between High and Low Self-Monitors

High Self-Monitors	Low Self-Monitors
Prefer variety in relational partners	Prefer relational partners who are similar to them
Prefer relationships that are flexible	Prefer that others adapt to them
Are adaptable in their relationships	Have a single and unified social network; prefer being exclusive
Have a number of segmented social networks; prefer being non-exclusive	Prefer to commit to fewer friends and relational partners
Have a tendency to not commit in relationships	Tend to feel comfortable being intimate with others
Tend to feel uncomfortable being intimate with others	Prefer significant others who are willing to be intimate with them
Fear that significant others will want them to be more intimate than they can be with the person	Seek forgiveness from partners they have wronged

Identity Management Strategies

There are a number of strategies that you can use to manage your identity. When using these strategies, it's very important to consider your audience. You probably manage a number of relationships, including the ones you have with your parents, siblings, friends, and teachers and the ones you have at work with your supervisor and co-workers and with your employees if you're a manager or supervisor. You simultaneously manage several different identities. You're a son or daughter, student, employee, friend, campus leader, and member of a religious congregation. It's important to consider your goal when managing your identity. How do you want other people to see you? What behaviors would they consider appropriate?

Following are some strategies that you might find helpful in managing your appearance, first impressions, and online identity.

Manage your appearance.   You begin managing your identity by first managing your **appearance**, or the personal factors that people use to shape an image of you. When managing their work or professional identity, most people wear clothing that is suitable for their profession or occupation. Because appearance is a highly personal identity management strategy, it's challenging to provide a list of strategies without a context for the strategies. Following is a list of identity management strategies using the context of appearance for a job interview or a semi-formal business meeting or social gathering.

- Wear clean and pressed clothes that cover the body appropriately and polished shoes.
- Be well groomed, including clean and styled hair, clean and appropriate length fingernails, and fresh breath.
- Wear a moderate amount of jewelry. Remove all hats, sunglasses, earphones, and chewing gum before entering the office where the interview is going to take place.
- Cover all tattoos, and remove non-traditional jewelry such as nose, tongue, or multiple ear studs.

Manage the first impression.   As you probably know, the first impression is the one that people tend to remember. For instance, you usually know within the first few minutes of meeting someone how the first date is going to end. Malcolm Gladwell coined the term "the blink" for this concept. In his bestseller, titled *Blink*, Gladwell describes how and why people have the ability to make important decisions in seconds. According to Gladwell, our instantaneous judgments are for the most part accurate and need to be trusted. Here are a few communication strategies that you might want to try to enhance other people's first impression of you.

© Ditty_about_summer/Shutterstock.com

For most people, a first date is one of those events where people carefully manage their appearance and first impression.

- *Use a firm handshake.* A firm handshake is one that is strong (but not so strong as to cut off the blood supply), vigorous (meaning that it conveys an appropriate amount of energy), adequate in duration (not too brief or too long), and complete in grip (meaning that full hands are gripped, with palms touching).
- *Use a confident voice.* A confident voice has energy and volume, a fast tempo, few and short pauses, varied pitch, expressiveness, and fluency.
- *Use expressive gestures.* Dale Leathers, who studied nonverbal communication extensively, recommends five ways to effectively use gestures. Gestures should (1) be used to add emphasis to the points we are making; (2) be spontaneous, relaxed, and unrehearsed; (3) be used to signal that we wish to speak or that we want someone else to speak; (4) be kept away from the body, thus increasing the persuasive impact; and (5) indicate our feelings and emotions.
- *Use responsive cues.* Nonverbally responsive behaviors that signal that you're paying attention to another person include using affirming head nods, maintaining eye contact, displaying an expressive face, showing interest by taking notes, sitting up and leaning forward, and using backchannel cues that suggest that you understand what the person is saying.

Manage your online identity. If you're a user of online social networking websites, such as Facebook or LinkedIn, it's important that you manage your online identity. There are an estimated 110 million monthly active users of social networking websites in the United States, and these individuals have access to your identity through the profile you create for your website. What would a potential employer learn about you from conducting an online search or reviewing your social networking profile? This was the case with administrators in the San Antonio, Texas, school district who were in the process of hiring new teachers for their schools. What they found were teacher applicants whose identities during the interview were inconsistent with their online identities.

Here are a few strategies that you might want to try to ensure that your online identity is managed well:

- *Google yourself.* Go to a popular search engine (Google.com, Yahoo.com, or MSN.com will do), and type your name within quotation marks. If you find something that you would rather the world not see, contact the site's owner and ask that the item be removed.
- *Clean up your Facebook page.* Some online social networking sites allow you to have multiple identities or profiles for different social networks. You might want to have two profiles—one for your personal network and one for your professional network.
- *Tune in to your blog buzz.* You can monitor your Web presence through sites such as Pubsub.com, which will alert you by email when your name is mentioned in Internet newsgroups, blogs, and securities flings.
- *Be in good company.* Research suggests that the online company you keep enhances your identity. One study found that your social capital increases as your number of online friends increases. **Social capital** is how valuable you are perceived to be in terms of your connections. For example, the popular kids in high school had a lot of social capital. Others wanted to be their friends. The same seems to be the case for online social networks. As your network increases, your identity is enhanced.

Learning Outcome 6

Be able to identify and use strategies to manage your identity.

Which item below is not a recommended identity management strategy?

- A. Managing your appearance.
- B. Managing the first impression.
- C. Manage your on-line identity.
- D. Manage your self-monitoring.

Which item below "best" matches strategies with recommended behaviors?

- A. Managing your appearance; Use a firm handshake and confident voice.
- B. Managing the first impression; Wear pressed clothes and be well groomed.
- C. Managing your on-line identity; Be in good company, sign up for alerts.
- D. Managing your self-monitoring; Become more aware of self and others.

Answer key in back of chapter.

TAKE-AWAYS

Interpersonal communication begins with your understanding of who you are as a person. Most people do not live in isolation from others. You're a product of the relationships that you have with others as well as the personality and communication traits that you possess. The purpose of this chapter was to introduce you to some new ways to think about who you are as a person. When you understand yourself better, you also begin to understand others better. This level of understanding enhances interpersonal communication. The following list of knowledge claims summarizes what you have learned in this chapter:

- Your self-concept is the sum total of your knowledge and understanding of yourself; it's descriptive. Self-esteem reflects your overall self-evaluation of your worth; it's evaluative.
- Your self-concept is complex and constantly evolving, and it develops through your self-perceptions, social comparisons, peer group influence, and reflected appraisals.
- Your self-esteem is affected by two large factors: biology and environment. A part of your self-esteem is inherited through the genes that have been passed down to you from your parents and grandparents, and a part of your self-esteem develops through your relationships, your educational experiences, and your exposure to and interaction with various forms of media.
- Your self-concept and self-esteem affect your communication in that they influence your motivation to communicate, the expectations you have for yourself and others, your relational messages, and how you interpret messages.
- Communication traits are enduring consistencies and differences in message-sending and message-receiving behaviors among individuals.
- Most people manage their identities in order to reach their interpersonal communication goals.
- Your identity is a set of characteristics that you recognize as belonging uniquely to you and no one else: private and public identities, pragmatic and principled selves.

Following are some of the ways you learned about how your personality and communication traits influence your interpersonal communication:

- By completing the communication apprehension (PRCA-24) measure, you learned about the anxiety you experience when communicating with others.
- By completing the socio-communicative orientation (SCO) measure, you learned about your social style and how to adapt to other people's social styles.

Following are a list of skills you can develop to enhance your interpersonal communication:

- Enhance your self-concept and self-esteem by developing supportive relationships, realistic expectations, skill competencies, rational beliefs, and a plan B that will help you when there's a setback.
- Manage your communication apprehension by guarding against negative attentional focus, finding a good fit, seeking out communication skills training, visualizing success, finding professional assistance, and avoiding the things that trigger your communication apprehension.
- Manage your identity by using a variety of strategies, including managing first impression, appearance, and online identity.

PRACTICE TEST ITEMS

Learning Outcome 1

Which statement best describes the differences between self-concept and self-esteem?

    A. Self concept is a person's overall self-evaluation of his or her own worth; Self-esteem is the sum total of a person's knowledge and understanding of his or herself. Incorrect answer. The definitions are reversed. Self-evaluation reflects self-esteem; sum total of a person's knowledge and understanding of his or herself is self-concept.

    B. When a person introduces himself as being an excellent athlete he is revealing his self-esteem; When he shares with others that being an athlete is a big part of his identity, he is revealing his self-concept. Correct answer. Being an "excellent" athlete reveals a self-evaluation. Sharing that he is an athlete reflects self-concept in that this person identifies with athletics.

    C. Research suggests that men and women differ in terms of self-concept. Incorrect answer. Research suggests that men and women differ in terms of self-esteem.

    D. Researchers have found that your biology, that is your genes or nature, is partially responsible for your self-concept. Incorrect answer. Research suggests that your biology is partially responsible for your self-esteem.

Learning Outcome 2

Which statement most accurately describes how self-concept and self-esteem impact communication?

    A. Communication researchers have found that what motivates people to communicate is their "real" or "actual" communication abilities rather than their "perceived" abilities. Incorrect answer. What motivates people to communicate with others is their perceived abilities, not their real or actual abilities.

    B. Self-esteem does not impact the expectations we set for others. Self-concept does impact the expectations we set for others. Incorrect answer. Self-esteem does impact the expectations we set for others; one's self-concept is unrelated to the expectations we set for others.

    C. High self-esteem people interpret messages similarly to low-self esteem individuals. Incorrect answer. With the exception of being persuaded, high and low self-esteem individuals have a tendency to interpret messages differently including constructive feedback and relational success.

    D. High and low self-esteem individuals are not persuaded as easily as people who have moderate levels of self-esteem. Correct answer. High self-esteem individuals are confident in their ability to critically examine issues. Low self-esteem individuals are less confident in their ability to critically examine issues and therefore avoid or ignore persuasive messages.

Learning Outcome 3

Which strategy would probably not lead to enhanced self-concept and self-esteem?

A. Developing supportive relationships enhance self-concept and self-esteem through your experiencing others "having your back" during challenging times. Incorrect answer. All of these have been shown to enhance self-concept and self-esteem.

B. Developing realistic expectations enhance self-concept and self-esteem by challenging you to reach "doable" expectations and the sense of fulfillment when accomplished. Incorrect answer. All of these have been shown to enhance self-concept and self-esteem.

C. Developing new competencies enhance self-concept and self-esteem through the self-confidence one achieves from learning something new. Incorrect answer. All of these have been shown to enhance self-concept and self-esteem.

D. Developing rational beliefs enhances self-concept and self-esteem by replacing rational behaviors with irrational behaviors through a cognitive restructuring process. Correct answer. The use of irrational and rational has been transposed. One enhances self-concept and self-esteem by replacing irrational behaviors with rational behaviors.

Learning Outcome 4

Which statement best describes how high levels of communication apprehension affect your communication with others?

A. High levels of communication apprehension cause people to avoid communication, experience communication disruptions, and overcommunicate in some situations. Correct answer.

B. High levels of communication apprehension causes people to avoid communication, withdraw from communication, experience communication disruptions, and undercommunicate in some situations. Incorrect answer. All are correct with the exception of undercommunicate. High communication apprehensive individuals have a tendency to overcommunicate in some situations.

C. High levels of communication apprehension causes people to avoid communication, withdraw from communication, and engage in high assertive and low responsive communication behaviors. Incorrect answer. Communication apprehension and socio-communicative orientation are two different communication personality variables. The text does not describe how these two variables are related.

D. High levels of communication apprehension causes people to avoid communication, withdraw from communication, and engage in low assertive and high responsive communication behaviors. Incorrect answer. Communication apprehension and socio-communicative orientation are two different communication personality variables. The text does not describe how these two variables are related.

Learning Outcome 5

Which item accurately describes the social styles?

A. Amiables are low on assertiveness and high on responsiveness whereas analyticals are high on assertiveness and low on responsiveness. Incorrect answer. Analyticals are low on both assertiveness and responsiveness.

B. Analyticals are excitable, versatile, reacting, ambitious, stimulating, enthusiastic, dramatic, and friendly whereas drivers are critical, indecisive, stuffy, picky, moralistic, industrious, persistent, serious, exacting, and orderly. Incorrect answer. The first set of adjectives describes expressives; the second set describes analyticals.

C. Drivers are high on assertiveness and low on responsiveness whereas expressives are high on assertiveness and high on responsiveness. Correct answer.

D. Expressives seem to be most comfortable working in environments in which they can provide services and be supportive and helpful in their relationships with others whereas amiables know how to use their communication skills to gain recognition and attention, and they like being seen and noticed by others. Incorrect answer. The first description reflects amiables; the second description reflects expressives.

Learning Outcome 6

Which item below is not a recommended identity management strategy?

A. Managing your appearance. Incorrect answer.
B. Managing the first impression. Incorrect answer.
C. Manage your on-line identity. Incorrect answer.
D. Manage your self-monitoring. Correct answer. Self-monitoring is a personality factor that influences identity management. Since it is a personality variable, it tends to be more challenging to change.

Which item below "best" matches strategies with recommended behaviors?

A. Managing your appearance; Use a firm handshake and confident voice. Incorrect answer. These are examples of managing first impression.
B. Managing the first impression; Wear pressed clothes and be well groomed. Incorrect answer. These are examples of managing your appearance.
C. Managing your on-line identity; Be in good company, sign up for alerts. Correct answer.
D. Managing your self-monitoring; Become more aware of self and others. Incorrect answer. Self-monitoring is an identity management influence and not a strategy.

STUDY GUIDE

1. What influences the development of self-concept and self-esteem? Based on the research, is self-concept or self-esteem more influenced by nature/nurture influences?
2. How does a person's self-concept and self-esteem impact how messages are received and interpreted?
3. How does communication apprehension impact one's ability to communicate with others?
4. If you are a highly communication apprehensive person, list and explain three strategies that may be able to help you manage your communication apprehension.
5. What are the four socio-communicative orientations? Provide an example of a person you know who exemplifies each style.
6. What role does self-monitoring play in how people manage their identities?

REFERENCES

Adapted from Bolton, R., & Grover-Bolton, D. (2009). *People styles at work: Making bad relationships good and good relationships better.* New York: American Management Association.

Adapted from Schiraldi, G. R. (2001). *The self-esteem workbook.* Oakland, CA: New Harbinger Publications.

Ayers, J., & Hopf, T. S. (1985). Visualization: A means of reducing speech anxiety. *Communication Education, 34,* 318–323; Ayres, J., & Heuett, B. L. (1999). An examination of the impact of performance visualization. *Communication Research Reports, 16,* 29–39.

Bandura, A. (1977). *Social learning theory.* Englewood Cliffs, NJ: Prentice-Hall.

Bandura, A. (2001). Social cognitive theory: An agentic perspective. *Annual Review of Psychology, 52,* 1–26.

Beatty, M. J., & Friedland, M. H. (1990). Public speaking state anxiety as a function of selected situational and dispositional variables. *Communication Education, 39,* 142–147.

Beatty, M. J., McCroskey, J. C., & Floyd, K. (2009). *Biological dimensions of communication: Perspectives, research, and methods.* Cresskill, NJ: Hampton Press; McCroskey, J. C., Daly, J. A., Martin, M., & Beatty, M. J. (Eds.) (1998). *Communication and personality: Trait perspectives.* Cresskill, NJ: Hampton Press.

Brophy, J. E., & Good, T. L. (1974). *Teacher-student relationships: Causes and consequences.* New York: Holt, Rinehart, & Winston.

Brown, B. L., Shwalb, D. A., Godfrey, K., & Larcher, A. M. (2007). The efficacy of selective serotonin reuptake inhibitors in adult social anxiety disorder: A meta-analysis of double blind, placebo-controlled trials. *Journal of Psychopharmacology, 21,* 102–111.

Chaplin, W. F., Phillips, J. B., Brown, J. D., Clanton, N. R., & J. L. Stein, J. L. (2000). Handshaking, gender, personality, and first impressions. *Journal of Personality and Social Psychology, 79,* 110–117.

Cooley, C. H. (1912). *Human nature and the social order.* New York: Scribner's.

Downey, G., Freitas, A. L., Michaelis, B., & Khouri, H. (2004). The self-fulfilling prophecy in close relationships: Rejection sensitivity and rejection by romantic partners. In H. T. Reis & C. E. Rusbult (Eds.), *Close relationships* (pp. 435–455). New York: Psychology Press.

Discussed on pages 67–78 in Richmond, V. P., & McCroskey, J. C. (1998). *Communication: Apprehension, avoidance, and effectiveness.* (5ᵗʰ ed.). Boston: Allyn and Bacon.

Edwards, R., & Pledger, L. (1990). Development and construct validation of the sensitivity to feedback scale. *Communication Research Reports, 7*, 83–89.

Ellis, A., Abrams, M., & Abrams, L. (2008). *Theories of personality.* New York: Sage Press.

Elisson, N. B., Steinfield, C., & Lampe, C. (2007). The benefits of Facebook "friends": Social capital and college students' use of online social network sites. *Journal of Computer-Mediated Communication, 12*, 1143–1168.

For a review of the research, see Burgoon, J. K., Birk, T., & Pfau, M. (1990). Nonverbal behaviors, persuasion, and credibility. *Human Communication Research, 17*, 140–169. Also refer to Pearce W. B., & Conklin, F. (1971). Nonverbal vocalic communication and perception of speaker. *Speech Monographs, 38*, 235–241; Street, R. L., & Brady, R. M. (1982). Speech rate acceptance ranges as a function of evaluative domain, listener speech rate, and communication context. *Communication Monographs 49*, 290–308.

For example: Glasser, W. (1999). *Choice theory.* New York: HarperCollins; Ledley, D. R., Marx, B. P., & Heimberg, R. G. (2005). *Making cognitive-behavioral therapy work: Clinical process for new practitioners.* New York: Guilford Press; Neenan, M. (2002). *Life coaching: A cognitive behavioural approach.* New York: Routledge.

From Richmond, V. P., & McCroskey, J. C. (1998). *Communication: Apprehension, avoidance, and effectiveness.* (5ᵗʰ ed.). Boston: Allyn and Bacon.

From p. 528 of Snyder, M. (1974). Self-monitoring of expressive behavior. *Journal of Personality and Social Psychology, 30*, 526–537.

Garber, J. & Flynn, C. (2001). Predictors of depressive cognitions in young adolescents. *Cognitive Theory and Research, 25*, 353–376.

Gass, R. H., & Seiter, J. S. (2006). *Persuasion: Social influence and compliance gaining* (3ʳᵈ ed.). Boston: Allyn and Bacon.

Gifford, R., Ng, C. F., & Wilkinson, M. (1985). Nonverbal cues in the employment interview: Links between applicant qualities and interviewer judgments, *Journal of Applied Psychology, 70*, 729–736.

Gladwell, M. (2005). *Blink: The power of thinking without thinking.* New York: Little, Brown, and Company.

Goffman, E. (1959). *The presentation of self in everyday life.* New York: Anchor Books.

Goss, B. (1995). *The psychology of human communication* (2ⁿᵈ ed.). Prospect Heights, IL: Waveland Press.

Harris, J. R., & Pinker, S. (1999). *The nurture assumption: Why children turn out the way they do.* New York: Free Press.

Harris, J. R. (2007). *No two alike: Human nature and human individuality.* New York: W. W. Norton; also refer to Harris, J. R., & Pinker, S. (1999). *The nurture assumption: Why children turn out the way they do.* New York: Free Press.

Infante, D. A., Rancer, A. S., & Womack, D. F. (2003). *Building communication theory* (4ᵗʰ ed.). Prospect Heights, IL: Waveland Press.

James, W. (1890). *The principles of psychology* (Vol. 1). Cambridge, MA: Harvard University Press.

Kelly, L., & Keaten, J. A. (2000). Treating communication anxiety: Implications of the communibiological paradigm. *Communication Education, 49*, 45–57.

Kleck, C. A., Reese, C. A., Behnken, D. Z., & Sundar, S. S. (2007, May). *The company you keep and the image you project: Putting our best face forward in online social networks.* Paper presented at the meeting of the International Communication Association, San Francisco, CA.

Leathers, D. G. (1988). Impression management training: Conceptualization and application to personal selling. *Journal of Applied Communication Research, 16*, 126–145.

Leone, C., & Hawkins, L. B. (2006). Self-monitoring and close relationships. *Journal of Personality, 74*, 739–778.

Lippert, L., Titsworth, B. S., & Hunt, S. K. (2005). The ecology of academic risk: Relationships between communication apprehension, verbal aggression, supportive communication, and students' academic risk status. *Communication Studies, 56*, 1–21; Limon, M. S., & France, B. H. (2005). Communication traits and leadership emergence: Examining the impact of argumentativeness, communication apprehension, and verbal aggressiveness in work groups. *Southern Communication Journal, 70*, 123–133; Wheeless, L. R., & Parsons, L. A. (1995). What you feel is what you might get: Exploring communication apprehension and sexual communication satisfaction. *Communication Research Reports, 12*, 39–45; Kim, M., & Storm, R. (2000). A test of a cultural model of patients' motivation for verbal communication in patient-doctor interactions. *Communication Monographs, 67*, 262–284; Lucchetti, A., Powers, W. G., & Love, D. E. (2002). The empirical development of the child-parent communication apprehension scale for use with young adults. *Journal of Family Communication, 2*, 109–131.

Mann, M., Clemens, M. H., Schaalma, H. P., & de Vries, N. K. (2004). Self-esteem in a broad-spectrum approach for mental health promotion. *Health Education Research, 19*, 357–372; Garber, J., & Flynn, C. (2001). Predictors of depressive cognitions in young adolescents. *Cognitive Theory and Research, 25*, 353–376.

Mann, M., Clemens, M. H., Schaalma, H. P., & de Vries, N. K. (2004). Self-esteem in a broad-spectrum approach for mental health promotion. *Health Education Research, 19*, 357–372.

Mann, M., Clemens, M. H., Schaalma, H. P., & de Vries, N. K. (2004). Self-esteem in a broad-spectrum approach for mental health promotion. *Health Education Research, 19*, 357–372; Garber, J., & Flynn, C. (2001). Predictors of depressive cognitions in young adolescents. *Cognitive Theory and Research, 25*, 353–376.

Markus, H., & Wurf, E. (1987). The dynamic self-concept: A social psychological perspective. *Annual Review of Psychology, 38*, 299–337.

McCroskey, J. C. (1978). Validity of the PRCA as an index of oral communication apprehension. *Communication Monographs, 45*, 192–203.

McCroskey, J. C., & McCroskey, L. L. (1988). Self-report as an approach to measuring communication competence. *Communication Research Reports, 5*, 108–113.

McCroskey, J. C., & Beatty, M. J. (1998). Communication apprehension. In J. C. McCroskey, J. A. Daly, M. M. Martin, & M. J. Beatty (Eds.), *Communication and personality: Trait perspectives,* (pp. 215–231). Cresskill, NJ: Hampton Press.

McCroskey, J. C., & Beatty, M. J. (2000). The communibiological perspective: Implications for communication in instruction. *Communication Education, 49*, 1–6.

Merton, R. K. (1968). *Social theory and social structure.* New York: Free Press.

Modified from Richmond, V. P., & McCroskey, J. C. (1992). *Organizational communication for survival.* Englewood Cliffs, NJ: Prentice Hall. See also Thomas, K. W., & Kilmann, R. M. (1974). *Thomas-Kilmann conflict mode instrument.* Tuxedo, NY: Xicom.

Mottet, T. P., & Thweatt, K. S. (1997). The relationships between peer teasing, self-esteem, and affect for school. *Communication Research Reports, 14*, 1–8; Hay, I., Ashman, A. F., & van Kraayenoord, C. E. (1998). Educational characteristics of students with high or low self-concept. *Psychology in the Schools, 35*, 391–400.

Mottet, T. P., Beebe, S. A., & Fleuriet, C. (2006). Students' influence messages. In T. P. Mottet, V. P. Richmond, & J. C. McCroskey (Eds.), *Handbook of instructional communication: Rhetorical and relational perspectives* (pp. 143–166). Boston: Allyn and Bacon.

Neiss, M. B., Sedikides, C., & Stevenson, J. (2006). Genetic influences on level and stability of self-esteem. *Self and Identity, 5*, 247–266.

Neiss, M. B., Sedikides, C., & Stevenson, J. (2006). Genetic influences on level and stability of self-esteem. *Self and Identity, 5,* 247–266; Roy, M. A., Neale, M. C., & Kendler, K. S. (1995). The genetic epidemiology of self-esteem. *The British Journal of Psychiatry, 166,* 813–820; Kendler, K. S., Gardner, C. O., & Prescott, C. A. (1998). A population-based twin study of self-esteem and gender. *Psychological Medicine, 28,* 1403–1409.

Richmond, V. P., McCroskey, J. C., & McCroskey, L. L. (1989). An investigation on self-perceived communication competence and personality orientations. *Communication Research Reports, 6,* 28–36.

Richmond, V. P., & McCroskey J. C. (1992). *Organizational communication for survival.* Englewood Cliffs, NJ: Prentice Hall. See also Thomas, K. W., & Kilmann, R. M. (1974). *Thomas-Kilmann conflict mode instrument.* Tuxedo, NY: Xicom.

Richmond, V. P., & McCroskey, J. C. (1998). *Communications: Apprehension, avoidance, and effectiveness.* (5th ed.). Boston: Allyn and Bacon.

Rill, L., Baiocchi, E., Hopper, M., Denker, K., & Olson, L. N. (2009). Exploration of the relationship between self-esteem, commitment, and verbal aggressiveness in romantic dating relationships. *Communication Reports, 22,* 102–113.

Rodriguez, K. (2007, Feb. 4). Kids can find what principals can't on a prospective teacher's character. *San Antonio Express-News,* B-1, B-3; see also Ferguson, T. (2007, March 28). Want a job? Clean up your Web act. Retrieved on March 30, 2007 from http://news.zdnet.com/2102-9588_22-6171187.html.

Rosenberg, M. (1965). *Society and the adolescent self-image.* Princeton, NJ: Princeton University Press.

Rosenberg, M. (1972). *Society and the adolescent self-image* (p. 5). Princeton, NJ: Princeton University Press. Richmond, V. P., & McCroskey, J. C. (1998). *Communication: Apprehension, avoidance, and effectiveness* (5th ed.). Boston: Allyn and Bacon.

Rosenfeld, P. (1997). Impression management, fairness, and the employment interview, *Journal of Business Ethics, 16,* 801–808.

Sadker, M., & Sadker, D. (1994). *Failing at fairness: How America's schools cheat girls.* New York: Simon & Schuster; see also Sadker, D., Sadker, M., & Zittelman, K. R. (2009). *Still failing at fairness: How gender bias cheats girls and boys in school and what we can do about it.* New York: Simon & Schuster.

Sahlstein, E., & Allen, M. (2002). Sex differences in self-esteem: A meta-analytic assessment. In M. Allen, R. W. Preiss, B. M. Gayle, & N. Burrell (Eds.), *Interpersonal communication research: Advances through meta-analysis* (pp. 59–72). Mahwah, NJ: Lawrence Erlbaum. See also Birndor, S., Ryan, S., Auinger, P., & Aten, M. (2005). High self-esteem among adolescents: Longitudinal trends, sex differences, and protective factors. *The Journal of Allergy and Clinical Immunology, 37,* 194–201.

Sawyer, C. R. (2016). Communication apprehension and public speaking instruction. In P. L. Witt (Ed.), *Communication and Learning, 16,* (pp. 397–425). New York: de Gruyter Mouton.

Sax, L. (2007). *Boys adrift: The five factors driving the growing epidemic of unmotivated boys and underachieving young men.* New York: Basic Books; Sommers, C. H. (2001). *The war against boys.* New York: Simon & Schuster.

Schwartz, C. E., Wright, C. I., Shin, L. M., Kagan, J., & Rauch, S. L. (2003). Inhibited and uninhibited infants grown up: Adult amygdala response to novelty. *Science, 300,* 1952–1953.

Seiter, J. S., & Sandry, A. (2003). Pierced for success?: The effects of ear and nose piercing on perceptions of job candidates' credibility, attractiveness, and hirability. *Communication Research Reports, 20,* 287–298. This information was adapted from "Dressing for success in interviews," n.d., retrieved on March 27, 2007, from http://www.wetfeet.com/Content/Articles/d/dressing%20for%20success%20in%20interviews.aspx.

Shimotsu, S. (2008). *The relationships between student self-reported perfectionism, communication apprehension, temperament, and learning outcomes.* Unpublished master's thesis, University of Texas-Pan American, Edinburg, Texas; Hill, R. W., & Zrull, M. C. (1997). Perfectionism and interpersonal problems. *Journal of Personality Assessment, 69,* 81–103.

Shimotsu, S., & Mottet, T. P. (2009). The relationships among perfectionism, communication apprehension, and temperament. *Communication Research Reports, 26,* 188–197.

Snyder, M., & Campbell, B. H. (1982). Self-monitoring: The self in action. In J. Suls (Ed.), *Psychological perspectives on the self* (Vol. 1. pp. 185–230). Hillsdale, NJ: Lawrence Erlbaum.

Taylor, S. E., Wood, J. V., & Lichtman, R. R. (1983). It could be worse: Selective evaluation as a response to victimization. *Journal of Social Issues, 39,* 19–40.

Walker, C. O., Greene, B. A., & Mansell, R. A. (2005). Identification with academics, intrinsic/extrinsic motivation, and self efficacy as predictors of cognitive engagement. *Learning and Individual Differences, 16,* 1–12.

Walther, J. B., Van Der Heide, B., Kim, S., Westerman, D., & Tong, S. T. (2008). The role of friends' appearance and behavior on evaluations of individuals on Facebook: Are we known by the company we keep? *Human Communication Research, 34,* 28–49.

Social Influence

OBJECTIVES

- Define persuasion and differentiate it from other forms of influence.
- Describe key characteristics of persuasion.
- Describe situations in which persuasion is commonly used.
- Consider the role of ethics in persuasion.

KEY TERMS

Assimilation
Attitudes
Authority heuristic
Behavioral intention
Beliefs
Central route
Cognitive complexity
Cognitive dissonance theory
Commitment and consistency
  heuristic
Constructivistic model
Controllability
Dogmatism
Door in the face technique
Ego-involvement
Elaboration likelihood model
Functional model of credibility
Inoculation theory
Latitude of acceptance
Latitude of noncommitment
Latitude of rejection

Liking heuristic
Machiavellianism
Multiple-act
Need for cognition
Need for social approval
Opinionated acceptance
Opinionated rejection
Perceived behavioural control
Perceived control
Peripheral route
Persuasibility
Reciprocity heuristic
Scarcity heuristic
Selective exposure
Self-efficacy
Self-esteem
Social proof heuristic
Subjective norm
Theory of reasoned action
Values

DEFINING CHARACTERISTICS OF PERSUASION

Persuasion has been defined in numerous ways, as is illustrated by the five definitions shown in Figure 5.1. Before we provide the definition to be used in this text, let's discuss some key characteristics that will help you understand why we define persuasion the way we do. First, **persuasion is a type of communication using a shared symbol system**. Persuasion uses messages in some kind of symbol system, and four of the five definitions in Figure 5.1 refer to communication. The one definition that does not directly refer to communication does imply communication. These messages may be verbal and involve language (e.g., English), or they may be nonverbal with symbols that have shared meanings (e.g., a smile, a picture of a flag). In either case, a message must be transmitted from a sender to a receiver in some commonly shared symbol system for persuasion to occur. All of Cara's influence situations clearly involve communication and a shared symbol system, so all have at least one characteristic of persuasion.

Second, **persuasion requires intent**. Without this requirement, we could argue that all communication is persuasive; however, only three of the five definitions in Figure 5.1 refer to intent in some way. When someone walks across campus and says "hello" to you, it is possible to interpret that as a persuasive intent to convince you that he or she is a friendly person and/or to convince you to respond in a friendly manner but, most often, it is nothing more than a greeting. A definition that doesn't require persuasive intent on the part of the sender doesn't help us distinguish persuasion from other related terms such as communication. The intent requirement means that persuasion focuses on messages that are intended to persuade the receiver. The first situation clearly

---

| Figure 5.1 | **Definitions of persuasion.** |

Bostrom (1983)

"Persuasion is communicative behavior that has as its purpose the changing, modification, or shaping of the responses (attitudes or behavior) of the receivers" (p. 11).

Petty and Cacioppo (1981)

"... any instance in which an active attempt is made to change a person's mind because the word is relatively neutral and because one person's propaganda may be another person's education" (p. 4).

Larson (2013)

"... the process of dramatic co-creation by sources and receivers of a state of identification through the use of verbal and/or visual symbols" (p. 20).

Perloff (2010)

"... a symbolic process in which communicators try to convince other people to change their attitudes or behaviors regarding an issue through the transmission of a message in an atmosphere of free choice" (p. 12).

O'Keefe (2002)

"A successful intentional effort at influencing another's mental state through communication in a circumstance in which the persuadee has some measure of freedom" (p. 5).

involves intent, but is Cara the intended target? The students arguing about baseball teams clearly intended to influence each other, but did they intend to influence someone who overheard their loud conversation? Clearly Larry intended to influence Cara about the group project, and Kellie intended to influence Cara to join the rowing club. Did the newspaper story about armed robbers intend to influence student behavior? Does Dr. Kalibo intend to influence Cara to change her eating habits? Maybe. Assuming Cara's teacher, Dr. Kalibo, is like most other teachers, she wants Cara to learn specific information about nutrition and dispel myths and misconceptions about food and diet. But that doesn't mean Dr. Kalibo intends to change Cara's eating habits, particularly the changes that Cara made. We would really need to ask Dr. Kalibo if she intended to change her students' eating habits. If that indeed was her intention, then the situation would have the second characteristic of persuasion. If Dr. Kalibo simply wanted students to learn the content, and she left it up to the students to decide what to do with that information, then we would likely conclude that this really is not persuasion. Education and persuasion overlap in numerous ways, and the similarities and differences are further discussed later in this chapter. Intent is a necessary requirement for persuasion, but it isn't always easy to determine.

Third, **persuasion need not be successful to be considered persuasion**. When we see a television advertisement attempting to sell a product, or watch a politician's campaign speech, we view those messages as persuasion. Even if we choose not to buy the product or to vote for the political candidate, we are aware that an attempt at persuasion has been made. We don't have to wait months for the election to be held to decide what is persuasion, and we wouldn't define the losing candidate's speeches as anything but persuasive messages. Thus, it is critical that the message is intended to be persuasive rather than it necessarily be successful. Only one definition in Figure 5.1 refers to success. The other definitions are consistent with our approach that success is not required for a message to be considered persuasion.

Fourth, **persuasion involves two or more persons**. There has to be a sender and a receiver for persuasion to occur. Some have considered whether nonhuman animals can be involved in persuasion, whether individuals can persuade themselves through intrapersonal communication, and/or whether inanimate objects (e.g., a tree) can be persuasion agents. Although each of these arguments has supporters, the persuasion discussed in this textbook (and in most persuasion -research) refers to persuasion attempts between at least two persons. All of the previous influence situations involve at least two persons, so they all have this characteristic.

Finally, we need to consider the outcomes of persuasion. Miller (1980) argues that persuasion is intended to shape, reinforce, or change the responses of the receiver, and all of the definitions in Figure 5.1 refer to some type of change. We generally expect persuasive messages to involve attempts to **change** the beliefs, attitudes, and/or behavior of the receivers. For example, you have probably heard and seen numerous public service campaigns that want smokers to stop smoking. In our situations, we can see change in behavior. Cara changes her eating habits and intends to sign up for the rowing club. We also assume that Cara's beliefs about her diet changed, which led to a change in her behavior. We can also assume that Cara developed positive beliefs about the rowing club; otherwise, she wouldn't plan to sign up. On the other hand, we don't know what Cara thinks about the Yankees or the Red Sox. However, not knowing the outcomes doesn't mean that these were not attempts to change Cara's beliefs, attitudes, and/or behaviors.

Not all persuasive messages try to invoke change, however. Some attempt to **reinforce** currently held beliefs or attitudes and/or current behavioral practices. For example, Pepsi wants current Pepsi drinkers to remain loyal to the product. Political candidates speaking to members of their own party want members to remain loyal to the party and vote along party lines. Typically, speeches at the Republican and Democrat National Conventions focus on their supporters and use persuasive messages designed to reinforce current political views. Check out the 2012 convention speeches online to examine their focus. Another example is antismoking campaigns targeted at teens. Such campaigns are focused more on encouraging them *not* to start smoking than on altering current behaviors. Much of the persuasion surrounding us is attempting to reaffirm current beliefs, attitudes, and/or behaviors.

Finally, some persuasion tries to **shape** responses. These are messages targeted toward receivers who have not developed an attitude toward an object and who often lack knowledge on the issue. For example, when a company introduces a new product, it tries to shape positive responses to that product. When Procter and Gamble introduced Febreze®, a product targeted at removing odors from fabric, the company needed to inform consumers and wanted them to think positively about such a product. Because receivers had no prior knowledge of this product, the company wasn't trying to change anything, and there was nothing there to reinforce. When AIDS was identified, the government was most concerned with shaping responses to that information. Now, the government is more concerned with reinforcing positive behaviors (e.g., safe sex) and trying to change the behaviors of those who are at risk for transmission of the disease (e.g., those who engage in sex without condoms, those who share needles). Thus, depending on the situation, the intended outcome for persuasion may be change, reinforcement, or shaping of receiver responses.

Of course, you may be wondering what is meant by "receiver responses." Depending on the situation, the desired response from the receiver may involve attitudes, beliefs, and/or behaviors. For example, at times, attitude change is desired. A political candidate may want voters to share favorable attitudes toward key campaign issues. A religious organization may want to target beliefs in receivers so that they would be in alignment with the particular religion. Many times, however, behavior is the ultimate target of persuasion attempts. Advertisers ultimately want products to be purchased. Political candidates want votes and/or financial contributions. Social issue organizations often want to persuade the public about acceptable behavior (e.g., not smoking, wearing seatbelts, adopting healthy exercise and eating patterns). We often expect attitudes and/or beliefs to be the basis for behavior, so targeting attitudes and beliefs may be an avenue to influence receiver behavior. As a result, when considering receiver responses, we need to consider attitudes, beliefs, and behaviors.

Thus, when all of these criteria are taken into account, we come to the following definition of persuasion, which draws on the multiple perspectives represented earlier: **Persuasion involves symbolic communication between two or more persons with intent to change, reinforce, or shape attitudes, beliefs, and/or behaviors of the receiver.**

At this point, we have discussed the situations presented at the beginning of this chapter in relation to the key characteristics of persuasion, but we really haven't answered the question of which of these is persuasion and which are not. We determined that Cara's change of eating habits might not be a result of persuasion if Dr. Kalibo did not intentionally try to influence her eating habits. However, the situations involving Larry asking for group work and Kellie encouraging Cara to join the rowing club seemed to have all of the characteristics of persuasion. The situation involving armed robberies brings up another issue in distinguishing persuasion from other forms of influence: coercion. **Coercion** is social influence that involves force or threat of force. The robbers used a threat to force students to turn over their property. For this reason, this situation is a better example of coercion than it is of true persuasion; however, the difference between coercion and persuasion is not always clear. Perloff's (2010) and O'Keefe's (2002) definitions of persuasion in Figure 5.1 refer to the receiver having free choice or freedom. The continuum that follows has *free choice* on one end and *forced choice* on the other.

Free choice _____ Forced choice

Having a gun pointed at your head with a demand for your laptop is clearly a forced choice. Cara's behavior in signing up for the rowing club was a result of free choice. However, not all circumstances easily fit into one end of the continuum or the other. In the group project situation, Cara's grade appeared to be threatened by a negative peer evaluation if she did not comply with Larry's request. Is that coercion? Consider the class you are in. The teacher controls the awarding of grades. Instructors set grading policies, work and attendance expectations, and so on. Students may choose to complete the work or not; however, there is a consequence in terms of grade received for choosing not to complete the work. Is that a free choice, or is there an element of threat in this situation? Is the public service announcement in Figure 5.2 an example of persuasion or coercion? Are you being threatened? Do you have free choice when it comes to wearing a seat belt? Situations that fall toward the forced choice end of the continuum are considered more coercion than persuasion, whereas situations that offer more free choice are considered more persuasion than coercion. However, where choice ends and force begins is not clear, making many situations ambiguous.

WHY STUDY PERSUASION?

The question of why we study persuasion is one that students may ask advisers and that researchers ask themselves. There are three major reasons people have for wanting to know more about persuasion. The most common reason students have given us for taking a class in persuasion is a very practical one. We all engage in persuasion in multiple contexts in our lives, and many want to study persuasion in order to be **more successful persuaders** themselves. That desire for mastery of the art of persuasion may be career oriented. Regardless of what career path is sought, most people want to be able to convince organizations to hire them and supervisors to promote them and award raises. People want to be able to sell their ideas to those in power and want to influence the choices made in their organizations. Some career paths call for particularly strong persuasive skills, such as in sales, law, marketing, public relations, and politics. In these areas, the ability to do a good job relies on strong persuasive abilities.

In addition, we all use persuasion in our personal lives. You might work to convince parents to send money or to buy you a new car. You might try to persuade others to engage in social activities with you, follow you on Twitter, or to join causes you support. Perhaps you try to persuade faculty to admit you to classes or to give you a better grade. You might attempt to persuade a car

Figure 5.2 Public service announcement for safety belt use.

NO EXCEPTIONS.

CLICK IT OR TICKET

YOU WILL GET A TICKET FOR NOT WEARING YOUR SAFETY BELT.

Safety belt enforcement is being stepped up everywhere. It doesn't matter where you drive, they'll be looking for you. Simply, law enforcement writes tickets to save lives. So buckle up or you will get a ticket. No exceptions.

National Traffic highway safety.

salesperson to give you a better deal on your next vehicle or try to negotiate a better price for a new house. In short, because we engage in persuasion on a regular basis in multiple aspects of our lives, one good reason for studying persuasion is to be better at this process.

Another common reason for studying persuasion is so that we can be **better consumers of information**. As we discussed previously, we are all bombarded with a broad variety of persuasive messages daily. Understanding persuasion allows us to make choices about when to be influenced and when not to be. By understanding the strategies, tactics, and methods employed by others, we can be better prepared to deal with persuasive messages targeted at us. This is particularly important in a democratic society where we trust that the typical citizen is able to process huge amounts of material and competing persuasive campaigns in order to make rational decisions about voting. Participation in a democratic society involves both the production and consumption of persuasive messages.

Finally, some people study persuasion in an attempt to **better understand** what they observe happening around them. When we look at behavior that doesn't fit our expectations and seems at times irrational to us, we try to understand how this can happen. Cult members engage in mass suicide in the belief that a spaceship hidden in the tail of a passing comet will take them to heaven. Seemingly useless products such as singing toy fish sell out of every store on the block. Trends in fashion come and go. Political candidates are elected to office although experts said they had no chance of being elected. A nation supports a leader conducting unspeakable atrocities, such as what happened in Germany with the Holocaust under Hitler's leadership. Studying persuasion can give us insight into these puzzling events and help to make sense of them.

The study of persuasion and the value of exploring this realm is certainly not new. Persuasion was studied and written about more than 2,500 years ago by the ancient Greeks. Arguably the most famous scholar of persuasion from that time was Aristotle. His work, *Rhetoric,* laid out many concepts about persuasion that are still considered valid today (Freese, 1991). Aristotle observed human interaction and persuasive attempts and taught his students how to persuade others. We discuss some of Aristotle's concepts as we explore persuasion, and much modern research draws on Aristotle's basic principles. For example we examine source factors that influence the success and failure of persuasion and draw on Aristotle's concept of ethos, which still guides how modern researchers define source credibility. Aristotle saw persuasion as a central part of society and human interaction then, and today we still ask questions and explore persuasion as a part of interactions.

WHERE AND WHEN DO WE PERSUADE?

We suggest in this chapter that we are immersed in attempts at influence every day. The daily lives of individuals often involve persuasion in interpersonal and small-group contexts as well as in myriad forms of mass media. Students try to persuade parents to support them financially and emotionally. Roommates try to persuade each other to clean living quarters and to respect each other's privacy. Students try to convince faculty to grade them more positively. Group projects involve persuasion about meeting times, locations, and the division of labor. The multiple forms of media, such as radio, television, smartphones, newspapers, magazines, Internet, posters, billboards, and corporate logos, surround us with messages constantly. It is hard to imagine a lack of persuasion in daily interactions for most people.

In addition, some segments of society depend on persuasion in order to achieve their goals. We have all been targeted as receivers by these segments, and some of you anticipate being senders in these contexts. We often think of advertising and marketing as bombarding us with persuasion. Certainly every form of media from television to newspapers to the Internet carries advertising, and it is clearly labeled as such. These advertising messages are open attempts to influence behavior, and they meet the criteria we established for persuasion. The messages are framed in words and nonverbal images that draw on culturally developed shared symbol systems. Persuasive intent is clearly involved in the purchase of advertising space, and the ads aren't always successful, but many are. The advertisements all have the purpose of changing, shaping, or reinforcing behavior toward the product or service being promoted.

Marketing encompasses advertising, but it moves beyond the purchase of advertising space in mass media outlets. Marketing can include promotional programs such as the popular, annual McDonald's Monopoly promotion. Consumers are encouraged to purchase McDonald's products in order to collect Monopoly game pieces for a chance at a variety of great prizes, including a million dollars. Although the odds against winning are great, McDonald's does great business during the promotion. Marketing can also include such promotional devices as hats or T-shirts with corporate logos, special events, direct mail, and more. In these cases, persuasion is operating and the receivers are generally aware that persuasion is being attempted. It still involves systems of verbal and nonverbal symbols, clear persuasive intent, varying degrees of success, and attempts to influence the purchasing behaviors of receivers.

Persuasion is also used in public relations and encompasses a broad range of activities such as media relations, special events, crisis management, grassroots lobbying, and more. Here, receivers may be unaware that they are targets of persuasion. When reading a newspaper, readers often assume that more or less objective journalists write the articles. However, those articles are often influenced heavily by public relations materials that organizations have sent to the newspapers to influence content. The same is true for other forms of mass media, including news programming, talk shows, game shows, and situation comedies. These activities still meet the established criteria for persuasion. They all involve an agreed on verbal and nonverbal symbol system, intent is clearly present in the hiring of public relations professionals, the level of success varies, and the targeted result includes changing, shaping, and reinforcing responses from the receivers.

Although we often think of marketing and corporate interests as involved in persuasion, public health organizations and social issue groups also engage in persuasion. For example, the Surgeon General has launched efforts to reduce smoking, encourage better eating patterns, reduce drug use, and encourage safer personal behaviors to avoid the spread of AIDS. Other groups, both public and private, have launched public health campaigns around specialized issues. For example, Mothers Against Drunk Driving (MADD) has worked for years to reduce driving while under the influence of alcohol. Chances are good that one or more of the health campaigns has influenced choices you make about what to eat and how to live your life safely. Similarly, there are social issue groups that are attempting to get you to recycle more, donate to the homeless, or care about abandoned pets. These campaigns generally draw on approaches from advertising, marketing, and public relations and they all involve persuasion.

PERSUASION AS ONE OF MULTIPLE FORMS OF INFLUENCE

We have used both the terms *influence* and *persuasion,* and we have used them somewhat differently. At this point we want to clarify how persuasion is different from influence as well as to clarify some related terms. Influence is a very general term that refers to a power that affects something. Persuasion, as we have discussed, is the use of communication to intentionally change, reinforce, or shape another's attitudes, beliefs, and/or behaviors. Clearly, persuasion is a form of influence. **Coercion** is also a form of influence that we discussed that involves force. Persuasion doesn't rely on force, although persuasion may involve pressure to change. Another term is *propaganda.* Propaganda is a term we often use to refer to persuasion attempts by those we do not agree with. When we are engaged in influence attempts, we call it persuasion. But when others are engaging in influence attempts that we disagree with, we often label that propaganda. This perspective represents the connotative meaning propaganda has for many people. **Propaganda** has been defined as a type of persuasion that involves mass audiences with a purpose of achieving the goals of the persuader. It often involves emotional appeals, concealment of purpose, and a lack of sound support. Propaganda carries negative connotations and, as a result, there are ethical questions about the techniques used in propaganda messages.

Education is another form of influence that overlaps somewhat with persuasion and is illustrated on the following continuum with persuasion. Whether we consider influence to be education or persuasion is dependent on the intent of the source and the outcomes of the influence. If the source intends to change the receiver's attitudes, beliefs, or behavior (or to reinforce or shape receiver responses), it would be considered persuasion. Many view persuasion and education as opposites with no overlap, yet education and persuasion share several qualities of persuasion.

Education _____ Persuasion

The difference lies in the intentions and outcomes. Purists argue that education does not have a persuasive intent, but instead has the intent of sharing information or knowledge. In the case of Cara and her nutrition class, it is quite likely that sharing of information was Dr. Kalibo's primary intent. It would be rare, however, for educators to not care about how that information is used. Most educators want their students to adopt the information and use it in their lives, and that runs pretty close to shaping, reinforcing, and changing responses. Dr. Kalibo might well have been pleased by the changes in Cara's diet. Certainly the public health campaigns have the intent of doing more than sharing information. Those campaigns want to affect how receivers think about health issues, and most want specific health behaviors to be the result. Because of the overlap between education and persuasion, a continuum is a more appropriate way of viewing the relationship between the two. Purely informational intents fall into the *education* end of the continuum, whereas those clearly intending to influence individuals fall into the *persuasion* end of the continuum; however, there are many situations that fall in the middle.

We've stated several times that persuasion involves communication, but how is it similar and different from persuasion? Communication is a broad term that encompasses a variety of messages, including those that influence people. Communication has been defined in a variety of ways; however, our preferred definition was put forth by McCroskey and Richmond (1996), who define **communication** as "the process by which one person stimulates meaning in the mind(s) of another person (or persons) through verbal and non-verbal messages" (p. 3). Certainly the definition of persuasion developed previously refers to persuasion as a type of communication, and influence

Figure 5.3 Venn diagram.

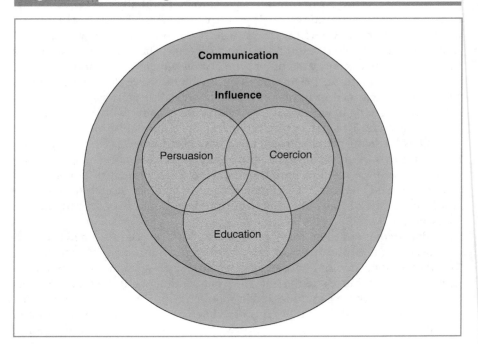

attempts involve communication. Thus, a hierarchy of terms would include communication as the umbrella term, influence next, with persuasion, coercion, and education fitting into the influence realm. The Venn diagram in Figure 5.3 illustrates the relationships among communication, influence, persuasion, coercion, and education.

ATTITUDES, VALUES, AND BELIEFS*

Beliefs. Inferences we make about ourselves and the world around us.

Values. Core beliefs or beliefs central to our cognitive system.

Attitudes. Collections of beliefs organized around an issue or event that predispose behaviour.

Integral to our frame of reference is the value and belief system upon which attitudes are based. One of the best explanations of human behavior and possibly the finest theory on attitude and attitude change was developed by Milton Rokeach. In this theory, beliefs are the fundamental building blocks of attitudes. Rokeach asserted that some beliefs are more central to an individual's cognitive system than others. These core beliefs, or values, are typically well-established and relatively stable. They are very difficult to change because they are most salient to the individual and his/her belief system. They function as "life guides," determining both our daily behavior and our life goals.

According to Rokeach, collections of beliefs organized around a focal point (like an issue, an event, or a person) constitute an attitude. He identifies two kinds:

*From *Strategic Communications Planning for Effective Public Relations and Marketing* by Laurie J. Wilson and Joseph D. Ogden. Copyright © 2008 by Kendall Hunt Publishing Company. Reprinted by permission.

1. attitudes toward **objects** and
2. attitudes toward **situations**.

The combination of these two kinds of attitudes will determine an individual's behavior in any given situation. Rokeach uses gardening as an example. The collection of an individual's beliefs—that gardening is fun, that it saves money, that it releases tension, and that it produces beautiful flowers—will result in a favorable attitude toward gardening. Given the absence of intervening attitudes, a person's collection of beliefs and resultant attitudes will motivate their gardening behavior.

For communications professionals to motivate behavior then, requires that they understand and tap into core beliefs and values that shape attitudes. In some cases, we may need to change beliefs and attitudes. Remembering that core beliefs are difficult to change, we may try to tap into a value and base the alteration of peripheral beliefs on that central belief. We may also need to motivate people to change the depth of a belief or value to help us build a foundation for attitude change. At any rate, it is important for us to recognize that people do not do something just because we want them to do it or because we think they should consider it in their self-interest. They behave in their own self-interest according to their own beliefs and attitudes. Changing behavior requires addressing those beliefs and attitudes.

Another set of theories that aids us in understanding how to change attitudes are the balance or cognitive consistency theories. This body of research has found that people are comfortable when their beliefs, attitudes, knowledge, and behaviors are consistent. The presence of conflict among those cognitive elements creates discomfort or dissonance. Leon Festinger contends that when the cognitive elements are in conflict, people tend to reduce or eliminate the dissonance by changing the elements or introducing new elements (like new information).

The classic example is that of a smoker. In today's environment with today's information, smoking behavior potentially causes great dissonance or conflict in the cognitive processes. The smoker will try to reduce the dissonance. One way would be to change one or more of the cognitive elements (like behavior) by stopping smoking. Another way would be to add a new element, like switching to a pipe which is perceived to be less harmful. A third way is to see the cognitive elements as less important than they used to be (i.e., longer life isn't such a desirable belief if I have to give up pleasure to achieve it). A fourth method would be to seek consonant information such as evidence contradicting the health hazard studies. Fifth, you might reduce the conflict among cognitive elements by distorting or misinterpreting (misperceiving) the information available on the ill effects of smoking. Finally, you have the option to flee the situation, or simply refuse to contemplate the conflict thereby avoiding the dissonance.

If we understand these cognitive processes, we are better able to work with people to bring about cognitive consonance. The process of changing the cognitive elements is the process of persuasion. We may conclude that the art of persuasion, to be effective in motivating behavior, must be implemented at the most basic level of public opinion: at the level of individual beliefs and attitudes.

Personality Traits and Persuasion*

Many communication studies have explored how personality influences communication, especially in persuasion situations. We will briefly survey some of the major personality traits that have been examined (for a review of this literature see Steinfatt, 1987).

PERSUASIBILITY.   Research reported in the book *Personality and Persuasibility* (Hovland & Janis, 1959) suggests that a personality trait predicts how much a person is influenced by persuasion attempts—regardless of the topic, source, or situation. This idea appears to be valid. Some people seem easy to persuade. They rarely resist pressure to move in one direction or another. This willingness to change can be viewed as **persuasibility**. Also, other individuals seem consistently difficult to persuade. They rarely budge on any issue. In essence, they seem resistant to persuasion.

The idea of a persuasibility trait appears to be an uncomplicated way to explain susceptibility to social influence. However, conceptually the matter is not so clear. Is there such a trait, or are there other personality traits sometimes related to persuasion that create the illusion of a general persuasibility trait? In that regard, the traits that follow have been found to be related to persuasion. The amount of persuasibility indicated by each trait, when viewed as a whole, could create the impression that there is a more global persuasibility trait.

Self-esteem refers to how favorably the individual evaluates self and is a trait related to persuasion.

SELF-ESTEEM.   Self-esteem refers to how favorably the individual evaluates self and is a trait related to persuasion. When individuals have low self-esteem, they lack self-confidence in general, and they have little faith that their positions on controversial issues are valid. They tend to be high in persuasibility. When told by a speaker that their positions should be changed, they tend to believe the speaker: "The speaker must know what is right on this, for I certainly do not know." High self-esteem, on the other hand, is thought to be related to low persuasibility. When people feel very good about themselves, they are also confident about their positions on controversial issues because opinions are a part of one's identity. Satisfaction with oneself usually discourages change. Therefore, individuals with high self-esteem tend to resist persuasion.

dogmatism The individual's willingness to consider other belief systems.

DOGMATISM.   Rokeach (1960) conceptualized dogmatism in terms of individuals' willingness to consider belief systems (what one associates with an object or issue) other than the ones they hold. Open-minded individuals are willing to consider other sets of beliefs, even if they feel very strongly about an issue. Dogmatic or closed-minded persons are unwilling to do so. They have a firm set of beliefs for an issue, and they do not want to be bothered by other belief systems.

Dogmatic people find it very difficult to separate a source from the source's message. Thus, if dogmatic people like a source, they tend to accept the source's message; if they dislike a speaker, rarely will the speaker's message persuade them. The open-minded person, however, has less trouble reacting differently to source and message—for example, "I can't stand the speaker, but he makes a good point." When the source is viewed as credible, dogmatism is associated with persuasion. This is especially true when the persuasion topic is not very important to the individual. Dogmatic people tend to be rather easy to persuade when given a credible source and a less important topic. This also suggests that open-minded persons are not necessarily easy to persuade. When the source is credible and the topic rather unimportant, open-minded people are more difficult to persuade than dogmatic individuals.

MACHIAVELLIANISM.   The trait of Machiavellianism refers to an orientation in which people believe that manipulating others is a basic strategy of social influence. Individuals who are high in Machiavellianism think it is ethical to tell people only what they want to hear, to use the receivers' doubts, fears, and insecurities to motivate action, and even to distort facts so they become more acceptable. Generally these people are willing to use whatever strategy works in persuasion; they are very pragmatic. High Machiavellians tend to act rather detached and to be less emotional than other people. They believe the end justifies the means. Persons with a high level of this trait have a strong need to influence others. They like leadership positions, and they are usually the dominant parties in their relations with other people.

Low Machiavellians, on the other hand, are very nonmanipulative in dealing with people. They want to avoid pressuring others, to allow others maximum freedom to decide for themselves. Low Machiavellians tend to have little need to dominate and influence others. They tend to be more emotional than high Machiavellians when discussing a controversial issue.

> **Machiavellianism**   An orientation in which people believe that manipulating others is a basic strategy of social influence.

COGNITIVE COMPLEXITY.   Cognitive complexity is sometimes conceptualized as a trait relating to our personal constructs. A construct is a bipolar pair of terms such as honest–dishonest or exciting–dull, which we apply to differentiate elements in our environment. People in a society learn a common core of constructs because of their shared culture, resulting in some fairly "standard" meanings. However, people also develop pairs of idiosyncratic constructs, opposites that are unique to the individual. The pair humorous–deadly would be an example of an unusual pairing. Individuals experience meaning in a situation depending on which constructs they apply and which pole of each construct they associate with the situation (for example, either *exciting* or *dull*). The basic idea is that people structure their reality based on their construct systems.

Someone who is cognitively complex has a greater number of constructs that are both more abstract and more interconnected than someone who is cognitively simple. Cognitive complexity is related to a number of important communication processes. The greater one's cognitive complexity, the better one is able to imagine how *other* people view a situation. Perspective-taking ability is a key determinant of successful communication. With this ability one is able to understand another person's concerns by seeing things from his or her perspective. This means the more complex person is better able to adapt a message to a particular receiver. If a message is not adapted to the audience, it seems impersonal, generic, and less relevant. Because the probability of success in persuasion is usually lower if the message is not tailored to the likes and dislikes of the receiver, cognitively complex sources should be better persuaders.

> **cognitive complexity**   The complexity of one's construct system affects their persuasive ability.

NEED FOR SOCIAL APPROVAL.   People vary in their need for social approval and the extent to which they fear social disapproval. According to this idea, a source who offers social approval or threatens social disapproval when the receiver has a strong need for approval ought to be very persuasive. Various forms of opinionated language specified by Rokeach (1960) provide

> **need for social approval**   A person's need for approval from others influences how they react to persuasive messages implying approval-disapproval.

opinionated rejection
Language that expresses an unfavorable attitude toward people who disagree with the speaker.

opinionated acceptance
Language that expresses a favorable attitude toward people who agree with the speaker.

a way to test this relationship. Opinionated acceptance language expresses a favorable attitude toward those people who agree with the speaker—for example, "Intelligent and responsible people will agree that my proposal is needed." Opinionated rejection language states a negative attitude toward those who disagree with the speaker's position—for example, "Only a bigoted fool would oppose this plan." Opinionated acceptance language represents social approval, whereas opinionated rejection constitutes social disapproval. Baseheart (1971) found support for the idea that opinionated language leads to more persuasion when people have a strong need for social approval. In such a circumstance, opinionated rejection was as successful as opinionated acceptance in stimulating persuasion. Having a strong need for social approval probably heightens a person's sensitivity to language that suggests the speaker is evaluating the receiver in some way.

Research on Message Variables

Throughout the last four decades, communication theorists have identified several message variables that appear to influence our reaction to persuasive messages (Sussman, 1973). Two will be examined here: fear appeals and evidence.

FEAR APPEALS.   The study of fear-arousing message content has its roots in antiquity. Aristotle discussed the use of fear and other emotions in the *Rhetoric*. Aristotle suggested that speakers must understand the emotional predispositions of their audience and then use that knowledge as one of the "available means of persuasion." Modern research considers fear appeals to be arguments that take the following form:

1. You (the listener) are vulnerable to a threat.
2. If you are vulnerable, then you should take action to reduce your vulnerability.
3. If you are to reduce your vulnerability, then you must accept the recommendations contained in this message.
4. Therefore, you should accept the recommendations contained in this message. (Boster & Mongeau, 1984, p. 371)

A typical fear appeal might be a variation on the following:

1. Smoking has been found to increase the chances for disease and death.
2. Because you do not want disease or death, you must do something to prevent them.
3. An effective way to prevent these outcomes is to stop smoking.
4. Therefore, you must stop smoking.

During an average evening, we may witness several fear-arousing messages in television commercials. From smoke detectors to life insurance, advertisers make frequent use of the fear appeal to influence consumers.

The contemporary study of fear in persuasion can be traced to the work of Irving Janis and Seymour Feshbach (1953). In their seminal study, high school students were randomly assigned to one of two experimental groups who heard messages on dental hygiene. For one group, a *moderate fear* appeal was used; for the other, a *high fear* appeal was created. A third group of students was also tested. They served as a *control group* and were exposed to an entirely different message on the structure and operation of the human eye. The high fear appeal urged dental care and recommended vigorous and proper brushing of the teeth; pictures of rotting gums and decaying teeth accompanied the message. In the moderate fear appeal, these pictures were omitted. Janis and Feshbach discovered that the moderate fear appeal was more effective than the high fear appeal in changing students' attitudes toward proper brushing and dental care.

These findings led to several decades of experimental research testing the relationship between the level of fear in a message and attitude change. Some studies discovered the opposite outcome: attitude change was more likely when a high fear appeal was used (Beck & Davis, 1978; see Miller, 1963, for a summary and analysis of the early research). Because experimenters sometimes arrived at different results when they studied fear appeals, scientists tried to reconcile these contradictions.

Boster and Mongeau (1984) reviewed six explanations of fear appeal effects. The *drive explanation* suggests that the fear aroused by a persuasive message creates a state of drive, which receivers find unpleasant. Individuals experiencing this state of drive are motivated to reduce it by changing their attitudes and/or behaviors. According to the drive explanation, the greater the amount of fear in a message, the greater the attitude change in the direction recommended by the message.

The *resistance explanation* finds that as perceived fear in a message decreases, individuals' attitudes and/or behaviors will move closer to those recommended in the message. The rationale is that receivers will pay attention to messages low in threatening content; they will resist more threatening messages. Low fear appeals are less threatening than high fear appeals. Thus, messages containing low fear appeals are more likely to be heard than messages containing high fear appeals.

According to the *curvilinear hypothesis,* when receivers are either very fearful or very unafraid, little attitude or behavior change results. High levels of fear are so strong that individuals block them out; low levels are too weak to produce the desired effect. Messages containing *moderate* amounts of fear-arousing content are most effective in producing attitudinal and/or behavior change.

The *parallel response explanation* suggests that fear-arousing messages activate fear control and danger control processes in listeners. *Fear control* is a coping process by which receivers strive to reduce the fear created by the message. *Danger control* refers to a problem-solving process in which listeners search for information on how to deal with the threat presented. These two processes interact to influence message acceptance. According to the parallel response explanation, when a fear-arousing message primarily activates the *danger control* process, a *high* fear appeal will most influence attitudes and/or behaviors. When a fear-arousing message primarily activates the *fear control* process, a *low* fear appeal is most influential.

The *protection motivation explanation* states that a receiver's attitude toward the topic is a result of the amount of "protection motivation" produced by the message. Protection motivation refers to receivers' drives to avoid or protect themselves from a threat. As protection motivation increases, conformity to attitudes and/or behaviors recommended in the message also increases. Thus, the greater the fear in a message: (a) the more likely a threat will occur; and (b) the greater the ability to deal with the threat by following the recommendations provided in the message; thus (c) the greater the attitude and/or behavioral change in the direction of the message.

The sixth explanation is labeled the *threat control explanation*. Reactions to fear appeals depend on logical, not emotional, factors. A fear-arousing message stimulates *response efficacy* and *personal efficacy* processes in listeners. Response efficacy refers to the receiver's perception of how effective the recommended attitudes or actions will be in reducing or eliminating the threat. Personal efficacy refers to whether or not the receiver is capable of taking the actions recommended by the message. These two responses combine to produce threat control. Threat control is a person's perceived probability of success in controlling the threat. This explanation suggests that, as threat control increases, listeners will adopt attitudes more closely corresponding to the recommendations of the message. As fear increases in a message, so too should the amount of attitude and/or behavioral change in the listener.

Boster and Mongeau concluded that all six explanations were less than adequate in explaining the results of experiments studying fear-arousing messages and persuasion. None of the six explanations was completely consistent with the evidence. Several problems were highlighted. First, researchers were not creating strong enough fear appeals. If manipulations of fear in messages were not strong enough to produce fear in listeners, then it was impossible for any relationship between fear and attitude or behavior change to emerge. Second, other demographic variables and personality traits interacted with fear appeals to affect attitudes and behavior. In particular, *age, trait anxiety* and whether the participant *volunteers* for the study were offered as potential moderators of the fear–attitude relationship. Contrary to conventional wisdom, low-anxiety, older volunteers seemed to be more susceptible to fear appeals than high-anxiety, younger nonvolunteers.

Sussman (1973) similarly suggested the influence of mediating variables on the fear–attitude relationship. "Such variables as coping style, self-esteem, perceived vulnerability to danger, and chronic anxiety may mediate the response to a fear appeal" (p. 209). Despite the attention paid by researchers to understanding the fear–attitude relationship, additional theory and research are needed to uncover more satisfactory explanations. Because the use of fear appeals in messages is very common, the results of such research should be of interest both to applied communicators (for example, advertisers) and to scholars.

EVIDENCE IN MESSAGES.   When we hear the term *evidence*, images of attorneys arguing cases come to mind. Television shows such as *Law and Order* depict the powerful effects of good evidence. Clearly evidence is a critical component in any trial. Evidence is also an important verbal behavior variable in less-formal communication contexts. When we become the target of a persuasive effort, we usually challenge our adversary to *prove* the case to us. When a new drug claims to prevent baldness, all but the most desperate or trusting of souls require some type of evidence before they spend huge sums of money on it.

Communication theorists beginning with Aristotle have focused on evidence as a determining influence on individual belief systems. Evidence consists of "factual statements originating from a source other than the speaker, objects not created by the speaker, and opinions of persons other than the speaker that are offered in support of the speaker's claims" (McCroskey, 1969, p. 170). A slightly different definition is "any statement of fact, statement of value, or definition offered by a speaker or writer which is intended to support a proposition" (Florence, 1975, p. 151). Contemporary communication courses, especially argumentation and public speaking, stress the relationship between evidence and persuasion. However, the findings of almost two decades of communication research do not appear to support a direct, positive association between evidence and persuasion. It has not been conclusively shown, for instance, that an audience will be more easily persuaded if more evidence is presented.

After reviewing over twenty studies on the influence of evidence in persuasion, James McCroskey concluded that several variables interact with evidence to produce changes in attitudes or increases in perceived speaker credibility: *evidence and source credibility, evidence and delivery effectiveness,* and *prior familiarity of evidence.*

There is a relationship between the use of evidence and the credibility or believability of the speaker. If a speaker is already perceived to be very credible, including "good" evidence will do little to change attitudes or enhance speaker credibility. However, speakers who are perceived as low to moderate in credibility may increase their credibility by employing evidence. This increase in perceived credibility may in turn increase attitude change.

In several studies on evidence and message topic, McCroskey believed that other factors were influencing the evidence–attitude change relationship. By interviewing participants after the experiments, he discovered that the quality of the delivery made a difference. To investigate the relationship further, he conducted several studies using live, audiotaped, and videotaped versions of a well-delivered and a poorly delivered presentation. The amount and type of evidence were the same for each version in each medium. From these studies, he found that: (a) including good evidence influences attitude change very little if the message is delivered poorly; and (b) including good evidence can influence attitude change and speaker credibility immediately after the speech if the message is well-delivered, the speaker initially has only low-to-moderate credibility, and the audience has little prior knowledge of the evidence. Because the results were consistent for all versions, he concluded that the medium of presentation has little effect on the use of evidence in persuasion.

McCroskey also believed that prior familiarity with evidence should be considered when assessing the evidence–persuasion relationship. Postexperimental interviews led him to conclude that "old" evidence does little to influence listeners. "Old" evidence has already been heard and processed cognitively. If any dissonance had been created by the message, it was already resolved or defense mechanisms were created to prevent a recurrence. These assumptions are consistent with explanations derived from information theories and cognitive dissonance theory (discussed later in this chapter). For evidence to affect listeners' attitude change or perceptions of the source immediately, McCroskey found that the evidence must be "new" to the listener. Including evidence has little, if any, impact on receivers if they are already familiar with it. McCroskey concluded that although considerable information has been uncovered about the influence of evidence in persuasion, communication theorists should continue their research efforts.

One researcher examined the theoretical foundations of previous research and reformulated the existing theories concerning evidence and persuasion (Florence, 1975). According to these findings, evidence influences persuasion only if the proposal, idea, or policy it supports is *desirable* to the audience. Both the credibility of a source of evidence and the evidence itself influence the desirability of a proposal. More recently, Dale Hample (1977, 1979, 1981) developed a theory of argument in which evidence plays a major role. In this theory, the relative power of evidence was measured. Hample argued that the power of evidence is one of the best predictors of attitude change. Because evidence is a key verbal message variable in the communication process, researchers will no doubt continue to examine its influence in persuasion.

A number of other variables may affect credibility: energy (dynamism), sociability, power, impact, mental balance, cultivation, and charisma. If credibility is a list of factors, critics wonder about the length of the list. Does a longer list imply a better understanding of credibility? This raises the issue of whether a "laundry list" of factors really tells us anything. Does each new factor increase understanding or cause confusion? Another criticism of the factor approach is that the model does not specify whether a receiver uses all the factors in assessing a source's credibility. A plausible expectation is that in some persuasion situations some factors matter more than other factors; some receivers will find certain factors more relevant than will other receivers. Thus, the characteristics used to judge the source's credibility can change with different sources, situations, and audiences. These and other criticisms of the factor model have led to the development of two additional models of credibility.

THE FUNCTIONAL MODEL. The functional model of credibility views credibility as the degree to which a source satisfies the receiver's needs. Three simultaneous processes occur in a persuasive situation. First, the receiver becomes aware of the source's characteristics. Some, like height and voice quality, are observable; others, like education and social status, must be inferred. Second, the receiver determines criteria for judging the source in the situation. That is, the receiver becomes aware of the functions that the source could serve for the receiver (for example, to provide recent information, to entertain). Third, the receiver compares the characteristics with the functional criteria. An audience at a banquet might judge the extent to which a speaker has both informed and entertained them. The more needs that are fulfilled by the source, the more credible the source is. For example, the more the audience enjoyed the speech, the more credible they consider the speaker (Cronkhite & Liska, 1980).

Another group of researchers developed a method for measuring credibility according to the functional approach and then compared the functional model to the factor model to determine which explains persuasion best. The two models performed equally well in explaining differences, so the test was inconclusive. However, because the factors did not explain persuasion better than a general measure of credibility, the functional model was judged to be promising (Infante, Parker, Clarke, Wilson, & Nathu, 1983).

THE CONSTRUCTIVISTIC MODEL. Our earlier discussion in this chapter of constructivism and cognitive complexity as a trait related to persuasion is relevant to understanding the constructivistic model of credibility. The basic idea is that people use their personal construct systems to construct their reality. That is, reality is not something that exists where everyone experiences the very same thing. Two people viewing the same situation can have radically different conceptions of that reality because they have applied very different personal constructs to the situation. Personal construct systems involve bipolar judgments such as valuable-worthless. Some constructs are acquired from culture, others from family, friends, or school. Some constructs can be unique to the individual and highly idiosyncratic. For instance, an economically oriented person might see a situation mainly as having great potential for yielding investment profit, whereas a scholarly individual might mainly perceive how that situation could produce certain knowledge that will advance understanding of a problem.

functional model of credibility   Credibility is determined by the extent to which a source fulfills the receiver's needs.

constructivistic model of credibility   How individuals use their personal construct systems to form, reinforce, and change impressions of sources.

These ideas can be applied to conceptualizing source credibility. Delia (1976) said understanding source credibility involves learning how individuals use their personal construct systems to form, reinforce, and change impressions of people in persuasion situations. Just as two people can have a very different conception of reality in viewing a given situation, they also can have very different impressions of the credibility of a given speaker. We need to determine which constructs the receiver of a message used in deciding to accept or reject the source's position on the object of persuasion. Although this seems to be a reasonable approach to understanding source credibility, a problem is that an appealing measurement model has not been developed. Whereas sets of rating scales have been used successfully for measuring credibility according to the factor approach, a comparable method of measurement has not been developed for the constructivistic approach. Research here typically has had the research subject write an impression of the communicator, which was then content analyzed later by researchers to determine the constructs used and how those identified constructs related to the degree of persuasion that took place (e.g., Delia, O'Keefe & O'Keefe, 1982). Not only is this a tedious, labor-intensive way to study credibility, but the results have not been promising enough to stimulate much further research. More progress in measuring source credibility is necessary, and if that is accomplished, it should have a very beneficial effect in stimulating future research.

Cognitive Dissonance Theory

Social psychologist Leon Festinger's cognitive dissonance theory (1957) is the most thoroughly researched of a family of cognitive consistency theories and therefore the one we shall discuss in this chapter (for a review of other consistency theories, see Kiesler, Collins, & Miller, 1969). Consistency theories of persuasion are based on the idea that inconsistency is psychologically uncomfortable. Inconsistency results when we believe A should have a certain relationship to B but does not, or when A has an unexpected, undesirable relationship with something. For instance, inconsistency would be felt if we see that a program to reduce poverty in our city is not reducing hunger among children as we had expected. Instead, the program is reducing hope and aspirations among poor people.

Cognitive dissonance theory assumes that two beliefs are related either in a state of consonance or dissonance. A state of **consonance** is characterized by consistency: "I like my sorority, and my good friend likes my sorority." **Dissonance** is marked by inconsistency: "I like my sorority, but my good friend does not like it." The idea is that it would "bother" us (we would feel dissonance) if our friend did not also value what we value, and we would be motivated to get rid of the uncomfortable feeling. A central tenet of the theory is: The more the mental discomfort (dissonance), the more we are motivated to change something to make things comfortable.

The theory identifies a number of factors that influence the amount of dissonance experienced. Perhaps the most important one is whether the person's self-concept is involved in the dissonant relationship. If one belief is, "I just said that I liked a task that I really hate" ("I lied"), and a second belief is, "I am an honest person," the dissonance involves self-concept—our mental picture of the kind of person we are. What will be done to reduce dissonance? Research suggests individuals tend to change so that their attitude toward the task is more favorable, "I actually do like that task." This change in attitude

cognitive dissonance theory   Assumes that two beliefs are related either in a state of consonance or dissonance.

permits consistency with the belief, "I am an honest person." We try to protect our self-concepts by rationalizing our actions and decisions so we do not "look bad" to ourselves. Changing the second belief to "I am dishonest" would also have restored consistency: "I lied" and "I am dishonest." However, we seldom reduce dissonance by changing a favorable belief about ourselves.

This principle can be used to explain the results of a classic study by Aronson and Mills (1959). To join a very dull discussion group, individuals were required either to recite a list of sexual terms (mild initiation) or to recite a list of "obscene" words (severe initiation). The research participants were then asked how much they liked the group. Did the severe or the mild initiation lead to greater liking for the group? In line with the theory's prediction, persons given the severe initiation liked the group more. Why? Because they experienced more dissonance. Their beliefs could be characterized as: "I am efficient," so "I just put forth a great effort, and I got something worthwhile." To conclude that the group was worthless would force the belief about self to be: "I am inefficient" because "I just put forth a great effort for little reward." Individuals who experienced the mild initiation did not distort their feelings about the group. "I am efficient," and "I got little benefit from the discussion, but I did not put much into it, so I have not lost."

Dissonance can be reduced in many ways besides changing beliefs, as in the preceding example. Attitude change toward a speaker's proposal and attitude change toward the speaker are two basic methods of resolving dissonance. Attitude change toward the speaker might involve criticizing the source of the information: "I won't listen to the American Cancer Society public service announcement warning about the health risks of smoking because the American Cancer Society is biased against cigarette smoking." Other methods of reducing dissonance are not as obvious. Selective exposure involves seeking information that supports your opinion but avoiding information that is unfavorable toward your opinion. The listener can also misinterpret the speaker's position so that the speaker seems to agree with the listener. One could also consider the dissonant elements unimportant so that the dissonance does not really matter. "The new car I just bought has little pickup, but I really don't need power and speed in a car anyway." Another alternative is to add consonant elements to "drown out" the dissonance. "Besides, my new car has great lines, a beautiful interior, an excellent stereo, and perfect handling."

A basic idea about persuasion from dissonance theory is that to persuade people, you must cause them to experience dissonance, then offer your proposal as a way to get rid of the dissonance. A persuader might try to make receivers feel dissonance about energy policies in the United States and then present a proposal for developing alternative and renewable energy sources such as hydrogen fuel cells or solar energy to free the United States from dependence on foreign oil. When a speaker arouses dissonance, the receiver will try to reduce it, using one of the methods just listed. However, dissonance can also be reduced by adopting or agreeing with the speaker's proposal. Although there is no guarantee that the audience will reduce dissonance by changing their minds, the speaker does have a chance to achieve persuasion.

According to the theory, if no dissonance is aroused, there will be no persuasion. People do not change an attitude unless they feel they need to change it. Feeling dissonance provides the motivation to change. The theory predicts that to persuade someone, you must first "upset" the person (make them feel dissonance) concerning the topic of your proposal. If you fail to persuade the audience, perhaps the dissonance they felt was not great enough to motivate action.

selective exposure
Exposing oneself only to agreeable messages; avoiding situations, such as public speeches by a political opponent, requiring us to listen to those with whom we disagree.

Figure 5.4 Cognitive dissonance.

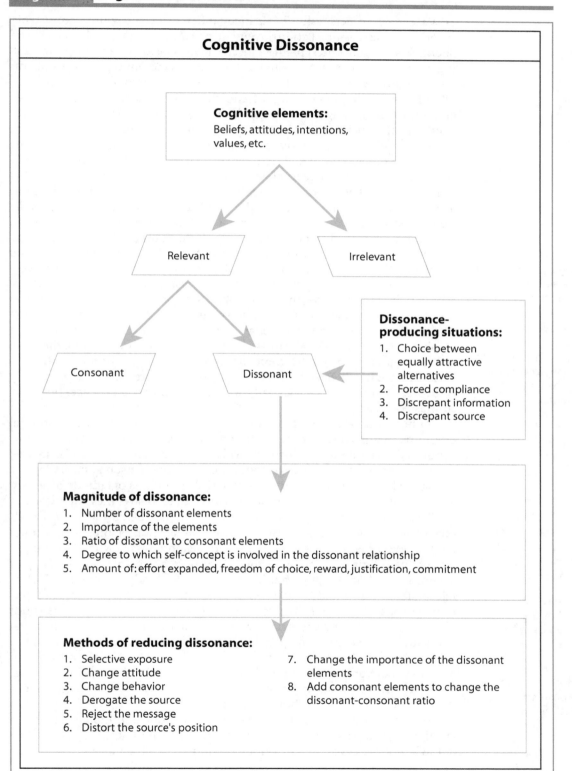

Cognitive Dissonance

Cognitive elements:
Beliefs, attitudes, intentions, values, etc.

Relevant

Irrelevant

Consonant

Dissonant

Dissonance-producing situations:
1. Choice between equally attractive alternatives
2. Forced compliance
3. Discrepant information
4. Discrepant source

Magnitude of dissonance:
1. Number of dissonant elements
2. Importance of the elements
3. Ratio of dissonant to consonant elements
4. Degree to which self-concept is involved in the dissonant relationship
5. Amount of: effort expanded, freedom of choice, reward, justification, commitment

Methods of reducing dissonance:
1. Selective exposure
2. Change attitude
3. Change behavior
4. Derogate the source
5. Reject the message
6. Distort the source's position
7. Change the importance of the dissonant elements
8. Add consonant elements to change the dissonant-consonant ratio

Ego-Involvement, or Social Judgment Theory

This approach to persuasion is distinctly different from cognitive consistency theories of persuasion. Ego-involvement or social judgment theory (Sherif, Sherif, & Nebergall, 1965) predicts successful persuasion by a message depending on how the message is related to the person's current beliefs. (The Sherifs were psychologists; Nebergall was a member of the communication discipline.) Research in physiological psychology indicates that if a person is given an "anchor" in making judgments, objects close to the anchor are seen as more similar to the anchor than they really are (they are assimilated). Objects far from the anchor are perceived as even more dissimilar than they really are (they are contrasted). If you were handed a bar and told it weighs 10 pounds, you would probably judge too low when asked to guess what a 12-pound bar weighs. You probably would judge the 12-pound bar as just about the same as the 10-pound anchor; you would assimilate it. Next, if asked to guess the weight of a 40-pound bar, you probably would judge it heavier than it really is. It would seem more distant from the anchor; the contrast effect would occur.

What does this have to do with persuasion? Ego-involvement or **social judgment theory** indicates that assimilation and contrast effects also occur in persuasion. Assimilation constitutes persuasion; a **contrast effect** represents a failure to persuade. In the case of persuasion, the receiver's position on the topic of the persuasive message serves as the **anchor**. If a speaker slightly opposes gun control and you moderately oppose it, you tend to interpret the speaker's position as basically the same as yours. On the other hand, the more you favor gun control and the more the speaker opposes it, the greater the likelihood that you will view the speaker's position as more extreme than it really is (that is, a contrast effect). Basically, we accept assimilated messages but reject contrasted messages.

Although interesting, the assimilation–contrast notion leaves several questions unanswered. Under what conditions are messages assimilated or contrasted? Why do two individuals with the same position on an issue react differently to the same message about the issue, one person assimilating the message while the other person contrasts it? The concepts of latitude of acceptance, rejection, and noncommitment are needed to answer these questions.

The latitude of acceptance consists of all statements the person finds acceptable, including the favorite position, the anchor. Figure 5.5 illustrates the latitudes of acceptance for two individuals on an issue with 11 positions. Notice that Chris and Pat have the same most acceptable position (A) or anchor belief: "Final exams should be optional for graduating seniors." Chris rejects statements 6 and 7, while Pat agrees with them. The latitude of rejection (r) consists of all of the positions on the issue the person rejects (finds objectionable). Pat and Chris have latitudes of rejection that vary in width. Pat rejects only statement 1, the position that final exams should be required of all students, whereas Chris rejects statements 1–7. The latitude of noncommitment (nc) consists of all positions the person neither accepts nor rejects. The person is noncommittal or neutral on these issues. Chris is neutral about statement 8; Pat is neutral about statements 2–5.

The latitudes of acceptance, rejection, and noncommitment determine whether a given person will assimilate or contrast a message. Messages falling in the latitudes of acceptance or noncommitment will be judged closer to the

ego-involvement Characterized by a wide latitude of rejection and narrow latitudes of acceptance and noncommitment.

assimilation The degree to which a person accepts the influence of the new culture or environment.

latitude of acceptance Consists of all statements the person finds acceptable. This can include the favorite position or the anchor.

latitude of rejection Consists of all of the positions on an issue the person rejects.

latitude of noncommitment Consists of all of the positions a person neither accepts nor rejects.

| Figure 5.5 | **Ego-involvement or social judgment theory.** |

Topic Positions			**Chris**									
	1	2	3	4	5	6	7	8	9	10	11
	r	r	r	r	r	r	r	nc	a	A	a

Topic Positions			**Pat**									
	1	2	3	4	5	6	7	8	9	10	11
	r	nc	nc	nc	nc	a	a	a	a	A	a

A = most acceptable position
a = other acceptable positions

r = positions which are rejected
nc = positions on that the person is neutral

POSITION STATEMENTS

11. Final exams should be optional for all students.
10. Final exams should be optional for graduating seniors.
 9. Final exams should be optional in elective courses.
 8. Final exams should be optional for students with an A average.
 7. Final exams should be optional for students with an A or B average.
 6. Final exams should be optional for students with an A, B, or C average.
 5. Final exams should be optional for students with a passing average.
 4. Final exams should be optional at the professor's discretion.
 3. Final exams should be required only of freshmen.
 2. Final exams should be required only of freshmen and sophomores.
 1. Final exams should be required of all students.

favorite position (anchor belief) than they really are (assimilated). Messages falling in the latitude of rejection will be judged farther away (contrasted). According to ego-involvement theory, a basic principle of persuasion is that to change a person's most acceptable position on a topic, the message must fall within the person's latitude of acceptance. A persuader can also attempt to widen the latitude of acceptance by advocating a position in the person's latitude of noncommitment. If successful, the persuader will widen the receiver's latitude of acceptance, thus creating a larger "target" for a second persuasion attempt.

The latitudes also indicate whether the person is ego-involved. According to the theory, high ego-involvement is characterized by a narrow latitude of acceptance (the person's own favorite position is about the only position accepted), a wide latitude of rejection (almost everything other than one's own position is rejected), and a narrow latitude of noncommitment (nearly all positions are either accepted or rejected; the person is neutral about very few positions). Low ego-involvement is the opposite. The latitude of acceptance is wide (people are able to accept several other positions on the issue besides their anchor position), the latitude of noncommitment is wide (there are many positions on the topic that the person is neutral about), and the latitude of rejection is narrow (there is not much left to reject if one accepts most positions and does not care about most of the remaining ones).

Chris is highly ego-involved, and Pat is not ego-involved with final exam regulations. According to the theory, even though they both hold the same most acceptable position (statement 10), they would react differently to a message that advocated position 6. Chris would contrast the message because it falls in the latitude of rejection; it would be "heard" as a more extreme message than it actually is. On the other hand, Pat would assimilate the message, perceive it closer to the anchor (position 10) than it really is because it is one of the acceptable positions. Thus, Pat would be persuaded by the message; Chris would not.

This theory permits us to conceptualize how persuasion can be achieved with a highly ego-involved individual. In our example, to persuade Chris to change from position 10 to position 2 would take many messages. One message would not be enough—it would be contrasted. Persuasion would require many messages over a long period of time, each gradually expanding the latitude of acceptance and slowly moving the favorite position (anchor belief). This probably is a realistic view of persuasion. It is very difficult to persuade someone who is very ego-involved in a topic. The theory represents this idea clearly. When a person is highly ego-involved, a "one-shot" attempt to persuade the individual is surely doomed to failure. A "persuasive campaign" composed of many messages over a period of time is a more realistic way to try to change someone who is ego-involved.

The Theory of Reasoned Action

theory of reasoned action
A theory of persuasion that is based on attitudes, belief strength, and the evaluation of the meaning of the belief.

The theory of reasoned action by psychologists Martin Fishbein and Icek Ajzen is included here because it has been used a good deal by communication researchers (e.g., see recent research by Edwards, 1998; Stewart & Roach, 1998; Park, 1998). It is also a good example of theory building. The theory was introduced in the 1960s and enhanced through the next two decades (for instance, see Ajzen, 1985; Ajzen & Fishbein, 1980; Fishbein & Ajzen, 1975).

The theory of reasoned action began with Fishbein's theory of attitude toward an object (an object could be a person, a physical thing, an idea, a social program, etc.); he conceptualized attitude as a sum of the beliefs that we have learned to associate with the object. Suppose we consider your attitude toward physical fitness. You might have learned to associate seven beliefs with physical fitness. The extent to which each belief contributes to your attitude depends on (a) belief strength and (b) evaluation of the meaning of the belief. You might have a belief that it is extremely likely (belief strength) that a physical fitness lifestyle results in a very favorable (evaluation) consequence, an attractive body shape. This belief would favorably affect your attitude toward physical fitness; you have a strong belief that the object produces something good. A second belief might be that you think it is slightly unlikely (belief strength) that you will get frequent colds if you are in good physical condition. This belief also is positive because it asserts that you will be less likely to experience something bad, but because it is not a very strong belief, it will have less impact on your attitude. If your remaining five beliefs followed the pattern of these two examples, you would have a moderately favorable attitude toward physical fitness. That is, if we add the degree of favorable feelings in your seven beliefs, the total would be much closer to the favorable end than to the unfavorable end of the attitude object continuum.

In the 1960s, psychology and sociology researchers found that attitude theories such as this one were poor predictors of a given behavior. For example, we could design a study to measure your attitude toward physical fitness. If your attitude was very favorable and we gave you a coupon for a free workout at a local gym, the prediction would be that you would use the coupon. Typically, that prediction would not be very accurate. In fact, flipping a coin might be just as accurate in predicting behavior as measuring attitude.

Fishbein, who was later joined by Ajzen, expanded the theory to deal with this problem of why attitude toward an object does not accurately predict a specific behavior relevant to the object. Fishbein declared that attitude does predict behavior, but not in the way that previous researchers had assumed that it should. The problem was the measure of behavior. A single act, observed once, was what most studies used as the criterion. This was a mistake because there is no theoretical reason why attitude toward an object should be closely related to a single behavior, unless there is only one behavior that is relevant to the object, which is seldom the case. Typically, many behaviors are relevant to an attitude object. When that is the case, attitude toward the object should be related to the total set of behaviors. Thus, one act, observed once, does not measure the entire set of relevant behaviors. The correct behavioral measure was what Fishbein called the multiple-act, repeated observations criterion. This means all the relevant behaviors should be counted; ideally, they should be observed more than once over a period of time.

In terms of our example, then, your attitude toward physical fitness probably would not predict whether you will show up at the gym. We would be a bit more accurate if we could observe you showing up next week, the week after, and the next week, and so on (this would be a single-act, repeated measures criterion). An even better predictor would be observations of all other relevant behaviors, observed more than once. Two possibilities would be observing you eating a healthy diet each day for a month, or noting that you watched physical fitness shows on TV for a month. If we designated ten behaviors and observed them for a month, the total number of occurrences of the ten would constitute a multiple-act, repeated observations criterion. Research by Fishbein and others found an improved behavioral measure such as this is strongly related to attitude toward the object.

What this means in terms of persuasion, then, is if you succeeded in persuading someone who had an unfavorable attitude toward physical fitness to have a favorable attitude (probably by arguing successfully that several good things would likely follow), you should expect the total pattern of the person's fitness-related behaviors to change. However, any single behavior might not change. For instance, the person might go to the gym often, watch exercise shows on TV, attend fitness lectures, etc., but continue eating high-fat fast food. We might wonder at this point whether it is possible to target a single behavior not only for prediction but also for change in persuasion situations.

The theory of reasoned action was developed to deal specifically with the problem of predicting a single behavior, even if it is only observed once. Fishbein and Ajzen built on their earlier research. A core idea of the theory of reasoned action is that behavior is intentional; very little behavior is accidental. When people engage in a given behavior, it is because they formed intentions to do so, and they had reasons for their decisions to actualize their intentions. Thus, much of our behavior can be characterized as "reasoned action."

multiple-act A behavioural prediction in research based on a set of relevant behaviors ideally more than once over a period of time.

Attitude toward the specific act is one of two major components of a behavioral intention. The second is what has been called the *normative component*. Keep in mind that the Fishbein and Ajzen model works backward from a specific behavior. That is, a specific behavior is predicted or controlled by an intention to behave; that intention is predicted and controlled by two factors, attitude toward the act and the normative component. Each of these two components is controlled by particular factors.

Attitude toward the specific act is controlled by the beliefs that the person has about the consequences of performing the act. As with Fishbein's earlier theory of attitude toward an object, two aspects of each belief are important: belief strength and evaluation. Continuing with our gym visit example, suppose you have five moderately strong beliefs about five somewhat desirable consequences of accepting the offer for a free workout at a gym: the gym has superior equipment; it is easy to get to the gym because of its location; membership rates could be cheaper after a trial visit; a gym membership would increase motivation to exercise; you could meet interesting people there. At this point it might be tempting to predict that you probably will go to the gym. The five beliefs are reasons for action or inaction. In this case the reasons tilt somewhat toward action. However, there is more to the theory. The second determinant of an intention is the normative component, and we need to consider it before making a prediction about behavior.

The normative component is composed of our beliefs about what valued others expect us to do regarding the behavior. Each belief is weighted by our motivation to comply with the wishes of other people. In terms of our example, suppose one normative belief is that your good friend would not want you to join that gym, because he is planning on having a gym in the basement of his home and wants you to work out there so the two of you can motivate one another. Perhaps another normative belief is that your significant other does not like the manager of the gym and therefore is less than enthusiastic about the prospect of you being a member there. Suppose further that you have fairly strong motivation to comply with these normative expectations.

On the basis of these two components, attitude toward the act and the normative component, can we now offer a prediction of whether or not you will go to the gym for the trial workout? Often information about these two components is enough to make an accurate prediction, However, in a case like this where you are being pulled one way by one component and another way by the second component, more information is needed. The *subjective weights* of each component help evaluate conflicting influences. For some behaviors we feel that we can do whatever we feel like doing (i.e., we let our attitude toward the act guide us and feel no constraint from other people). For other behaviors we decide what we do must be compatible with the preferences of valued others (i.e., we look to the normative component for guidance).

In our example, suppose on a 1–10 scale your weight for attitude toward the act is 3 and your weight for the normative component is 8. In view of this data the theory would predict that you will not go to the gym for the trial workout. Suppose that the theory is accurate (as it has been most of the time), and you do not go to the gym. However, what would have happened if we had made a prediction based only on the first attitude that we considered, attitude toward physical fitness? Because the attitude in the example was moderately favorable, the prediction would have been that you would go to the gym. The prediction would have been wrong. If the prediction had been based only on attitude toward the act, once again it would have been wrong. An accurate prediction was achieved only when both components were considered and weighted. The theory became more accurate as it developed—an excellent illustration of the advantages of theory building. The theory of reasoned action has been a popular one in communication research because of its accuracy.

In addition to prediction strengths, the theory provides implications for persuasion. For example, if you want to influence a person to perform a specific behavior, do not devote much time to trying to change attitude toward the object. Instead, try to determine what the person's current attitude is toward that act and also the normative component. Importantly, how is each component weighted? Such analysis directs your focus for the persuasive attempt. The fundamental persuasion tactics would involve arguing the consequences of performing the act. For a favorable attitude toward the behavior you would claim good consequences would be likely and bad consequences would be unlikely. For an unfavorable attitude, the opposite would be argued (i.e., that good things would not happen, but bad things would occur). Influencing the normative component involves maintaining that persons valued by the individual either expect certain behaviors or do not want certain things to happen. Sometimes it could be necessary to convince people that they should have high motivation to fulfill the expectations of valued others. In other circumstances persuading people to perform a given behavior necessitates moving them to ignore the wishes of others and to act mainly on the basis of self-interest. This tactic could be especially difficult to accomplish because it is not unusual in persuasion situations for need for approval to be a major factor.

The Theory of Planned Behavior

As explained in the previous section, the core of Fishbein and Ajzen's theory of reasoned action is the notion of the behavioral intention; a person's intention of performing a given behavior is the best predictor of whether or not the person will actually perform the behavior. It may have occurred to you, however, that several factors can work against this behavioral intention → behavior sequence. Think about some examples where you, to use a cliché, "had the best intentions" to perform a behavior (e.g., taking your sibling to the mall to go shopping next Saturday morning) but certain personal limitations (e.g., you were too tired and overslept) and/or external obstacles (e.g., you didn't have a car available to you that day) prevented you from actually performing that behavior. The successful performance of a behavior also depends on one's ability to control factors that either allow or prevent performance of that behavior (Ajzen, 1988).

To resolve some of the difficulties in predicting behavior precisely, Ajzen (1985, 1988, 1991) proposed the theory of planned behavior (TPB), an extension of the theory of reasoned action (TORA). TPB is also based on the premise that the best predictor of an actual behavior is a person's behavioral intention. However, unlike its predecessor theory, TPB suggests that there are three, rather than two factors associated with a person's behavioral intention (see Figure 5.6).

In TPB, the first two factors associated with a behavioral intention are the same as in TORA: (1) attitude toward the specific act (or behavior), and (2) the normative component, our beliefs about what valued others expect us to do

behavioral intention
A person's intention of performing a given behaviour is the best predictor of whether or not the person will actually perform the behavior.

Figure 5.6   Theory of planned behavior.

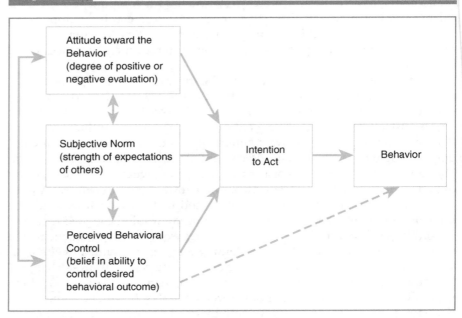

regarding the behavior in question. Ajzen (1985, 1988, 1991) added a third factor, perceived behavioral control, to TPB. Perceived behavioral control refers to "the degree to which a person believes they can control the behavior in question" (Roberto, Meyer, & Boster, 2001, p. 316)—how easy or difficult the person believes it will be to perform a given behavior.

TPB suggests that, in general, more favorable attitudes toward the specific act (or behavior), more favorable subjective norms (normative component), and greater perceived behavioral control (the ease of performing the behavior in question) strengthen the intention to perform the behavior. According to TPB, perceived behavioral control is directly related to behavioral intentions and to actual behavior.

Ajzen (2001) suggests that perceived behavioral control influences a person's confidence that they are capable of performing the behavior in question. Perceived behavioral control is, in essence, a combination of two dimensions, self-efficacy (ease or difficulty in performing the behavior or likelihood that the person can actually do it) and controllability (people's beliefs that they have control over the behavior, that the performance of the behavior is—or is not—up to them).

Returning to the physical fitness lifestyle example, let's say you want to predict whether a person will walk on a treadmill in a physical fitness center for at least 30 minutes each day in the next month (Ajzen, 2001). To assess the self-efficacy dimension of perceived behavioral control, you might ask the person to respond to an item such as, "For me to walk on a treadmill for at least 30 minutes each day in the forthcoming month would be" [impossible—possible]. To assess the controllability dimension of perceived control, you could ask, "How much control do you believe you have over walking on a treadmill for at least 30 minutes each day in the forthcoming month" [no control—complete control].

perceived behavioural control   The degree to which a person believes that they control any given behavior.

self-efficacy   The degree of ease or difficulty in performing the behavior or likelihood that a person can actually perform a behavior.

controllability   People's belief that they have control over the behavior, that the performance of the behaviour is-or-is not up to them.

Thus, if you want to assess more accurately whether a person will actually perform a given behavior, you will need to measure perceived control, along with an assessment of the person's *behavioral intention*, "I plan to walk on a treadmill for at least 30 minutes each day in the forthcoming month" [strongly disagree—strongly agree], their *attitude toward the behavior*, "I believe walking on a treadmill for at least 30 minutes each day in the next month is [harmful—beneficial, worthless—valuable], and their subjective norm, "Most people who are important to me think that [I should—I should not] walk on a treadmill for at least 30 minutes each day in the next month" (Ajzen, 2001, pp. 4–7).

When put to the test, TPB has been able to predict a number of health-related behaviors such as weight loss (Schifter & Ajzen, 1985), adolescent use of alcohol (Marcoux & Schope, 1997), and adolescent abstinence from sex and/or use of condoms during sexual relations (Basen-Engquist & Parcel, 1992). Communication researchers have recently adopted TPB to predict actual behavior. For example, Roberto, Meyer, and Boster (2001) used TPB to predict adolescent decisions about fighting. In their study, several hundred seventh-grade boys and girls were questioned about their participation in physical fights "where two or more people hit, punch, slap, push, or kick each other in anger" (p. 317). They completed a survey instrument that measured their actual behavior (e.g., "During the last month how many times did you get into a fight?), their behavioral intentions (e.g., "How many times do you think you will get into a fight in the next month?"), the perceptions of subjective norms (e.g., "Do most of the kids you know think you should get into fights?"), their attitudes toward fighting (e.g., very cool—very uncool), and their *perceived behavioral control* (e.g., "How easy or hard is it for you to stay out of fights," and "When someone tries to start a fight with you, how easy or hard is it for you to avoid the fight?").

The results supported several of the assumptions of TPB in that attitudes toward fighting and perceived behavioral control were both related to an individual's behavioral intentions. That is, those adolescents who felt they were more "in control" of their fighting behaviors and who expressed unfavorable attitudes toward fighting were less likely to get into fights. Both behavioral intentions and perceived behavioral control emerged as predictors of actual behavior (Roberto et al., 2001).

TPB has also been used to predict smokers' interests in participating in a smoking-cessation program (Babrow, Black, & Tiffany, 1990). TPB suggests that measuring a person's attitudes toward participating in a particular smoking-cessation program allow better prediction of participation in the program than attitudes toward smoking in general or attitudes toward quitting smoking in general. Intentions to participate (behavioral intentions), attitude toward participation, beliefs about the consequences of participating, perceptions of the subjective norm, and perceived behavioral control were measured ("how frequently would the following factors: flexibility of program hours, participation with other friends, convenience of location, etc. affect your ability to participate in this particular smoking-cessation program" [never—constantly]). Babrow et al.'s (1990) findings generally supported TPB. Beliefs about the consequences of participating in the program were related to attitude toward participation. Most important, attitude, subjective norm, and perceived behavioral control beliefs were strongly related to individuals' intentions to participate in the smoking cessation program.

perceived control   The degree to which people believe that they have control over a situation or behavior.

subjective norm   The pressure a person feels to conform to the will of others to perform or not perform a behavior.

The development of TPB in response to an earlier theory, TORA, allows us to see how theories are built by extension where new theories emerge from expansion of existing theories. By adding new information, factors, and knowledge to existing theories, we can better explain, predict, and thus, control behavior.

Elaboration Likelihood Theory

We will now examine a theory that has been described as "the most promising recent theoretical development in persuasion research" (O'Keefe, 1990, p. 109). Social psychologists Petty and Cacioppo (1986) developed the elaboration likelihood model (ELM). They recognized that persuasion results primarily from characteristics of the persuasive message or from characteristics of the persuasion situation. ELM analyzes the likelihood that receivers will cognitively elaborate—engage in issue-related thinking—on the information presented in a persuasive message. Because of its focus on the conditions of certain types of thinking in persuasion, ELM fits the laws tradition of theories.

At times persuasion occurs because the receiver of a message considers the content of the persuasive message carefully and has favorable thoughts about the content. The favorable thinking about the message content causes a favorable attitude to form toward the object of the message. This represents one type of persuasion—the central route to persuasion, characterized by a good deal of persuasive, issue-related thinking. At other times persuasion occurs because the receiver is guided not by his or her assessment of the message but because the receiver decides to follow a principle or a decision-rule derived from the persuasion situation. The rule might be: "When everyone else goes along with the speaker's recommendation, I should too unless I have a very good reason to deviate from the group." This is an example of persuasion through a peripheral route.

According to Petty and Cacioppo, when persuasion takes a peripheral route, there is little or no elaboration of message content; that is, there is a lack of issue-related thinking. When a decision on a persuasive message is not based on the message itself, the receiver looks to other things to guide the decision, as in the preceding example. The persuasive situation provides many principles for evaluating a message if one does not want to engage in a critical assessment of the message content. We sometimes base message acceptance on the trustworthiness of the source, the expertise of the source, or even the physical attractiveness of the source. Also, a decision-rule can be based on rewards or punishments. "I will accept the source's position if I can realize a financial gain from it or if I can avoid a punishment such as higher taxes." Sometimes we are guided by our relationship with the persuader, as in "I need to return a favor."

The ELM is based on the idea that people realize their attitudes are important because attitudes guide decisions and other behaviors. This importance motivates people to form attitudes that are useful in their lives. Although attitudes can result from a number of things, persuasion is a primary source. When a persuasive message attempts to influence an attitude the receiver realizes is significant to his or her life, the likelihood increases that the receiver will cognitively elaborate on the content of the message. This process takes a good deal of effort, so it is avoided whenever possible. That is, people generally prefer not to have to work hard mentally and will follow the "easy way" whenever possible. This probably is due not so much to people being lazy as to the reality

elaboration likelihood model   A model of persuasion that assumes persuasion results primarily from characteristics of the persuasive message or from characteristics of the situation.

central route   The favorable thinking about the message content causes a favorable attitude to form toward the object of the message.

peripheral route   When there is little or no elaboration of a message. Situational cues persuade people instead of the message.

of our cognitive limits. Our physical limits are pretty obvious. For instance, we cannot run a marathon as a sprint. The central route to persuasion is probably more like a "mental sprint." You can only do it for a limited period of time.

A peripheral route to persuasion is "easy" because not much thinking is necessary. All one has to do is realize an appropriate guiding principle and make a decision on the persuasive message based on the principle. "The source is a real expert so I can trust what she is saying." Little, if any, elaboration takes place when a simple principle, like this example, is used to guide assessment of a persuasive message.

It is important to note that persuasion, or lack of it, can take place with either route. What matters is the *cognitive product* of the process. When one takes the central route, thinking about the content of the message might result in unfavorable assessments of the source's arguments. This negative reaction would inhibit persuasion. Similarly, persuasion could fail to occur through a peripheral route when a receiver utilizes the negative side of a principle. "The source has no real credentials to speak on this topic, so I would not even consider changing my opinion."

Because elaboration or issue-related thinking is central to this theory, a good deal of research has explored the factors that influence how much we elaborate when we receive a persuasive message. Basically, two types of factors have been identified: (a) factors that influence our *motivation* to elaborate, and (b) factors that influence our *ability* to elaborate.

Motivation to elaborate has been investigated in terms of the receiver's involvement in the persuasive issue; the more the person is personally involved in the topic, the more likely he or she will elaborate on the message. Also, motivation to elaborate is increased when several sources present arguments on the topic. The variety of arguments presents a sense of conflict, and conflict tends to attract attention. The research also has discovered that some people are more likely than others to elaborate. Specifically, people who have a strong need for cognition (they enjoy thinking a lot) are more likely to elaborate on the content of a message.

need for cognition
A stable individual difference in people's tendency to engage in and enjoy effortful cognitive activity.

The need for cognition trait is defined as "a stable individual difference in people's tendency to engage in and enjoy effortful cognitive activity" (Cacioppo, Petty, Feinstein, & Jarvis, 1996, p. 198). Cognitive activity refers to the degree of critical thinking a person engages in. People range from being high to being low in need for cognition. Individuals high in need for cognition enjoy thinking about abstract issues and often engage in contemplative thought, whereas people low in need for cognition tend to rely more on simple social cues that provide a shortcut to effortful thought. These cues can be things such as attractiveness and source credibility, as illustrated in the Elaboration Likelihood Model of Persuasion. That is, people who are high in need for cognition have a tendency to process information through the central route, whereas people low in need for cognition have a tendency to process information through the peripheral route.

Although it may appear that people high in need for cognition are somehow smarter than people low in need for cognition, this is not the case. Of course people high in need for cognition have to have a degree of critical thinking capacity. Sanders, Gass, Wiseman, and Bruschke (1992) compared Asian Americans, Hispanic Americans, and European Americans in need for cognition, argumentativeness, and verbal aggressiveness. The results of this study reveal that need for cognition was positively related to argumentativeness and negatively related to verbal aggressiveness. Further, Asian Americans reported being lower in need for cognition than both Hispanic Americans and European Americans. A similar link between need for cognition and argumentativeness was also observed by Mongeau (1989).

It is important to note that need for cognition is a motivational trait, not a behavior skill-related trait. Similar to the competing motivational tendencies that comprise the trait of argumentativeness, need for cognition simply suggests that we either enjoy abstract thinking or we do not.

You may be thinking, "Why is need for cognition in the Persuasion Approaches chapter and not in the Trait Approaches chapter?" The answer is that unlike other traits, need for cognition is an important motivational factor in the Elaboration Likelihood Model of persuasion. The need for cognition is a very important trait for researchers and theorists interested in a source-based factor that influences how people are persuaded.

The ability to elaborate is also influenced by several factors. Distractions are a key element. If people are distracted during the presentation of a message, they are less likely to elaborate on the content. They are more likely to take a peripheral route. For instance, distracting a friend by dining in a good restaurant while trying to persuade him or her makes it less likely that your friend will exert the cognitive effort to elaborate on the message (attention to the food subtracts from the attention available for message elaboration). In this example, it is again more likely that a peripheral route to persuasion will be taken. "Coming from so generous a friend, the message is probably valid." Knowledge of the topic also is a factor that influences ability to elaborate. Knowing little about the topic makes elaboration very difficult, and peripheral routes are welcomed when we find ourselves in such a circumstance. Similarly, the comprehensibility of a message influences elaboration. A very vague message or one that relies heavily on very difficult material reduces the ability to elaborate. However, this might not reduce persuasion if, instead of elaborating on the message content, the receiver relies on a principle such as "the speaker is such an expert that the message position surely is correct." Diverting receivers to a particular peripheral route at times could be a successful strategy of persuasion.

It should be noted that the two routes to persuasion are not mutually exclusive. Probably only one route is taken under circumstances of extremely high or extremely low elaboration. Thus, when elaboration of the message content is very extensive, no consideration might be given to a peripheral route. On the other hand, when there is no elaboration of the message, a peripheral route is taken exclusively. Between those extremes, however, probably both characteristics of the message and characteristics of the persuasion situation matter. For instance, after receiving a persuasive message, a person might say: "After thinking extensively about what was said, I must conclude that I am persuaded a bit, but not as much as I would have been if the speaker had been motivated less by self-interest." Research by James Stiff (1986) suggests people are influenced in persuasion not only by cues associated with the central route but also by cues pertaining to peripheral routes. Stiff demonstrated that, when they want to, people can "stretch" their capacity for processing information and process both message and situation information. Therefore, it is overly simplistic to view persuasion in an "either/or" (as in either a central or a peripheral route) sense. Allowing for both provides a richer explanation of persuasion.

We can avoid being overly simplistic also by saying that characteristics of sources (such as expertise or attractiveness) do not always pertain to peripheral routes. For instance, an actor's beautiful tan could be considered part of the persuasive message when trying to sell suntan lotion; the tan would constitute data (an example) for the claim that having a tan enhances physical attractiveness. In other circumstances, such as the actor talking about aiding the homeless, the tan would function as a component of attractiveness that, for some receivers, might be a peripheral route to persuasion.

O'Keefe's (1990) assessment of the ELM being most promising as a theoretical development is probably quite accurate. The theory is generating a good deal of research and is attracting the attention of a sizeable body of researchers. Although cognitive dissonance theory was the dominant theory of persuasion in earlier periods of persuasion research, the ELM might very well play a similar role in the future.

Compliance-Gaining Message Selection

A good deal of social influence research in the communication discipline through the 1980s focused on **compliance gaining**. Recall our earlier distinction that compliance gaining and persuasion are two different types of social influence (persuasion involves attitude change). The main emphasis of compliance-gaining research was on the various strategies that people use under different circumstances to influence another person to behave in a particular manner (see Dillard, 1990, for an analysis of this literature). This line of research had its beginning in the field of sociology, where Gerald Marwell and David Schmitt (1967) derived sixteen different compliance-gaining strategies from previous research and theory, which were later introduced to the communication field (Miller, Boster, Roloff, & Seibold, 1977). Figure 5.7 presents a definition of each strategy with an example from the Marwell and Schmitt study. Generally, research was conducted by presenting a hypothetical situation (for example, your roommate is playing the stereo too loudly). The set of compliance-gaining strategies was then presented, and participants were asked to rate the likelihood that they would use each strategy in the hypothetical situation. Another method was to ask participants to write what they would say in such a situation. Researchers then analyzed the written content to determine preferred strategies.

We will examine John Hunter and Franklin Boster's (1987) model of compliance-gaining message selection because it is a good example of the new direction taken in social influence theory building. The model posits that the source's selection of compliance-gaining messages is influenced greatly by the way the source thinks the receiver will react emotionally to the message. Emotional reactions to a message can range from extremely positive to extremely negative. Persuaders generally select messages that create a favorable emotional reaction in their receivers, and they would rather avoid messages that produce negative emotional states. However, this is a general pattern, and it does not apply to everyone. Some people are more willing than others to select messages that stimulate very unfavorable reactions in receivers. Some people only select messages that arouse positive emotions.

Willingness to select negative affect-producing messages is an individual difference, a variable from person to person. The persuader's willingness to stir

Figure 5.7 Compliance-gaining strategies: Family situation examples.

The situation analyzed here involved a father attempting to persuade his son, Dick, to study.

1. Promise
If you comply, you will be rewarded.
Offer to increase Dick's allowance if he increases his studying.

2. Threat
If you do not comply, you will be punished.
Threaten to forbid Dick the use of the car if he does not increase his studying.

3. Expertise (Positive)
If you comply, you will be rewarded because of "the nature of things."
Point out to Dick that if he gets good grades he will be able to get into a good college and get a good job.

4. Expertise (Negative)
If you do not comply, you will be punished because of "the nature of things."
Point out to Dick that if he does not get good grades he will not be able to get into a good college or get a good job.

5. Liking
Actor is friendly and helpful to get target in "good frame of mind" so that he will comply with request.
Try to be as friendly and pleasant as possible to get Dick in the right "frame of mind" before asking him to study.

6. Pre-Giving
Actor rewards target before requesting compliance.
Raise Dick's allowance and tell him you now expect him to study.

7. Aversive Stimulation
Actor continuously punishes target, making cessation contingent on compliance.
Forbid Dick the use of the car and tell him he will not be allowed to drive until he studies more.

8. Debt
Compliance is owed because of past favors.
Point out that you have sacrificed and saved to pay for Dick's education and that he owes it to you to get good enough grades to get into a good college.

9. Moral Appeal
You are immoral if you do not comply.
Tell Dick that it is morally wrong for anyone not to achieve good grades and that he should study more.

10. Self-Feeling (Positive)
You will feel better about yourself if you comply.
Tell Dick he will feel proud if he studies more.

11. Self-Feeling (Negative)
You will feel worse about yourself if you do not comply.
Tell Dick he will feel ashamed of himself if he gets bad grades.

12. Altercasting (Positive)
A person with "good" qualities would comply.
Tell Dick that since he is mature and intelligent, he naturally will want to study more and get good grades.

13. Altercasting (Negative)
Only a person with "bad" qualities would not comply.
Tell Dick that only someone very childish does not study.

14. Altruism
Your compliance is very badly needed, so do it as a favor.
Tell Dick that you fervently want him to get into a good college and that you wish he would study more as a personal favor to you.

15. Esteem (Positive)
People you value will think better of you if you comply.
Tell Dick that the whole family will be very proud of him if he gets good grades.

16. Esteem (Negative)
People you value will think worse of you if you do not comply.
Tell Dick that the whole family will be very disappointed in him if he gets poor grades.

From Marwell & Schmitt, Dimensions of Compliance-gaining Behavior, 1967, pp.357–58..

negative emotional reactions in receivers serves as a "go, no-go" trigger for message selection. Sources are willing to use messages that stimulate negative reactions up to a certain degree. A given message is a candidate for use if it does not exceed the degree of negative arousal persuaders are willing to cause in receivers; it triggers a "go" response. If a persuader believes a particular message will exceed the amount of negativity the persuader is willing to stir, the message selection process triggers a "no-go." This means the source finds the message "unacceptable" as a means of persuasion.

Hunter and Boster reanalyzed the data from several earlier compliance-gaining studies and found considerable support for the idea that sources' anticipations about the emotional reactions of receivers to messages provide a foundation for the message selection process. According to this idea, a fundamental concern in persuasion theory involves understanding the persuader's willingness to use messages that cause negative affect. Hunter and Boster suggested that variability in willingness to create negativity might be explained by certain traits such as argumentativeness and verbal aggressiveness.

Hunter and Boster derived several speculations about how these traits might pertain to one's willingness to create negativity. For instance, high verbal aggressives may have a higher willingness because they like inflicting psychological pain on others. Thus, they should be more likely than other people to use compliance-gaining messages that threaten the receiver with some form of punishment. Low verbal aggressives, on the other hand, probably have a very low threshold for creating negative impact because they are very sensitive to others' self-concepts and try not to cause psychological pain. In terms of argumentativeness, it could be predicted that high argumentatives use a diverse group of messages (positive and negative) because they like arguing and will try numerous arguments to succeed. Low argumentatives, however, probably use few negative compliance-gaining messages to avoid an argument being instigated by such messages. Other research has supported these ideas (Boster & Levine, 1988; Boster, Levine, & Kazoleas, 1989; Infante, Anderson, Martin, Herington, & Kim, 1993).

Although a person's traits probably exert considerable influence on his or her willingness to create a negative emotional impact on receivers, a possibility is that factors in the particular persuasion situation also may have an impact. That is, situational influences may cause the willingness to create negativity to be a little higher or lower in some situations than in others. Although Hunter and Boster's model did not deal much with this idea, expanding the model to include situational influences seems like a natural development. Thus, we might speculate that there are several important situational factors. The nature of the receiver might influence the source's willingness to stimulate negativity. For instance, if the receiver is extremely stubborn, the source might become more negative than usual. The persuasive topic could be another factor. Persuaders might be willing to stir more negative reactions on some topics than on others. For example, willingness to cause negative emotional impact may be lower when the topic is a delicate, sensitive one. For some receivers, this might pertain to their religion, their physical appearance, or their sexual orientation. The emotional climate in the situation could alter the source's willingness to be negative. For instance, if the mood in a crowd of people turns very aggressive, the source's willingness might increase; the source might find negative messages more acceptable than at other times.

Although only a few studies have been based on Hunter and Boster's model, the focus on compliance-gaining message selection is of obvious relevance to communication theory. Moreover, the ideas that make up the model are intuitively valid and lead to interesting implications. Thus, it deserves continued attention from researchers.

Cialdini's Persuasive Heuristics

Robert Cialdini (1988) developed six principles of compliance gaining based on his experience in a variety of occupations, including advertising, public relations, and fund-raising. He defines compliance as "action that is taken only because it has been requested" (Cialdini, 1987, p. 165). He noted that there are consistencies across all occupations in terms of getting people to comply with a request, which he labeled "persuasive heuristics." The six heuristics consist of reciprocity, commitment and consistency, social proof, liking, authority, and scarcity.

The reciprocity principle assumes that when someone gives you something, you should give them something in return. The sense of owing someone something is believed to be a powerful compliance-gaining strategy. People are constantly being given things in an effort to enhance compliance. Whether it is free food samples in a supermarket, free mailing labels from a charity, or free Avon products, the feeling of obligation is powerful and transcends cultures. In a study of charitable solicitations, Cialdini and Ascani (1976) used the reciprocity principle to increase blood donation. A request was made for people to join a long-term blood donor program. When this initial request was rejected, the researchers then made a second smaller request of a one-time blood donation. This smaller request resulted in a 50% compliance rate as opposed to a 32% compliance rate for simply asking for the one-time donation. This compliance technique is also known as the door in the face technique.

The commitment and consistency principle assumes that when people take a stand on an issue, there is internal pressure to be consistent with what you committed to. For example, it is common practice in the toy industry to purposely understock the more popular toys around the holiday season. Parents promise their children the most popular toys for the holidays. When the parent goes to the toy store and finds that the promised toy is out of stock, other toys are purchased to make up for the promised toy. Conveniently, after the holidays there is an ample amount of the most popular toys. The parent, more often then not, will return to get the promised toy, thus increasing the toy stores' overall sales.

The social proof principle states that "we determine what is correct by finding out what other people think is correct" (Cialdini, 1988, p. 110). This is especially powerful when we are uncertain about what is correct behavior. To determine what is correct behavior, we look around us to see how other people are behaving. This serves as a guide as to what is correct. Consider your favorite television comedy. The producers will purposely include "laugh tracks" to cue the viewer when to laugh. It is common practice in churches to "salt" the collection plate (i.e., put a one or five dollar bill in the plate before it is passed to the parishioners). By doing this, it sets a standard amount for the donation. This also works in bars, where the bartender will "salt" the tip jar to indicate the standard rate of tipping.

The liking principle assumes that we comply with requests because we like the person. The police use this principle when interrogating suspects. If you have ever seen an episode of *CSI* or *Law and Order,* you most certainly are familiar with the "good cop/bad cop" interrogation technique. The principle behind this technique is that one interrogator will threaten and be aggressive to the suspect, and the other will be more understanding and calm. When the aggressive interrogator leaves the room, the suspect will have a greater tendency

reciprocity heuristic
A compliance gaining strategy that assumes when someone gives you something, you should give them something in return.

commitment and consistency heuristic
A compliance gaining strategy that assumes when people take a stand on an issue, there is internal pressure to be consistent with what you committed to.

social proof heuristic
A compliance gaining strategy that assumes that we determine what is correct by finding out what other people think is correct.

liking heuristic
A compliance gaining strategy that assumes we comply with requests because we like the person.

authority heuristic
A compliance gaining strategy that assumes people should be more willing to follow the suggestions of an individual who is a legitimate authority.

scarcity heuristic
A compliance gaining strategy that assumes people want to try to secure those opportunities that are scarce.

door in the face technique   A compliance gaining strategy that utilizes a large request followed by a smaller request. People are more likely to agree to the smaller request after rejecting the larger request.

to give information to interrogator that he or she "likes" more. It is a common practice in sales to build a relationship with your clients and then work toward the sale. It is well documented that **homophily**, or similarities of attitudes and backgrounds, increases liking (Byrne, 1971; Stotland & Patchen, 1961). In a study of peace marchers, Suedfeld, Bochner, and Matas (1971) found that people were more likely to sign a petition if the person requesting the signature was similarly dressed.

The authority heuristic holds that "one should be more willing to follow the suggestions of an individual who is a legitimate authority" (Cialdini, 1987, p. 175). Our culture is filled with authority figures that tell us what to think, who to vote for, and what to buy. One study revealed that people were three and a half times more likely to follow a jaywalker into traffic when he wore a suit as opposed to just a shirt and pants (Lefkowitz, Blake, & Mouton, 1955). The authority heuristic, similar to that of social proof, is particularly effective in times of uncertainty. When we are uncertain, we look to authority figures to help us determine what is appropriate.

The final persuasive heuristic is scarcity. Ciladini (1987) defined this principle as "one should want to try to secure those opportunities that are scarce" (p. 177). The fact that something is offered for a limited time or in limited quantity makes the item that much more valuable. This concept is illustrated in television infomercials. It is a common tactic for vendors to put a counter in the corner of the television screen informing the viewer of how many units are left. This strategy gives the viewer the perception that once they are sold out of product, there will be no more available.

The persuasive heuristics developed by Robert Cialdini continue to represent one of the most comprehensive efforts in explaining the complex process of compliance gaining. Recall in the Elaboration Likelihood Model (ELM) of persuasion that people process messages either through the central route (critical thinking) or the peripheral route (cues in the environment). The persuasive heuristics presented here would be processed through the peripheral route of the ELM.

Preventing Persuasion

We turn now to theories that explain how to prevent persuasion. In emphasizing how to persuade people, it is easy to forget that the reverse is often our goal. It is not unusual for us to want another person to resist being influenced by a third party. We might want a wavering Democrat to resist appeals to vote Republican. In a sense, we try to "persuade" a person not to be persuaded. There have been five approaches in persuasion research to the problem of how to prevent persuasion.

The *behavioral commitment* approach advises public statements about positions. If you know that someone supports your proposal, you would want him or her to express that opinion publicly. When other people learn someone holds a given position, it is more difficult for that person to change the position. Because the position has been associated with the individual, "losing face" might result from changing what was previously declared.

The *anchoring approach* is based on the idea that someone will be less likely to change a position if the position is anchored or "tied" to things that are significant for that person. With this approach you would try to convince an individual who valued others (friends, family, etc.) to agree with a position by pointing out that other people and/or reference groups (religious, political groups, etc.) also agree. You might add that important values (freedom, for instance) are upheld by the position. Changing an opinion would involve disagreeing with family and friends, would violate group norms, and would undermine values.

A third approach is creating *resistant cognitive states*. People are more difficult to persuade when they are in certain frames of mind. The major research finding in this area is that when persons experience an increase in self-esteem, they are particularly resistant to persuasion because people who feel high self-esteem believe they are valuable; they are confident and therefore less likely to say they were wrong in holding a position that a persuader tries to change. It is relatively easy to raise or lower self-esteem in a research laboratory. The main technique for raising self-esteem is to lead individuals to believe they have succeeded at an important task. Conversely, believing they have failed lowers self-esteem. Because a person with low self-esteem is particularly easy to persuade, an ethical issue arises. Is it acceptable to try to persuade someone who has just experienced failure? The person may be especially vulnerable at that time, and attempting persuasion may be taking advantage of him or her (Infante, 1976).

Training in critical methods is an approach that has met with mixed results. The idea appears sound. Train people to think critically when listening to a speech, to recognize fallacies in reasoning, and to detect propaganda techniques; they will then not be so easily persuaded. In one study, students were trained in methods for critically evaluating speeches. Later they listened to a tape-recorded speech. Women in the study were persuaded less than the control group of women who had not been taught the evaluation methods. However, male participants were persuaded more than the control group of untrained men. American culture may have influenced men to be more dogmatic in their positions than women; therefore, men may pay less attention to opposing positions in the message. The training might have neutralized this cultural effect and made men more sensitive to the content of the message (Infante & Grimmett, 1971), thus yielding the variable results.

inoculation theory
Approach to preventing persuasion based on the biological analogy of preventing disease.

Inoculation theory from social psychology is the fifth approach (McGuire, 1964). This theory assumes that preventing persuasion is like preventing a disease. To keep a dangerous virus from causing a disease, the body can be inoculated with a weakened form of the disease-producing virus. The body's immune system will then create antibodies to destroy that type of virus. If the actual virus does invade the body at a later date, the defense will be in place and will prevent the disease. To prevent persuasion, according to this biological analogy, the person's cognitive system needs to be inoculated so a defense is in place when a strong persuasive message "invades the mind." How does *cognitive inoculation* work? The counterpart of the weakened virus would be weak arguments in support of an opponent's position. In theory, when an audience hears the weak arguments, they think of refutations for them. These refutations, like antibodies against a disease, form the foundation for attacking stronger arguments heard later. Thus, preventing persuasion from this approach involves "strengthening" the mind's defense systems so it will be able to destroy strong, attacking arguments.

Persuasion is an integral topic for communication study because the skill of the persuader in using verbal and nonverbal symbols affects the interaction. In this chapter, we defined persuasion as attitude change toward a source's proposal. Persuasion differs from coercion because audience members can choose to agree or disagree. In this framework, belief change leads to attitude change, which can then produce behavior change. Adapting to the audience and the situation makes persuasion more effective.

As we said at the beginning of this chapter, persuasion research has changed greatly in recent years. We think it is important for persuasion research to continue with the enthusiasm it has enjoyed in the past. Current researchers are especially interested in how people influence one another in interpersonal relationships. The advertising and public relations professions provide another important persuasive context for the application of communication theory.

Research that enhances our understanding of the persuasion process is inherently valuable. Of course, there are other ways of influencing another person's behavior. Two particularly distasteful methods are physical aggression and coercion. Persuasion is infinitely more desirable than these alternatives because the process of persuasion respects the dignity of others and their right to choose among alternatives based on their beliefs. Persuasion offers hope for people to resolve differences in a satisfying and constructive manner.

Interpersonal Conflict

OBJECTIVES

- Plan and conduct a conversation using the five stages of conversational development.
- Understand the cooperative principle and the benefits of dialogue.
- Recognize the importance of seeking productive conflict.
- Appreciate the variety and value of different conflict management techniques.
- Apply principles of confirmation and negotiation to work through conflict.
- Develop skills for handling difficult conversations and for de-escalating conflict situations.

KEY TERMS

Accommodating	Facework
Altercasting	Feedback
Avoiding	Feedforward
Coercive power	Focus
Collaborating	Formal feedback
Competing	Informal feedback
Compromising	Information/persuasive power
Confirmation	Legitimate power
Conflict	Monologue
Conversational disclaimers	Negotiation
Cooperative principle	Phatic communication
Destructive conflict	Power
Dialogic negotiation	Principled negation
Dialogue	Productive conflict
Disconfirmation	Referent power
Expert power	Reward power

Imagine you're discussing an upcoming presentation for this class with your instructor. Let's eavesdrop on part of that conversation.

"I'm lost on this assignment."

"What confuses you?"

"I just don't get it."

"Don't get what?"

"The whole thing. Your instructions are so unclear."

"The instructions are very explicit. Did you read them?"

"Of course I read them. You don't have to insult me. I'm leaving!"

Oh, dear! We just overheard a very ineffective conversation. The exchange might be fun to read, but it exemplifies significant, ongoing issues that affect our everyday communication. How often have you had a conversation that didn't go the way you wanted? Think of the worst date or social experience you ever had. Chances are that a major part of your disappointment began with a less-than-ideal conversation. We talk with each other all the time, yet too often we talk past each other, not connecting on deeper levels and failing to accomplish what we had hoped.

The first part of this chapter deals with the process of conversation, a form of communication we easily take for granted although it often forms the foundation of fulfilling relationships. A growing body of evidence suggests that everyday conversations play a key role in relationship satisfaction (Alberts et al., 2005). Research on same-sex couples confirms that conversational quality and relationship quality go hand in hand (Gottman et al., 2003).

The second part of this chapter focuses on conflict, which we can understand as situations where our goals, desires, or expectations differ from those of someone else. Agreement with others might seem more comfortable or easier than conflict, but too much agreement actually reduces creativity and productivity. Research has shown consistently that small groups where conflict and difference of opinion occur tend to be more productive and innovative than groups without significant disagreement (Likert & Likert, 1976).

We complete our tour of conversation and conflict with reflection on how to address some common challenges in both areas. We will probe some practical ways to prevent conversations and conflicts from getting out of hand. These recommendations can help you prepare for difficult communication situations and avoid communication breakdowns.

UNDERSTANDING AND ENHANCING CONVERSATIONS

Becoming a better conversationalist can be extremely beneficial. Skillful conversationalists find it easier to approach and interact with a wide variety of people, equipping them well for the highest positions in their profession (Murphy, 2005). Others increasingly approach you as someone who can engage in lively conversation. As a student and as a professional, your conversational skills will enable you to give and get more out of your talks with professors, supervisors, and colleagues.

If we know conversation skills are so valuable, why do we take them for granted? Perhaps we assume that we can converse effectively just because we have been communicating with others since we were very young. Unfortunately, we don't always recognize the importance of conversation until the conversation takes a negative turn or we end up hurting someone we care about. In this section, we will focus on understanding conversational structure and recognizing key elements of conversation. The best part about studying conversation is that you can put the principles and strategies into practice immediately.

A good way to begin understanding conversations is with their structure. We will track how to manage conversations by tracking stages adapted from DeVito (2005): opening, feedforward, focus (a stage DeVito labels "business"), feedback, and closing. We cover what happens within each conversational stage, offering ongoing examples from some of the most important conversations you can conduct as a student: consultations with your instructors. Through these examples, you will be able to gain a basic understanding of each stage of conversation as well as practical advice for appropriately handling conversations with instructors.

Opening

Although we often search for ways to begin a conversation, the very beginning is simple: Acknowledge the other person with a greeting. Surprisingly, many people forget this obvious step in e-mail messages. Instead of greeting the recipient with something as simple as "Hi, Cheryl," correspondents often simply dive right into a detailed message, which can disorient the recipient. During face-to-face conversations, the absence of an opening greeting is much more obvious. Consider this scenario. You are out with your significant other and a friend that you haven't seen or talked to in five years walks up and immediately asks you intimate details about your romantic relationship. You are likely stunned and not willing to disclose this type of information at this moment. You needed an opening greeting to help you and the friend ease into conversation.

Typically, a greeting leads to small talk that seems trivial but actually serves a vital social maintenance function. This small talk, known as **phatic communication**, simply keeps the lines of communication open, clearing a path for further interaction. Phatic communication works because it avoids controversy and does not require an emotional commitment, consequently inviting connection instead of conflict (Gill & Adams, 1998). Figure 6.1 provides examples of phatic communication.

Small talk has big consequences. Phatic communication acknowledges the presence of the other person, and this recognition reaffirms his or her value. In medical settings, phatic communication can make the difference between a patient feeling reassured or ignored by the nurses (Burnard, 2003). This is certainly not limited to the medical field, but important in all personal and professional interactions.

Figure 6.1   **Examples of Phatic Communication**

Common Phatic Communication Phrases

- "Hi, how are you?"
- "Nice day today, isn't it?"
- "Good to see you."
- "What's up?"

Sample Phatic Communication Between Instructor and Student

Student: "Hi, Dr. Doolittle, how are you?
Instructor: "I'm well, Biffy, and you?"
Student: "I'm doing pretty well."
Instructor: "Are you glad it's Friday?"
Student: "Yes, I'm looking forward to the weekend."

Another good way to begin a conversation is by referring to some shared knowledge or experience. You could note something about the other person or about what connects you. <u>Example</u> (at the gym): "Wow, we're working out at the same time again." An especially effective opener is to begin with an observation of something you have in common. This technique worked well for me one morning. An older gentleman at the gym caught my eye because he was wearing a sweatshirt from my alma mater. I approached him and said, "Oh, I see we're both Hawkeyes." He immediately warmed up to me, excited to encounter someone familiar with his beloved University of Iowa.

Feedforward

The second stage, **feedforward**, previews the content and tone of the upcoming conversation. Think of feedforward as the preview of main points in a speech or as a road sign alerting you to what lies ahead. Attention to feedforward can improve conversational quality by predicting the course of conversation and preparing participants to manage it appropriately. Feedforward often provides the preview of the conversational content, format, or emotional dimension. As with other oral communication, the preview should follow introductory material (the opening) that invites others to participate. Plunging directly into feedforward might disorient or antagonize your conversational partners, especially on a sensitive topic. Figure 6.2 provides examples of feedforward in a conversation between an instructor and a student.

Feedforward can set guidelines and boundaries. You might explicitly lay down the format of the conversation: "Each person will speak for five minutes"; "We will discuss the problem and then the possible solutions." Feedforward also can set limits to conversational topics or methods: "No interrupting"; "Everyone gets a chance to speak"; "Don't talk about anyone else's family."

We covered disclaimers in as a form of powerless language. Now we can expand our understanding of disclaimers. In conversations, different kinds of disclaimers can serve more diverse purposes. Conversational **disclaimers** are statements that set guidelines to "regulate the impact of utterances" by warding off potential criticisms or channeling interpretations in a particular direction (Beach & Dunning, 1982, p. 178). Disclaimers can serve many purposes, such as the following:

- Warnings ("Anything you say may be used against you in a court of law").
- Image management ("Don't consider me homophobic when I say ...").

Figure 6.2 Examples of Feedforward

Common Feedforward Phrases

- "Here's something that will really surprise/disappoint you."
- "I have some very good/bad news."
- "Let's try to understand why ..."
- "We need to talk about ..."

Sample Feedforward Between Instructor and Student

Student: "I have a few concerns about my performance in this class."
Instructor: "Okay, let's talk them through."
Student: "I will present my concerns and then ask for any ideas you might have."
Instructor: "I will be happy to do that."

- Establishing expectations or credentials ("This is just the opinion of an amateur," "As someone with vast experience on this topic …").
- Setting other conditions for interpreting what someone says ("Hypothetically speaking, what if …").

Used in these ways, disclaimers shape expectations about how the conversation should proceed.

Feedforward can include setting up the roles conversational participant play in relation to each other. **Altercasting**, or designating a role for the other person in the conversation, could help you accomplish your conversational goals (Weinstein & Deutschberger, 1963). Altercasting sets up the expected roles that will structure response. For example, I have had students altercast by saying, "I'd like your reaction as if you were my parent, not my professor." Altercasting can distinguish which among several possible roles someone should occupy. It also controls the direction of conversation if each participant responds in accordance with their role (Malone, 1995).

Focus

Now we will consider what to do in the heart of the conversation, or the **focus**. Each conversation will develop its own character depending on the topic, context, goals, and the people involved. Because there is not a specific set of statements that usually occurs during the focus of the conversation, this section offers some hints on ways to approach the substance of your conversations. Regardless of the topic, any conversation can improve by addressing some fundamental principles.

Cooperative Conversations. Paul Grice, a philosopher of language, observed that conversations operate on a **cooperative principle**, which calls us to be aware of the accepted rules and expectations of any conversation (1975). It isn't enough for someone just to be a lively conversationalist. Conversations proceed on mutual assumptions that each participant expects the other to fulfill (Bach, 2006). Conversations fizzle and spark conflicts or misunderstanding when these conditions are not met. Exactly what do we expect from each other in conversations? Grice identified four conversational maxims, shown in Figure 6.3. If we choose not to abide by the maxims, we might find ourselves in awkward situations or even worse—our conversational partner may leave. Understanding and following these maxims can invite productive participation in conversations.

Let's go back to the instructor–student relationship and apply these maxims to a conversation that may take place when you see your instructor at the local movie theater. You will need to consider the following issues:

- *Quantity:* Ask open questions that allow for both parties to expand on ideas. If you are asked a closed question, try to answer and then expand on your idea. Speak for a few minutes but don't continue talking for a long period of time.
- *Quality:* Speak about what you know and don't attempt to make things up or pretend to know something that you don't. Don't lie; after all, instructors are human beings and appreciate honesty.
- *Relation:* Try to recognize early (during feedforward) what you will discuss during this time. Will you talk about class? Will you talk about the movies you will be seeing? Just pick a topic or two and stay with it.

Figure 6.3   Grice's Conversational Maxims

Maxim	Explanation	Rationale	Example of Violation
Quantity	Contribute as much information as required, but no more than necessary.	Too little Conversation can't be sustained without interaction. Too much Conversationalists cannot process the flood of information.	Too little Conversation shuts down if one conversant only grunts or says "yes" and "no" Too much A "motormouth" who endlessly spews all possible information
Quality	Make statements that are true. Don't say false things. Don't say anything that lacks adequate support.	Conversation breaks down if we can't judge whether information is true or accurate.	False statements Lies, fantasies Statements without support Generalizations or extreme exaggerations
Relation	Stay relevant.	Conversations that wander from their focus accomplish little.	Random topic changes that interrupt the direction or focus
Manner	Remain clear. Avoid obscurity and ambiguity. Be brief and orderly.	We must enable others to interpret what we say.	Stream of consciousness babbling; saying one thing and meaning another; vague references

- *Manner:* Converse in a way your instructor can follow logically. Consider how to move the conversation progressively forward instead of randomly jumping from topic to topic. Achieve clarity by using a straightforward vocabulary instead of trying to impress your instructor with terms you don't understand.

Developing Dialogue.   Try answering the following questions:

1. Do you frequently use negative criticism and judgment?
2. Do you usually refuse to talk when others don't agree with you?
3. Do you often praise yourself and your accomplishments?

If you answered yes to these questions, you may often engage in a conversational style known as monologue. **Monologue** is communication in which one person does the majority of the speaking and maintains most of the attention. Effective communication is transactional. This shared responsibility for communication would suggest that monologue may not be the best style for an effective conversation. Monologue prevents interaction and only allows for one individuals' goals and ideas to be heard.

Many philosophers, psychologists, communication theorists, and social activists note the advantages of moving conversations toward **dialogue** (Cissna & Anderson, 1994). When we discussed dialogue as part of listening, we noted that participants collaborate in conducting a conversation using honest, open communication based on mutual respect. Now we delve deeper into how to build dialogue through conversations.

Dialogues strive for shared understanding even if participants have different viewpoints. Engaging in genuine dialogue requires the willingness to cooperate with others to find common ground that enables participants to talk *with* each other rather than at each other. Dialogue isn't just about the personal satisfaction of self-disclosure, but of opening ourselves to what others have to offer (Arnett & Arneson, 1999). Participants in dialogue feel secure enough about the conversation and each other to advocate passionately and question assertively.

Exactly what does dialogue involve?

- *Turn-taking:* No one person or group monopolizes the conversation. Everyone has an equal opportunity to participate as a speaker and as a listener (even if some people choose to participate more or less than others).
- *Agreement on procedures:* Participants share basic rules or conversational practices that guide interaction and establish boundaries. Examples: no profanity, no yelling.
- *Sincerity:* All participants in dialogue feel "safe" enough in the conversation to speak honestly, expressing ideas and feelings genuinely. Examples: no "trick questions," melodrama, or refusal to engage others.
- *Equal power and status:* No one automatically gains a superior position simply because of who or what they are. Conversation proceeds without prejudice or privilege. Example: a first-year undergraduate and a university president in dialogue get an equal hearing.
- *Civility:* Everyone is respected, regardless of whether we agree with individual views. Each person has inherent value that he or she retains regardless of how the conversation goes.
- *Openness:* Dialogue requires openness to new viewpoints and willingness to concentrate on the strengths of ideas rather than tearing them down (Franco, 2006).

Not every conversation will exhibit characteristics of dialogue. In fact, few do. As we move closer toward achieving the characteristics of dialogue, we may find that our conversations become more interesting and rewarding.

Developing dialogue isn't easy, since dialogue isn't simply agreement and obedience (Arnett & Arneson, 1999). Indeed, "'dialogue' is not some saccharin-filled, consensual 'group-hug' affair! It refers instead to the ongoing tensionality of multiple, often competing, voices" that interplay in conversation (Baxter, 2007, p. 118). Approaching dialogue—even if we don't achieve it entirely—can move conversation to a more challenging but also deeper, more satisfying, and more productive level.

> **THAT'S DEBATABLE**
>
> Dialogue represents a conversational ideal. Like any ideal, it might fit some situations better than others. What are some examples of situations that might call for communication approaches in addition to or instead of dialogue? What might those approaches be? How should they be implemented?

Feedback

Feedback is defined as the process of responding to the communication of others. Within any conversation, feedback reviews what has occurred. Certainly both verbal and nonverbal feedback occur throughout the stages of conversation; however, the feedback stage allows the speaker to see and hear how the bulk of the message has been interpreted. This type of verbal or nonverbal feedback is known as **informal feedback** and can be as simple

Figure 6.4   Examples of Conversational Feedback

Common Feedback Phrases

- "OK, so you're going to ... and I'm going to ..."
- "As I understand it, you are concerned about _____. Is that correct?"
- "Thank you for sharing your story with me. I hear that ..."

Sample Feedback Between Instructor and Student

Student: "So, based on what I have heard, you believe that I have been writing strong papers; however, I need to continue to work on my oral presentations."
Instructor: "Yes, I believe you can improve your performance on presentations."

as a smile or frown. Often feedback used to review or summarize what has been said or what the participants will do as a result of the talk. Based on the feedback received, the speaker can determine whether the conversation has accomplished its goal. If not, return to feedforward to set a new agenda. Figure 6.4 provides examples of feedback.

Some entire conversations revolve around feedback, and these they can have a big impact. These conversations represent **formal feedback**. If you have not already experienced a performance review at your job, you will likely engage in one of these conversations in your future career.

For now, let's consider a formal feedback conversation that may happen in any of your college classes. If your professor requires meetings with students to review progress in the course and discuss grades, you might feel anxious, uneasy, or just unsure of what might happen. You might even have some of the following thoughts:

- "I must have done something wrong. Otherwise, why would I be meeting with my professor about my performance?"
- "If he says something bad about the work I've done after I've worked so hard this semester, I'll tell him a thing or two. I'll let him know just what a jerk he is."
- "Gosh, she's the professor and I'm the student. I guess I'd better just sit there silently the whole time, thank her, and then be glad it's over."

While you might have had the previous thoughts, they are actually all misguided and may harm the conversation. For this reason, it is important to prepare mentally before entering a feedback-oriented conversation. First, we need to eliminate negative and destructive thoughts such as those expressed in the examples above. Second, you will need to engage in positive mental preparation. Figure 6.5 lists some basic preparatory actions you can take before receiving feedback. For mental preparation to be effective, it has to be implemented, not just understood. You should actually be saying to yourself the kinds of statements that appear in the "self-talk" column of the list.

While receiving constructive feedback, be sure to demonstrate your effective listening skills and participate in the conversation. If any feedback is vague or confusing to you, ask for clarification. Effective feedback should leave you with clear indications of how your work can improve. Your questions should be courteous and presented in a tone that shows you value the person's comments, not that you are annoyed or want to retaliate.

DO ask questions such as ...

- "As I understand it, you are concerned about _____. Is that correct?" (asks for verification, checks for proper interpretation)

Figure 6.5   Preparing for Feedback

Basic Mindset	Self-Talk	Actions
Constructive feedback evaluates performance, not the person. Regardless of what happens, feedback will not damage my personal worth.	"The other person is evaluating my performance, not judging my character."	Treat all comments as remarks about your work, not directed to you personally.
Constructive feedback focuses on ways to improve.	"Feedback is how I can become a better student."	Anticipate potential limitations of your own performance to avoid surprises.
Constructive feedback is a partnership among students and teachers to move toward better performance.	"My instructor and I have the same goal: for me to become the best student I can. If the instructor didn't care, I wouldn't be getting any feedback."	Treat the evaluator as someone trying to help you, not as an adversary.

- "Would you please help me understand which things I did that were not up to standards?" (moves toward getting precise targets for improvement)

  DO NOT ask questions such as …
- "So you're saying I'm a poor student, are you?" (leading question, sounds accusatory)
- "What do you mean my work was not up to standards?" (sounds challenging)

  DO ask questions such as …

- "Thank you for your comments. What would you suggest as the best ways to improve in these areas?"
- "If you were in my position, what would you do to perform better?"
- "What concrete actions can I take to do better next time?"

  DO NOT ask questions such as …

- "So, what do you want me to do?" (sounds as if you have no control over improving your own performance)
- "How am I supposed to do better with all this pressure and so little time?" (offers excuses, not a positive desire to improve)

Feedback can be a critical step in your personal and professional success. Generally, the higher the stakes in a feedback session, the more formal the feedback will be. Ordinarily formal feedback that is tied to determining job performance will be conducted in a performance appraisal interview. In such an interview, the supervisor typically meets personally with each employee to discuss strengths and areas for improvement. An employee cannot expect to advance by maintaining the same level of performance. Consistent improvement merits advancement in position, in pay, and in responsibilities. A major way supervisors determine improvement is to examine how well an employee implements suggestions from formal feedback sessions. It becomes vital to understand how to make the most of feedback.

Receiving feedback from various individuals with whom you interact is critical. Aside from receiving feedback from co-workers, feedback from clients has a major impact on employees. Many organizations have formalized the flow of feedback from clients by distributing comment cards or client satisfaction surveys. The practice of follow-up surveys to patients has become routine in many hospitals throughout the nation. Client feedback gives an important perspective to supervisors about how an employee is representing the organization to the public. A lot of positive feedback from clients (both formal and informal) about an employee can impress supervisors and ultimately enhance the employee's career. Conversely, a pile of client complaints can cause a worker to be reprimanded or fired.

Closing

Have you ever been conversing with someone and felt deep frustration that the person simply refuses to end the conversation? How about the guest who lingers on and on at a party or event you are hosting, ignoring every hint to leave? If these situations sound familiar, you know the value of conversational closure. Endless conversations can play havoc with schedules and disrupt plans, so we need to offer clear signs that the interaction has ended. Verbal signals of closure include remarks that call attention to time constraints. A closing may not explicitly reference time, but instead use the past tense to describe the interaction. Figure 6.6 provides some examples.

Regardless of the closing you use, remember to allow for the possibility of future interactions. "I'll text you" is just one common closing phrase that suggests a future interaction. Simply hanging up to end a phone call certainly closes the conversation, but it also may close the potential for more interaction. You can prepare for closure nonverbally, behaving in ways that signal your preparation to terminate the exchange: gather up books, close a briefcase or purse, put on a coat, take out your keys, or glance at a clock. All closures, however, should include some expression of appreciation. Conversation is a privilege, and anytime someone engages in conversation with us, we should consider it a gift. Remarks such as "I've enjoyed our conversation" or "This talk meant a lot to me" reaffirm the value of interaction.

Tech Talk: Managing E-mail Conversations

Because we cannot interact directly with others in computer-mediated communication, we must take extra steps to help conversations flow.

- **Include a subject heading as feedforward for every message.**
  A blank subject heading gives no clue how the receiver should process the message. Blank subject lines also invite the receiver to delete the message, suspecting it might be unimportant or spam (unwanted or "junk" e-mail).
- **Address the receiver directly, as in a personal letter.**
  Since you can't wave or shake hands through e-mail, you need a way to acknowledge the other person. Simply beginning with a greeting such as "Hi, Frodo ..." recognizes the other person as an individual.
- **Treat e-mail conversations as public communication.**
  Every e-mail is just one mouse click away from being forwarded to anyone with an e-mail address. Countless conflicts have arisen from supposedly "confidential" e-mails that (accidentally or intentionally) got into the wrong inboxes. For highly personal information, select more private media such as the telephone.
- **Remember to close the e-mail by referencing the next communication step**
  (e.g., "Please talk to me about this after class") or meeting time. You may even want to specify what type of feedback you are hoping to receive and when. Always sign your e-mails appropriately.

| Figure 6.6 | **Examples of Conversational Closure** |

Common Closing Phrases

- "Well, you need to get back to what you were doing."
- "Too bad we can't continue our talk any longer."
- "I'll let you go now."
- "It's been nice speaking with you."

Sample Closing Between Instructor and Student

Student: "Well, I really appreciate your time and advice today."
Instructor: "I'm glad you came to talk to me."
Student: "I'll let you get back to your grading."
Instructor: "Great, and I'll see you tomorrow in class."

CONFLICT AND NEGOTIATION

When was the last time you saw a reality TV show or movie that included at least one conflict scene? You probably did not need to think too hard to recall several examples. It seems that many of us are drawn to these conflicts and we can't wait to see who will be yelling and cursing in the next episode of our favorite reality show or who finally "wins" the "fight" on any number of TV dramas.

Why are we so interested in conflict? A few reasons explain our focus on conflict (Melchin & Picard, 2008). First, war and violence have been prevalent during the twentieth and twenty-first centuries. From World War I to more recent wars in Iraq and Afghanistan, conflict has been a part of our present and past. Second, there is great concern about scarcity of our planet's resources. This crisis not only evokes strong feelings and emotions, but it also promotes competition and fear. Third, diversity increasingly surrounds us in our workplaces, homes, schools, and communities. While this diversity carries enormous benefits, differing opinions and lifestyles raise the potential for conflict.

In addition to world trends, the media frames our views and understanding of conflict. From TV to video games, we have created a world that appears to be full of conflict and competition (Brigg, 2008). Because of all of these factors, we often see "social and political life as saturated with difference and dissension" (Melchin & Picard, 2008, p. 3).

While we may be drawn to and surrounded by conflict, we often recognize this conflict as "difficult, complex, and frequently mismanaged" (Kellett & Dalton, 2001, p. 3). Despite the fact that conflict and competition can be frightening, it is unavoidable. In fact, some scholars suggest that it is not only inevitable but also necessary in human relationships (Kellett & Dalton, 2001). Conflict can cause damage, but we must separate violent attacks from productive disagreements. In work groups, for example, "while relationship conflicts based on personality clashes and interpersonal dislike are detrimental to group functioning, task conflicts based on disagreements regarding the specific task content are beneficial in many situations" (Jehn, Chadwick, & Thatcher, 1997, p. 287).

This inevitability of conflict explains why this chapter talks about "managing" instead of "eliminating" conflict. The choices we make concerning conflict management will undoubtedly affect our personal relationships and the greater society. The way we handle conflict can prove helpful or harmful to our relationships. This is why we must reflect on our individual experiences with conflict and work to develop effective strategies for managing conflict—even recognizing it as positive and constructive.

You might be asking yourself: "What is this thing called conflict that is so prevalent and what causes it?" or "Can't I just pretend I don't know something that I think might cause a conflict between me and a friend?" In the next few sections, we will address these questions and more.

What Is Conflict?

So, you and a friend are talking about your differing religious beliefs, or you and your parents are brainstorming different gifts that you might like to receive for your birthday. Are these examples of conflict? Probably not, although if the conversations escalate and both parties in the conversation begin to argue over competing views, it could become a conflict. **Conflict** can be defined as "an expressed struggle between at least two interdependent parties who perceive incompatible goals, scarce rewards, and interference from the other party in achieving their goals" (Hocker & Wilmot, 2006, p. 201). This definition recognizes that two people must be aware of the problem for conflict to occur, and it emphasizes the interconnectedness of both people. We can understand conflict as "a difference that matters" (LeBaron, 2003, p. 11). This definition allows us to focuses on the difference of opinions and beliefs that we often openly see during a conflict.

Now that we know what conflict is, we need to break it down a little further. You probably know from experience that conflict can be extremely destructive to a relationship. This **destructive conflict** usually "results in a worse situation and sometimes, harm to the participants" (Kellett & Dalton, 2001, p. 4). But another type of conflict might actually enhance a relationship. This type of healthy, or **productive conflict**, allows people involved to move "toward resolution" and protects the "psychological and relational health of the participants" (Kellett & Dalton, 2001, p. 4). Productive conflict may benefit the relationship and the people in it in several ways: (1) Conflict can create energy and motivation; (2) conflict can bring out different viewpoints and increase creativity; and (3) conflict can help people understand the argument and themselves as communicators (Walton, 1987).

So, what is required if we seek to have and manage productive conflict in our lives? Four suggestions can help you to continuously seek productive conflict and reduce destructive conflict (Kellett & Dalton, 2001). Figure 6.7 identifies these suggestions and provides an example of self-talk that might be helpful in achieving this.

Seeking productive conflict will not be a one-time event, nor is it something that you can do without hard work. As you notice from the previous suggestions, we should be asking deep questions about the nature of the conflict, prioritizing conflict and concerns, continuously learning, and continuously examining and inquiring about conflict and how it can best be managed. You will want to pay attention to your own needs and tendencies as well as those of your relational partners. This takes time and commitment—and of course, effective communication!

Figure 6.7	**Four Ways to Seek Productive Conflict**

Suggestion	Example
1. **Ask deep questions about conflict experiences.**	Why are we fighting? What are my beliefs and goals? What are the key negotiation principles I should remember? NOT: What's wrong with you?
2. **Learn from your own and other people's conflicts.**	I will focus on understanding this and not brush it under the rug or save it until later.
3. **Make understanding conflicts a priority.**	What has happened in the past that may have started this pattern? What happens with me during conflict?
4. **Manage conflicts by continuously examining and inquiring.**	How might forgiveness change our relationship? How might I manage my communication skills to prevent this from happening in the future?

Hopefully, you have chosen to invest the effort required for productive conflict; however, if it were as simple as choosing one type over another, we certainly would not be spending so much time studying this material. As with conversations, actually managing conflict in the moment is extremely difficult. We are often so emotionally invested and care so much that we forget that the other person is a human being and we use hurtful words, react inappropriately, and make the situation much worse than it originally was. The next section is designed to give you a few pointers for managing conflict and a strong foundation for understanding what is happening in that difficult moment.

How Can Conflict Be Managed?

Before we consider how to manage conflict, it will be important for us to openly recognize the misconceptions that often make conflict even worse. The follow examples illustrate common myths concerning communication and conflict (James, 1996):

- Myth: "If I communicate more, I will clarify everything."
- Myth: "I don't care what people say, there is an easy solution."
- Myth: "I'll just change what I am doing and it should fix everything."
- Myth: "If everything seems peaceful, that must mean there is no conflict."

Many of us have thought or said the previous myths. We need to consider why each of points is in fact a myth (Kellett & Dalton, 2001).

- First "communication concerns quality, not quantity." The type of communication matters more than the amount of communication. Therefore, more communication is not always better and in fact sometimes makes conflicts worse.
- Second, conflicts are often deeply rooted in historical patterns and cultural beliefs. Even when we understand a conflict and work toward an agreement, the conflict does not always disappear. Furthermore, it takes time and hard work to move through many conflicts. Even with hard work, there are still times when you may need to "agree to disagree."

- Third, initially conflicts need to be understood. The understanding should always come before the action. Simply changing behavior will likely not address the root of the problem.
- Fourth, people often choose to avoid conflict or continue to be peaceful around one another even if there is a problem. This is why we must continue to utilize dialogue throughout relationships.

Now we know that we shouldn't handle conflict based on our assumptions and societal myths. The question becomes: How should we handle conflict? We will now focus on foundational conflict management styles, influential factors, and suggested ways to negotiate a conflict.

Conflict Management Styles

Now that we have a foundation for seeking productive conflict, let's consider five conflict management styles (Kilmann & Thomas, 1975). Each style is associated with its degree of cooperativeness or assertiveness and its concern for self or others. Figure 6.8 contains a breakdown of each style. We can use these management styles to improve our understanding of how we individually tend to handle conflict situations (Kellett & Dalton, 2001). While we may tend to prefer a particular conflict management style, it is also important to remain flexible when choosing a style to address a specific situation (Folger, Poole, & Stutman, 2005). Being an effective communicator often requires you to use different styles of conflict management. As you consider each of the following styles, try to determine which style of conflict you use most frequently, but also consider which styles you might use in specific situations.

Let's imagine that you and your best friend have just discovered that both of you are attracted to the same person—we'll name the object of your affection

Figure 6.8   Styles of Conflict Management

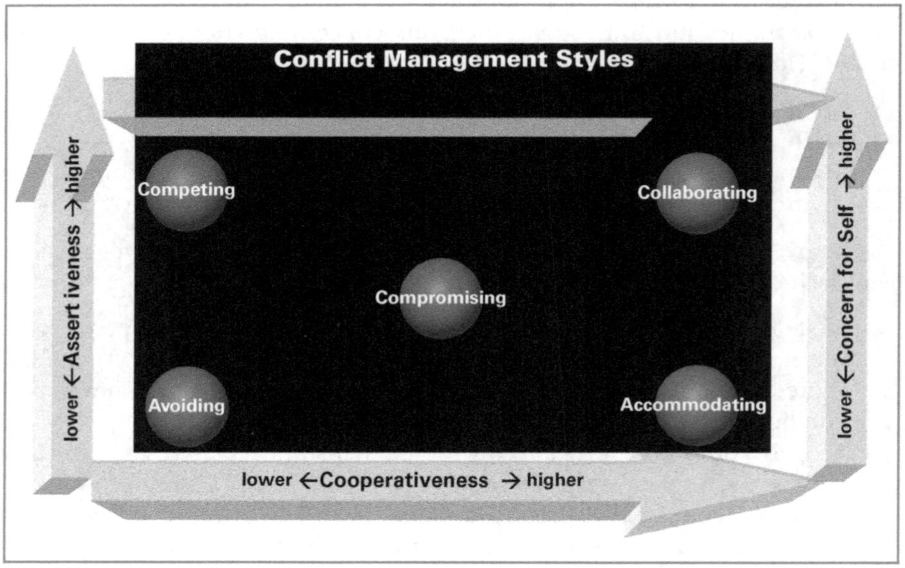

Sources: Folger, Poole, & Stutman (2005); Rahim, Antonioni, & Psenicka (2001)

Jordan. You really like Jordan and think there is potential for a relationship, but you also now know that your best friend feels the same way about Jordan. Both of you want to date Jordan. This has caused a lot of tension. Your friend suggests that the two of you talk. Assuming that Jordan likes both of you, what should you do? This will all depend on the style of conflict management that you choose. Let's look at the options.

Avoiding: You could choose a style that is not assertive or cooperative. Avoiding can be described as trying to ignore the fact that there is a problem. It is the most passive style of conflict management. You might say to yourself, "I'll just pretend that I don't know, and we will just let it blow over." You might choose to simply not respond to the request for conversation, or you may try to delay the conversation. Both of these strategies would suggest that you are avoiding the conflict. The pro of utilizing this style might be that you can side-step confrontation for the moment, but of course the con is that you are also eliminating the chance of working this out. Avoiding conflict is commonly recognized as a no-win style, and as you can see, it reflects low concern for your own needs or the needs of other people.

Accommodating: Your second style option is not assertive, but it is highly cooperative. Accommodating involves going along with what others want, just to appease them and keep everything conflict free. You might agree to the meeting and tell your friend, "I'll just let you date Jordan, you deserve this opportunity more than I do." If you don't openly give in to what your friend wants, you may find yourself continuously apologizing or excessively using disclaimers. Any of these strategies may be used to manage conflict through accommodation. The pro of accommodating might be that you make your friend happy, but the con is that you completely abandon your own needs and desires. Accommodating is commonly known as a lose-win style. It allows your friend to reap all the benefits, but you leave empty-handed.

Competing: Your third option is very assertive, but not very cooperative. Competing can be described as looking to achieve your own goals. If you choose to compete, you will likely agree to the meeting and try to use power, status, or force to convey your ideas. If you think or say something like, "We'll see who wins Jordan over," you are likely competing. The pro of competing might be that you get want you want, but the con is that you may hurt or silence others in doing so. Competing is commonly known as a win-lose style. It allows you to gain, but at someone else's expense.

Compromising: Your fourth option is moderately assertive and moderately cooperative. Compromising can be described as giving something to get something in return. If you choose to compromise, you might continuously restate your desires and summarize your friend's ideas. You might make statements like, "If you are willing to let me go out with Jordan on Friday, then I will let you go out with Jordan on Saturday." The pro of compromising is that both parties have some of their needs and desires met, and it is a quick way to come to a decision. Conversely, the con is that both parties have some needs and desires that remain unmet. For this reason, compromising is commonly known as a lose-lose style. Everybody sacrifices something in the process.

Collaborating: Your final option is highly assertive and highly cooperative. Collaborating can be described as seeking a mutually agreeable solution. You may find yourself deeply exploring a disagreement to see each other's perspectives and then openly sharing all concerns and desires in hopes that the underlying issues can be discovered and an appropriate solution can be implemented.

Suppose as a result of dialogue with your friend, you find that one of you wants Jordan as a date to a specific formal occasion while the other is interested in pursuing an ongoing romance. By sharing the rationales behind your attraction for Jordan, you can help each other. You might encourage Jordan to accompany your friend to the formal event, and during that event your friend could note how eligible you might be for longer-term companionship. The pro of collaborating is that everyone is validated and consensus is reached. The con of collaborating is the time and effort required. If managed effectively, collaborating is commonly known as a win-win style. All parties have their needs met.

So, it is time to choose your style. Figure 6.9 summarizes the five styles. Which approach do you normally use? Do you use this style in all situations? Let's consider a few more factors that may affect or confirm—or challenge—your decisions.

Figure 6.9   Comparison of Conflict Management Styles

Style	Approach	Explanation	Advantages	Drawbacks
Collaborating	Win/win	Seeks mutually beneficial outcomes, inclusive toward others; cooperative partnership	High level of buy-in from all participants; usually yields mutually satisfying outcomes	Time-consuming; requires mutual trust (rare and challenging to develop); requires willingness to share power
Competing	Win/lose	Zero-sum mentality: benefits to one party must come at the expense of others; style often involves dominating or coercing others	Maximizes personal benefits; can motivate high performance to "defeat" competitors	Encourages cutthroat practices; sets up conflict as antagonistic
Accommodating	Lose/win	Voluntary surrender; giving in to someone else	Maximizes generosity toward others; effective as showing obedience	May be seen as weakness; minimizes chance of personal gain; presumes other party is correct
Compromising	Lose/lose	Each party sacrifices something in order to gain something else; "give a little to get a little"	Does not insist on total "victory" for satisfactory outcome; highly flexible as each party can adjust what it gives/gets	All parties may remain dissatisfied; all parties must be willing to sacrifice; high degree of compromise may equal capitulation (e.g., appeasement of Hitler prior to WWII)
Avoiding	Don't play	Refusal to acknowledge or address conflict	Prevents pain and time expenditure of working through conflict	Fails to address root causes of conflict; unaddressed conflict can smolder and intensify

Source: Covey (1989)

THAT'S DEBATABLE

Of the five styles presented we might assume that compromising and col-laboration are the best styles for managing any conflict. However, are there circumstances when avoiding, accommodating, and competing might be more appropriate? Furthermore, how can we effectively collaborate in an individualistic and often competitive society? What resistance might you encounter?

Factors Influencing Conflict Management

As we learned earlier, difference can spark and even define conflict. Certainly, various types of difference can influence your conflict management style and the potential for conflict in the relationship. Power, gender, culture, experience, and context are just a few factors that may highlight differences and conse-quently play a role in conflict and its management.

Power Factors.   Whether we realize it or not, power has the potential to be present in any relationship, and it can affect how conflicts are approached and managed. The classic types of social power originally discussed by French and Raven (1959) can apply to interpersonal conflict. **Power** here refers to the "resources that an influencing agent can utilize in changing the beliefs, atti-tudes, or behaviors" of someone else (Raven, 2001, p. 218). To illustrate how power operates during conflict, suppose you and your instructor are disputing a grade on an assignment.

Referent power: When you have referent power, others identify with you. They look up to you or want to be like you. Referent power describes how someone can serve as a role model. Celebrities use their referent power when they endorse products or services. Example: Your instructor might have referent power because you admire this person's teaching style and connect with the examples and humor during class discussions. You might have referent power because you could represent the type of student the instructor used to be, so the instructor relates to you.

Legitimate power: The power that results from a job title (e.g., president, CEO, military rank), appointment (e.g., the designated leader of a group), or role (e.g., "I'm the oldest") represents what is known as legitimate power. "Legitimate" here does not necessarily mean correct; it describes the way an official position entitles you to exert power. Example: The instructor has legiti-mate power (as part of the job's duties) to determine course policies and assign final grades. You have legitimate power as a student to communicate with your instructor and to ask questions.

Expert power: The special knowledge or skill you possess can confer expert power. The saying "Knowledge is power" refers to expert power. Example: The instructor's expert power depends on proficiency in the subject matter, dem-onstrated by experience, education, publications, or other professional accom-plishments. You might bring expert power to an assignment based on some specialized background you have in a particular topic.

Reward power: This type of power enables you to provide someone with tangible or intangible incentives. If you have reward power, you can offer benefits to someone else for seeing things your way. Example: The instructor has reward power to write you a letter of recommendation in the future. You have the reward power to submit a positive evaluation of the instructor or to nominate the instructor for a teaching award.

Coercive power: Your ability to punish someone or withhold rewards constitutes coercive power. Example: The instructor could threaten to lower any grade that you challenge. You could threaten to lodge a formal complaint with the instructor's supervisor.

Information/Persuasive power: When a full explanation can justify something as desirable, information (also called persuasive) power is at play. You might have information power in a conflict if further information can clear up a misunderstanding. Example: The instructor's information power might lie in revealing details of the assignment that you had overlooked. Your information power might result from noting a portion of your work that the instructor accidentally skipped over while grading.

These types of power often operate together. Rarely does someone hold power in only one of the six dimensions. Understanding the types of power also reveals that while different degrees of power may be present in a conflict, no one is permanently powerless. A skillful communicator should understand how to adapt to each conflict by understanding the proportion of each type of power involved. Example: A teacher could approach conflicts in different classes by adapting power dynamics according to how students respond to various types of power (Tauber, 2007). Reward power might come into play more often with students who respond well to incentives. If students do not value academic credentials, the solution may be to cut back on legitimate power while exercising power in other dimensions.

Knowing the types of power you *can* wield opens up several questions to ask about the power components you *should* use within a conflict:

- Which dimension of power plays the most important role in this conflict? (The answer might be more than one type of power.)
- How do power differences between you and the other party affect your choice of conflict management styles? Which styles are you more or less likely to use given these power dynamics?
- How might different outcomes of this conflict affect the distribution of power? How could your relationship change if the power distribution shifts (with each party gaining or losing various types of power)?
- Which types of power are you willing to use in this conflict? What other sources of power might you choose? What effect might exercising different dimensions of power have on the relationship?

A few patterns have emerged in how the types of power play out during conflicts. Coercive power alone "is generally ineffective in influencing individual outcomes" (Rahim, Antonioni, & Psenicka, 2001, p. 195). The reason is that a threat of punishment might convince someone to avoid harm, but it fails to address the root of the conflict itself. Coercive power and reward power also tend to work best when the person who can punish or reward is present to check for compliance (Raven, 2001). After all, someone may comply with your wishes only to avoid punishment or obtain a reward, not out of respect for you or to resolve the conflict. The other types of power tend to exercise influence without the need for such constant monitoring.

If you are perceived to hold greater power in one or more key power dimension in a relationship, your relational partner may be more likely to avoid or accommodate. Consequently, whoever considers him- or herself more powerful in one or more key dimensions might be more likely to compete. If relational partners hold equal power, they may be more likely to collaborate or compromise. Of course, gaining and losing power may actually cause relational conflict to occur.

Gender and Cultural Influences. Gender and culture may affect the way you express yourself and what you prioritize in conflicts. Everyone enters into conflicts and tries to manage them as "situated actors" (Avruch, 1998, p. 40), meaning that our group identities and cultural values affect our actions. Some researchers have claimed that gender seems to determine how people behave in conflicts (Gray, 1992; Tannen, 1990), but the situation is much more complex.

Gender does influence how people approach conflicts (Campbell, 1993), although it operates alongside other cultural factors (Wood, 2002). In the workplace, research shows that men gravitate toward more competing conflict management styles; however, a person's rank in an organization affects his or her choice of style more than gender (Thomas, Thomas, & Schaubhut, 2008). The more assertive styles (collaborating and competing) tend to be used by higher-ranking workers, while lower-ranking employees use less assertive styles (accommodating and avoiding). Women tend to opt for less competitive styles of conflict management, but gender alone does not explain which style someone will prefer in a specific situation (Folger, Poole, & Stutman, 2005; Shockley-Zalabak & Morley, 1984). Many assumptions about gender and conflict are too simplistic and lack sufficient evidence. For example, "no support was found from either population [students or non-students] for the perspective that females more than males prefer conflict styles requiring concern for relationship orientations or cooperativeness" (Shockley-Zalabak & Morley, 1984, p. 31).

The dimensions of culture have important connections with approaches to conflict. The cultural dimensions of individuality and achievement (masculinity) show stronger tendencies toward competitive styles (Mohammed, White, & Prabhakar, 2008). In high power distance cultures, those who occupy lower-power positions tend to avoid challenging those in positions of power or accommodate them. Highly individualistic cultures will gravitate toward styles that emphasize more concern for self, while more collectivist cultures will prefer styles that prioritize concern for others (Kaushal & Kwantes, 2006).

Confirmation and Disconfirmation

Now let's turn our attention to a few specific skills that can help you to manage conflict in the moment. We discussed the importance of confirmation for healthy relationships (Laing, 1961). **Confirmation** is simply a message that conveys the idea that an individual exists and matters. This type of communication would be especially beneficial during a conflict. Even if you disagree with someone's position, you still can recognize that person's inherent value. Certainly we would not want to utilize **disconfirmation**, or messages that suggest that an individual does not matter or even exist. Specific methods of confirmation can make a positive difference in conflict situations (Cissna & Sieberg, 2009).

Recognition.   This is the most basic type of confirmation, yet unfortunately we don't always remember to use it. If you have ever not responded to a text message or not acknowledged someone that you know when you see him or her in the store, then you may have missed an opportunity for confirming. By simply saying, "Hi," making strategic eye contact, or calling someone by name, we can recognize and confirm someone. Sometimes the failure to issue recognition can begin a conflict.

Acknowledgment.   One step up from recognition is acknowledgment. When we acknowledge someone, we intentionally summarize or reflect on the content or emotions that we hear. To practice acknowledgment we will need to listen actively, perhaps asking questions to clarify the message. We might also paraphrase the other person's ideas or note his or her feelings. Example: "I can see you find Jordan very attractive." In the heat of a serious conflict, acknowledgment immediately offers a point of agreement. No matter how opposed your viewpoints are, you and the other person can agree on what each of you is saying and feeling.

Endorsement.   The highest level of confirmation is endorsement. This means that we find something in the other's message that we agree with and share this with them. Endorsement does not mean we must agree with everything the person says, but we select at least one piece of the message to support. We might agree with the individual that the issue at hand is something we both need to address and take responsibility for, or we might agree that the problem is important.

If it sounds like you use confirmation in your daily interactions and during conflict situations, you are on the right track. Remember that like the opening of a conversation, confirmation is important for moving forward in the discussion.

Negotiation

Exactly how does the process of handling a conflict proceed? Here we move into the territory of **negotiation**, defined as "a process of communication between at least two parties, from individuals to states (in which case it goes by a special name, diplomacy). In negotiation, the two parties become interlocutors: they engage in an extended conversation about their dispute" (Avruch, 1998, p. 39). More specifically, negotiation refers to the strategic movement through concerns that involves a process of give and take to address the needs and values of all parties (Fisher & Ertel, 1995; Johnson, 1993). Fisher and Ury (1981) developed four foundational principles that have helped many people to work through conflict. These principles outline a method known as **principled negotiation**, which enables all parties to seek mutual benefit and helps them to develop and implement fair standards for evaluation. Figure 6.10 contains a basic overview of the four principles (Fisher & Ury, 1981, p.11).

The first aspect of principled negation to consider is to focus on the *people* and not the problem. Have you ever lashed out at your best friend or attempted to humiliate your significant other? If so, you were probably more focused on the problem than you were the people involved. We must remember to always recognize (beginning with confirmation) the individual perceptions

Figure 6.10	**Principled Negotiation**		
Area of Concern	**Basic Principle**	**Rationale**	**Example in Negotiations**
People	Separate the people from the problem.	Personal attacks cause defensiveness and shut down open, honest communication.	Adopt a "nothing personal" rule for discussions: Criticize ideas but not the people who offer them.
Interests	Focus on interests, not positions.	Find potential connections among underlying values that can lead to solutions.	Ask what needs or core values the other party wants to fulfill through his or her positions.
Options	Generate a variety of possibilities before deciding what to do.	Maximize opportunities for finding desirable outcomes.	Entertain proposals that neither party had considered before.
Criteria	Insist that the result be based on some objective standard that does not favor one party over the other.	Everyone needs ground rules to determine what would be agreeable outcomes.	Settle on what a "good" outcome must include, preferably based on shared interests.

of everyo ne involved. We need to protect the feelings of others as well as ourselves and understand the emotions being expressed. Anyone who feels personally vulnerable to attack will not communicate openly and honestly in negotiations. Understanding emotions does not mean that it is appropriate to react without checking your emotions—so use your emotional intelligence (Cooper & Sawaf, 1997). Remain calm and focus on working jointly to build the relationship. The participants in negotiations operate best as partners trying to find solutions together, not as adversaries trying to beat each other (Nierenburg & Ross, 1985).

Recognizing individual *interests* and not just the positions that the parties are taking will be critical for negotiation. If you have ever viewed the people in a conflict as being on "two different sides of the coin," then you were probably focusing more on the position they were taking and not their interests. If you can determine the interests (or values) of each individual, then you should be able to define the problem. Consider not only what the other party wants, but why he or she wants it. There may be ways to satisfy those interests aside from the positions being taken. The goal here is to find shared interests. Remember that Maslow's hierarchy of needs showed we all have the same basic needs, so this might be a great place to start. Finding interests might require that you ask "why" someone is advocating a specific plan or seeking a particular goal.

Seeking *options* may sound fairly simple, yet the problem that many people encounter is not seeking enough options. On the surface it may seem that there are only two options: "We move to the mountains" or "We move to the beach." In reality, there are many more options. Just think of all of the different places to live in the world. As we learned earlier, there may not be only one solution, so remain open-minded. Be careful not to present options that simply solve the "current problem." Again, as mentioned before, there is a possibility that the most recent "fight" is a symptom of a deeper problem. Finally, use brainstorming methods and always avoid the trap of "either-or" think that assumes choosing one option excludes all others. Seek options that help both parties to benefit equally.

The principle that is often the most difficult, and overlooked, is *criteria*. Have you ever had a class assignment that included the criteria for earning a passing grade? Conflict negotiation can work in a similar way. Recall when one of your instructors assigned a paper with several requirements or rules (e.g., the paper must be between 8 and 10 pages; references must be cited in a certain format; it must contain a thesis, literature review, methodology, and discussion). Now, hopefully this has never happened to you, but what if you decided to ignore or overlook these requirements and instead created a fictional story with no references that was 20 pages long? My guess is that the outcome you had hoped for—a good grade—was not achieved. Now, what if you never had any criteria in the first place? There would be no way for you or your instructor to determine successful completion. What does this teach us? Just as we must have and follow criteria to create a product, we must do the same to have a strong negotiation process. The criteria that you create should not favor either party and recognize fair standards and procedures. All parties in the conflict must agree to abide by the criteria in choosing and implementing a solution. Then comes the hard part: Both parties must actually use the criteria during their discussion.

Principled negotiation is not the only negotiation method for managing conflict. **Dialogic negotiation** focuses on understanding the meaning of a conflict by understanding the ways the stories of participants intersect (Kellett, 2007). This strategy combines key elements of negotiation with the basic principles of dialogue. In dialogic negotiation, each party has the opportunity to explain his or her story of how the conflict originated and progressed. The stories include reflections on how the conflict affects each participant. Instead of telling "my side" or "your side," the participants commit to appreciating the feelings and needs expressed in each other's story—not simply advocating their own side. By revealing the stories that surround and ground the apparent conflict, each person can begin to understand how the other is constructing the meaning of the conflict. From that understanding, an approach to the conflict can emerge that addresses the values and meanings each person seeks from the conflict.

Dialogic negotiation can delve into the personal history each person brings into a specific conflict. This type of deep revelation requires a firm foundation of trust that enables open disclosure. Dialogic negotiation therefore may require a lot of time to develop, and it presumes everyone's readiness to risk telling how a conflict intersects with other aspects of their life. The reward, however, is that participants may find new and more permanent ways to connect with each other by noticing how the story of the conflict fits within larger life stories.

HONE YOUR SKILLS IN CONVERSATION AND CONFLICT MANAGEMENT

In previous sections of this chapter, we addressed specific aspects of conversation and conflict. But wait—didn't we say that perhaps the hardest part of managing conflict is actually developing skills and determining what you will say in the moment? The final section of this chapter is dedicated to helping you to (1) identify specific skills for difficult conversational moments and (2) recognize some ways to de-escalate conflicts that start to get out of control.

Skills for Difficult Conversational Moments

Because we now have a foundational understanding of conversation and the potential conflicts that may occur, we should consider specific challenging situations that we may encounter. For each of the situations that follow you will find specific suggestions for how to handle the difficult conversational moment.

How to Express Feelings.   Conversations about people, events, or things might not present much of a challenge; talking about how we feel is a different matter altogether. How do we express feelings honestly without letting our emotions run wild and possibly damage our relationships? Four steps can enable progress toward communicating feelings constructively (Fox-Hines, 2001; Gilles, 1974).

1. *Acceptance:* Accept that you are human, and humans have feelings and emotions *as well as* thoughts and ideas. Acknowledge your feelings and then consider what you want to do with them.
2. *Nondestructive expression:* Once you have acknowledged you do feel a certain feeling or combination of feelings, it is important to find some way to express those feelings ("good" and "bad") in a way that is safe and not harmful to yourself or to others. This might include physical and nonphysical methods such as running, crying, writing feelings, or talking about feelings.
3. *Redirection:* After expressing feelings, it is often good to stop and take several nice, deep slow breaths. As relaxation increases, ask yourself: "What do I want to do about this?" "Are there any actions that would be helpful to take?" "What would be the most helpful, useful thing to do now?" "Do I want to talk to someone else about my feelings? Do I want to talk now?"
4. *Action:* After considering the facts, the situation, the consequences, etc., you are ready to put things into perspective make decision to act (make an assertive request, lodge an assertive complaint, leave a relationship) or to not act (truly let go of the feeling, decide that "in the great cosmic picture" it isn't worth your energy).

How to Handle Egocentric Communicators.   "It's all about me, me, me." "If I want your opinion, I'll give it to you."

The preceding statements describe the attitude of an **egocentric** communicator: someone who focuses on him- or herself while ignoring or dismissing others. This person is likely to engage only in monologue and not dialogue. What should you do when confronting an egocentric conversationalist? Several responses could rechannel the conversation to its proper focus:

- Reframe the conversation, establishing explicit guidelines. Example: "Let's approach the issue as something that affects both of us."
- Set procedural or content guidelines. Example: "Let's make a deal: Nobody uses the pronouns 'I' or 'me' in our conversation."

- Reciprocate by responding to each personal example or story with one of your own. Example: "OMG, that happened to me last week too." By contributing more of your own content to the interaction, you place yourself on a more equal footing within the conversation.

How to Revive Conversations. We've all experienced those awkward moments of conversational silence. Luckily, you might be able to employ some tactics to restore lively interaction (Aaker, Kumar, & Day, 2007).

- *Chain reaction:* If you are in a group, ask each person to comment on an idea someone else expressed earlier. Not only does this tactic build on each person's contributions, but it encourages better listening because everyone has to connect what one person says to someone else's comments. Example: "We just heard from Hildegaard. Now, Rajiv, how would you react to her proposal?"
- *Devil's advocate:* Take an extreme position on an unexpected viewpoint to stimulate more reaction. The surprise might energize the entire conversation. Caution: Use this tactic carefully, since you must remain within the bounds of propriety for the conversation to continue. An extreme position also does not mean an offensive one. Example: "Our discussion of pesticide safety has reached an impasse. I think we should simply ban all pesticides and see what happens."
- *False termination:* Act as if the conversation has ended by offering closure and ask for final questions. Just as the "last call" at a bar generates a flurry of drink orders, this conversational "last call" might spur a slew of new ideas. Example: "I'm glad we've had this talk. Anything else before I go?"

Skills for Coping with Conflict

Sometimes you might find a conflict spiraling out of control. The dispute might threaten to become too nasty to permit any approach toward negotiation. A few communication tools might de-escalate a conflict so that everyone becomes more willing to manage the situation.

How to Deal with Anger. In many settings, people operate under severe stress. While it is tempting to lash out at people who might complain or even verbally abuse you, remember that the distress of coping with fear, pain, or loss can make others edgy. When you feel your own anger building or encounter an angry person, the following techniques can help avoid a bitter dispute (Williams & Williams, 1994).

- *Validate the person's feelings.* Say that you understand and recognize that the person is angry. If you say, "I certainly see you're upset," you preserve the person's right to his or her feelings. You can accept that a person feels a certain way even if you do not agree with the reasons for his or her reactions.
- *Establish a connection with the other person.* If you find some basis for common ground, you will show that you and the other person are on the same side and can work together to solve the problem. A comment as

Anger and verbal aggression can undermine the productive aspects of conflict.

Source: © 2010 by Yuri Arcurs. Used under license from Shutterstock, Inc.

simple as "I also can't stand it when people give me the runaround" can show you are an ally, not an antagonist.

- *Maintain a calm tone.* Don't raise your voice, even if the other person rants and raves. Usually, someone who shouts will lower the volume quickly if the other person does not shout back. Since we tend to adapt to the communication behaviors of others, calmness breeds calmness.
- *Listen carefully and try to understand why the person is angry.* Sometimes dissatisfaction results from a simple misunderstanding. Don't interrupt, let the other person have his or her say, and then try to understand the other person's viewpoint.

How to Help Others Save Face.   The idea of **facework** deals with a communicator's attempt to maintain a positive sense of worth and dignity for themselves and others in public (Ting-Toomey & Kurogi, 1998). When we employ **face-saving** approaches to conflict, we communicate in ways that preserve the dignity and value of ourselves and others. Face-saving encourages respect for differing viewpoints and discourages personal attacks. **Face-detracting** communication robs someone of dignity, humiliating or shaming the person. To help others save face, you could try the following techniques:

- *Do seek understanding with others:* "I don't quite understand the question" or "I disagree with the premise of that question."
  Don't say: "That's a stupid question."
- *Do seek common ground:* "Let's see if we can find something we agree on."
  Don't say: "There are two approaches here: my way and the wrong way."
- *Do allow graceful exits:* "Could we agree to disagree?"
  Don't say: "We're going to continue until you admit everything was your fault."
- *Do value others:* "I understand your point, although I don't agree with it because…"
  Don't say: "There you go again. Blah, blah, blah. Yada, yada, yada."
- *Do use indirectness:* "Your proposal may not be among the most attractive options after we consider all the alternatives."
  Don't say: "Your proposal is absurd."

Saving face has important consequences in conflicts. "Repeated face-loss and face-threat often lead to escalatory conflict spirals or an impasse in the conflict negotiation process" (Ting-Toomey, 2007, p. 257). One way to separate the person from the problem in negotiations would be to commit to saving the face of the other party.

Saving face traditionally has played an important role in many Asian cultures. The government of South Korea expressed collective shame when it was disclosed that the murderer of 32 Virginia Tech students in April 2007 was a Korean American. South Korea is concerned with its public image (i.e., its face), and "its group-oriented culture means the achievements of the few are marshaled into rallying cries for the many" (Herman, 2007). We also must remember that high collectivism does not mean that every person will act or react the same way—only that each person feels more connected to other cultural cohorts.

Skillful management of conflict allows participants to save face even if they "lose." The sense of fair play in athletics practices face-saving by celebrating the efforts of all players, not just the winners. In conflicts, you can save face by appreciating the *process* of managing the conflict even if the outcome was not what you desired. Saving face includes being gracious to opposing sides in victory or defeat.

Throughout this chapter, we have presented both theoretical concepts and practical suggestions for creating effective conversations and managing productive conflict. Now it is your turn. The next time you need to have a conversation with one of your professors or a conflict arises with your best friend, try implementing some of the techniques we have discussed. You might find you not only get more accomplished, but you also might develop more satisfying relationships.

HIGHLIGHTS

1. Conversations proceed in several stages.
   a. The opening generally includes a greeting, phatic communication, and perhaps reference to something that connects the participants.
   b. Feedforward prepares for the conversation to follow. It establishes the rules and roles that govern the interaction.
   c. The focus of conversation is its substance. Cooperative principles guide our interactions. Dialogue can enrich participation and deepen understanding during conversation.
   d. Feedback offers information about the conversation. Some conversations are conducted primarily to exchange feedback.
   e. The closing concludes conversation while remaining positive about the interaction.
2. Conflict is common and unavoidable, but does not have to be destructive.
3. The five conflict styles represent different ways to deal with conflict.
   a. Avoiding is withdrawing from or ignoring the situation.
   b. Accommodating is giving in to appease others and keep peace.
   c. Competing is trying to gain an advantage at the expense of someone else.
   d. Compromising is sacrificing something in order to get something.
   e. Collaborating is cooperating with others to reach a mutually agreeable outcome.
4. Gender and culture will likely play a role in relational expectations and conflict management.
5. Confirmation is a key step in recognizing the other person during a conflict.
6. Principled negotiation allows you to focus on finding ways for both parties to benefit and find objective ways to solve the conflict.
   a. Separate people from the problem.
   b. Focus on interests and not positions.
   c. Seek a variety of options.
   d. Establish and follow objective criteria.
7. Dialogic negotiation focuses on creating shared meaning of the conflict in an effort to reach a mutually satisfactory outcome.
8. Difficult conversational moments require specific skills and considerations.
   a. Constructive communication of feelings links expressing emotions with deciding what to do about them.
   b. You can rechannel a conversation so egocentric communicators do not monopolize discussion.
   c. Conversations that lapse can be revived.

9. Communication techniques can prevent a conflict from escalating.
   a. Anger is best met with acknowledgment and not with further anger.
   b. Face-saving can preserve your own and the other party's dignity.

APPLY YOUR KNOWLEDGE

SL = Activities appropriate for service learning
🖳 = Computer activities focusing on research and information management
🎬 = Activities involving film or television
♫ = Activities involving music

1. SL Identify a conflict that your community partner has encountered. Critically examine the nature of the conflict according to the following dimensions.
   A. What approach to "winning" did the primary participants take in the conflict? How productive was this approach?
   B. What conflict management style did each participant use? Provide specific examples from the conflict that support your assessment.
   C. In your opinion, what conflict management style or styles *should* the participants have used? What could these different styles accomplish in the situation?
2. Reflect on a conflict you have had with a friend or family member. Now, write out an effective conversation that would help you and your relational partner work through the conflict. Be specific and remember to implement confirmation and the principles of negotiation. Based on your new discoveries, what will you do differently to handle your next conflict with this individual?
3. 🖳 Track a current event that involves a conflict between nations or within a nation. According to your research in reliable news sources, what is causing the conflict? Describe how the conflict might be approached using each of the conflict styles discussed in this chapter. Which of these styles offers the best promise for managing the conflict? Why would this style make the best choice?
4. 🎬 ♫ Identify a movie, sitcom, or song that depicts two characters in dialogue. How are they upholding the requirements of dialogue? Are there any challenges or obstacles that may threaten their use of dialogue?
5. 🖳 Save all of the (non-confidential) e-mails you receive over the next few days. Examine these e-mails for effective or ineffective conversational techniques. What specific examples do you find of miscommunication in each of the following areas? How would you recommend the e-mails be altered to make better use of conversational techniques?
   A. Opening
   B. Feedforward
   C. Focus
   D. Feedback
   E. Closing

REFERENCES

Aaker, D. A., Kumar, V., & Day, G. S. (2007). *Marketing research* (9th ed.). New York: John Wiley and Sons.

Alberts, J. K., Yoshimura, C. G., Rabby, M., & Loschiavo, R. (2005). Mapping the topography of couples' daily conversation. *Journal of Social and Personal Relationships, 22*, 299–322.

Arnett, R. C., & Arneson, P. (1999). *Dialogic civility in a cynical age: Community, hope, and interpersonal relationships*. Albany: State University of New York Press.

Avruch, K. (1998). *Culture and conflict resolution*. Washington, DC: United States Institute of Peace.

Bach, K. (2006). The top 10 misconceptions about implicature. In B. J. Birner & G. Ward (Eds.), *Drawing the boundaries of meaning: Neo-Gricean studies in pragmatics and semantics in honor of Laurence R. Horn* (pp. 21–30). Amsterdam: John Benjamins.

Baxter, L. A. (2007). Problematizing the problem in communication: A dialogic perspective. *Communication Monographs, 74*(1), 118–124.

Beach, W. A., & Dunning, D. G. (1982). Pre-indexing and conversational organization. *Quarterly Journalof Speech, 68*, 170–185.

Brigg, M. (2008). *The new politics of conflict resolution: Responding to difference*. New York: Palgrave Macmillan.

Burnard, P. (2003). Ordinary chat and therapeutic conversation: Phatic communication and mental health nursing. *Journal of Psychiatric and Mental Health Nursing, 10*, 678–682.

Campbell, A. (1993). *Men, women, and aggression*. New York: Basic Books.

Cissna, K. N., & Anderson, R. (1994). The 1957 Martin Buber-Carl Rogers dialogue, as dialogue. *Journal of Humanistic Psychology, 34*(1), 11–45.

Cissna, K. N. L., & Seiberg, E. (2009). Patterns of interactional confirmation and disconfirmation. In J. Stewart (Ed.), *Bridges not walls* (9th ed.; pp. 429–439). New York: McGraw-Hill.

Cooper, R. K., & Sawaf, A. (1997). *Executive EQ: Emotional intelligence in leadership and organizations*. New York: Perigee.

Covey, S. R. (1989). *The seven habits of highly effective people: Restoring the character ethic*. New York: Simon and Schuster.

DeVito, J. A. (2005). *Essentials of human communication* (5th ed.). Boston: Allyn and Bacon.

Fisher, R. & Ertel, D. (1995). *Getting ready to negotiate: A step-by-step guide preparing for any negotiation*. New York: Penguin.

Fisher, R. & Ury, W. (1981). *Getting to yes: Negotiating agreement without giving in*. Boston: Houghton Mifflin.

Folger, J. P., Poole, M. S., & Stutman, R. K. (2005). *Working through conflict: Strategies for relationships, groups, and organizations* (5th ed.). New York: HarperCollins.

Fox-Hines, R. (2001). *Four steps in dealing with feelings*. Unpublished manuscript.

Franco, L. (2006). Forms of conversation and problem structuring methods: A conceptual development. *Journal of the Operational Research Society, 57*, 813–821.

French, J. R. P., Jr,, & Raven, B. H. (1959). The bases of social power. In D. Cartwright (Ed.), *Studies in social power* (pp. 150–167). Ann Arbor, MI: Institute for Social Research.

Gill, D., & Adams, B. (1998). *ABC of communication studies* (2nd ed.). Cheltenham, UK: Nelson Thornes.

Gilles, J. (1974). *My needs, your needs, our needs*. New York: Doubleday.

Gottman, J. M., Levenson, R. W., Gross, J., Frederickson, B. L., McCoy, K., Rosenthal, L., Ruef, A., & Yoshimoto, D. (2003). Correlates of gay and lesbian couples' relationship satisfaction and relationship dissolution. *Journal of Homosexuality, 45*, 23–43.

Gray, J. (1992). *Men are from mars, women are from Venus*. New York; Harper-Collins.

Grice, H. P. (1975). Logic and conversation. P. Cole & J. Morgan (Eds.), *Syntax and semantics, volume 3: Speech acts* (pp. 41–58). New York: Academic Press.

Herman, B. (2007, April 20). Sympathy and shame in South Korea. *Washington Post.* Retrieved April 20, 2007, from http://www.washingtonpost.com/wpdyn/content/article/2007/04/20/AR2007042001042.html

Hocker, J. L., & Wilmot, W. W. (2006) Collaborative negotiation. In K. Galvin & P. Cooper (Eds.), *Making connections* (4th ed.; pp. 201–208). Los Angeles: Roxbury.

James, J. (1996). *Thinking in the future tense: Leadership skills for a new age.* New York: Simon & Schuster.

Jehn, K., Chadwick, C., & Thatcher, S. (1997). To agree or not to agree: The effects of value congruence, individual demographic dissimilarity, and conflict on workgroup outcomes. *International Journal of Conflict Management, 8*(4), 287–305.

Johnson, R. A. (1993). *Negotiation basics: Concepts, skills, and exercises.* Newbury Park, CA: Sage.

Kaushal, R., & Kwantes, C. T. (2006). The role of culture and personality in choice of conflict management strategy. *International Journal of Intercultural Relations, 30,* 579–603.

Kellett, P. M. (2007). *Conflict dialogue: Working with layers of meaning for productive relationships.* Thousand Oaks, CA: Sage.

Kellett, P. M., & Dalton, D. G. (2001). *Managing conflict in a negotiated world: A narrative approach to achieving dialogue and change.* Thousand Oaks, CA: Sage.

Kilmann, R. H., & Thomas, K. W. (1975). Interpersonal conflict handling behavior as reflections of Jungian personality dimensions. *Psychological Reports, 37,* 971–980.

Laing, R. D. (1961). *Self and others.* New York: Pantheon.

LeBaron, M. (2003). *Bridging cultural conflicts: A new approach for a changing world.* San Francisco, CA: Jossey-Bass.

Likert, R., & Likert, J. G. (1976). *New ways of managing conflict.* New York: McGraw-Hill.

Malone, M. J. (1995). How to do things with friends: Altercasting and recipient design. *Research on Language and Social Interaction, 28,* 147–170.

Melchin, K. & Picard, C. (2008). *Transforming conflict through insight.* Toronto: University of Toronto Press.

Mohammed, U. K., White, G. R. T., & Prabhakar, G. P. (2008). Culture and conflict management style of international project managers. *International Journal of Business and Management, 3*(5), 3–11.

Murphy, P. (2005, May 7). How to master the art of conversation. *Ezine Articles.* Retrieved December 17, 2009, from http://ezinearticles.com/?How-To-Master-The-Art-of-Conversation&id=33622

Nierenburg, J., & Ross, I. S. (1985). *Women and the art of negotiating.* New York: Simon and Schuster.

Rahim, M., Antonioni, D., & Psenicka, C. (2001). A structural equations model of leader power, subordinates' styles of handling conflict, and job performance. *International Journal of Conflict Management, 12*(3), 191–211.

Raven, B. H. (2001). Power/interaction and interpersonal influence: Experimental investigations and case studies. In A. Y. Lee-Chai & J. A. Bargh (Eds.), *The use and abuse of power: Multiple perspectives on the causes of corruption* (pp. 217–240). Philadelphia: Psychology Press.

Shockley-Zalabak, P., & Morley, D. (1984). Sex differences in conflict style preferences. *Communication Research Reports, 1*(1), 28–32.

Tannen, D. (1990). *You just don't understand: Women and men in conversation.* New York: Ballantine.

Tauber, R. T. (2007). *Classroom management: Sound theory and effective practice* (4th ed.). Westport, CT: Praeger.

Thomas, K., Thomas, G., & Schaubhut, N. (2008). Conflict styles of men and women at six organization levels. *International Journal of Conflict Management, 19*(2), 148–166.

Ting-Toomey, S. (2007). Intercultural conflict training: Theory-practice approaches and research challenges. *Journal of Intercultural Communication Research, 36*(3), 255–271.

Ting-Toomey, S., & Kurogi, A. (1998). Facework competence in intercultural conflict: An updated face-negotiation theory. *International Journal of Intercultural Relations, 22,* 187–225.

Walton, R. E. (1987). *Managing conflict: Interpersonal dialogue and third-party roles* (2nd ed.). Reading, MA: Addison-Wesley.

Weinstein, E. A., & Deutschberger, P. (1963). Some dimensions of altercasting. *Sociometry, 26,* 454–466.

Williams, R., & Williams, V. (1994). *Anger kills: Seventeen strategies for controlling the hostility that can harm your health.* New York: Harper Perennial.

Wood, J. T. (2002). A critical essay on John Gray's portrayals of men, women, and relationships. *Southern Journal of Communication, 67,* 201–210.

Initiating Relationships:
"Haven't We Met Somewhere Before?"

OBJECTIVES

- Explain four primary reasons people initiate interpersonal relationships.
- Identify three types of attraction: physical, social, and task. Describe the impact of demographic differences on perceptions of attraction.
- Recognize the three dimensions of similarity that influence decisions to initiate relationships.
- Describe the role of disclosure and reciprocal disclosure on relationship initiation.
- Discuss the role of question-asking in reducing uncertainty in relationship initiation.
- Explain five stages in the process of forming relationships.

SCENARIO: SOUND FAMILIAR?

Amelia went to Southwest University's first home football game with a group of friends. As she was cheering on the team with her friends, her roommate grabbed her arm and whispered in her ear, "Don't look now, but there's a cute guy seated in the next section and he keeps looking over here!" Amelia sneaked a glance and noticed a classmate from her biology class looking at her. He quickly glanced away when she caught him looking and immediately got up to go to the concession stand. As he returned, he stopped next to Amelia's seat and said, "Hey, my name is Patrick. Don't you sit behind me in BIOS 1010? Are you ready for our midterm on Monday?" They chatted about the exam for a few minutes, then Patrick asked if anyone was sitting next to Amelia. She smiled and moved over to make room on the bleacher. They spent the rest of the game talking about their love of football, discovering that they had attended rival high schools, and they made plans to get together the following day to study for their biology exam.

KEY TERMS

Attachment security	Context	Experimenting
Attitude similarity	Costs	False homophily
Background similarity	Demographic	Flirtatious
Bonding	similarity	communication
Breadth	Depth	Goals
Complementarity	Duration	ideal-self Similarity

From *Interpersonal Communication: Building Rewarding Relationships*, Second Edition by Melissa Bekelja Wanzer, Kristen Campbell Eichhorn, and Candice Thomas-Maddox. Copyright © by Kendall Hunt Publishing Company. Reprinted by permission.

Impression management	Predicted outcome value	Similarity to current self
Initiation	Private communication	Social attractiveness
Integrating	Proximity	Social exchange theory
Intensifying	Reciprocal self-disclosure	Social penetration theory
Interpersonal attraction	Relationship	Social goals
Intimate communication	Rewards	superficial communication
Obligatory relationships	Role	Task attractiveness
Personal communication	Rules	Task goals
Physical attractiveness	Self-disclosure	Uncertainty reduction theory
	Self-monitoring	Voluntary relationships
	Similarity	

OVERVIEW

Recalling how a relationship began often results in the telling of stories in which individuals share their perceptions of what prompted their initial inter-action. As the telling of the story unfolds, partners may find that each of their views of events differs slightly. While one person may insist that it was his witty opening line that started it all, the other person may insist that she was ini-tially attracted by a shy smile. We are intrigued by stories of "first encounters." Consider the popularity of the television series *How I Met Your Mother*. The show focuses on Ted's narrative, in which he explains to his children how he initiated his relationship with their mother.

As viewers watched Ted's story evolve during nine seasons of *How I Met Your Mother*, it became apparent that relationships aren't easy. A vari-ety of factors cause us to be initially attracted to one another, and these ultimately influence our decision to further pursue relationships. After all, relationships require a significant amount of time and energy. Consider the fact that *every* relationship we are involved in had to start somewhere. In this chapter we take a close look at how we define the term *relationship* and how and why relationships are initially established. We also look at the communication behaviors and strategies used in the early stages of a relationship.

THE ROLE OF COMMUNICATION IN RELATIONSHIP DEVELOPMENT

The decision to begin a new relationship is filled with a myriad of emotions—confusion, excitement, anxiety, and perhaps even apprehension. First, a person must decide whether to approach another person to initiate a conversation. Then the challenge involves determining *how* to make the initial approach in order to convey a positive image. What opening line or verbal message should be used to make the all-important first impression? In addition to finding the right words, let us not forget the impact of nonverbal messages on the relation-ship initiation process. After all, we form our initial perceptions about others based on nonverbal cues such as how someone is dressed and whether they make eye contact.

In addition, we also need to consider the role that self-perception plays in the process. As discussed in Chapter 2, someone with a low level of self-esteem will face unique challenges when initiating a relationship compared to a person who has a positive self-image.

As we begin our discussion of relationship initiation, it is important to define what we mean by the term *relationship*. If you are involved in a relationship at this very moment, please raise your hand. Do you have your hand up? If not, you should probably reconsider how you define this term. When we have asked this question in our interpersonal communication classes, only a few students initially raise their hands. But after much prompting with questions such as, "Are you *sure* you're not involved in *any* relationships right now?" every member of the class has a hand in the air. Our culture biases our perception about what it means to be "in a relationship." Immediately, most people think of a "relationship" as involving romance. However, we are all involved in a number of different types of relationships at any given time. Examples of these include:

- Friendships
- Family relationships
- Coworker relationships
- Teacher-student relationships
- Employee-customer relationships
- Patient-physician relationships

Throughout this chapter, we encourage you to consider how each of the concepts applies in the various relationships you have formed in your own life.

RELATIONSHIP DEFINED

We encounter countless messages about relationships on a daily basis. While waiting in the supermarket checkout line, you will see magazine covers that make claims about the status of celebrity relationships. Tweets or news stories speculating about who's dating whom are constantly updated on Internet sites. Facebook ads beckon us to "click now" to learn how to attract others with a sensuous new hairstyle, clever banter, or trendy apparel. Even if you do not venture near the magazine section or notice the Internet headlines, take a moment to consider common themes of popular songs. Many contain references to the various stages of relationships, from first encounters to breakups. Messages about relationships are everywhere!

A work relationship can start out as obligatory, but it may later transform into a voluntary friendship.

A relationship can be defined as a connection between two individuals that results in mutual interaction with the intent of achieving shared meaning. In this chapter, we focus primarily on voluntary relationships, which differ greatly from those that are obligatory or involuntary. Our relationships with friends, roommates, and romantic partners are considered

relationship a connection between two individuals that results in mutual interaction with the intent of achieving shared meaning.

voluntary interpersonal relationships entered into by choice or of one's own volition.

obligatory/involuntary often occur by chance and not by choice. Also referred to as "involuntary" relationships.

voluntary because we enter into them of our own volition. Relationships with family members and coworkers are often defined as obligatory/involuntary because they often occur by chance and not by choice. Some relationships, like those we form with coworkers, may start out as obligatory and transform into voluntary ones. We begin by describing important elements of relationships.

THE NATURE OF RELATIONSHIPS

We often use descriptors or referents to describe and categorize the numerous relationships in which we are involved. Three categories often used to describe the nature of a relationship include references to duration, context, and roles.

Duration references used to describe the length of time we have known the other person.

Duration. Duration references are used to describe the length of time we have known the other person. Statements such as "my friend from kindergarten," "my new coworker," and "an acquaintance I met last week" are used to describe the duration or how long we have known the other person. These terms provide insight as to the amount of time that the relational partners have had to share information about each other.

context references regarding the setting in which the relationship was initiated.

Context. In some instances, relationships are described by referring to the context, or setting, in which the relationship was initiated. "Friends from the soccer team," "committee members from the PTO," or "coworkers on a project team," provide information about the environment in which the relationship exists.

By making reference to the relationship context, clues are offered with regard to the rules or expectations for communication. Rules may be explicitly stated. A boss may openly state to employees that there is an "open door"

rules expectations for communication in relationships. May be explicitly stated or implicit.

> **Figure 7.1** **Referents used to categorize or define the nature of relationships**

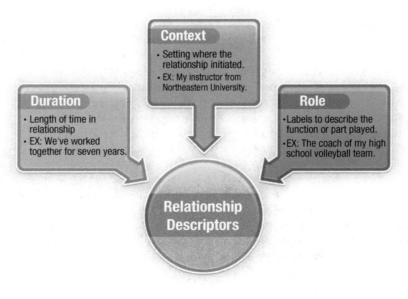

policy in the office, indicating that employees should feel comfortable walking in without an appointment to discuss issues. Other rules are implicitly understood. Teammates have a mutual understanding that emotions have an impact on how messages are created and interpreted on game day. If a teammate has a bad game, the unspoken rule may be that it is probably not wise to discuss the errors that were made in the game. It is important to note that rules regarding the appropriateness of topics and the acceptable depth of discussions may differ from context to context. While an individual may be comfortable disclosing her intimate feelings about her newest romantic partner with a family member, such information could be viewed as highly inappropriate in the workplace.

role   labels or descriptors used to define the nature of a relationship.

Role.   Finally, references to a person's **role** may be used to describe the nature of a relationship. Terms such as *mother, teacher, supervisor, friend, colleague,* or *coach* are used to describe the role an individual plays in a particular relationship. It is important to note that labels used to describe roles can provide insight into the contextual nature of the relationship and shed light on the rules and expectations for interactions. More formality is needed when a student engages in an interaction with a teacher than when calling up a family member to discuss a bad grade on an assignment. By making reference to our relationships in terms of duration, context, or roles, we let others know what our initial expectations are for communication.

What are the communication expectations associated with the role of a coach?

DECIDING TO MAKE THE FIRST MOVE: WHY WE INITIATE RELATIONSHIPS

Think back to your first day in this class. As you walked through the door, you scanned the classroom and were faced with the decision of where to sit. Were there any familiar faces in the room? If not, you ended up sitting next to someone you had never met before. At that point, you had two decisions to make. Should you (a) initiate a conversation with that person, and if so, (b) how should you begin the interaction? As you reflect on that first day of class, consider how quickly some of these decisions were made. Even if the decision of where to sit was influenced by the fact that there were a limited number of seats available, you still had to choose whether to start a conversation, and thus, initiate a relationship with a fellow classmate. Every relationship has a unique history that includes an explanation of why we chose to initiate the relationship in the first place.

Over the years, scholars in the fields of communication, psychology, and sociology have been fascinated by the question of *why* we initiate relationships. For example, when writing about why people initiate long-term romantic relationships, interpersonal communication researcher Anita Vangelisti (2002) describes the number of factors that contribute to mate selection as "daunting." While there appear to be many different reasons, years of research have identified four common explanations for why humans begin relationships. The four primary reasons we establish relationships with others are attraction, proximity, similarity, and purpose. In the next sections, we take a closer look at each of these reasons for beginning a relationship.

INTERPERSONAL ATTRACTION

The four primary reasons we establish relationships with others are attraction, proximity, similarity, and purpose.

Identifying the reasons for being attracted to one person and not to another is perhaps one of the greatest mysteries in life. Researchers have dedicated countless studies to exploring the phenomenon of initial attraction. After all, attraction is perhaps one of the most influential factors in setting the relationship initiation process in motion. While references to attractiveness are often assumed to be directed toward physical characteristics, interpersonal attraction refers to a general feeling or desire that impacts our decision to approach and initiate a relationship with another person. Many different forms of attraction influence our decision to begin relationships.

interpersonal attraction a general feeling or desire that impacts our decision to approach and initiate a relationship with another person.

Attraction is one of the primary determining factors for choosing to initiate relationships, and it is the basis for forming initial impressions of others. While most people may argue that forming first impressions of others simply based on their appearance is superficial and trivial, the fact remains that in the United States many of our decisions to initiate romantic relationships are rooted in our perceptions of the physical attractiveness of the other person. While our initial impressions typically focus on the physical features associated with attractiveness, other factors can come into play as well. In Chapter 7 we introduced the concept of attraction as it relates to physical attributes. McCroskey and McCain (1974) identified three dimensions of attractiveness used when deciding whether to initiate relationships: physical, social, and task attractiveness.

Figure 7.2   **Types of interpersonal attraction**

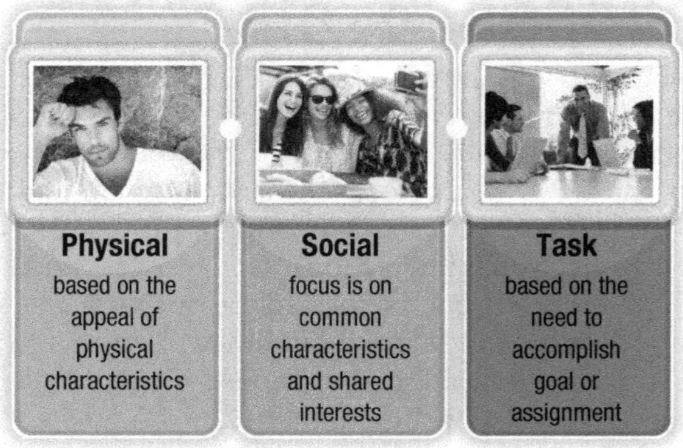

© Kendall Hunt Publishing Co.

Physical
based on the appeal of physical characteristics

Social
focus is on common characteristics and shared interests

Task
based on the need to accomplish goal or assignment

Physical Attractiveness

More often than not, we decide whether to initiate conversations with a potential relationship partner based on our perceptions of the person's physical attractiveness (Vangelisti, 2002). According to research by Reis and his colleagues (1980), we are more likely to evaluate interactions as enjoyable when we view the person we interact with as physically attractive.

How do we determine whether someone is physically attractive? Judgments about what constitutes physical attractiveness are often answered by asking the question, "What do I think makes someone pretty or handsome?" When characteristics such as body shape or size, hair color or length, and facial features are used in making a determination of whether to initiate a relationship, this dimension is referred to as physical attractiveness. Aristotle recognized the value of physical attractiveness when he stated, "Personal beauty is a greater recommendation than any letter of reference."

Recall our discussion of perception in Chapter 2. The phrase "beauty is in the eye of the beholder" addresses the perceptual nature of physical attraction and provides insight as to why one person may be attracted to blondes while another is attracted to brunettes. Sometimes we are baffled as to how individuals who appear to be so completely opposite with regard to their physical appearance could be attracted to each other. Our perception causes us to view physical characteristics in unique ways. While some studies report that men may value physical attractiveness more than women (Buss, 1989; Sprecher, Sullivan, & Hatfield, 1994), it is clear that both men and women report physical attractiveness as a factor influencing their decision to initiate relationships (Hatfield & Sprecher, 1986).

So why does physical attractiveness play such an important role in the early stages of relationship development? One explanation is that people tend to associate other positive and favorable characteristics with physical attractiveness. Take a moment and consider how much emphasis our culture places on physical attractiveness. An overwhelming amount of research (see, for example, Eagly et al., 1991) seems to support the bias that individuals have toward those perceived as physically attractive.

Several demographic factors such as age, gender, and culture influence our perceptions of physical attractiveness.

Age and Attractiveness. Beginning at a very young age, we are taught that physical attractiveness is often rewarded or valued. After all, the princesses in Disney movies are always beautiful young women, while the evil characters are portrayed as being ugly. Hasbro's Barbie doll is presented to young children as an ideal image of female attractiveness. She has long, blond hair and blue eyes, and is big-breasted, tall, and thin. Young children are able to identify her and many idolize her. However, Barbie's bra size has been estimated to be a DDD compared to the average C cup size of most women, and her body dimensions have been translated to the equivalent of 38-18-34 if she were a real woman. Nonetheless, young girls adore Barbie! They receive the message that being physically attractive, like Barbie, is associated with having friends and receiving more attention, not to mention a host of other rewards: great clothes, cars, beach houses, and a "cool" lifestyle.

physical attractiveness characteristics such as body shape or size, hair color or length, and facial features used in making a determination of whether to initiate a relationship.

Why is physical attractiveness important early in a relationship?

RESEARCH IN REAL LIFE: HONESTY IN ONLINE DESCRIPTIONS OF PHYSICAL ATTRIBUTES

The emphasis placed on physical attraction in decisions to initiate a relationship via an online dating site often result in the posting of deceptive information. A 2010 study by Toma and Hancock asked those who had created online dating profiles to identify inaccuracies in their descriptions of themselves. Next, researchers evaluated the physical attractiveness of the participants. Results found that:

- Those who were rated lower in physical attractiveness were more likely to edit or enhance their profile photos and post inaccurate information about their weight, height, or age.
- While they were deceptive about physical attributes, participants reported accurate information about other demographic information such as income level and occupation.

Why do you think we place so much importance on physical attraction in initiating relationships via online dating sites?

Several demographic factors such as age, gender, and culture influence our perceptions of physical attractiveness.

In addition to messages about physical attractiveness that are depicted in toys and media sources, messages regarding the importance of physical attractiveness are also conveyed in classrooms:

- Attractive children are perceived as being more popular with both classmates and teachers.
- Elementary-age students who are perceived as being physically attractive receive more attention from their teachers (Richmond, 1992).
- Attractive high school and college-age students receive higher grades than those who are perceived to be less attractive.
- Teachers provide higher evaluations and establish higher expectations for attractive students. Attractive people are perceived as being happier, more likeable, popular, and friendly (Berscheid & Reis, 1998).

As we get older, physical attractiveness impacts our own perceptions as well as the perceptions others have of us. Research has found that people under the age of 30 have been rated as being more physically attractive than people over the age of 50 (McClellan & McKelvie, 1993). In addition, various studies have examined how perceptions of physical attraction are influenced by age:

- Young and middle-age adults rate younger faces as more attractive than older faces. Older adults rate faces across all ranges as equally attractive (Foos & Clark, 2011).
- Johnson and Pittinger (1984) discovered that physically attractive males and females aged 60 to 93 were rated more positively than those in the same age group who were perceived to be less attractive.
- As males increase in age, they rate younger women as being more attractive than older women. However, the same was not true for women. Women in the older age categories rate males similar in age to be more physically attractive (Mathes, Brennen, Haugen, & Rice, 1985).

While both men and women indicate that they view physical attractiveness as important in the initiation of romantic relationships, the level of intensity that each sex uses in expressing their value for attractiveness differs.

Gender and Attractiveness.

While both men and women indicate that they view physical attractiveness as important in the initiation of romantic relationships, the level of intensity that each sex uses in expressing their value for attractiveness differs.

Many research studies point to the positive and negative aspects associated with physical attractiveness:

- In the workplace, physically attractive women often encounter biases *against* them when applying for administrative or executive positions (Zebrowitz, 1997).
- In an experiment examining the impact of a female employee's physical attractiveness on the decision to terminate her, participants indicated that they would be more likely to terminate an unattractive woman than an attractive woman (Commisso & Finkelstein, 2012).

- Lewis and Bierly (1990) examined the impact of female perceptions of male political candidates' attractiveness. Women rated physically attractive political candidates as being more competent than less attractive candidates.

Decisions to initiate dates are most often based on physical attractiveness. In a meta analysis of 2,247 personal ads, Feingold (1990) found that males are more likely than women to indicate physical attractiveness as a desired characteristic in a relationship, including descriptors of specific physical attributes as criteria for potential dates. In addition, men tend to indicate a strong preference for women who are younger than themselves. While women may identify general physical criteria such as *athletic, tall,* or *attractive* in personal ads, references to a partner's status were included more often and emerged as a stronger predictor of attraction (Davis, 1990).

Culture and Attraction.   Culture is an influential factor in our perception of physical attractiveness. What one culture establishes as a standard of physical attractiveness may be perceived differently in other cultures. Within a culture, media play an influential role in depicting the accepted standards of beauty. Images are found on television and billboards, in magazines, movies, and books, and on the Internet. These messages influence our consumer decisions to meet the standards of beauty promoted by the media. In the United States, physical beauty is so highly valued that Americans spent more than $38 billion dollars on cosmetics in 2007, nearly double or triple the amount spent by people in other countries (see Figure 7.3).

Figure 7.3 | Money spent on cosmetics around the world

WHO WANTS IT THE MOST?

Total national spending on cosmetics (2007 statistics)

	USA	JAPAN	FRANCE	GERMANY
Men	$11.059 bn	$5.927 bn	$4.163 bn	$3.879 bn
Women	$27.638 bn	$19.780 bn	$10.268 bn	$9.285 bn
Total	$38.698 bn	$25.708 bn	$14.321 bn	$13.164 bn

Source: Americans Spend Billions on Beauty Products But Are Not Very Happy. (n.d.). Retrieved September 14, 2014, from http://jezebel.com /5931654/ americans-spend-billions-on-beauty-products-and-are-still-pretty-unhappy/

Perceptions of physical attractiveness can differ across ethnic groups. A very curvaceous figure is often considered to be unattractive among Caucasian women, but African American women may not agree (Hebl & Heatherton, 1998). In fact, African American women are perceived as being more attractive by African American males if they have a curvaceous bottom, as opposed to being able to fit into a pair of size-four jeans.

As we cross cultural boundaries, it becomes apparent that there are universal perceptions of beauty as well. One particular physical feature that has been judged across cultures as a focal point for physical attraction is the human face. In particular, the more "feminine" a face appears, the greater its perceived level of attractiveness. In a study comparing the attractiveness of men and women by looking at close-up photographs of their faces, both Caucasian and Japanese participants rated pictures of men and women whose facial features had been "feminized" or softened as being more attractive (Perrett, Lee, & Penton-Voak, 1998).

Social Attractiveness

Social attractiveness common interests or similar patterns of communication that cause individuals to perceive each other as someone with whom they would like to spend time.

Once we initiate a conversation with another person, it is likely that our attention shifts from the physical attributes, which drew us to start talking in the first place, to identifying commonalities. Social attractiveness can be defined as common interests or similar patterns of communication that cause individuals to perceive one another as someone they would like to spend time with. Questions used to identify the level of social attraction with another person might include, "Would I like to hang out with this person?" and "Is this someone who would fit in with my friends?"

While physical attraction has a substantial impact on our decision to initiate relationships with others, social attraction is equally important. Some people exert considerable effort to ensure that others perceive their social behavior favorably. Recall our discussion of impression management in Chapter 3, defined as the process of maintaining a positive image of self in the presence of others. Consider the time and energy dedicated to making sure our physical appearance is "just right" when we meet or approach someone for the first time. When interviewing for a job, it is essential that the suit is pressed, the shoes are polished, and the hair is neat and clean. As the expression advises, "You never get a second chance to make a good first impression."

impression management process of maintaining a positive image of self in the presence of others.

Self-monitoring personality construct that causes a person to respond to social and interpersonal cues for appropriate communication behaviors in a variety of situations.

Individuals vary greatly in the extent to which they are self-aware of the impressions that others have of them. Self-monitoring refers to a personality construct that causes a person to respond to social and interpersonal cues for appropriate communication behaviors in a variety of situations. High self-monitors are constantly aware of behaviors others perceive to be appropriate in interpersonal situations, and continuously strive to control how they are portraying themselves. By contrast, low self-monitors dedicate little, if any, energy to responding to the cues of social appropriateness. They do not spend a lot of time worrying if they break the social rules by wearing jeans to an event where everyone else is dressed more formally, or by belching in front of a potential romantic partner.

What questions do you ask to determine your level of social attraction to someone?

To examine the relationship of self-monitoring and relationship initiation, participants were given file folders containing photographs and descriptions of personal attributes of potential dates. High self-monitors dedicated more time to reviewing the photographs in the folders, while low self-monitors spent more time reviewing the personal descriptions (Snyder, Berscheid, & Glick, 1985). Thus, it appears that high self-monitors place more emphasis on physical attraction when selecting a potential partner for a date, while low self-monitors focus more on social attractiveness.

© Aila Images/Shutterstock.com

While physical attractiveness plays an important role in our decision to initiate romantic relationships, social characteristics are also part of the evaluation process. Humor is one communication strategy that contributes to our perceptions of social attractiveness. When asked to describe characteristics associated with social attractiveness, descriptors such as "humorous," "low-drama," and "easygoing" are often used. While our initial attraction may be based on physical attributes, social attractiveness may emerge as we engage in conversations and share information. Wilbur and Campbell (2011) identified several gender differences in the use of humor on first dates:

- Men are more likely to use humor when getting to know a potential date.
- Women tend to evaluate "how" and "why" humor was used and then respond accordingly.
- In dating profiles, men tend to focus on describing their own sense of humor; women indicate their desirability for humor in a potential partner.

A 2011 survey of those who posted profiles on the eHarmony online dating site examined the types of humor that males and females found to be attractive in the initial stages of a relationship (see Figure 7.4). Men indicated a preference for women who engage in a sarcastic style of humor, while women favor men with a dry sense of humor. Recall our earlier discussion of self-monitoring. Being aware of others' reactions to our use of humor is important in creating perceptions of social attractiveness.

Task Attractiveness

While physical and social attributes may be influential in the initial phase of relationships, as individuals pursue their professional goals, decisions based on attractiveness may take on a much different perspective. Task attractiveness refers to the characteristics or qualities that are perceived as appealing when initiating relationships in which the goal is to complete a task or assignment. Suppose your professor allows you to select the team members you wish to work with on a major term project. Are you going to select the most physically attractive person to work with on this assignment? Possibly, if your goal is to get a date for Saturday night. Are you going to choose the funniest person in the class to be on your team? Maybe, if your goal is to have

Task attractiveness characteristics or qualities that are perceived as appealing when initiating relationships in which the goal is to complete a task or assignment.

> Being aware of others' reactions to our use of humor is important in creating perceptions of social attractiveness.

Figure 7.4 **eHarmony 2011 Online Dating Survey—Gender and perceived attraction to various humor styles**

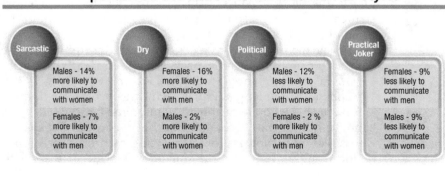

Sarcastic
Males - 14% more likely to communicate with women
Females - 7% more likely to communicate with men

Dry
Females - 16% more likely to communicate with men
Males - 2% more likely to communicate with women

Political
Males - 12% less likely to communicate with women
Females - 2 % more likely to communicate with men

Practical Joker
Females - 9% less likely to communicate with men
Males - 9% less likely to communicate with women

© Kendall Hunt Publishing Co.

plenty of laughs as you work on the project. Most likely, you will seek out people with characteristics and qualities that are essential to accomplishing your goal. A question used to identify perceived task attractiveness might be, "Does this person have what it takes to help get the job done?" Depending on the task, the list of qualities used to assess task attractiveness might be very different. If you consider yourself to be "technologically challenged," you may seek someone whom you consider to be proficient with computers. Suppose there is a strict timeline for the project. In such a situation, you will probably seek a person who is dependable and organized.

While physical, social, and task attractiveness influence our decisions to initiate relationships, other variables play an important role as well.

PROXIMITY

Proximity the physical distance between two people.

Consider our earlier question regarding your decision to initiate a relationship with the person seated next to you in this class. In essence, the decision to begin the relationship was influenced by proximity. Proximity refers to the physical distance between two people. The fact that you sit next to the same person for an entire semester increases the chance that you will communicate with each other and ultimately choose to form a relationship. Segal (1974) supported this notion in a study that examined friendships formed in a college classroom. At the beginning of the term, students were given seat assignments. When asked to indicate the persons whom they considered to be friends in the class, most students reported that they were friends with those who were seated next to them. Relationships are often formed with our neighbors because of our close proximity to these individuals.

So why is proximity such a strong predictor of interpersonal attraction? One explanation may be found in the diminished effort required to establish relationships with those who are close in distance. It is just easier to strike up a conversation with your next-door neighbor, chat with the person who works out at the same gym, or to share stories with the coworker whose cubicle is directly adjacent to yours. Much more effort is required to start relationships with those who sit on the other side of the room or who work on different floors.

similarity common interests, backgrounds, goals, and/or resemblances in appearance shared by two people. Also referred to as "homophily."

SIMILARITY/HOMOPHILY

After initiating a conversation, identifying potential topics to discuss can be the next hurdle to overcome. The goal of our discussions at this phase in a relationship is to identify common interests between ourselves and the other person. Remember the phrase, "Birds of a feather flock together?" This phrase refers to an influential element of interpersonal attraction known as similarity, or homophily.

Research confirms that we seek out relationships with those who have common interests, backgrounds, and goals, and who are similar in appearance (McCroskey, Richmond, & Daly, 1975). This phenomenon might explain why friendships are formed among people who are members of an online fan club site for a band, or how romantic relationships begin between two people who strike up a conversation after seeing each other at various political rallies. Both of these situations provide partners with common topics for discussion.

© bikeriderlondon /Shutterstock.com

Friendships may form on the basis of similar interests or hobbies.

Figure 7.5   Categories of Similarity

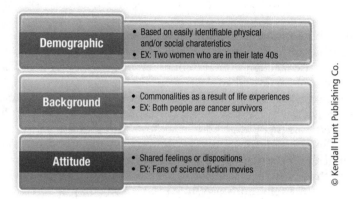

© Kendall Hunt Publishing Co.

Our similarity with others can be categorized based on demographic, background, or attitude commonalities. Demographic similarity is based on physical and social characteristics that are easily identifiable. Consider the relationships that you have initiated with others who are of a similar age or are the same sex. Background similarity refers to commonalities that we share as a result of our life experiences. Chances are that many of your friendships began as a result of experiences that you had in common with others—going to the same summer camp, playing on the same athletic team, working in the same organization, or simply growing up in the same hometown. Finally, attitude similarity focuses on our commonly held feelings or dispositions toward people, things, or events. Some relationships are formed as a result of our cultural, religious, or political affiliations. When two friends express similar attitudes toward music, movies, or sports, they are exhibiting attitude similarity.

In their examination of interpersonal attraction and similarity, Klohnen and Luo (2003) identified four dimensions of similarity that individuals consider in initial attraction:

Claiming that you have interests or beliefs in common with another person just to appear more attractive creates unrealistic expectations in the relationship.

- similarity to current self;
- complementarity;
- attachment security; and
- ideal-self similarity.

Similarity to current self refers to the belief that individuals are attracted to those who are similar to themselves. The dimensions we use to identify the congruence between ourselves and others differ from person to person. You may seek someone whose sense of humor is similar to your own, while another person may view similar levels of intelligence as being more important.

The complementarity hypothesis explains the saying "opposites attract." It predicts that people will be more attracted to those whose personality characteristics complement their own. This may explain why persons who have a high level of communication apprehension seek romantic relationships with those who have low levels of apprehension. To someone who is apprehensive about communicating, it is attractive to have someone who will initiate and carry out interactions.

Demographic similarity commonalities based on physical and social characteristics that are easily identifiable.

Background similarity refers to commonalities that we share as a result of our life experiences.

attitude similarity our perception of the attitudes, beliefs, and values that we hold in common with another person(s).

Similarity to current self one of four dimensions of similarity considered in initial attraction. Refers to the belief that individuals are attracted to those who are similar to themselves.

complementarity one of four dimensions of similarity considered in initial attraction. Often referred to as "opposites attract" and predicts that people will be more attracted to those whose personality and/or communication characteristics complement their own.

Attachment security   one of four dimensions of similarity considered in initial attraction. Predicts that individuals will be most attracted to those who are secure.

ideal-self similarity   one of four dimensions of similarity considered in initial attraction. Proposes that we are attracted to those who are similar to our view of how we would like others to perceive us.

False homophily   presentation of a deceptive image of self in an attempt to appear more similar to another person.

goals   refers to a desired or preferred outcome which motivates us to behave in particular ways.

Social goals   desired end states that fulfill the need for inclusion or affection.

Task goals   desired end states that fulfill the need for the completion of a task.

Attachment security predicts that individuals will be most attracted to those who are secure. Thus, we find individuals who are confident and trusting more attractive than individuals who are preoccupied by emotions of jealousy, neediness, or worry.

Finally, some individuals are most attracted to those whom they perceive to possess ideal-self similarity (as opposed to their actual or current self). We tend to view those who are similar to our view of how we would ultimately like to be perceived more favorably.

When we attempt to portray ourselves as being more similar to the other person than we really are just to appear more attractive, we run the risk of creating a relationship pitfall known as false homophily. False homophily refers to the presentation of a deceptive image of the self that appears to be more similar than it actually is. Claiming that you have interests or beliefs in common with another person just to appear more attractive creates unrealistic expectations in the relationship. While this strategy may be effective for gaining attention in the initial stages of the relationship, eventually the differences will emerge and could potentially cause problems.

Social media sites encourage us to identify commonalities with other users by posting information about music interests, favorite athletic teams, and places we have visited. We invite others to join games of Candy Crush Saga and Farmville and help one another reach goals. Online dating sites are designed to help singles quickly identify shared interests that can serve as the foundation for initiating conversations. Even in the absence of visible cues, online sites provide us with countless opportunities to identify similarities with others.

INTERPERSONAL GOALS

A final reason people choose to initiate relationships with others is to fulfill a purpose, or goal. Charles Berger (1995) defines goals as "desired end states toward which persons strive" (p. 143). Many of our interpersonal interactions are initiated to fulfill two primary goals: social and task.

Social goals refer to desired end states that fulfill the need for inclusion or affection. Both parties involved in the initial relationship can experience the fulfilled need. Consider the new kid in school. In order to ease some of the anxiety of starting a new school, the student might approach a table of students in the cafeteria and ask, "Is this seat taken?" One explanation for the initiation of this interaction is to fulfill a social goal—the student seeks to fulfill the need for inclusion at school.

Task goals are defined as desired end states that fulfill the need for the completion of an objective or task. Consider your current relationship with your hair stylist or barber. You initiated the relationship because the task of getting your hair cut needed to be fulfilled. A phone call was made to a local hair salon with the goal of finding a competent stylist to complete the task. As you initiated a conversation with the stylist, the task goal was to describe your desired hair cut. Consider all of the relationships you have initiated to fulfill task goals. Relationships are initiated with teachers to fulfill the task goal of achieving your educational objectives, and teachers form relationships with colleagues to accomplish tasks associated with the job. Interpersonal communication is instrumental in achieving our goals.

© Andresr/Shutterstock.com

What social and task goals do you find in classroom relationships?

RESEARCH IN REAL LIFE: WHAT ARE THE PRIMARY GOALS OR MOTIVES FOR FIRST DATES?

In a study of first-date goals, 144 college students identified their primary reasons for going on a first date with someone (Mongeau, Serewicz, & Therrien, 2004). Males and females who reported their goals for first dates included the following:

GOAL	FEMALES	MALES
Reduce uncertainty/get to know the other person	52	36
Escalate the relationship/explore possibility of pursuing the relationship further	48	25
Have fun	40	26
Companionship	16	7
Ego boost	6	6
Sexual activity	2	8
Hedonistic (get something for "free"— dinner, concert ticket)	8	0
Guilt/avoid hurting the other person's feelings	5	0

Recall your reasons for agreeing to a date or an invitation to hang out with friends. What motivated you to agree to go out?

Dillard (1990) points out that our goals serve three functions in interpersonal relationships. First, goals are used to take action and fulfill an interpersonal need. Individuals determine what need to fulfill, and the goal prompts the initiation of the relationship. If your social goal is to form new friendships at school, you will introduce yourself in an attempt to take action to fulfill the need. Second, goals assist us in defining the purpose for the interaction or behaviors. Suppose a woman asks a colleague to join her for a cup of coffee to discuss an upcoming presentation for an important client. She realizes that the purpose of the interaction is to accomplish a task goal. However, if she had a romantic interest in the colleague, the ulterior motive for the meeting may have been prompted by social goals. Finally, goals provide us with a standard by which to judge the behaviors and outcomes of interpersonal interactions. We evaluate our interpersonal interactions with others and judge their effectiveness based on whether or not we accomplish our goals. After a blind date we typically evaluate the date as being "good" or "bad," based on the interaction that took place. If conversation was forced and awkward, we are likely to evaluate the date negatively.

Online interactions can also be initiated to fulfill goals. Katz and Rice (2002) pointed out that sometimes Indian parents use the Internet as a source to seek suitable mates for their children as a modern extension of their traditional matchmaking processes. Signing up to post and browse online personal ads signals a social goal—the intent to form a romantic relationship.

INTERPERSONAL COMMUNICATION THEORIES: *HOW* WE INITIATE RELATIONSHIPS

While attraction, proximity, similarity, and goals help explain *why* we pursue relationships, several theories are useful in understanding *how* we use communication to initiate these connections. Social penetration theory, uncertainty reduction theory, predicted outcome value theory, liking, and social exchange theory provide us with explanations to explain *how* we start relationships with others. Before we address these interpersonal theories and concepts, we will first examine the role of initial impression formation and self-disclosure in establishing relationships.

Starting the Conversation

To identify things we have in common with others, we typically need to engage in some type of communication. For some people, this is one of the most difficult tasks in a relationship. Consider the last time you attempted to start a conversation. Figuring out the most appropriate way to break the ice and create a positive initial impression can be intimidating. Should you offer a compliment or tell a joke? Mimic the shy smile or quick glances that you saw being used in a recent movie or television show? Knowing what communication behavior to use and predicting how it will be interpreted is challenging. Recall the scenario from the beginning of the chapter. Rather than using a humorous pick-up line with Amelia, Patrick initiated the conversation by asking if they were in the same class . Over the years, many of our students have shared "pick-up lines" or relational openers that have been used to initiate conversations with a potential romantic partner. Table 7.1 includes examples of pick-up lines listed on www.pickuplinesgalore.com.

Table 7.1	Sample Pick-Up Lines from www.pickuplines galore.com

SAMPLE PICK-UP LINES

"Do you have a sunburn, or are you always this hot?"

"Are you a camera? Because every time I look at you I smile!"

"I seem to have lost my phone number. Can I have yours?"

"Do you know what my shirt is made of? Boyfriend material."

It is important to note that pick-up lines are not necessarily the most effective conversation starters, although they may succeed in getting someone's attention. Our advice is that the next time you think about using one of these pick-up lines to begin a conversation, don't. Informal surveys of our students have revealed that the vast majority feel a simple and sincere introduction is the most effective way to initiate a conversation.

Flirtatious communication involves the use of verbal and nonverbal behaviors to indicate our interest in initiating a potential relationship. Our reasons and motives for flirting often vary depending on our relational goal. A 2008

Flirtatious communication involves the use of verbal and nonverbal behaviors to indicate our interest in initiating a potential relationship.

study comparing flirting motives of students and employees identified six primary reasons that guide our decisions to engage in flirtatious communication (Henningsen, Braz, & Davies, 2008). These motives are highlighted in Table 7.2.

Table 7.2	Motives for Engaging in Flirtatious Communication
MOTIVES	**GOAL**
Sexual	Indicate a desire to pursue a sexual relationship
Relational	Express desire to pursue an intimate relationship that involves the sharing of personal information
Fun	Pass time; participate in playful interactions as a distraction
Exploring	Gauge the other person's interest in pursuing a relationship
Esteem	Inflate one's self esteem by seeing if the other person engages in reciprocal flirting
Instrumental	Influence or manipulate others to gain assistance or compliance with requests

The results of the study found that the motives for flirting in both work and social contexts were similar. We tend to flirt in an attempt to have fun, to build our self-esteem, and to gauge how interested the other person may be in pursuing a relationship. While flirting may be viewed as primarily a fun and innocent activity, it's important to note that miscommunication may occur as a result of misinterpretations. For example, a receiver may perceive a wink as indicating sexual interest when the intent was to communicate agreement (Hecht, DeVito & Guerrero, 1999). While flirting has been proven to be a popular strategy for gauging interest in pursuing a relationship, the sharing and exchanging of personal information provides valuable insight regarding the potential for the relationship to continue.

Self-disclosure sharing or revealing personal information about oneself with others.

Self-Disclosure

While it is difficult to determine which opening line or nonverbal behavior should be used to initiate our interest, continuing the conversation can be an even greater challenge. Deciding what information to share about yourself and what information you should seek from the other person can be daunting. During the early stages of relationship formation, partners will often self-disclose information in an effort to increase intimacy (Reis & Shaver, 1988; Reis & Patrick, 1996). Self-disclosure is "the process of revealing personal information about oneself to another" (Sprecher & Hendrick, 2004, p. 858). Sharing information results in increased attraction and liking in relationships. Self-disclosing is important not only in the initial stages, but also in sustaining relationships over time. It helps others learn who we are and our expectations for the relationship. You can assess your own preferences for disclosing information by completing the Revised Self-Disclosure scale located at the end of this chapter.

Breadth variety of topics that we are willing to disclose about in our discussions with others.

Breadth of disclosure refers to the variety of topics we are willing to discuss with others. During the initial stages of a relationship, we tend to "play it safe" and stick to sharing superficial information such as our hobbies and general demographic

What topics do you feel comfortable disclosing in a new relationship?

depth level of intimacy or amount of detail that is disclosed about a particular topic.

information. For example, speed dating events provide participants with the opportunity to experience a series of multiple "mini-dates" in which they share information about a wide variety of topics in several five- to eight-minute sessions. At the end of the speed dating event, individuals indicate whom they would be interested in meeting again. The level of intimacy or the amount of detail shared about a specific topic is referred to as the depth of disclosure. How much detail we share is often influenced by societal or cultural norms. For example, revealing our income level, sharing our fears, or exposing details about past relationships would involve disclosing more details than we would typically expect upon meeting someone for the first time.

Once we reveal personal information about ourselves, we expect that the other person will also share similar information. Reciprocal self-disclosure involves the mutual sharing of information between two people. Collins and Miller (1994) identified a link between self-disclosure and liking. We like those who disclose with us, and we are more willing to disclose information to those whom we like. It is best when the disclosures of both partners are similar in terms of breadth of topics discussed and depth of disclosure. Consider the following initial disclosures between two classmates on the first day of class:

Reciprocal self-disclosure involves the mutual exchange or disclosure of information between two people. Enhances relationship satisfaction when disclosures are similar in terms of topics discussed and depth of information shared.

Sabina: Hi, I'm Sabina. Have you ever taken a class with Dr. Yost before?

Natalie: Hey Sabina, I'm Natalie. No, I haven't had a class with her, but my roommate took the class last semester.

Sabina: Really, what did he say about it?

Natalie: He said she's tough but fair.

Sabina: Ouch! That's what I was afraid of. I have to take this class for my major, and this is the only time that it fit into my schedule. If she's a difficult teacher, then why did you take this class?

Natalie: Well, even though she's tough, I've also heard that you learn a lot that will help you down the road in other classes in the major.

Sabina: Oh, are you a communication major?

Natalie: Yes, this is my second year. What year are you?

Sabina: I'm a junior, but I just transferred into the major at the beginning of the semester. I feel like I'm so far behind. Everyone else has their schedules all planned out and they know exactly who and what to take.

Natalie: Don't stress yourself out about it. We've all been there before. If you have any questions about who you should take, just ask me. Have you met with your advisor yet? They're pretty good about helping you map out your long-term schedule.

Consider the reciprocity of disclosure in this initial interaction. Both women share information about their majors as well as their fears about the class. As one asks a question, the other answers it. When one woman discloses information, so does the other. In situations where others fail to disclose similar information, we become uncomfortable and may perceive them to be hiding something, or engaging in deceptive communication. Understanding the social expectations for appropriate self-disclosure is important to enhancing our relationships with others. Table 7.3 offers suggestions for both engaging in and responding to self-disclosure.

| Table 7.3 | **Suggestions for Delivering and Receiving Self-disclosure** |

DELIVERING	RECEIVING
Begin by self-disclosing information on safe or neutral topics.	*Do not overreact when someone shares personal information with you.*
During initial conversations, talk about where you went to school, hobbies, talents, etc., before sharing any private information.	Try not to become overly emotional or provide judgmental feedback when someone shares private information with you. For example, screaming, "YOU DID WHAT?" when a friend shares information is not recommended.
If possible, attempt to match your partner's disclosures in depth.	*Provide verbal and nonverbal support.*
If your partner shares intimate information (e.g., fears, future goals, insecurities), he may expect you to reciprocate. Remember that reciprocal disclosures between partners often indicate trust and liking.	Make an attempt to display warm, receptive nonverbal cues during your conversation by maintaining eye contact, sitting near the person, nodding your head to indicate listening, and, if appropriate, smiling. Engage in active listening behaviors, which might include paraphrasing and appropriate empathic responses (e.g., "I can see why you would be upset").
Before disclosing private information, ask yourself if this is someone you can trust.	*If you do not feel comfortable discussing a topic or issue, tell your friend or relationship partner.*
If you feel you cannot trust this person or feel this person will share this information with others, it is probably not a good idea to share private information.	Rather than avoid the person and risk damaging your relationship, tell the person why you are uncomfortable discussing the topic.

Social Penetration Theory

When we become more comfortable and trusting of others, the breadth and depth of our disclosures change. Altman and Taylor (1973) created social penetration theory to explain how self-disclosure changes as relationships move from one level to the next. It explains how and why we move from superficial topics of conversation in the initial stages of relationships to more intimate conversations as the relationship progresses.

Altman and Taylor use the analogy of an onion to describe the layers of information that are revealed as relationships become more intimate. This analogy helps illustrate the various levels of information that we share as our relationships progress from initiation to more intimate stages. There are four levels of information that we are willing to disclose depending on the nature of our relationships: superficial, intimate, personal, and private.

Superficial communication is revealed in initial interactions. Communication focuses on safe topics such as one's major, occupation, or hometown. As the relationship intensifies, a layer of the onion is "peeled" away and more personal information is revealed. Personal communication focuses on topics of a more personal nature such as likes, dislikes, and experiences.

social penetration theory explains how information is exchanged during relationship development. Describes the process of moving from superficial topics of conversation in the initial stages of relationships to more intimate conversations as the relationship progresses.

Superficial communication outer layer of the social penetration theory model. Information shared in the initial stages of relationships that focus on safe topics such as one's major, hometown, or occupation.

Personal communication self-disclosure topics that focus on personal aspects such as likes, dislikes, and experiences.

Figure 7.6 Social penetration "onion" model

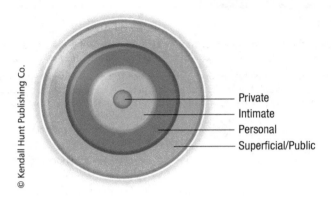

Intimate communication information that is self-disclosed to those with whom we have established a high level of trust or comfort. Topics may include concerns and aspirations.

private communication core of the social penetration theory onion model. Information that is reserved for our closest relationships.

As the relationship progresses to a more intimate level, so does the communication. Intimate communication topics are shared with those with whom we have a high level of trust and comfort. We may share our career concerns and aspirations with a close friend or colleague. At the innermost core of the onion model, we engage in private communication in which specific topics of discussion topics of discussion are reserved for our closest relationships. Topics may include our secrets, fears, hopes, and motivations.

As we disclose information with each other, we "peel" away the layers of the onion. This enables us to reduce our level of uncertainty or ambiguity about the other person.

Uncertainty Reduction Theory

Uncertainty reduction theory describes the process of exchanging information in an attempt to reduce ambiguity about others. Questions are a primary communication strategy used for reducing levels of uncertainty.

Recall Amelia's initial encounter in the scenario at the beginning of this chapter. When her biology classmate chose to occupy the seat beside her at the football game, she knew very little about him. As they asked each other questions and shared information, they reduced their level of ambiguity about each other. Uncertainty reduction theory (Berger & Calabrese, 1975) identifies question asking as a primary communication strategy we use to encourage reciprocal disclosure and to reduce our levels of uncertainty about others. In a test to examine the relationship between our initial attraction to someone and how we use questioning or disclosure, Douglas (1990) asked pairs to engage in a six-minute initial interaction. He found that the majority of questions were asked in the initial two minutes of the conversation, and greater disclosures were made in the final two minutes of the discussion.

Nonverbal cues can also provide valuable information in the uncertainty reduction process. A quick scan of a room may reveal someone wearing a t-shirt from your alma mater, or perhaps you enter a meeting and see someone who appears to be close in age to you. We can use a variety of nonverbal cues to decrease our level of ambiguity and guide our initial encounters.

As we reduce our uncertainty about someone, we engage in a "strategy selection" process. This procedure requires us to maximize our efficiency in gaining information about others while utilizing behaviors that are viewed as socially appropriate. Speed dating is an example of a trend that provides singles with the opportunity to initiate conversations with multiple prospective dates at a singles event. The context, speed dating, itself reduces the level of uncertainty of "How long do I have to pretend to be interested?" by establishing a time limit for the interactions. If the conversation is uncomfortable, participants know that their time spent with one another will be brief.

Predicted Outcome Value Theory

Once we have reduced our level of uncertainty about a new relationship, the next step involves deciding what we expect or want from the new relationship. Predicted outcome value theory focuses on the perceived rewards or benefits associated with the new relationship (Sunnafrank, 1986). There is a shift from focusing on the need for more information about the other person to analyzing the potential value that can be obtained from the relationship. Consider when you meet someone for the first time. Is this person someone you could see becoming a good friend or a potential romantic partner? Chances are you evaluate the potential for the future of the relationship without even realizing it. At some point, you make a decision regarding whether to pursue the relationship, how the relationship should progress, and what type of relationship you are interested in pursuing with the other person (e.g., friendship, romantic).

> Predicted outcome value theory that explains the process of evaluating the perceived rewards or benefits associated with a relationship.

To evaluate predicted outcome value, Mottet (2000) developed a seven-question scale that asks individuals to rate future relationship potential by evaluating them using the following adjectives:

- Positive—Negative
- Good—Bad
- Satisfying—Unsatisfying
- Valuable—Not valuable
- Worthwhile—Not worthwhile
- Rewarding—Unrewarding
- Comfortable—Uncomfortable

As you review the list of items used to assess the potential benefits of pursuing a relationship, consider the criteria you have used in deciding whether to pursue some of your current relationships.

> Once we have reduced our level of uncertainty about a new relationship, the next step involves deciding what we expect or want from the new relationship. —Rudyard Kipling

Social Exchange Theory

During the process of predicting the potential value of initiating a relationship, we consider the costs and rewards associated with connecting with the other person. Have you ever heard the phrase "on the market" to refer to a person who is single and searching for a new romantic relationship? While at first this reference may seem degrading, it accurately describes the strategies we use when evaluating new relationships. This process is actually quite similar to shopping—we examine the options available and seek the best "deal."

Social exchange theory (also known as interdependence theory) refers to an assessment of costs and rewards in determining the value of pursuing

> Social exchange theory refers to an assessment of costs and rewards in determining the value of pursuing or continuing a relationship.

RESEARCH IN REAL LIFE: SPEED DATING AND PREDICTING THE POTENTIAL FOR FUTURE DATES

A 2008 study by Houser, Horan, and Furler asked 157 speed daters to evaluate the predicted outcome value (POV) for pursuing a relationship after engaging in a brief initial conversation at a speed dating event. Of the 75 participants who reported positive POV ratings about another person, 100% indicated that they would be interested in pursuing a future date. Interestingly, almost half (43%) of the participants who provided a negative POV evaluation indicated they would still be interested in pursuing a future date, despite the fact that their initial impression was negative.

or continuing a relationship (Thibaut & Kelley, 1959). Rewards refer to aspects that are desirable, which the recipient perceives as enjoyable or fulfilling. By contrast, costs are perceived as being undesirable. As we exchange information in the initial stages of a relationship, decisions are made regarding the relative value of continuing to pursue the relationship. While your initial conversation with the person seated next to you on an airplane may be rewarding in the sense that you felt comfortable discussing common interests to pass the time on a three-hour journey, the costs of maintaining the relationship (effort involved in emailing or calling the person) may outweigh the benefits. You weigh the rewards and costs in making your prediction about the value of the relationships. As a result, you may decide to shake hands at the end of the flight, exchange pleasantries, and go your separate ways. Suppose that person seated next to you is employed at Google, an organization that you would love to work for after graduation. In that instance, the costs involved in continuing to communicate across the distance are minimal compared to the potential reward of having an inside connection when you apply for employment at the company in the future.

Rewards consist of behaviors or things that are desirable, which the recipient perceives as enjoyable or fulfilling.

costs perceived undesirable behaviors or outcomes that influence our decision regarding the relative value of continuing to pursue the relationship further.

Stages of Relationship Development

Now that we have explored the reasons why we initiate relationships and some theoretical explanations for how we use communication, we turn our attention to understanding the process of moving from one stage of a relationship to another.

Knapp (1978) proposed a "staircase" model depicting the stages of relationship development and dissolution. The first five steps of this model, known as coming together, will be discussed here (see Figure 7.7). Chapter 9 will discuss Knapp's (1978) stages of relationship disengagement, or coming apart. Before discussing the stages of relationship initiation and development, it is important to note the following caveats about the movement from one stage to the next (Knapp & Vangelisti, 2003):

- Movement from one stage of the model to the next is typically sequential. This allows us to make predictions regarding the future of the relationship.
- Our decision to move to the next level involves an analysis of the potential benefits of continuing the relationship and increasing the level of intimacy in communication.
- At times, relationships may experience a "backward" movement to a prior stage. This is often due to a decline in the communication behaviors prescribed in the present stage.
- Movement through the stages occurs at different paces for each relationship. One may move very quickly from one stage to the next, while another may stall at one stage while the partners work through the communication challenges of that phase and make the decision of whether to progress to the next level.

Initiation stage of relationship development in which one person decides to initiate conversation with another. Communication typically consists of the polite formalities of introduction.

Initiation.   Initiation occurs when one party decides to initiate conversation with another person. Communication during this phase typically consists of the polite formalities of introduction. Statements such as "How are you?"

Figure 7.7 Knapp's (1978) Stages of "coming together" in a relationship

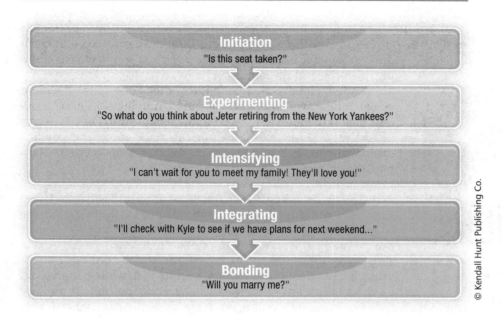

Initiation
"Is this seat taken?"

Experimenting
"So what do you think about Jeter retiring from the New York Yankees?"

Intensifying
"I can't wait for you to meet my family! They'll love you!"

Integrating
"I'll check with Kyle to see if we have plans for next weekend..."

Bonding
"Will you marry me?"

© Kendall Hunt Publishing Co.

or "Is anyone sitting here?" are used to break the ice. We evaluate the person's attractiveness and may scramble to come up with the perfect opening line. During this phase, impression management is essential. Our goal is to present ourselves in the most positive way possible. While some people may be tempted to use one of the pick-up lines discussed earlier in this chapter, the best strategy for making a good first impression is to be confident and sincere.

Experimenting. You know that you have reached the experimenting phase when the communication involves extensive questions and discussions about topics such as classes, hobbies, or other demographic information. Whereas physical attraction has a strong influence on the decision to engage in the initiation phase, social attraction is discovered during the experimenting phase. Reciprocal disclosures are common, with one person asking questions such as, "So have you lived in Los Angeles your entire life?" and the other person responding with "No, I grew up in Chicago and moved to L.A. last year to escape the cold winters. Did you grow up in California?" Uncertainty reduction is the primary goal of this stage of relationship development.

experimenting stage of relationship development in which partners exchange information about a variety of superficial topics and interests to identify potential commonalities.

Intensifying. As we progress to the intensifying stage of the staircase model, our disclosures with each other increase in depth. Whereas in the experimenting stage we disclosed information on a variety of topics (breadth), during this phase the information shared becomes more personal and private (depth). Messages communicated between partners involve a lot of "tests" to determine the intensity of commitment felt by the other. Knapp and Vangelisti (2003) identify specific verbal characteristics that are common during the intensifying stage. These include using nicknames or terms of endearment to refer to each other (think "Boo Bear" or "Babe"), referring to each other through the use of first-person plural pronouns ("*We* should go to the movies with Joe and Cara

intensifying stage of relationship development in which our disclosures with each other increase in depth. Messages are used to determine the intensity of commitment felt by the other person.

integrating stage of relationship development that is marked by a merging of personalities and identities. Relational partners are viewed by others as "a couple."

on Friday"), and making explicit references to the commitment like "I think about you all the time when you're not here."

Integrating.   The integrating stage is marked by a merging of personalities and identities. Not only do the partners see themselves as a couple, but others recognize and refer to them as a unit as well. Relationship rituals that occur during this stage include exchanging personal items such as clothing, pictures, and rings that can be worn or displayed to communicate their identity as a couple to others, engaging in similar verbal and nonverbal behaviors, and identifying common "property" that is identified as special to the relationship ("our" song or purchasing a pet together). During this stage of coming together, one partner might say to the other, "What are our vacation plans for the summer?"

Marriage communicates a long-term commitment to a relationship.

Bonding   the final stage of relationship development, which involves a perceived contractual agreement of commitment between partners.

Bonding.   Bonding, the final stage of coming together, is viewed as a formal contractual agreement that declares to the world that the couple has made a serious commitment to each other. This stage can be marked by performing public rituals such as exchanging class rings to show that you are "going steady," or getting engaged, or getting married. It is important to note that, while bonding can be viewed as a contract at any stage of the relationship, the message communicated between a couple during this stage is that there is a serious commitment that implies the goal of pursuing a long-term relationship.

Relationship Initiation Contexts

Another factor impacting the decision to initiate a relationship focuses on the setting in which the initial interaction takes place. Reflect on your own relationships and recall where those relationships began. A 1981 study of college women asked them to report the settings where their significant relationships were initiated (Jason, Reichler, & Rucker, 1981). Five settings were identified by single women as the location where their significant relationships were initiated (see Table 7.4 below). Given that the women were currently enrolled in

Table 7.4	**Contexts of significant relationship initiation for college women**

Setting	Percentage
School	25
Work	20
Through Friends	14
Bar	9
Party	9

Source: Jason, L. A., Reichler, A., & Rucker, W. (1981). Characteristics of significant dating relationships: Male versus female initiators, idealized versus actual settings. *The Journal of Psychology, 109,* 185–190. Reprinted with permission of the Helen Dwight Reid Educational Foundation. Published by Heldref Publications, 1319 Eighteenth St., NW, Washington, DC 20036-1802. Copyright © 1981.

college classes, it should come as no surprise that they most often listed school as the place where their most important relationships began.

A study of preferred meeting places for gays and lesbians reveals a slight difference in setting choices. Gay bars are often identified as a popular place for initiating relationships, given the fact that patrons of the bars are similar in terms of their sexual preference. Among lesbians, the second most preferred meeting place is at political functions, such as feminist or lesbian rallies (Huston & Schwartz, 2003). It is important to note that some environments are not open or welcoming to the initiation of homosexual relationships. Thus, frustration in locating a common place to meet similar others is often reported by gay men and lesbians.

Relationship Initiation and Technology

Online Relationship Initiation.   As the number of people who form relationships online continues to grow, there is a greater need to understand the unique nature of interactions in cyberspace. In face-to-face interactions, the initial decision to approach another person is often based on physical characteristics. We see the person, make a decision of whether or not to approach him, and subsequently spend time getting to know each other by progressing through the relationship stages identified by Knapp and Vangelisti (2003). Online relationship initiation differs because of the absence of physical cues, which can affect the course of the relationship. Individuals meet via written messages or text. From there, they decide whether to talk with the other person via phone and, ultimately, in person. In essence, online relationship initiation could be considered a "test drive"—we can dedicate as little or as much time as we want to getting to know the person before deciding if we want to meet face-to-face.

Is an on-line relationship right for me?

While we might doubt the sustainability of relationships that are initiated online, research suggests otherwise. One study examined the stability of a variety of online relationships (acquaintances, friends, and romantic partners) over a two-year period and found 75 percent of respondents indicated that they were still involved in a relationship that had been initiated online (McKenna, Green, & Gleason, 2002).

Relationship Initiation and Culture

While you might think that perceptions with regard to relationship initiation differ across cultures, you might be surprised to find out that we are more alike than different. Pines (2001) examined the role of gender and culture in initial romantic attraction by comparing Americans with Israelis. She asked participants to describe how they met their romantic partner and indicate what attracted them to the other person initially (see Table 7.5).

The only significant differences occurred when comparing U.S. and Israeli perceptions relating to status, proximity (propinquity in Table 7.5), and similarity. Some Americans reported that they were attracted by the status of their

Table 7.5	Attraction Variables (Percentage) by Country	
Attraction Variable	**USA**	**Israel**
Appearance	63	70
Status	8	0
Personality	92	94
Need filled	54	6
Propinquity	63	46
Mutual attraction	41	40
Arousal	22	25
Similarity	30	8

Reprinted with permission from *European Psychologist*, Vol. 6, No. 2, June 2001, pp. 96–102. © Hogrefe & Huber Publishers (now Hogrefe Publishing). www.hogrefe.com DOI: 10.1027//1016-9040.6.2.96

relational partner, while none of the Israeli respondents indicated this was a factor. Physical proximity between partners was listed as being more influential to Americans who reported being more attracted to partners who lived, worked, or studied at the same place. Similarity of partners was found to be more important to Americans. Having similar experiences, values, interests, attitudes, and personalities was rated as being far more important to Americans than to Israelis.

SUMMARY

In this chapter we have answered some of the questions regarding *why* we form interpersonal relationships with others and *how* we use communication to initiate them. While each relationship is unique, the reasons we choose to interact with others are fairly similar. Our hope is that you have gained both an understanding of, and the confidence for, using effective communication behaviors to pursue new relationship journeys. Perhaps the most important piece of advice we could offer as you begin a relationship with another person, whether it is a platonic or a romantic relationship, is to just be yourself.

DISCUSSION QUESTIONS

1. Throughout this chapter, various goals and motives for initiating relationships were discussed. Which of these goals and motives do you perceive as most influential in your own decisions to initiate various relationships (e.g., friendships, romantic relationships, workplace relationships)?

2. Recall a time when you were successful at initiating a romantic relationship. Offer several suggestions or guidelines for individuals who want to be successful when initiating conversations or beginning a romantic relationship. What types of things should you avoid saying or doing during this critical time period?

3. In what context or under what circumstances did most of your important relationships begin? Do you initiate different types of relationships in different contexts? Are there similarities and differences in the questions asked/strategies employed during the initiating stages of platonic and romantic relationship development?

REFERENCES

Altman, I., & Taylor, D. A. (1973). *Social penetration: The development of interpersonal relationships.* New York: Holt, Rinehart, & Winston.

Berger, C. (1995). A plan-based approach to strategic interaction. In D. E. Hewes (Ed.), *The cognitive bases of interpersonal interaction* (pp. 141–180). Hillsdale, NJ: Lawrence Erlbaum.

Berger, C. R., & Calabrese, R. J. (1975). Some explorations in initial interaction and beyond: Toward a developmental theory of interpersonal communication. *Human Communication Research, 1,* 99–112.

Berscheid, E., & Reis, H. T. (1998). Attraction in close relationships. In D. T. Gilbert, S. T. Fiske, & G. Lindzey (Eds.), *The handbook of social psychology* (4th ed.). New York: McGraw Hill.

Buss, D. M. (1989). Sex differences in human mate preferences: Evolutionary hypotheses tested in 37 cultures. *Behavioral and Brain Sciences, 12,* 1–49.

Collins, N. L., & Miller, L. C. (1994). Self-disclosure and liking: A meta-analytic review. *Psychological Bulletin, 116,* 457-475.

Commisso, M., & Finkelstein, L. (2012). Physical attractiveness bias in employee termination. *Journal of Applied Social Psychology, 42*(12), 2968–2987.

Davis, S. (1990). Men as success objects and women as sex objects: A study of personal advertisements. *Sex Roles, 23,* 43–50.

Dillard, J. P. (1990). A goal-driven model of interpersonal influence. In J. P. Dillard (Ed.), *Seeking compliance: The production of interpersonal influence messages* (pp. 41–56). Scottsdale, AZ: Gorsuch-Scarisbrick.

Douglas, W. (1990). Uncertainty, information seeking, and liking during initial interaction. *Western Journal of Speech Communication, 54,* 66–81.

Eagly, A. H., Ashmore, R. D., Makhijani, M. G., & Longo, L.C. (1991). What is beautiful is good, but...: A meta-analytic review of research on the physical attractiveness stereotype. *Psychological Bulletin, 110,* 109–128.

Feingold, A. (1990). Gender differences in effects of physical attractiveness on romantic attraction: A comparison across five research paradigms. *Journal of Personality and Social Psychology, 59*(5), 981–993.

Foos, P. W., & Clark, M. C. (2011). Adult age and gender differences in perceptions of facial attractiveness: Beauty is in the eye of the beholder. *The Journal of Genetic Psychology, 172*(2), 162–175.

Hatfield, E., & Sprecher, S. (1986). *Mirror, mirror: The importance of looks in everyday life.* Albany, NY: SUNY Press.

Hebl, M. R., & Heatherton, T. F. (1998). The stigma of obesity in women: The difference is black and white. *Personality and Social Psychology Bulletin, 24,* 417–426.

Hecht, M. L., DeVito, J. A., & Guerrero, L. K. (1999). Perspectives on nonverbal communication: Codes, functions, and contexts. In L. K. Guerrero, J. A. DeVite, & M. L. Hecht (Eds.), *The nonverbal communication reader: Classic and contemporary readings* (2nd ed.) (pp. 3–18). Prospect Heights, IL: Waveland Press.

Henningsen, D. D., Braz, M., & Davies, E. (2008). Why do we flirt?: Flirting motivations and sex differences in working and social contexts. *Journal of Business Communication, 45*(4), 483–502.

Houser, M. L., Horan, S. M., & Furler, L. A. (2008). Dating in the fast lane: How communication predicts speed-dating success. *Journal of Social and Personal Relationships, 25*(5), 749–768.

Huston, M., & Schwartz, P. (2003). The relationships of lesbians and of gay men. In K. M. Galvin & P. J. Cooper (Eds.), *Making connections: Readings in interpersonal communication* (3rd ed.) (pp. 171–177). Los Angeles, CA: Roxbury.

Jason, L. A., Reichler, A., & Rucker, W. (1981). Characteristics of significant dating relationships: Male versus female initiators, idealized versus actual settings. *The Journal of Psychology, 109,* 185–190.

Johnson, D. F., & Pittinger, J. B. (1984). Attribution, the attractiveness stereotype, and the elderly. *Developmental Psychology, 20,* 1168–1172.

Katz, J. E., & Rice, R. E. (2002). *Social consequences of Internet use: Access, involvement and interaction.* Cambridge, MA: The MIT Press.

Klohnen, E. C., & Luo, S. (2003). Interpersonal attraction and personality: What is attractive—self similarity, ideal similarity, complementarity, or attachment security? *Journal of Personality and Social Psychology, 85,* 709–722.

Knapp, M. L. (1978). *Social intercourse: From greeting to goodbye.* Boston: Allyn & Bacon.

Knapp, M., & Vangelisti, A. (2003). Relationship stages: A communication perspective. In K. M. Galvin and P. J. Cooper (Eds.), *Making connections: Readings in interpersonal communication* (3rd ed.) (pp. 158–165). Los Angeles, CA: Roxbury.

Lewis, K. E., & Bierly, M. (1990). Toward a profile of the female voter: Sex differences in perceived physical attractiveness and competence of political candidates. *Sex Roles, 22,* 1–12.

Mathes, E. W., Brennan, S. M., Haugen, & Rice, H. B. (1985). Ratings of physical attractiveness as a function of age. *The Journal of Social Psychology, 125,* 157–168.

McClellan, B., & McKelvie, S. J. (1993). Effects of age and gender on perceived physical attractiveness. *Canadian Journal of Behavioral Science, 25,* 135–142.

McCroskey, J. C., & McCain, T. A. (1974). The measurement of interpersonal attraction. *Speech Monographs, 41,* 261–266.

McCroskey, J. C., Richmond, V. P., & Daly, J. A. (1975). The development of a measure of perceived homophily in interpersonal communication. *Human Communication Research, 1,* 323–332.

McKenna, K. Y., Green, A. S., & Gleason, M. E. (2002). Relationship formation on the Internet: What's the big attraction? *Journal of Social Issues, 58,* 9–31.

Mongeau, P. A., Serewicz, M. C., & Therrien, L. F. (2004). Goals for cross-sex first dates: Identification, measurement, and the influence of contextual factors. *Communication Monographs, 71,* 121–147.

Mottet, T. P. (2000). The role of sexual orientation in predicting outcome value and anticipated communication behaviors. *Communication Quarterly, 48,* 233–240.

Perrett, D. I., Lee, K. J., & Penton-Voak, I. (1998). Effects of sexual dimorphism on facial attractiveness, *Nature, 394*(August, 27), 884–886.

Pines, A. M. (2001). The role of gender and culture in romantic attraction. *European Psychologist, 6,* 96–102.

Reis, H. T., & Patrick, B. C. (1996). Attachment and intimacy: Component processes. In E. T. Higgins and A. W. Kruglanski (Eds.), *Social psychology: Handbook of basic principles* (pp. 523–563). New York: Guilford Press.

Reis, H. T., & Shaver, P. (1988). Intimacy as interpersonal process. In S. Duck (Ed.), *Handbook of personal relationships: Theory, research, and interventions* (pp. 367–389). Chichester: John Wiley & Sons Ltd.

Richmond, V. P. (1992). *Nonverbal communication in the classroom.* Edina, MN: Burgess.

Segal, M. W. (1974). Alphabet and attraction: An unobtrusive measure of the effect of propinquity in a field setting. *Journal of Personality and Social Psychology, 30,* 654–657.

Snyder, M., Berscheid, E., & Glick, P. (1985). Focusing on the exterior and the interior: Two investigations of the initiation of personal relationships. *Journal of Personality and Social Psychology, 48,* 1427–1439.

Sprecher, S., & Hendrick, S. (2004). Self-disclosure in intimate relationships: Associations with individual and relationship characteristics over time. *Journal of Social and Clinical Psychology, 23,* 857–877.

Sprecher, S., Sullivan, Q., & Hatfield, E. (1994). Mate selection preferences: Gender differences examined in a national sample. *Journal of Personality and Social Psychology, 66,* 1074–1080.

Sunnafrank, M. (1986). Predicted outcome value during initial interactions: A reformulation of uncertainty reduction theory. *Human Communication Research, 13,* 3–33.

Thibaut, J., & Kelley, H. (1959). *The social psychology of groups.* New York: Wiley.

Toma, C. L., & Hancock, J. T. (2010). Looks and lies: The role of physical attractiveness in online dating self-presentation and deception. *Communication Research, 37*(3), 335–351.

Vangelisti, A. L. (2002). Interpersonal processes in romantic relationships. In M. L. Knapp & J. A. Daly (Eds.), *Handbook of interpersonal communication* (pp. 643–679). Thousand Oaks, CA: Sage.

Wilbur, C. J., & Campbell, L. (2011). Humor in romantic contexts: Do men participate and women evaluate? *Personality and Social Psychology Bulletin, 37*(7), 918–929.

Zebrowitz, L. A. (1997). *Reading faces: Window to the soul?* Boulder, CO: Westview Press.

Sustaining Relationships:
Relationship Maintenance and Conflict Management

OBJECTIVES

- Discuss the four goals of relationship maintenance.
- Explain equity theory and discuss how it is related to the process of relationship maintenance.
- Describe the five most common relationship maintenance strategies.
- Identify individual differences that affect relationship maintenance strategy choices.
- Define conflict and identify the key aspects of conflict episodes.
- Explain the three most common conflict management styles and describe advantages and disadvantages of each.
- Explain the four most typical conflict responses.

SCENARIO: SOUND FAMILIAR?

Maria was tired of fighting with her roommates. It seemed as though they were always arguing about cleaning the apartment, guests, food purchases, and a range of other roommate-related concerns. At times, the comments the roommates made to one another were verbally aggressive. Maria worked hard to maintain her relationships with her roommates, but she was becoming increasingly frustrated with their constant bickering and the lack of effort her roommates put into maintaining their friendships. She began to question whether she wanted to live with these same women next year.

KEY TERMS

Advice	Conflict management	Face management
Antisocial behaviors	styles	Fair fighting
Assurances	Control mutuality	Humor
Avoidance	De-escalatory conflict	Incompatible goals
Avoidant	spirals	Interdependence
Collaborative/	Ego support	Interference
integrative	Empathy	Joint activities
Comforting skills	Equity theory	Liking (or affinity)
Commitment	Escalatory conflict	Loyalty
Competitive/	spirals	Mediated
distributive	Exit	communication
Conflict	Expressed struggle	Neglect

No flirting	Relationship	Strategic maintenance
Openness	maintenance strategies	behaviors
Overbenefited	Routine maintenance	Trust
Perceived scarce	behaviors	Underbenefited
resources	Sharing tasks	Verbal aggression
Positivity	Skill similarity model	Voice
	Social network	

OVERVIEW

In Chapter 7 we examined the process of initiating relationships. In this chapter we examine how and why individuals maintain their relationships with others and manage conflict. Perhaps you can relate to Maria's roommate situation and the frustration she is experiencing. Some people seem to have more trouble staying together than building new bonds. The difficulty in sustaining a high level of commitment in romantic relationships is best illustrated by the current divorce rate in the United States: approximately 50 percent of current marriages will fail, and, sadly, most second marriages have an even greater chance of ending. In the first sections of this chapter we take a closer look at the goals of relationship maintenance, the reasons we maintain relationships with others, and the strategies used. We use a number of strategies to maintain relationships with our romantic partners, friends, family members, and colleagues. In this chapter we explore the use of different strategies and examine their effect on relationship maintenance.

> We use different strategies to maintain relationships with our romantic partners, friends, family members, and colleagues.

In the second section of this chapter we examine the role of conflict in our relationships. Conflict is inevitable, and in fact, all of us experience it at one time or another in our interpersonal relationships. To maintain relationships with those we care about, it is important to manage conflict appropriately. In the conflict section of this chapter, we present information on conflict in order to help you: (1) understand what conflict is and how it can be both good and bad in relationships and (2) approach and respond to conflict situations appropriately.

SIGNIFICANCE OF RELATIONSHIP MAINTENANCE

According to Duck (1988), individuals involved in committed relationships spend much more time maintaining a relationship than in any other phase of the relationship. Relationship maintenance is not an easy task. It often takes a great deal of time, effort, and skill. To better understand the process of relationship maintenance, let us consider four common relationship maintenance goals as proposed by Dindia and Canary (1993). They state that individuals who are focusing on relationship maintenance have one of the following four goals in mind: (1) maintaining the existence of the relationship, (2) maintaining a desired state or condition in the relationship, (3) maintaining a satisfactory state in a relationship, or (4) repairing a relationship in an attempt to either restore it or sustain it in a satisfactory state (1993, p. 163). We will consider each of these goals.

Maintaining the Existence of the Relationship

Have you ever had a friend whom you call or text only once or twice a year? Or perhaps there are friends or family members who send you an annual holiday card with a letter updating the events of the past year, and that is the only communication you have with them until the next Christmas card arrives. In both of these examples, the goal of relationship maintenance is to keep the relationship in existence, or to keep it from dying.

Relationship maintenance is often an ongoing task.

Maintaining a Desired State in the Relationship

The second goal of relationship maintenance focuses on maintaining a desired state in a relationship. Some of you may have already experienced a situation that illustrates this goal. Perhaps you learned a close friend was interested in you romantically but you did not feel the same way about this friend. Instead of terminating the relationship with your close friend, you decided to avoid flirting with this friend, self-disclosing private information to this friend, or doing anything that might increase the level of intimacy in your relationship. To maintain your desired level of closeness with this friend, you purposely and strategically altered your communication in an effort to stay "just friends." This strategy of regulating the state of the relationship enables one partner to keep the relationship at a level that is satisfactory rather than dissolving the relationship altogether.

Maintaining a Satisfactory State

A third goal focuses on attempts made by both partners to maintain a level of relationship satisfaction that they find to be mutually agreeable. Depending on the type and status of the relationship, what partners define as "mutually satisfying" can differ from one relationship to the next. In our example, Maria and her roommates might agree that, in order to maintain the quality of their relationships, they have to set time aside to have fun together. They might also agree that it is important for each of them to spend time with other friends so that they do not spend too much time together, which could negatively affect their relationships as well. The roommates find this arrangement agreeable.

routine maintenance behaviors relationship maintenance behaviors that are performed every day in an effort to keep the relationship alive.

Routine and Strategic Relationship Maintenance

Dindia and Canary (1993) point out that relationship maintenance involves both routine and strategic maintenance behaviors. Relationship maintenance is often an ongoing task. Just as you would seek routine maintenance to repair any issues that might keep your car from running smoothly, individuals engage in relationship maintenance to make sure that relationships run smoothly. According to researchers, routine maintenance behaviors "foster relational maintenance more in the manner of a 'by-product'" (Stafford, Dainton, & Haas, 2000, p. 307). Routine maintenance behaviors are performed every day in an effort to keep the relationship alive and may include behaviors such as giving advice and managing conflict (Stafford et al., 2000). While these behaviors may seem mundane at times, they are needed to maintain relationship satisfaction.

© ProStockStudio/Shutterstock.com

Spending time together helps friends reconnect and maintain their friendships.

strategic maintenance behaviors   relationship maintenance behaviors enacted to repair or fix the relationship in some way. These behaviors are often triggered by some type of transgression.

Individuals also engage in strategic maintenance behaviors. These behaviors are often enacted to repair or fix the relationship in some way. Perhaps you realize that your relationship with a friend has become more distant since you started a new romantic relationship. In an attempt to maintain your friendship, you realize that you have to fix some things—namely, spend more time together and engage in more communication with one another. Dindia and Canary (1993) note that it is important to remember that some aspects of these four goals can overlap with one another. Further, they point out that a relationship can be maintained even though one or both partners find it to be unsatisfactory, and even satisfactory relationships end for a number of reasons.

WHY WE MAINTAIN SOME RELATIONSHIPS AND NOT OTHERS

So why is it that we choose to maintain some relationships and not others? There are numerous factors that are central to interpersonal communication and relationship maintenance, including: intimacy, immediacy, investment, attraction, similarity, liking, commitment, and affection (see, for example, Burgoon & Hale, 1984). Rather than providing an exhaustive list of all of the characteristics that have been identified as relevant to sustaining relationships, interpersonal scholars have narrowed the list to the four relational characteristics that are generally perceived as universal to most relationships: control mutuality, trust, liking, and commitment (Canary & Stafford, 1994). Research has shown that relationships without these characteristics often lack substance, and as a result may not be able to be maintained.

Control mutuality is defined as "the extent to which couples agree on who has the right to influence the other and establish relational goals" (Canary & Stafford, 1994, p. 6). Relationships in which partners experience a high level of control mutuality are the result of both partners agreeing on who takes control in decision-making situations. Suppose two friends are planning a vacation to celebrate the end of the school year. If one of them is extremely organized, both friends may agree that he should be the one to plan their itinerary for the trip.

Trust has emerged as an equally important relationship characteristic. Individuals are often reluctant to reveal information to those they do not trust, and refusing to disclose about oneself often hinders relationship development. According to Rotenberg and Boulton (2013), individuals are considered trustworthy based on a number of different behaviors exhibited in a relationship. In order to be "trusted," a person must exhibit the following characteristics: (1) reliability, or the extent to which the individual keeps his or her promises; (2) emotional expression, or the extent to which the person does not cause any emotional pain for the partner—the individual is receptive to the partner's disclosures, does not share private information with others, and avoids saying or doing anything to embarrass the partner; and (3) honesty, or the extent to which the person is forthright with information.

Another characteristic required for sustaining a relationship is liking, or affinity. Mutual liking, or expressed affect, is a universal feature of all relationships. We prefer to be around individuals who know and like us. Not surprisingly, it is often very difficult for us to say no to requests that come from individuals we like (Cialdini, 2003).

Control mutuality   the extent to which couples agree on who has the right to influence the other and establish relational goals.

Trust   an important quality of relationships; a strong belief that someone is reliable and honest.

liking (or affinity) relational characteristic that indicates partners feel positively toward one another.

RESEARCH IN REAL LIFE: HOW IMPORTANT IS TRUST IN CHILDHOOD PEER RELATIONSHIPS?

To learn more about the importance of trust in children's peer relationships, Rotenberg and Boulton (2013) surveyed 505 nine-year-old children about their perceptions of how trust was expressed in their friendships. They made the following conclusions about the significance of trust:

- When children felt their peers were able to keep secrets shared, they viewed these same peers as more trustworthy.
- Children who reported greater feelings of trust toward their peers were also less likely to report being bullied. They were less likely to be called names, get left out of group situations, and/or be targeted physically by their peers.
- The researchers measured children's ratings of peer trustworthiness over time and found they were consistent over an eight-month period.

commitment an important relational characteristic that refers to the desire to continue or maintain a relationship.

Equity theory states that a relationship is considered equitable when the ratio of inputs to outputs is equal for both individuals involved.

A fourth and final characteristic of successful relationships is commitment, which refers to our desire to continue a relationship. When we say we are committed to a relationship, this is usually interpreted to mean that we are in it "for the long haul" and "for better or for worse." While commitment is important in romantic relationships for obvious reasons, it is also relevant to familial and platonic relationships. Commitment, trust, control mutuality, and liking are characteristics that most of us desire in our communication and relationships.

In addition to understanding these relational characteristics, it is also important to recognize the theoretical explanations for why we choose to maintain relationships. Equity theory offers perhaps one of the most widely understood explanations for why some individuals engage in relationship maintenance activity and others do

© Liquorice Legs/Shutterstock.com

Committed relationships are in it "for the long haul."

> Overbenefited individuals may be less satisfied in their relationships because they feel guilty about not contributing equally to the relationship.

not (Canary & Stafford 1992). According to this theory, a relationship is considered equitable when the ratio of inputs to outputs is equal for both individuals involved. If, for example, you contribute more inputs compared to the outputs you receive from your partner, you will feel underbenefited in the relationship, possibly resulting in anger at getting less than you deserve.

Conversely, if your output to input ratio is greater than that of your relationship partner, then you will feel overbenefited. Some of you may wonder why those who are overbenefited in relationships report feeling dissatisfied. Is it possible that individuals who receive too much attention, affection, or gifts could possibly be unhappy in a relationship? Absolutely! Overbenefited individuals may be less satisfied in their relationships because they feel guilty about not contributing equally to the relationship. Perhaps you have a friend who is always the one who sends you text messages or who calls you. Eventually, you may feel guilty that you fail to return the friend's text messages or calls because you have failed at contributing equally to the relationship.

underbenefited when a relationship partner contributes more to the relationship than he or she receives in return.

overbenefited when an individual is not contributing as much to the relationship as her partner.

If we rank, in order, the level of satisfaction experienced in relationships, it is not surprising that partners who are in equitable relationships report the greatest level of satisfaction. Those who feel overbenefited are the next most satisfied, and the least satisfied individuals are those who report feeling underbenefited.

HOW WE MAINTAIN RELATIONSHIPS: THE ROLE OF COMMUNICATION SKILLS

Now that you have a better understanding of the four relational characteristics associated with maintenance and the theory explaining why we choose to sustain our relationships, let us take a closer look at the role that communication skills plays in maintaining relationships with others.

Interpersonal researchers continually explore new ways that communication can be used as a tool to maintain relationships. For example, Burleson and Samter's (1994) research emphasizes the importance of similarity in communication skills in maintaining relationships. They state, "Similarity in the nature and level of partners' social skills may be more important to relationship maintenance than the absolute level of skill sophistication of the partners" (p. 62). They propose a skill similarity model (SSM) that portrays relationship maintenance as a process requiring the involvement of both partners. According to the SSM, relationship partners' communication skills will not change dramatically over time; therefore, it is important for partners to possess skills perceived as similar. Across several different studies, the researchers found that relationship partners with the same level of communication skills possessed the highest levels of satisfaction (Burleson & Samter, 1996). Interestingly, both the low communication skill and the high communication skill dyads in their studies reported the same levels of relationship satisfaction. See the text box below for a summary of the results of another SSM study.

skill similarity model proposes that relationship partners' communication skills will not change dramatically over time; therefore, it is important for partners to possess communication skills perceived as similar.

RESEARCH IN REAL LIFE: THE IMPORTANCE OF SKILL SIMILARITY IN FATHER-DAUGHTER RELATIONSHIPS

Dunleavy, Wanzer, Krezmien, and Ruppel (2011) were interested in learning whether daughters and fathers with similar communication skills would report higher relationship satisfaction and more frequent communication than those with dissimilar skills. They used the skill similarity model as the framework for this research.

- 388 college-aged females completed an interpersonal communication competence measure on themselves and their fathers. Daughters also completed measures that assessed how satisfied they were in their relationships and how often they communicated with their fathers.
- As the SSM would predict, when daughters indicated their skills were different from their fathers' skills, they tended to be less satisfied in their relationships and communicate less frequently with their fathers.
- When daughters reported greater discrepancies between their skills and their fathers' skills, they were less likely to have open and ongoing conversations with their fathers about a wide range of issues.

Burleson and Samter (1994) also argue that maintaining relationships typically involves mastery of specific types of communication skills such as comforting, ego support, empathy, and face management. Those who are able to master these valuable communication skills are more likely to experience success and satisfaction in their relationships. Comforting skills can be verbal and/or nonverbal in nature and include the ability to reduce another's emotional distress. Comforting can be communicated verbally ("I can see why you're so upset about this situation!") or via nonverbal channels, such as with a hug or an encouraging look.

Ego support, which is described as the ability to make others feel positive about themselves, is another essential relationship maintenance communication skill. Giving a compliment to a close friend about his artwork is an example of ego support.

Empathy involves the ability to see things from the other person's point of view. Employing empathy communicates to others that their perspective is important in maintaining the relationship. Consider the relationship in which one partner is devoted to his religious beliefs, but the other partner was not raised to value religion. By respecting each other's differences in values and beliefs, maintenance is achieved. Perhaps the couple agrees to attend church services together for particular events, and also agrees not to force their beliefs on each other.

Face-management skills are an essential part of relationship maintenance. The concept of *face* is described as one's self-perception that they wish to portray a particular image when interacting with others. Avoiding communication that could be perceived as face-threatening can strengthen a relationship. Examples of communication facework include: being polite, avoiding topics that could potentially cause embarrassment to another, and using disclaimers to help manage the other's perception of self (e.g., "I know I may be crazy to think that this means that you don't care . . .").

Comforting, ego support, empathy, and face management skills are all important and desirable communication skills that can assist in the relationship maintenance process. Researchers have also studied a wide range of specific strategies individuals use to maintain the quality of their relationships.

How do you comfort those who are close to you?

Comforting Skills verbal and/or nonverbal messages enacted by a source to reduce another's emotional distress.

Ego support the ability to make others feel positive about themselves by giving compliments or engaging in other behaviors that increase self-esteem.

Empathy involves the ability to see things from the other person's point of view.

Face management essential communication skills linked to relationship maintenance that involves avoiding communication with a partner that could threaten her/his self-esteem and being polite and considerate.

RELATIONSHIP MAINTENANCE STRATEGIES

Because our relationships cannot sustain themselves, it is up to us to engage in behaviors that will prolong them. Relationship maintenance strategies are defined as the behaviors and activities used strategically "to sustain desired relational qualities or to sustain the current status of the relationship" (Canary & Stafford, 2001, p. 134).

What are some of the most common relationship maintenance strategies people use? Researchers Laura Stafford and Dan Canary (1991) examined all of the studies that focused on how partners maintain relationships and identified the five most common types of relationship maintenance strategies: positivity, openness, assurances, social networks,

Relationship maintenance strategies behaviors and activities used routinely and strategically to sustain desired relational qualities or to sustain the current status of the relationship.

Sharing household tasks helps maintain a relationship.

© Minerva Studio /Shutterstock.com.

Positivity a relationship maintenance strategy that involves being polite, acting cheerful and upbeat, and avoiding criticism.

Openness relationship maintenance strategy involving open and ongoing discussions partners have about the status of the relationship.

Assurances relationship maintenance behaviors that include expressing love and commitment as well as making references to the future of the relationship.

social network a relationship maintenance strategy that involves relationship partners spending time with mutual friends and family members.

sharing tasks a relationship maintenance strategy that focuses on the extent to which partners share the chores and responsibilities associated with the relationship.

Joint activities relationship maintenance strategy that involves partners doing activities together: for example, "hanging out" with each other, watching television together, taking dance lessons, and going on trips with each other.

and sharing tasks. Positivity involves being polite, acting cheerful and upbeat, and avoiding criticism. Isn't it easier to maintain a relationship with someone who has a positive outlook on life and on the relationship than with someone who is always pessimistic? Openness refers to the open and ongoing discussions partners have about the status of the relationship. When individuals employ openness, they share their thoughts and feelings about the relationship. Assurances refer to expressions of love and commitment as well as making references to the future of the relationship. Relationship partners also sustain relationships by spending time with the mutual friends and family members who create a social network. The fifth and final strategy, sharing tasks, focuses on the extent to which partners share the chores and responsibilities associated with the relationship. Depending on the type of relationship, these tasks could include sharing responsibility for exchanging emails or phone calls, or allotting household tasks.

Since Stafford and Canary's initial investigation, there have been a number of follow-up studies exploring relationship maintenance strategies employed in a variety of relationships. For example, researchers have examined relationship maintenance in married adults (Dainton & Stafford, 1993; Dainton & Aylor, 2002; Ragsdale, 1996), in gay and lesbian relationships (Haas & Stafford, 1998), in dating couples (Dainton & Aylor, 2002), in same-sex (Canary et al., 1993) and cross-sex friendships (Messman, Canary, & Hause, 2000), and in family relationships (Canary et al., 1993; Myers & Weber, 2004). Once researchers began investigating the use of maintenance strategies in the various types of relationships listed above, it became apparent that there were numerous taxonomies, or ways of classifying, relationship maintenance behaviors. At this point, you will probably be happy to know that we are not going to cover all of the relationship maintenance strategies that exist. However, we will provide a brief overview of some of the additional maintenance strategies individuals might use with friends, romantic partners, family members, or coworkers such as: joint activities, mediated communication, advice, humor, no flirting, avoidance, and antisocial behaviors (Canary et al., 1993). Joint activities refer to those behaviors relationship partners do together: "hanging out" with each other, watching television together, and going on trips with each other. Mediated communication includes the exchange of email messages, letters, text messages, or phone calls to ensure a satisfying relationship. Advice typically involves disclosing personal information to the relationship partner or giving or seeking advice on some issue. Humor is also sometimes used as a means of maintaining relationships and might include the use of jokes and sarcasm in either positive or negative ways. A positive example of using humor would be "trying to make each other laugh" (Canary et al., 1993, p. 11), while a negative example of using humor might include being sarcastic or making fun of someone's appearance or personality.

Interestingly, there are also strategies individuals use to reduce the amount of intimacy in a relationship. One such strategy is labeled no flirting. By not encouraging "overly familiar behaviors" in our relationships, we are able to help maintain a desired state or level of intimacy. As mentioned earlier in the chapter, if your goal is to be "friends" with some-one, you would probably refrain from flirting with this person.

> To maintain the quality of a relationship and, at the same time, preserve a sense of autonomy, it might also be necessary to establish times when we are away from our partners.

The relationship maintenance strategies labeled avoidance and antisocial behaviors would initially appear to be antithetical to prolonging any type of relationship. However, individuals employ these types of "maintenance" behaviors in certain situations. Strategies labeled avoidant include dodging "sore," or difficult, subjects that we should avoid discussing with our romantic partners, family members, or friends, to steer clear of conflict. To maintain the quality of a relationship and, at the same time, preserve a sense of autonomy, it might also be necessary to establish times when we are away from our partners. Hence, relationship partners might have a "girls' night" or "boys' night" out.

Partners also engage in either direct or indirect antisocial behaviors, which are described as behaviors that might seem unfriendly or coercive (Canary et al., 1993). To gain a relationship partner's attention or to signal something is wrong in the relationship, one partner might act moody or difficult (indirect strategy) to gain the other person's attention. Dainton and Gross (2008) identified a number of antisocial behaviors couples used to maintain their relationships. Partners in romantic relationships might start a fight (destructive conflict) or try to determine personal or private information about a partner (spying) in an effort to maintain their relationships. Not surprisingly, couples who exhibit more of these negative maintenance strategies also report lower amounts of trust, commitment, satisfaction, and liking (Goodboy, Myers, & Members of Investigating Communication, 2010). Read the textbox below to learn more about research on the use of negative relational maintenance strategies in romantic relationships.

Mediated communication relationship maintenance strategy that includes exchanging email messages, letters, text messages, or phone calls with one's partner.

Advice relationship maintenance strategy that involves disclosing personal information to the relationship partner or giving or seeking advice on some issue.

Humor a relationship maintenance strategy that might include the use of jokes and sarcasm in either positive or negative ways to elicit laughter and smiling from one's partner.

no flirting a relationship maintenance strategy that is used to reduce the amount of intimacy in a relationship. One or both partners agree to refrain from exhibiting flirtatious behaviors.

avoidant relationship maintenance strategies that include dodging "sore" or difficult subjects that we should avoid discussing with our romantic partners, family members, or friends; to steer clear of conflict.

antisocial behaviors relationship maintenance strategy that involves acting in an unfriendly, unkind, or coercive manner to maintain the level of desired intimacy relationship.

RESEARCH IN REAL LIFE: ATTACHMENT AND THE USE OF NEGATIVE RELATIONAL MAINTENANCE BEHAVIORS IN ROMANTIC RELATIONSHIPS

Goodboy and Bolkan (2011) conducted research to understand why individuals might use negative relational maintenance strategies in their relationships. They studied the relationship between college students' attachment styles (Chapter 2) and use of negative relationship maintenance strategies.

- 232 college students in romantic relationships completed the Attachment Style Measure and the Negative Maintenance Scale.
- Secures were less likely to use negative relationship maintenance behaviors (i.e., jealousy induction, avoidance, destructive conflict, allowing control, spying, and infidelity) than non-secures.
- Dismissives and fearful-avoidants, who tend to have poor working models of relationships, reported using more negative relationship maintenance strategies than secures.

See Table 8.1 for additional examples of relationship maintenance strategies.

As relationship partners become more connected, or interdependent, the use of relationship maintenance strategies generally increases (Canary &

| Table 8.1 | Relationship Maintenance Strategies |

Strategy	Examples
1. Positivity	Engage in cheerful communication; ask "How was your day?"
2. Openness	Solicit discussion on status of relationship; ask partner to share feelings about the relationship
3. Assurances	Emphasize commitment to one another; say "I love you" to each other
4. Social network	Express interest in spending time with mutual friends; focus on building friendships that are mutual/shared
5. Sharing tasks	Help partner with various tasks or household chores such as cooking and cleaning
6. Joint activities	Spend time hanging out with each other; go to the movies, football games, dinners
7. Mediated communication	Use email to communicate; call partner on the phone; send partner a card
8. Avoidance	Avoid talking about certain issues; avoid the relationship partner
9. Antisocial behaviors	Be mean or rude to him/her; act moody when around him/her
10. Humor	Call him/her a funny or silly name; use sarcasm when communicating
11. No flirting	Do not flirt with him/her; do not show any sign of romantic interest
12. Advice	Give/seek advice on a variety of issues (e.g., love, relationships, school, future)

Source: Adapted from Canary and Stafford (1994, 1992); Canary et al. (1993); Messman et al. (2000).

Stafford, 2001). It should come as no surprise that decreases in relationship maintenance behaviors by one or both partners often signals that a relationship is in trouble (Ayres, 1983). Canary and Stafford's (1994) research indicates that the "use of positivity, sharing tasks, and offering assurance helps sustain control mutuality, trust, liking and commitment" (p. 19). They also note that not all relationships will benefit equally from the use of these five strategies (positivity, assurances, etc.). Thus, it is important to examine research that summarizes how these strategies function in different types of relationships, paying special attention to the outcomes of their use.

RELATIONSHIP MAINTENANCE IN DIFFERENT TYPES OF RELATIONSHIPS

Not surprisingly, the tactics, or behaviors, you use to maintain your friendships are different from those you use to sustain your relationship with your romantic partner. Researchers found the use of relationship maintenance strategies differs depending on relationship type. While there is a vast amount of research available on relationship maintenance in different types of relationships, we will overview a small portion to understand how relationship maintenance strategy use varies in relationships based on the *type of relationship* (i.e., romantic, platonic, family), *cultural differences*, and *sexual orientation*. We also discuss the outcomes associated with the use of these strategies.

Relationship maintenance has been studied extensively in different types of romantic relationships (see, for example, Canary, Stafford, Hause, & Wallace, 1993; Dainton, 2000; Dainton & Stafford, 1993). Researchers have investigated how relationship maintenance strategies differ based on (1) relationship length; (2) type of commitment, e.g., married or dating; (3) cultural differences; and (4) sexual preferences. Romantic partners use relationship maintenance strategies (e.g., positivity, openness, assurances, sharing tasks, and cards/letters) more than friends do (Canary et al., 1993). This finding is not particularly surprising since most of us put more energy into maintaining our romantic relationships. In another related study on married couples' use of relationship maintenance strategies, researchers found that married couples' use of relationship maintenance behaviors decreased over time (Dindia & Baxter, 1987; Ragsdale, 1996). Additionally, the use of relationship maintenance strategies in romantic relationships tends to become more *routine* and *less strategic* over time. In essence, we become comfortable with our partner and fall into a routine in which we use the same behaviors that have been proven to work in the past. In newer relationships, partners usually have to devote more time and energy to thinking about how they will strategically use assurances, positivity, or even openness as a means of stabilizing their relationship. For individuals in long-term relationships, the use of these behaviors becomes part of the daily routine and is not something partners are always cognizant of doing. One example of a relationship maintenance routine exhibited in married couples or long-term relationships is an expression of affection such as "I love you." Couples who ask each other questions about their daily activities such as "How was work?" or "How was school?" are also engaging in routine relationship maintenance.

© Goran Bogicevic /Shutterstock.com.

What relationship maintenance strategies do romantic partners use?

Some strategies appear to be more effective than others in increasing relationship satisfaction and stability, but it depends on the type of relationship and the individuals involved.

Some strategies appear to be more effective than others in increasing relationship satisfaction and stability, but it depends on the type of relationship and the individuals involved. For example, romantic relationship partners' use of assurances has been linked repeatedly to relationship satisfaction and commitment (Dainton & Aylor, 2002; Stafford & Canary, 1991). There are very few of us who do not like to hear our relationship partner say, "I love you" or "I really care about you." When comparing relationship maintenance behaviors of married couples to dating couples, married partners use more assurances and social networks, while dating couples engage in more openness than married couples (Stafford & Canary, 1991). Partners in dating relationships are still getting to know each other, and so individuals must be more open and willing to share information with each other for the relationship to develop.

Researchers have also investigated relationship maintenance in family contexts. Maintaining relationships with our grandparents, parents, siblings, aunts, uncles, and cousins takes a significant amount of time and energy. Because sibling relationships are often described as "lifelong" types of relationships, several studies have examined siblings' use of relationship maintenance strategies (Mikkelson, Myers, & Hannawa, 2011; Myers & Members of COM

200, 2001; Myers & Goodboy, 2013). From the research on siblings we can draw several conclusions:

- Adult siblings reported more positive relationships with their siblings when they used relationship maintenance strategies (i.e., positivity, assurances, openness, networks, and tasks) (Myers & Members of COM 200, 2001).
- Individuals of all ages (i.e., 18 and over 55) reported more positive relationships when their siblings engaged in relationship maintenance strategies.
- Female siblings tend to engage in relationship maintenance strategies more often than male siblings (Myers & Members of COM 200, 2001).
- Siblings who are more genetically related or share more genetic material with each other engage in relationship maintenance behavior more often than less-genetically related siblings. In other words, identical twins and fraternal twins, who share a great deal of genetic material, used positivity, openness, assurances, social networks, and shared tasks more frequently in their relationships than did adopted siblings or stepsiblings (Mikkelson, Myers, & Hannawa, 2011).
- Myers and Goodboy's (2013) research on adult sibling relationships indicated that siblings will engage in more relationship maintenance (e.g. openness) when the relationship is perceived as equitable. Siblings also report greater trust, liking, and satisfaction when the relationship is perceived as equitable.

Culture also plays a role in the types of relational maintenance strategies we employ. When comparing the impact of culture on marital partners, African American couples indicated using task-sharing as a maintenance strategy less often than European American couples (Diggs & Stafford, 1998). Researchers explain this result by pointing out that, generally, African American males and females tend to be more focused on sharing roles and responsibilities in their relationship when compared to their European American counterparts. Task-sharing might be discussed more frequently by European American couples because they have struggled historically with creating more equity in their romantic relationships. This study illustrates that partners' individual differences, which might include factors such as culture, personality, age, or even maturity, may also affect the types of relationship maintenance strategies used.

Sexual orientation also plays a role in the type of relationship maintenance strategies partners use with each other. Haas and Stafford (1998) discovered that heterosexual and homosexual couples employ many of the same strategies in their relationships. Two strategies unique to gay and lesbian relationships include (1) being "out" as a couple when communicating with their social networks, and (2) seeking out social environments supportive of gay and lesbian relationships. Additional research by Eldridge and Gilbert (1990) emphasizes the importance of perceived equity in relational power and high levels of emotional intimacy in enhancing relationship satisfaction in lesbian relationships. Gay men indicate a preference for low levels of conflict and high levels of cooperation as factors that help maintain a satisfying relationship (Jones & Bates, 1978). Heterosexual and homosexual couples appear to exhibit similar behaviors in their relationships to maintain satisfaction.

Heterosexual and homosexual couples appear to exhibit similar behaviors in their relationships to maintain satisfaction.

As researchers continue to explore the different ways partners sustain relationships, they are also turning their attention to the increasing role technology plays in how people maintain these associations.

FACEBOOK AND RELATIONSHIP MAINTENANCE

Facebook, an online social networking site, has been studied extensively by researchers from a number of different academic fields. Several researchers indicate that many people use Facebook to maintain relationships with friends, family, romantic partners, and coworkers (Craig & Wright, 2012; Dainton, 2013).

College students express positivity, openness, and assurances on Facebook as a means of maintaining their romantic relationships (Dainton, 2013). Does using these behaviors on Facebook contribute significantly to romantic partners' perceptions of relationship satisfaction? Dainton (2013) examined whether college students' use of relationship maintenance behaviors on Facebook and general face-to-face relationship maintenance behaviors contributed to reported relationship

Does Facebook help you maintain relationships?

satisfaction. When college students indicated their relationship partners used positivity and assurances on Facebook as a means of maintaining their romantic relationships, they reported *somewhat higher levels* of relationship satisfaction compared to college students who did not report the use of these same maintenance strategies (Dainton, 2013). However, when comparing Facebook relationship maintenance behavior with general relationship maintenance activity, the Facebook relationship maintenance behavior did not contribute meaningfully to relationship satisfaction. Dainton stated, "Facebook might not be an important tool for maintaining romantic relationships as compared to other relational types" (Dainton, 2013, p. 120). When looking at which behaviors were most instrumental in fostering satisfying romantic relationships, college students indicated that general maintenance behaviors such as "assurances" and "managing conflict" were more important to relationship satisfaction than Facebook maintenance behaviors.

CONCLUSIONS ABOUT RELATIONSHIP MAINTENANCE

There is an extensive body of research on strategic and routine relationship maintenance behaviors. Below, we highlight a number of important conclusions from the relationship maintenance literature:

- Relationships are not self-sustaining and, as such, require a significant amount of time and effort.

- Individuals are most motivated to maintain relationships in which partners exhibit high amounts of trust, commitment, control mutuality, and liking.
- Most individuals want to be in relationships that are perceived as equitable (inputs=outputs).
- Both routine and strategic relationship maintenance behaviors are used most frequently in equitable relationships.
- Five relationship maintenance strategies are used consistently regardless of the type of relationship, or whether the interactants communicate face-to-face or online: positivity, assurances, openness, sharing tasks, and social networks.
- Individuals' use of assurances, networks, and sharing tasks is consistently recognized as a significant predictor of relationship commitment.
- When researchers further examined relationship maintenance behaviors in other types of relationships, additional strategies emerged, including, among others: humor, avoidance, antisocial behaviors, mediated communication, advice, and conflict management.
- Effectiveness and frequency of strategy use depends on the type of relationship being investigated.
- Female siblings use more relationship maintenance strategies with one another than male siblings and male-female siblings.

CONFLICT: A NATURAL COMPONENT OF ALL RELATIONSHIPS

The key to sustaining our relationships often rests in our ability to manage the conflicts that arise from time to time. To maintain stability in our relationships, it is necessary to manage conflict appropriately. Many relationship scholars have identified conflict management as an important and necessary maintenance behavior. If individuals are unable to manage conflict in their different types of relationships (i.e., romantic, platonic, family, or work), it is likely that they will report less satisfaction with these relationships and may even terminate them. This section of the chapter explains what conflict is, why it occurs, how it can affect individuals and relationships (both positively and negatively), and how to manage it appropriately.

Definition of Conflict

conflict an expressed struggle between at least two interdependent parties who perceive incompatible goals, scarce resources, and interference from the other party in achieving their goals.

Regardless of whether disagreements occur between two coworkers, between a husband and wife, or between two neighbors, there are aspects that all conflict episodes share. A number of definitions for conflict exist in the literature; however, we want to focus on one that approaches conflict from a communication perspective. Hocker and Wilmot (1991) define conflict as "an expressed struggle between at least two interdependent parties who perceive incompatible goals, scarce resources, and interference from the other party in achieving their goals" (p. 12). To understand how and why conflict occurs, it is important to examine the main components of this definition in detail.

There are five consistent aspects, or components, of conflict episodes, as listed below:

| Figure 8.1 | **Five Components of Conflict Episodes** |

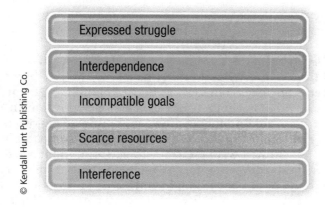

© Kendall Hunt Publishing Co.

- Expressed struggle
- Interdependence
- Incompatible goals
- Scarce resources
- Interference

Expressed Struggle. The first consistent component of conflict is that it typically involves expressed struggle or open communication about the issue or problem. How do we know if a conflict with a friend, coworker, or family member is really a conflict? From an interpersonal communication perspective, it is important to consider the communicative interchanges that make up the conflict episode (Hocker & Wilmot, 1991).

> Consider this dialogue between two roommates, Molly and Tiona:

Molly: Hey Tiona, do you want to go and get some coffee after you're done studying?

Tiona: No, thanks. *(Makes no eye contact, stares at her book.)*

Molly: Is something wrong, you seem a little annoyed? I thought you said you wanted to go and get coffee later this evening?

Tiona: I did, but now I really don't.

Molly: Fine, don't tell me what is wrong!

Do you think both roommates are aware that there is a problem? It is no wonder that Molly is confused! This example illustrates the importance of expressing conflict openly. When there are joint communicative representations of conflict, that is, both partners openly express their concerns or emotions, we typically say that conflict has occurred. Some individuals might feel angry or frustrated with a relationship partner but choose not to express their concerns openly. Once people openly communicate their feelings or concerns with their relationship partners, interpersonal conflict has occurred. Interpersonal communication scholars agree that communication is an essential element in all interpersonal conflict. Additionally, they stress that communication both affects, and is affected by, aspects of relationships (Canary, Cupach, & Messman, 1995; Hocker & Wilmot, 1991).

expressed struggle open communication about the issue or problem in a conflict situation.

Interdependence when individuals rely on one another and are aware of how their decisions or behaviors affect one another.

Interdependence.   The second key element of conflict addresses the significance of partner interdependence. Stated simply, if individuals rely on one another and are aware of how their decisions or behaviors affect one another, they are more likely to experience conflict than individuals who do not rely on one another. If you rely on your roommate to pick you up at the airport and he fails to do so, this might result in conflict. The more interdependent relationship partners are, the greater the chances are for conflict to occur (Braiker & Kelley, 1979).

incompatible goals an important component of conflict that occurs when relationship partners experience opposition in attempting to reach a goal.

Incompatible Goals.   A third factor of conflict is incompatible goals. According to Hocker and Wilmot (1991) people are most likely to "engage in conflict over goals they often deny as being important to them" (p. 17). All of us, at one time or another, will experience opposition in trying to reach a goal. Hocker and Wilmot describe two common types of goal incompatibility that can lead to conflict. One type of goal incompatibility occurs when relationship partners want the same thing. Think about two basketball players who are both competing for the same position on the team or two employees who are both contending for the same position in a company. Another type of goal incompatibility occurs when two individuals want different things. Recall the last time you and your relationship partner disagreed on the restaurant you would go to for dinner. How long did you argue about this? Do you remember how you finally decided where you would eat? Sometimes conflict is about actual differences in restaurant choices, while other times it is about who gets to choose the restaurant. Whether individuals perceive their goals as similar or different, perceived incompatibility in objectives is a consistent aspect of conflict episodes (Hocker & Wilmot, 1991).

perceived Scarce Resources anything an individual identifies as valuable or meaningful and can include, among other things: people, relationships, opportunities, material objects, or time.

Perceived Scarce Resources.   A fourth component of conflict is perceived scarce resources. Resources refer to anything an individual identifies as valuable or meaningful and can include, among other things: people, relationships, opportunities, material objects, or time. Hocker and Wilmot (1991) point out that "The resources might be real or perceived as real by the person. Likewise, the perception of scarcity, or limitation, may be apparent or actual" (p. 19). This is illustrated when an only child protests the addition of another sibling in the family and argues that the parents cannot possibly have enough love to go around for both children. Conflict experts say the best route to take in this situation is to try to change the child's perception of the available resource by assuring the child that there is more than enough love available for two children. Most interpersonal struggles revolve around perceived scarcity in power and self-esteem. As illustrated in the example above, the child was worried about receiving confirmation from the parents that would directly affect his or her self-esteem. Not surprisingly, when people fight or disagree, they often express sentiments that illustrate power and self-esteem struggles (Hocker & Wilmot, 1991).

interference an important component of conflict that occurs when a relationship partner perceives that someone is attempting to hamper or obstruct his or her ability to achieve a goal or objective.

Interference.   The fifth and final component of conflict is interference. Is it possible for individuals who depend on one another and perceive incompatible goals and scarce resources not to experience conflict? Yes, it is. Hocker and Wilmot (1991) point out that even when incompatible goals and limited resources are present, individuals must perceive interference from the other in their attempt to achieve a goal. As soon as someone interferes with, or blocks, your goals, it is likely that you will experience conflict. When we feel like someone is trying to stand in our way of accomplishing a goal, conflict is likely to emerge.

Remember, in order for conflict to occur between individuals, the following criteria must be evident: (1) differences must be expressed openly and recognized by both partners, (2) partners must be interdependent, (3) partners must have incompatible goals, (4) partners must perceive competition for scarce resources, and (5) partners must perceive interference in goal achievement. Next, we examine how conflict can be beneficial or detrimental to maintaining stability in a relationship.

WHY CONFLICT OCCURS

A common theme in all interpersonal conflict situations is incompatibility (Roloff & Soule, 2002). While we are often drawn to others because they are different, these differences can cause conflict. The list of reasons why conflict occurs in relationships is an endless one. In the next sections we highlight some of the more common types of relationship conflict.

- Individuals might argue about *principles*. This type of conflict has to do with discrepancies in values or ideals relationship partners possess. Perhaps one partner wants to get married in a church and have a big wedding ceremony while the other wants to continue the relationship but does not see a reason to get married.
- Individuals might have *realistic conflicts* that result from a variety of external situations or demands that the relationship partners face. Couples might argue about financial hardships, work demands, or difficult family members. These demands are all certainly stressful and can lead to conflict in relationships.
- *Personal conflict* results from one person acting based on her/his self-interests and not thinking about others. A personal conflict might occur when one roommate drinks all the milk and then places the empty container back in the refrigerator.
- Conflict also occurs when *rules* are broken in relationships. Most people establish a set of rules or expectations in their relationships and when these rules are broken, conflict occurs. For example, if you told a friend to keep certain information about you private and then she shared this information with another friend, you would probably be angry with her (Roloff & Soule, 2002).

This is certainly not an exhaustive list of all of the types of conflict that occur in relationships; however, the common theme across these situations is incompatibility between people. Because we are all so incredibly different, conflict is an inevitable part of our relationships. We now turn our attention to the benefits and drawbacks of conflict in relationships.

© conrado /Shutterstock.com

Have differences in your relationships caused conflicts?

CONFLICT CAN BE PRODUCTIVE OR UNPRODUCTIVE FOR INDIVIDUALS AND FOR RELATIONSHIPS

Depending upon how it is managed in interpersonal relationships, conflict can be productive or unproductive. When conflict is managed effectively, it can be good for both the relationship and the individuals involved. First, to establish meaningful relationships with others and survive in a social world, you must understand both the role of emotions (your own and others') and the social and cultural norms for conflict situations. By doing so, conflict actually becomes an important part of your personal development and growth. People's expectations and emotional states going into a conflict episode can affect the outcomes of these events (DiPaola, Roloff, & Peters, 2010). Read the textbox below to learn more about how college students' expectations of conflict intensity impacted their conflict interactions.

A second benefit of experiencing and managing conflict in interpersonal relationships is that it tests the strength and character of relationships more vigorously than other types of social interaction (Canary, Cupach, & Messman, 1995).When couples learn how to manage conflict effectively, they can strengthen their bond with each other and increase relationship satisfaction. Hence, individuals involved in the most rewarding relationships are able to manage conflict by using productive communication practices. For example, couples who manage conflict effectively and report higher relationship satisfaction refrain from aggression and focus more on confrontational (Cahn, 1992) and collaborative communication (Sillars & Wilmot, 1994).

RESEARCH IN REAL LIFE: COLLEGE STUDENTS' EXPECTATIONS OF CONFLICT INTENSITY: A SELF-FULFILLING PROPHECY

Researchers examined how college students' expectations about conflict episodes affected their interactions. They predicted that students with more intense expectations about conflict episodes would experience more negative outcomes than those with less intense expectations (DiPaola, Roloff, & Peters, 2010).

- Working from a *self-fulfilling prophecy* perspective (see Chapter 2), the researchers argued that "individuals who expect an emotionally intense conflict engage in behavior that facilitates its occurrence" (p. 60).
- 203 college students provided information on specific aspects of the conflict episode: relationship with person, conflict topic, expectation of conflict intensity, actual conflict intensity, attacking behavior, and emotional interference.
- As expected, college students' expectations for conflict intensity were related positively to the extent to which the conflict episodes were emotionally upsetting and involved personal attacks.
- Individuals who *initiated* conflict perceived more emotional intensity and more attacking behaviors than the targets of the initiation.

Another way conflict can be good for individuals in relationships is because it exposes them to different perspectives. For example, think about the last time you and your roommate argued about politics, religion, or even your favorite band. The process of actively disagreeing with another person can be personally beneficial because it exposes us to views that are different from our own. When we encounter views or perspectives that are different from ours, we usually reexamine our perspectives and reflect on why we feel or think a certain way in order to defend our views. This process of self-reflection can help individuals to either (1) develop a better understanding of their current perspective, or (2) develop a new perspective linked to the interaction with the relationship partner. Conflict can benefit individuals and relationships in a number of different ways.

Conflicts are typically described as unproductive, or destructive, when individuals walk away feeling frustrated or cheated by the end result. One type of destructive conflict is known as escalatory conflict spirals. This type of conflict is "characterized by a heavy reliance on overt power manipulation, threats, coercion and deception" (Hocker & Wilmot, 1991, p. 34). In escalatory spirals, the conflict intensifies each time individuals communicate with each other and the conflict escalates with more destructive communication occurring each time the individuals encounter each other. Individuals might also engage in unfair fighting tactics and make attempts to "get even" with each other.

When it comes to conflict situations, not everyone likes to fight it out. Rather than fight, some individuals might engage in de-escalatory conflict spirals that often involve flight responses (Hocker & Wilmot, 1991). Some individuals avoid volatile situations and instead adopt withdrawal types of behaviors. Why do individuals avoid or withdraw from conflict situations? As stated earlier in this section, individuals who are highly interdependent are more likely to experience conflict. Conversely, individuals who are not dependent on each other are less likely to engage in conflict. Perhaps relationship partners become bored with each other, apathetic about the relationship, or experience other problems in their relationship. If this is the case, then individuals might lose faith in the relationship, withdraw from interaction, and invest less time and effort into maintaining the relationship. Conflict in escalatory spirals is overt while conflict in de-escalatory spirals is covert. Individuals might avoid each other, or, when confronted, deny there is a problem. When conflict is not out in the open, it cannot be addressed or managed. Thus, expressing conflict in a covert or indirect way is clearly unproductive.

escalatory conflict spirals a type of conflict that intensifies each time individuals communicate with each other. Conflict escalates with more destructive communication occurring each time individuals communicate.

de-escalatory conflict spirals type of conflict where individuals might avoid each other, or, when confronted, deny there is a problem.

CONFLICT MANAGEMENT STYLES

Conflict can actually be healthy and productive in relationships if it is managed effectively. Researchers have identified a variety of strategies that are used by individuals. The strategies can be pictured on a continuum, with violence at one end and collaboration at the other (Hocker & Wilmot, 1991). When a conflict occurs, individuals typically decide whether they will avoid or confront it. Essentially, we make a decision to adopt various conflict management styles or habitual responses to conflict situations. The three most common conflict management styles individuals use to manage conflict are labeled *avoidance*, *competition* (*distributive*), and *collaboration* (*integrative*). Each of these conflict management styles has unique advantages and disadvantages, depending on how and when they are used.

conflict management styles habitual responses to conflict situations.

Avoidance

Avoidance is often used by partners who deny having a problem in the first place, or by someone who is uncomfortable at the prospect of engaging in conflict. In an effort to avoid conflict with another person, relationship partners might directly or indirectly deny there is a problem, use equivocation or evasive comments to avoid discussing issues, change topics, act noncommittal on an issue, or use jokes or humor. While occasionally avoiding conflict might not be problematic for relationships, consistently avoiding conflict has been found to be counterproductive for individuals in any type of relationship. Avoidance styles of conflict management are generally not productive because they often indicate a low concern for self, others, and the relationship, and are perceived as ineffective in solving problems (Hocker & Wilmot, 1991).

See the textbox in the next column for examples of avoidance messages and the disadvantages and advantages of this style.

It is important to think about the benefits and drawbacks of using avoidance as a means of managing conflict. There are times when conflict should not be addressed because it is not the right time or place to discuss an issue with someone. Also, depending on an individual's culture, they may be more or less predisposed to avoid conflict with others. Finally, avoiding a conflict does not make it go away.

AVOIDANCE CONFLICT MANAGEMENT STYLE

Sample Messages:

- Direct Denial: "There is no issue here, really."
- Topic Shift: "Let's not discuss this right now and instead focus on eating lunch."
- Noncommittal Questions: "What do you think we should do about this situation?"

Advantages:

- Buys time to contemplate issues
- Best to use with trivial or minor issues
- May protect each other's feelings

Disadvantages:

- Shows you do not really care about the relationship
- Problem will never be fixed or resolved
- Situation can escalate and relationship can end

Source: Adapted from Hocker and Wilmot (1991)

Competitive/Distributive

The second conflict management style is described as competitive or distributive. It involves the use of aggressive and uncooperative types of behaviors during conflict episodes. Individuals using this style pursue their own goals and objectives at the expense of others (Hocker & Wilmot, 1991). The primary goal when adopting this style is to win the argument using whatever means necessary. Individuals using this style view conflict as a battle or competition and address conflict situations in either assertive or aggressive ways. When individuals use a competitive style of conflict, they might offer personal criticism, rejection statements, hostile remarks, jokes or questions, presumptive remarks, or denial of responsibilities. This style of managing conflict is not always unproductive. Examine the table below for examples of this conflict style as well its as advantages and disadvantages.

COMPETITIVE/DISTRIBUTIVE CONFLICT MANAGEMENT STYLE

Sample Messages:

- Criticism: "You have no sense of humor at all!"
- Hostile Questions: "Who really cares the most and works the hardest to make this relationship work?"
- Rejection: "You have no clue at all, do you?"

Advantages:

- May be good in emergency situations
- Can generate new and creative ideas
- Can illustrate the significance of the issue

Disadvantages:

- Can harm relationship partner's self-esteem
- People become entrenched in their positions and want to win
- Can lead to covert conflict and games

Source: Adapted from Hocker and Wilmot (1991)

As we can see in the textbox above, there are situations when using competition as a means of managing conflict can be beneficial. For example, when an individual in a work setting is in a time crunch, lacks the time to debate all available alternatives, and feels strongly about his or her position, adopting a competitive stance to "win" an argument may be necessary. Or, if an issue has been discussed extensively and the individuals experiencing conflict have not made any progress toward resolving the disagreement, adopting a competitive stance may facilitate conflict resolution. Also, when individuals compete they often exert a great deal of energy, which sends a metamessage that the topic is important to the parties involved. However, competition can also damage relationships and isolate individuals who tend to avoid conflict situations. Unassertive or highly reticent individuals may avoid conflict situations when others adopt a competitive stance. Use of this style depends largely on the context, the goals of the interaction, and the unique characteristics of the individuals involved.

Collaborative/Integrative

The final conflict management style, collaborative or integrative, is often described as a productive means of managing conflict because it requires open and ongoing communication. When relationship partners adopt this style, they

collaborative/Integrative often described as a "win-win" approach to managing conflict because both parties walk away satisfied with the outcome. The goal of this conflict management strategy is to identify mutually satisfying solutions.

Collaboration is often described as a "win-win" approach to managing relationship issues because both parties walk away satisfied with the outcome.

offer descriptive and disclosive statements during the conflict episode and, at the same time, make attempts to gain similar information from others (Hocker & Wilmot, 1991). Partners work together to develop solutions to their disagreements that are mutually satisfying. Collaboration is often described as a "win-win" approach to managing relationship issues because both parties walk away satisfied with the outcome. See the textbox below for an overview of this strategy.

COLLABORATIVE/INTEGRATIVE CONFLICT MANAGEMENT STYLE

Sample Messages:

- Supportive Remarks: "I can see why you might want to do that."
- Concessions: "I promise not to interrupt you."
- Soliciting Criticism: "What are some of my communication weaknesses?"
- Disclosive Statement: "I was definitely in a bad mood last night."

Advantages:

- Best when solutions must be mutually satisfying
- Good for preserving the relationship
- Can lead to increased relationship satisfaction and solidarity

Disadvantages:

- Sometimes not worth the time and effort
- Can be used manipulatively
- Partners must have strong communication skills
- Partners must embrace this style

Source: Adapted from Hocker and Wilmot (1991)

This style of conflict management is not without its own set of constraints. For example, there are times when decisions need to be made quickly. Think about a football coach arguing with his assistant coaches about which play to run to win the game; it would not be realistic for him to consult each coach before sending out the final play. Another challenge with this approach is, because it takes time and effort, people may be reluctant to use it. Also, people might feel that by soliciting feedback from everyone and getting issues out in the open, it might "open a whole other can of worms." Collaboration, by its nature, encourages open expression of multiple perspectives. Sometimes encouraging others to openly express concerns can result in "tangents," lengthy discussion of unimportant or unrelated issues, and poor use of time. In other words, this approach could be viewed as time-consuming and challenging.

However, there are many benefits to using the collaborative/integrative approach to manage conflict management situations. When partners in romantic relationships report increased use of integrative styles of conflict management, relationship satisfaction increases (see, for example, Canary & Cupach, 1988; Canary & Spitzberg, 1989). Conversely, when partners in romantic relationships employ more distributive or avoiding styles of conflict, relationship satisfaction decreases significantly (Canary & Cupach, 1988; Canary &

Spitzberg, 1989; Rands et al., 1981; Spitzberg et al., 1994; Ting-Toomey, 1983). It should come as no surprise that those individuals who employ integrative conflict management strategies with relationship partners are generally perceived as more communicatively competent (Canary & Spitzberg, 1989). Perceptions of relationship partners' competence mediate the relationship between conflict messages and relational outcomes. More specifically, Canary and Spitzberg (1989) note that "conflict messages are assessed as more or less appropriate, effective, and globally competent, and these assessments then affect relational features of trust, control mutuality, intimacy and relational satisfaction" (p. 644). Thus, use of integrative conflict management styles, which are generally perceived as more appropriate and effective, increases relationship partners' reported satisfaction and trust.

> Collaboration, by its nature, encourages open expression of multiple perspectives.

THE DARK SIDE OF CONFLICT: VERBAL AGGRESSION

When partners lack communication skills, they are more likely to employ verbally aggressive communication behaviors, often resulting in violent episodes (deTurck, 1987; Infante, Chandler, & Rudd, 1989; Infante et al., 1990). **Verbal aggression** involves assaulting or criticizing another person's sense of self and typically involves attacks on one's character, competence, background, or appearance. These types of messages not only damage an individual's perceptions of self-worth, but can also negatively affect relationship satisfaction. It is important for relationship partners to minimize the use of verbally aggressive messages during conflict episodes.

Loreen Olsen (2002) conducted a qualitative investigation of romantic couples' conflict episodes to study the relationship between communication competence and aggression. In general, relationship partners felt the use of aggressive communication indicated a lack of communication competence. However, the researcher also found that there were times when individuals felt the use of aggressive communication in relationship disputes was justifiable. For example, participants described the use of aggressive communication as a constructive way to clear the air, gain their partner's attention, and reach a resolution faster. Some participants felt aggression was appropriate in certain situations because it became a relationship-changing event and permanently altered the way the couple managed conflict episodes. Olsen points out that her results should be interpreted with caution because most of her participants were female European Americans and because the participants recalled a conflict event that got out of hand. Thus, while these findings might not extend to all conflict episodes, they identify descriptive accounts of when relationship partners might view aggression as appropriate. In other words, because this study had participants recall conflict events, these results suggest that in hindsight there might have been productive results from aggressive behaviors.

© VGstockstudio /Shutterstock.com

Are there times in a relationship when expressing aggression is acceptable?

verbal aggression communication that involves assaulting or criticizing another person's sense of self and typically involves attacks on one's character, competence, background, or appearance.

MANAGING CONFLICT

In the final sections of this chapter, we offer a number of useful suggestions for approaching conflict productively, regardless of the communication situation. First, when approaching a conflict situation, you should consider the advantages and disadvantages of using avoidance or competitive or collaborative conflict management strategies. Each of these strategies requires a different set of communication behaviors and produces a variety of outcomes. From a relational perspective, collaboration is consistently viewed as the most competent way to manage conflict and often results in higher reported satisfaction for relationship partners. Conversely, avoidance and competition are regarded as less effective and appropriate strategies, often resulting in less relationship satisfaction.

Individuals should also consider the way they respond or react to problems in their relationships. Carl Rusbult and his colleagues (1982) found that when individuals experience problems in relationships, there are typically four different ways to react: exit, voice, loyalty, and neglect. These responses vary in the extent to which they are perceived as productive or unproductive and passive or active.

Exit responses to conflict situations that typically involve threats of physical separation between partners.

Exit responses typically involve threats of physical separation between partners. Consider a time when you had a conflict with another person and one of you physically left the room during the episode. Did you view this as a productive way to respond to the situation? Probably not. Exit is a passive strategy that is unproductive to conflict resolution.

neglect response to conflict that might include avoiding the relationship partner, refusing to discuss problems they are experiencing, and communicating in a hostile or aggressive manner.

Similarly, when relationship partners adopt a neglect response to conflict, they might avoid the relationship partner, refuse to discuss problems they are experiencing, and communicate with each other in a hostile and aggressive manner. This type of response is described as active and destructive. Rusbult and his colleagues (1982) found that college couples in satisfying relationships were less likely to use neglect and exit responses.

Couples reporting higher satisfaction in their relationships were more likely to use *loyalty* and *voice* responses as a response to conflict (Rusbult et al., 1982). When individuals adopt a loyalty response, they remain loyal to one another by not addressing the conflict. They may decide to "wait it out" in the hopes that, by doing so, the relationship will improve on its own. Loyalty is described as a passive strategy that could be viewed as productive or unproductive, depending on the situation. On the one hand, loyalty indicates that a partner is committed to the relationship and will stick with the other partner during both good and bad times. However, because the loyalty response is passive, and the partner adopting this response to a relationship problem is not actively addressing an issue, it could also be described as an unproductive response. As mentioned previously, avoiding conflict does little to bring it to a resolution.

A more productive response to problems in relationships is the voice response. When individuals adopt this response, they discuss relationship concerns openly and often offer suggestions for repairing the relationship transgression. Rusbult, Johnson, and Morrow (1986) noted that adopting a voice response during mild relationship transgressions assisted in stabilizing the relationship's health. Use of the voice response has been positively associated with both relationship satisfaction and commitment.

© wavebreakmedia /Shutterstock.com

Refusing to discuss problems is unproductive to conflict resolution

loyalty a response to conflict that involves remaining loyal to one's partner by not addressing the problem in the relationship.

voice a response to conflict that involves openly discussing relationship concerns and offering suggestions for repairing the relationship transgression.

Not surprisingly, individual differences such as sex affect the way people approach and respond to conflict situations. Men and women differ in the extent to which they use voice and loyalty responses in their romantic relationships. Women, more so than men, use the voice response as a means of managing minor problems and use loyalty for a wide range of problems. Men were more likely to use neglect responses than women (Rusbult et al., 1986). These gender-based differences in conflict responses illustrate that some women might feel that they must be the "relationship experts" or the keeper of the relationship standards.

RESEARCH IN REAL LIFE: GENDER DIFFERENCES AND SIMILARITIES IN MANAGING CONFLICT IN RELATIONSHIPS

Research by Keener et al. (2012) examined gender differences and similarities in preference for conflict goals and strategies in same-sex friendship and opposite-sex romantic relationships. The researchers predicted that men and women would differ in their preference for communal or agentic conflict strategies and goals in same-sex friendship and opposite-sex romantic relationships (Keener, Strough, & DiDonato, 2012). Communal conflict strategies and goals are more receiver oriented and emphasize *collaboration* in solving problems in relationships (e.g., "I would talk with my friend about where he wanted to eat dinner"), while agentic conflict strategies and goals emphasize autonomy and *independence* in solving problems (e.g., "I would be firm about where I wanted to eat dinner and not back down"). Male and female college students completed personality measures and then read scenarios that depicted a conflict with a same-sex friend or an opposite-sex romantic partner. Study participants indicated whether they would respond to the situations using either communal or agentic conflict strategies or goals.

* As expected, the researchers found that female college students were more likely to use communal strategies than men when approaching conflict situations with same-sex friends.
* When approaching conflict situations with an opposite-sex romantic partner, female college students were more likely than male students to support the use of agentic conflict strategies.
* Males and females were very similar in their preference for using communal conflict strategies in romantic relationships.
* These findings illustrate the complex relationships among the relationship partner's sex, type of relationship, and preference for conflict strategies and goals.

Men and women differ in their preference for communal or agentic conflict strategies and goals in same-sex friendship and opposite-sex romantic relationships (Keener, Strough, & DiDonato, 2012). Communal conflict strategies and goals are more receiver-oriented and emphasize collaboration in managing problems while agentic conflict strategies and goals emphasize autonomy and independence. As expected, researchers found that female college students were more likely to use communal strategies than men when approaching conflict situations with same-sex friends.

A final suggestion for managing conflict effectively and appropriately has to do with using "fair fighting" tactics in relationships. When we use the

fair fighting the use of productive or competent communication practices that promote problem solving, compromise, and collaboration.

term fair fighting, we are not referring to physical fighting in relationships. Instead, we are referring to the use of productive or competent communication practices that promote problem solving, compromise, and collaboration. The textbox below provides additional information regarding productive and unproductive communication responses to conflict.

To manage conflict in a productive and healthy way, it is important to adopt communication patterns that create an environment in which individuals feel comfortable sharing their concerns without being belittled, embarrassed, or ridiculed. It is important to choose an appropriate time and place to discuss the problem, listen actively when the other person is talking, and refrain from using negative listening behaviors such as pseudo-listening or defensive listening. Also, it is important be empathetic when communicating with the other person. Always try to understand the other person's feelings as you discuss the issue. Individuals often experience problems in their relationships because they do not really listen to one another. It is important to show individuals you are listening by using active listening behaviors, paraphrasing their messages, and asking relevant questions to help understand their perspective.

PRODUCTIVE AND UNPRODUCTIVE CONFLICT COMMUNICATION

Productive Communication:

- Active listening
- Using empathy (e.g., stating, "I can see why you might feel that way.")
- Choosing the right time and place to discuss the problem
- Communicating with respect (e.g., refraining from interruptions)
- Describing the problem clearly
- Using "I" statements versus blaming the other person (e.g., saying, "You did this to me.")
- Staying in the present
- Only focusing on issues relevant to the discussion

Unproductive Communication:

- Engaging in any of the listening misbehaviors (e.g., pseudo-listening, defensive listening, monopolizing, etc.)
- Choosing the wrong time and place to engage in conflict (e.g., in a public setting versus a private one)
- Being disrespectful and/or verbally aggressive
- Being ambiguous when describing the problem
- Bringing up the past or issues that are not relevant

SUMMARY

Relationships require work and effort! In this chapter we explored reasons for maintaining relationships, identified various maintenance strategies, and discussed the outcomes of strategy use. In the last sections of this chapter, we focused on managing conflict effectively as a means of stabilizing our relationships. More specifically, we focused on the definition of conflict, different types of conflict management strategies, conflict responses, and using productive communication during conflict episodes.

DISCUSSION QUESTIONS

1. Identify several relationship maintenance strategies you use to sustain your work relationships. Are they similar to those identified in this chapter?

2. Can you identify five or more skills needed to maintain effective relationships with family members, friends, or romantic partners?

3. Reflect on a recent conflict you experienced with a friend, roommate, or coworker. What was your approach to this situation? What conflict management style did you use? What was the outcome of this situation? In retrospect, do you feel that you could have handled this situation more effectively? What would you have done differently?

REFERENCES

Ayres, J. (1983). Strategies to maintain relationships. *Communication Quarterly, 31,* 62–67.

Braiker, H. B., & Kelley, H. H. (1979). Conflict in the development of close relationships. In R. L. Burgess & T. L. Huston (Eds.), *Social exchange in developing relationships.* New York: Academic Press.

Burgoon, J. K., & Hale, J. L. (1984). The fundamental topoi of relational communication. *Communication Monographs, 51,* 19–41.

Burleson, B., & Samter, W. (1994). A social skills approach to relationship maintenance: How individual differences in communication skills affect the achievement of relationship functions. In D. J. Canary & L. Stafford (Eds.), *Communication and relational maintenance* (pp. 61–90). New York: Academic Press.

Burleson, B., & Samter, W. (1996). Similarity in the communication skills of young adults. *Communication Reports, 9,* 127–139.

Cahn, D. (1992). *Conflict in intimate relationships* (pp. 72–112). New York: The Guilford Press.

Canary, D. J., & Spitzberg, B. H. (1989). A model of perceived competence of conflict strategies. *Human Communication Research, 15,* 630–649.

Canary, D. J., & Stafford, L. (1992). Relational maintenance strategies and equity in marriage. *Communication Monographs, 59,* 243–267.

Canary, D. J. & Stafford, L. (1994). Maintaining relationships through strategic and routine interaction. In D. J. Canary & L. Stafford (Eds.), *Communication and relational maintenance* (pp. 3–22). San Diego, CA: Academic Press.

Canary, D. J. & Stafford, L.(2001). Equity in the preservation of personal relationships. In J. H. Harvey & A. Wenzel (Eds.), *Close romantic relationships: Maintenance and enhancement* (pp. 133–151). Mahwah, NJ: Lawrence Erlbaum Associates.

Canary, D. J., & Cupach, W. R. (1988). Relational and episodic characteristics associated with conflict tactics. *Journal of Social and Personal Relationships, 5,* 305–325.

Canary, D. J., Stafford, L., Hause, K. S., & Wallace, L. A. (1993). An inductive analysis of relational maintenance strategies: Comparison among lovers, friends, relatives, and others. *Communication Research Reports, 10,* 5–14.

Canary, D. J., Cupach, W. R., & Messman, S. J. (1995). *Relationship conflict.* Thousand Oaks, CA: Sage Publications.

Cialdini, R. B. (2003). *Influence: Science and practice* (4th ed.). International Edition. Boston: Allyn and Bacon.

Craig, E., & Wright, K. B. (2012). Computer-mediated relational development and maintenance on Facebook. *Communication Research Reports, 29,* 119–129.

Dainton, M. (2013). Relationship maintenance on Facebook: Development of a measure, relationship to general maintenance, and relationship satisfaction. *College Student Journal, 47,* 113–121.

Dainton, M. (2000). Maintenance behaviors, expectations for maintenance and satisfaction: Linking comparison levels to relational maintenance strategies. *Journal of Social and Personal Relationships, 17*, 827–842.

Dainton, M., & Aylor, B. (2002). A relational uncertainty analysis of jealousy, trust, and maintenance in long-distance versus geographically close relationships. *Communication Quarterly, 49*, 172–188.

Dainton, M., & Gross, J. (2008). The use of negative behaviors to maintain relationships. *Communication Research Reports, 25*, 179–191.

Dainton, M., & Stafford, L. (1993). Routine maintenance behaviors: A comparison of relationship type, partner similarity, and sex differences. *Journal of Personal and Social Relationships, 10*, 255–272.

deTurck, M. A. (1987). When communication fails: Physical aggression as a compliance gaining strategy. *Communication Monographs, 51*, 106–112.

Diggs, R. C., & Stafford, L. (1998). Maintaining marital relationships: A comparison between African American and European American individuals. In V. J. Duncan (Ed.), *Towards achieving MAAT* (pp. 192–292). Dubuque, IA: Kendall Hunt.

Dindia, K., & Canary, D. J. (1993). Definitions and theoretical perspectives on maintaining relationships. *Journal of Social and Personal Relationships, 10*, 163–173.

Dindia, K., & Baxter, L. (1987). Strategies for maintaining and repairing marital relationships. *Journal of Social and Personal Relationships, 4*, 143–158.

DiPaola, B. M., Roloff, M. E., & Peters, K. M. (2010). College students' expectations of conflict intensity: A self-fulfilling prophecy. *Communication Quarterly, 58*, 59–76.

Duck, S. (1988). *Relating to others*. Buckingham, PA: Open University Press.

Dunleavy, K., Wanzer, M. B., Krezmien, E., & Ruppel, K. (2011) Daughters' perceptions of communication with their fathers: The role of skill similarity and co-orientation in relationship satisfaction. *Communication Studies, 62*, 581–596.

Eldridge, N. S., & Gilbert, L. A. (1990). Correlates of relationship satisfaction in lesbian couples. *Psychology of Women Quarterly, 14*, 43–62.

Goodboy, A., & Bolkan, S. (2011). Attachment and the use of negative relational maintenance behaviors in romantic relationships. *Communication Research Reports, 28*, 327–336.

Goodboy, A., Myers, S., & Members of the Investigating Communication. (2010). Relational quality indicators and love styles as predictors of negative maintenance behaviors in romantic relationships. *Human Communication, 11*, 71–86.

Haas, S. M., & Stafford, L. (1998). An initial examination of maintenance behaviors in gay and lesbian relationships. *Journal of Social and Personal Relationships, 15*, 846–855.

Hocker, J. L., & Wilmot, W. W. (1991). *Interpersonal conflict* (pp. 4–42, 103–144). Dubuque, IA: Wm C. Brown Publishers.

Infante, D. A., Chandler, T. A., & Rudd, J. E. (1989). Test of an argumentative skill deficiency model of interspousal violence. *Communication Monographs, 56*, 163–177.

Infante, D. A., Sabourin, T. C., Rudd, J. E., & Shannon, E. A. (1990). Verbal aggression in violent and nonviolent disputes. *Communication Quarterly, 38*, 361–371.

Jones, R. W., & Bates, J. E. (1978). Satisfaction in male homosexual couples. *Journal of Homosexuality, 3*, 217–224.

Keener, E., Strough, J., & DiDonato, L. (2012). Gender differences and similarities in strategies for managing conflict with friends and romantic partners. *Sex Roles, 67*, 83–97.

Messman, S. J., Canary, D. J., & Hause, K. S. (2000). Motives to remain platonic, equity, and the use of maintenance strategies in opposite-sex friendships. *Journal of Social and Personal Relationships, 17*, 67–94.

Mikkelson, A. C., Myers, S. A., & Hannawa, A. F. (2011). The differential use of relational maintenance behaviors in adult sibling relationships. *Communication Studies, 62*, 258–271.

Myers, S., and Members of COM 200. (2001). Relational maintenance behaviors in the sibling relationship. *Communication Quarterly, 49,* 19–37.

Myers, S., & Weber, K. (2004). Preliminary development of a measure of sibling relational maintenance behaviors: Scale development and initial findings. *Communication Quarterly, 52,* 334–347.

Myers, S., & Goodboy, A. (2013). Using equity theory to explore adult siblings' use of relational maintenance behaviors and relational characteristics. *Communication Research Reports, 30,* 275–281.

Olsen, L. (2002). "As ugly and as painful as it was, it was effective": Individuals' unique assessment of communication competence during aggressive conflict episodes. *Communication Studies, 53,* 171–188.

Ragsdale, J. D. (1996). Gender, satisfaction level, and the use of relational maintenance strategies in marriage. *Communication Monographs, 63,* 354–369.

Rands, M., Levinger, G., & Mellinger, G. D. (1981). Patterns of conflict resolution and marital satisfaction. *Journal of Family Issues, 2,* 297–321.

Roloff, M. E., & Soule, K. P. (2002). Interpersonal conflict: A review. In M. L. Knapp & J. A. Daly (Eds.), *Handbook of interpersonal communication* (pp. 475–528). Thousand Oaks, CA: Sage Publications.

Rotenberg, K. J. & Boulton, M. (2013). Interpersonal trust consistency and the quality of peer relationships during childhood. *Social Development, 22,* 225–241.

Rusbult, C. E., Johnson, D. J., & Morrow, G. D. (1986). Determinants and consequences of exit, voice, loyalty, and neglect: Responses to dissatisfaction in adult romantic involvements. *Human Relations, 39,* 45–63.

Rusbult, C. E., Zembrodt, I. M., & Grunn, L. K. (1982). Exit, voice, loyalty, and neglect: Responses to dissatisfaction in romantic involvements. *Journal of Personality and Social Psychology, 43,* 1230–1242.

Sillars, A. L., & Wilmot, W. W. (1994). Communication strategies in conflict and mediation. In J. A. Daly and J. M. Wiemann (Eds.), *Strategic interpersonal communication* (pp. 163–190). Hillsdale, NJ: Lawrence Erlbaum.

Spitzberg, B. H., Canary, D. J., & Cupach, W. R. (1994). A competence based approach to the study of interpersonal conflict. In D. D. Cahn (Ed.), *Conflict in personal relationships* (pp. 183–202). Hillsdale, NJ: Lawrence Erlbaum.

Stafford, L., & Canary, D. J. (1991). Maintenance strategies and romantic relationship type, gender and relational characteristics. *Journal of Social and Personal Relationships, 8,* 217–242.

Stafford, L., Dainton, M., & Haas, S. (2000). Measuring routine and strategic relational maintenance: Scale revision, sex versus gender roles, and the prediction of relational characteristics. *Communication Monographs, 67,* 306–323.

Ting-Toomey, S. (1983). An analysis of verbal communication patterns in high and low marital adjustment groups. *Human Communication Research, 9,* 306–319.

Terminating Relationships:
Knowing When to Throw in the Towel

OBJECTIVES

- Discuss the investment model and how it relates to relationship termination.
- Identify common reasons romantic relationships terminate.
- Describe Duck's five phases of relationship termination.
- Explain Knapp's model of relationship dissolution by describing each stage of coming apart and offer an example of typical communication that occurs in each stage.
- Explain ERA or Empathy, Rationale, Action and how it can be used in relationship termination situations.
- Identify effective strategies to "remain friends" with ex-romantic partners.
- Offer examples of strategies individuals use to cope with relationship dissolution.

SCENARIO: SOUND FAMILIAR?

Cole and Addison dated all through high school. Last year they enrolled in different colleges and found it difficult to maintain their relationship via long distance. Cole was highly involved in extramural sports, and Addison was extremely busy with clubs and organizations on campus. Cole was excited to finally visit Addison at her school and spend time with her. When he arrived on campus she was very busy with classes, volunteering, hanging out with her roommates, and talking about unfamiliar people and places. During his visit, he found that they had a difficult time connecting on anything except the past. Toward the end of his trip, he was certain that their relationship would not last. While he respected Addison for her commitment to her studies and leadership roles, he did not feel their relationship was working. He contemplated telling her before he left for home. Would this come as a shock to her? Would they maintain a friendship? He didn't want to hurt her feelings but it was clear they were evolving as individuals, but not evolving together as a couple.

KEY TERMS

Avoiding	Commitment	Differentiating
Circumscribing	Cost Escalation	Direct methods
Closure	De-escalation messages	Dissimilarity

Dyadic process	Investment Model	Resurrection Process
Equity theory	Investment Size	Satisfaction Level
ERA	Justification Messages	Self-determination
Fundamental	Lack of Commitment	theory
attribution error	Negative identity	Self-forgiveness
Granting forgiveness	management	Social exchange theory
Grave dressing process	Outside pressure	Social process
Indirect methods	Positive tone messages	Stagnating
Infidelity	Pseudo De-Escalation	Terminating
Interpersonal solidarity	Quality Of Alternatives	Withdrawal/avoidance
Intrapsychic process	Reframing	tactics

OVERVIEW

The last several chapters have examined how our interpersonal relationships are initiated, maintained, and how they may turn dark. In this chapter, we turn to the process of relationship disengagement. Breaking up is not easy. It usually results in pain for one or both partners. Throughout this chapter, we examine how to assess relationship problems and how to determine if these problems are significant enough to terminate a relationship. We introduce the investment model, which can help explain why seemingly unhealthy relationships stay together much longer than they should. Next, we will introduce the stages of dissolution and discuss the type of communication that is expected across the stages. We will then explore characteristics in termination across different relationship types such as friendships, heterosexual romantic, and homosexual romantic. Finally we will discuss what happens after the breakup, including remaining friends, rebounding, and finding closure. We describe the aftermath of relationship disengagement and explore suggestions for surviving relationship disengagement and ultimately moving on.

ASSESSING RELATIONSHIP PROBLEMS: ATTRIBUTIONS, SATISFACTION, EQUITY

When considering whether to stay in a relationship or not, we often assess the trouble occurring in the relationship and the explanations for these problems. For example, we ask ourselves questions such as:

- Why does he act that way?
- Why did she say that to me?
- Why would he or she hurt me?

To address these questions, it is necessary to recall our discussion of attribution theory and the fundamental attribution error from Chapter 5. These theories provide a framework for understanding how we explain our own and others' behaviors. Recall our discussion of the fundamental attribution error, which holds that people tend to attribute others' negative behaviors to internal, rather than external, causes. Rather than consider external or situational causes for others' behavior (for example, "the weather"), we often tend to take the "easy way out" and attribute others' behaviors to internal factors. Internal factors we typically use to describe behavior tend to be stable over time, such as personality traits (for example, "rude," "inconsiderate," "lazy")."

fundamental attribution error   when attempting to explain others' negative behaviors, we tend to overestimate the internal factors or causes and underestimate the external factors or causes.

Not surprisingly, appraisals of our relationship partner's intentions relate to how satisfied we are in the relationship. Researchers have identified a consistent link between the attributions, or explanations, about relationship partners' intentions and reported relationship satisfaction (Waldinger & Schulz, 2006). Much of the research on attributions in romantic relationships has examined how an assessment of a partner's accountability for a relationship transgression affects relationship satisfaction (Waldinger & Schulz, 2006). It is natural to want to understand why our partner is acting a certain way, and eventually, the explanations for the partner's behavior influence our evaluation of our relationship.

When relationship partners offer consistently negative attributions or explanations for a partner's behavior, they are more likely to report lower relationship satisfaction (Fincham & Bradbury, 1993; Miller & Bradbury, 1995). Thus, when a relationship partner forgets to buy a birthday present or forgets to recognize an important date, the offended partner may offer negative explanations for the behavior, especially if the negative behavior has been repeated over time. The offended partner may say, "He didn't get me a present because he is lazy," or "She didn't remember our anniversary because she is so self-absorbed." When individuals view a partner's behavior as selfishly motivated and dispositional rather than situational, they are more likely to view their partner in a negative way and to report decreased relationship satisfaction (Fincham, Harold, & Gano-Phillips, 2000).

Once we assess the relational problems, we may conclude that there is some form of inequity. Recall our discussion of equity theory in Chapter 8, which suggests that couples are happiest in relationships when there is a balance of inputs and outputs.

If you perceive you are receiving too little from the relationship compared to what you are contributing, this will impact your satisfaction.

Alternatively, if you are receiving more outputs from the relationship than you are contributing, you will feel a sense of guilt from the imbalance. However, this process is highly subjective in terms of one's personal view of inputs, outputs, and fairness in relationships.

Couples are happiest in relationships when there is a balance of inputs and outputs.

equity theory couples are happiest in relationships when there is a balance of inputs and outputs.

If you perceive you are receiving too little from the relationship compared to what you are contributing this will impact your satisfaction

HOW DO YOU DETERMINE IF A RELATIONSHIP PROBLEM IS SIGNIFICANT?

Interpersonal communication researchers study relationships to shed light on significant problems or challenges that should be addressed by couples. Vangelisti (1992) examined the link between specific types of relationship problems and relational dissatisfaction. She recognized a problem as *significant* for relationship partners when it meets at least two of the following criteria:

1. The behavior has a negative effect on the relationship;
2. It occurs often in the relationship; and
3. It is important enough for one or both partners to remember it and recall it as a continuing source of dissatisfaction within the relationship.

It is important to realize that even seemingly benign behaviors can become problematic over time. For example, if your partner displays a negative behavior such as not looking at you while listening (criterion 1) and it is consistent over time (criterion 2), it may reach the point where it becomes a significant relational problem. However, a salient (criterion 1) and negative behavior that is recalled over time (criterion 3), such as kissing a colleague at happy hour, may happen only once, but may be prominent enough to continually cause displeasure in the relationship, even though the behavior was never repeated.

Interestingly, the most frequently reported communication problem in relationships concerns withholding negative emotions. These may include feelings of anger, fear, distress, disgust, and shame.

INVESTMENT MODEL: WILL YOUR RELATIONSHIP PERSIST OR DIE?

investment Model identifies four factors that can be used to assess or predict the likelihood of a relationship continuing and prospering, or terminating.

We think the investment model proposed by Rusbult, Martz, and Agnew (1998) provides the most succinct conceptualization and clear understanding of the type of relationships that continue and those that end. By examining the model in Figure 9.1, you will notice it consists of four variables that help predict the extent to which a relationship will continue. The authors define these variables as follows:

Satisfaction level the level of positive or negative emotions or feelings toward the partner or the relationship.

Quality Of alternatives addresses the potential for fulfilling one's needs by someone outside of the current relationship.

Investment size includes the tangible and intangible qualities that are associated with being involved in a relationship; the resources that are invested in continuing the relationship.

Commitment the extent of our dedication to continue a relationship.

1. Satisfaction level Satisfaction level which is determined by how well the relationship partner fulfulls their partner's needs.
2. Quality of alternatives refers to the perceived desirability of the best available alternative to a relationship" (Rusbult et al., 1998, p. 359). Quality of alternatives refers to whether or not a partner's needs could be met in other ways or outside of the existing relationship.
3. Investment size refers to the resources attached to the relationship. Resources may include time, money, children, furniture, houses, and/or pets.
4. Commitment is central to a relationship's success and refers to the relationship partner's choice to stay in the relationship as well as the feeling of being connected to the other person.

Rusbult, Martz, and Agnew (1998) draw several important conclusions about how these variables are related to one another and predict relationship success and stability:

- When relationship partners report greater *commitment*, they also report feeling more *satisfied* with their relationships.
- When relationship partners feel more *committed*, they perceive *fewer alternatives* as meeting their relationship needs.
- Finally, partners who report greater *commitment* to their relationships also report greater *investments* in their bonds.

Therefore, important factors to consider when deciding whether to remain in a relationship are the level of commitment in the relationship, the number of alternatives, the amount of your relationship investments, and perceived relationship satisfaction. We encourage you to examine one of your own relationships by completing the Investment Model Scale provided at the end of the chapter.

Figure 9.1 **The relationship investment model**

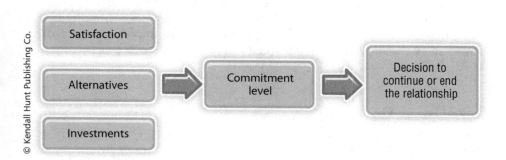

© Kendall Hunt Publishing Co.

PROCESS MODEL OF RELATIONSHIP TERMINATION

Ending a relationship is stressful because of the amount of time, feelings, and energy involved in this process. Communication scholars have examined the decision-making processes involved in ending relationships and note that it is not a singular event but rather a drawn-out process that often involves a number of different individuals (Duck & Rollie, 2003; Rollie & Duck, 2006). In 1982, Duck proposed a four-phase model of decision making that impacts communication patterns, social networks, and conversational topics. In 2006, Duck and Rollie modified the model by identifying a fifth process of relationship dissolution. The five phases of this model are:

1. Intrapsychic process
2. Dyadic process
3. Social process
4. Grave dressing process
5. Resurrection process

Intrapsychic Process

During the first phase, labeled the intrapsychic process, one partner recognizes that something is wrong in a relationship and no longer feels satisfied. The individual begins to spend more time thinking about the status of the relationship and considering the costs and rewards associated with it. There are two possible outcomes of this phase. First, the leaver may spend enough time ruminating about the negative aspects of the relationship that he is ready to move on and forgive the partner. Or, on the other hand, the leaver may spend considerable amounts of time thinking about the negative aspects of the relationship and find sufficient faults to justify ending the relationship.

Importantly, the leaver does not express concerns directly to the partner during the intrapsychic phase; instead, the partner may

intrapsychic process initial phase in the relationship termination process where the leaver spends considerable time contemplating whether the relationship is worth saving.

© wavebreakmedia /Shutterstock.com

How did your last relationship end and what processes did you experience?

vent, but only to individuals who do not know the relationship partner, such as a hairdresser or a mechanic (Duck & Rollie, 2003). Individuals in long-term relationships experience this phase often throughout the lifetime of their bonds. It is certainly not unusual for individuals to think about areas of improvement in their relationships; however, if this process becomes drawn out and more emotionally grueling, then the individual will move to the next process of relationship dissolution.

Dyadic Process

dyadic process when the leaver officially announces to the partner that he or she is leaving or thinking of leaving.

When the leaver officially announces to the partner that he or she is leaving or thinking of leaving, the dyadic process begins. This process opens the floodgates for discussion about the status of the relationship and justifications for ending it. This emotionally exhausting phase is characterized by long talks, conflict, and rationalizations of how the partnership "got to this place." During this phase, the other partner may make attempts to reconcile the relationship and attempt to illustrate the costs of terminating the relationship. This phase provides an opportunity for both partners to discuss the status of the relationship and, if possible, to fix it. If it does not get fixed here, the partners move to the next phase.

Social Process

social process relationship termination goes public and focuses less on the relationship and more on the relationship partners' friends and family.

If the relationship cannot be salvaged, the relationship termination then goes public. When the relationship termination is focused less on the couple and more on the relationship partners' friends and family, it is a sign that the couple has moved to the social process. The primary decision the couple has to make is: What are we going to tell people? Stories, blaming, and accounts of situations are shared with friends, coworkers, and family. At this time, friends will often choose sides, and the relationship partners now become socially available to others. In terms of the relationship partners, the rules and roles of their post-breakup status are discussed. Once the breakup has been shared with others, it becomes official. Sadly, many of the bonds formed with couple friends, family members, or coworkers will end.

Grave Dressing Process

grave dressing process partners are able to articulate the explanation of the termination and create their own versions of the relationship, whether truthful or not.

The next process is grave dressing. This phase is called grave dressing because partners typically "dress up" the dead relationship (or grave) by promoting a positive image of their role in their particular version of the relationship story. Grave dressing also refers to "officially burying" the relationship. Relationship partners fulfill psychological and social needs through sharing their stories of the breakup (Duck & Rollie, 2003). Partners offer their explanation of the termination and save face for future relationships. Some people in this stage will engage in ceremonial burying behaviors such as burning pictures and returning, giving away, or selling items given to them by their "ex." A primary decision in this process is for individuals to create a version of the "breakup story" that depicts them in a positive light so they look desirable to others.

Resurrection Process

The last phase is called the resurrection process and it is characterized by trying to "enlist others as supporters for one's own view of the breakup" (Rollie & Duck, 2006, p. 236). This process focuses on the need for individuals to prepare themselves for future relationships (Rollie & Duck, 2006). Seeking advice and perspectives from others in order to "do things differently next time" is typical in this process. Individuals who have ended a relationship may actively attempt to avoid others who remind them of their ex-partner. In addition, when they start to interact with prospective relational partners, they may communicate that they are looking for anyone who does not remind them of their ex-partner.

resurrection process   final phase of relationship termination in which one seeks the support of others to rationalize the end of the partnership in an effort to prepare for future relationships.

This five-stage process model helps us understand the complexity of the relationship termination process. Duck's model sheds light on the people involved in the process as well as the communication that occurs from start to finish.

Next, we turn our attention to the actual communication between the relational partners during the process of relationship dissolution—which sometimes helps us understand the ever-so-popular relational question, "How did we get here?"

FIVE STAGES OF RELATIONSHIP DISSOLUTION

You may recall our discussion of Knapp's (1978) stages of coming together in Chapter 7; he also developed a five-stage model that depicts how relationships typically come apart, as depicted in Figure 9.2. The five stages of dissolution are labeled *differentiating, circumscribing, stagnating, avoiding,* and *terminating.* It is possible that: (1) partners could perceive that the

Figure 9.2 **Knapp's five stages of relationship formation and of dissolution**

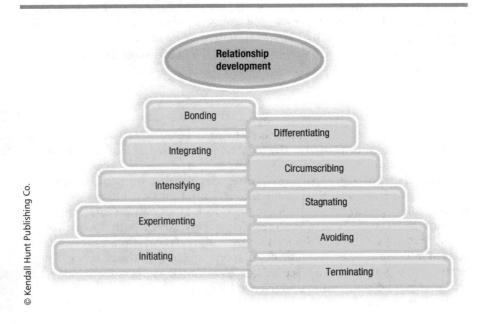

relationships is in different stages; they don't necessarily always agree on the stage of their relationship, (2) some stages last longer than others, and (3) partners often skip stages. It is important to note that this model seems to depict what actually happens when relationships deteriorate, not what "should" happen (Knapp, 1978).

Differentiating

During the stages of coming together, couples tend to emphasize hobbies, interests, and values they have in common; however, in the differentiating stage, partners highlight their differences. Individuals accentuate their unique attributes and use more "I" and "me" statements. During this phase of relationship dissolution, partners may engage in a great deal of conflict that often emphasizes all of the ways they differ from each other. For example, if one partner states that she likes eating out, the other partner may express a preference for cooking at home. If one person states that he likes action movies, the other person may express her affinity for romantic comedies.

differentiating partners highlight their differences.

When there is not a conscious decision to keep the partner involved, the relationship may drift apart.

One's independence in the relationship is the central focus of this stage, which has both positive and negative implications. On one hand, when individuals reassert their individual needs, they may choose to do things on their own, spend more time with friends, and reestablish their identity. This process can be healthy for a relationship. For example, before two individuals entered into a relationship, one partner may have enjoyed playing hockey while the other enjoyed participating in a yoga class. But as the relationship developed, there was less time for each person to enjoy his or her personal activities due to favoring more collaborative activities with the partner. As the relationship progressed, these interests were neglected. In the differentiating stage, those roots may be revisited, with hockey or yoga classes being resumed. This may provide a much-needed "spark" in the relationship and provide alternative topics for the partners to discuss. On the other hand, if the individual taking part in the activity excludes the significant other from his or her feelings and experiences, this independence may ultimately create more emotional distance in the relationship. If the partner is kept involved, this stage may have beneficial outcomes.

Circumscribing

When there is not a conscious decision to keep the partner involved, the relationship may drift apart. The next stage of relationship dissolution is labeled the circumscribing stage. During this stage, the communication between the relationship partners is often described as restricted, controlled, or constrained. Akin to the "don't talk about politics or religion" standard, relationship partners in this stage only choose to talk about safe topics that will not lead to some type of argument (Vangelisti, 2002). Both the quality and quantity of information exchanged between the relationship partners deteriorates significantly as each attempts to avoid subjects that may spark a fight. Relationship partners only discuss "safe"topics such as plans for the day, current events, and the weather, which are topics that would be discussed with casual acquaintances.

circumscribing communication between the relationship partners is often described as restricted, controlled, or constrained.

Stagnating

The third stage of relationship dissolution is the stagnating stage. This stage is often described as two people who are merely "going through the motions" in their relationship because communication has come to a virtual standstill. There is very little interaction within the relationship, and partners continue to engage in activities separately. When partners think of bringing up any issues regarding the relationship, they tell themselves, "It will just turn into an argument," and so they resort to holding issues inside to avoid a conflict. They conserve their energy for their daily activities and do not exert any energy on preserving the relationship.

Roommates, friends, and even family members may feel stagnant in their relationships with one another. Extended time in this stage can be particularly problematic as the partners may lose their motivation to fix the relationship. Over time, the thought of having to face the partner may seem like an arduous task. Therefore, it is often easier to just avoid the partner or minimize communication in this stage of coming apart.

stagnating   two people who are merely "going through the motions" in their relationship because their communication has come to a virtual standstill.

Avoiding

The fourth stage of coming apart is labeled the avoiding stage. During this stage, relationship partners will actively fill their schedules to avoid seeing their partners. Vangelisti (2002) describes this stage as particularly difficult, noting that when the partners do talk to each other, "they make it clear that they are not interested in each other or in the relationship" (p. 666). Relationship partners will arrive early to work and come home late in an effort to avoid each other. The idea of seeing the relationship partner is exhausting and any dialogue with this person is short, to the point, and often superficial. On the inside, individuals are exhausted from creating activities to avoid their partner and have increased disdain for one another. Any communication between the partners that occurs during this stage may focus on ways to avoid seeing each other. For example, one partner may ask the other, "What time will you be home from work?" in an effort to rearrange a work schedule to avoid contact.

avoiding   relationship partners will actively fill their schedules to avoid seeing their partners.

RESEARCH IN REAL LIFE:
COMPLAINING IN HETEROSEXUAL ROMANTIC COUPLES

Hall, Travis, and Anderson (2013) attempted to examine gender differences in complaints across Knapp's relationship stages. While this study did not find significant gender differences between the stages of the model, they did find some gender differences in types of complaints overall:

- Women were more likely to complain to their significant other regarding topics that they have no power to change and that are beyond their control.
- Males were more likely to complain to their significant others regarding something they do on a regular basis or specific behaviors she may or may not do in the future.

The authors suggested that since women usually complain to others who are not the source of the problem, it could be that they are using it as a relationship-building strategy. Alternatively, perhaps males use more task-orientation approaches such as instrumental complaints because they are trying to solve problems in the relationship.

Terminating

As we grow increasingly disappointed in a relationship, how do we send signals that our relationship needs attention?

terminating   this stage marks the end of a relationship.

As we grow increasingly disappointed in a relationship and in our partner, we reach a threshold and want to move on. This is when we reach the final stage of coming apart, the terminating stage, which marks the end of the relationship. Relationship partners may choose to divorce the partner, move out, or call an end to any type of formal or contractual commitment with the partner. When relationship partners do communicate during this stage, they make attempts to put physical and/or psychological distance between themselves and their relationship partner. Relationship partners will also make attempts to disassociate themselves from their relationship partner. Some married individuals will disassociate themselves from their partners by using their maiden names or explicitly stating to friends, coworkers, and family members, "We are not a couple anymore." See Table 9.1 for examples of typical messages that are exchanged during the stages.

Table 9.1	**Sample messages in Knapp's Stages of Coming Apart**
Stage	**Communication Example**
Differentiating	*"You are just so different from me!"* *"I hate when you don't wash the dishes!"*
Circumscribing	*"It's going to rain tomorrow."* *"Did you let the dog out yet?"* *"I am not going to answer that because it will just lead to a fight!"*
Stagnating	*"Oh, you're home."* *"What is the point of discussing this anymore?"* *"I know, I know. The usual."*
Avoiding	*"I have to work nights all this week."* *"I will not be home for dinner."* *What time are you going to be at John's game?*
Terminating	*"I don't want to be in this relationship."* *"Sorry, but we can't date anymore."* *"I'm moving out."*

STRATEGIES USED TO TERMINATE RELATIONSHIPS

Determining how one should end a relationship can be quite stressful. Whether you are terminating a relationship with a romantic partner, a roommate, or a neighbor, it can create much anxiety. When we are stressed we often turn to easily accessible solutions that are not always effective.

Once the leaver decides to verbalize his or her intentions, he or she typically relies on relational disengagement tactics. During the relational disengagement period, there is obviously a great deal of conflict. Leavers will use different strategies, depending on the type of the relationship and the timing of the disengagement. For example, more polite and face-saving tactics are typically used in the beginning of the relationship termination phase. However, if the rejected partner does not respond to these tactics, or if the leaver is in a dangerous relationship and immediate action is needed, more forceful and direct tactics may be necessary. Researchers have studied what people specifically recall saying during a breakup (Baxter, 1982; Cody, 1982), and they have identified five common tactics used during relational disengagement.

When the relationship is not working, you may feel justification to end it.

Positive Tone Messages

First, positive tone messages are created to ease the pain for the rejected partner. These messages have a strong emotional tone and usually imply that the leaver would like to see less of the other person, but not entirely end the relationship. When individuals employ this strategy, they usually want to try to end the relationship in a positive and pleasant way. An example of a positive tone message would be, *"I really like you as a friend, but I think we perceive this relationship differently."* In other words, the classic "It's not you, it's me." Here the leaver tries to ease the pain of the breakup by suggesting that he or she still likes the rejected partner and is interested in a friendship.

positive tone messages created to ease the pain for the rejected partner.

De-escalation Messages

The second tactic also involves reducing the amount of time spent with the partner. De-escalation messages are less emotional than positive tone messages and typically provide a rationale for wanting to see less of the rejected partner. For example, *"I think we need a break from each other,"* or *"My feelings for you have changed since the start of this relationship."* This strategy may be problematic because it is perceived as a partial or temporary type of relationship termination strategy. Individuals who want to end the relationship for good may want to follow up with a more direct strategy for ending the relationship.

De-escalation messages less emotional than positive tone messages and typically provide a rationale for wanting to see less of the rejected partner.

Withdrawal

A third tactic, withdrawal, refers to actively spending less time with the person. This includes dodging phone calls, blocking texts, and rerouting daily activities in order to avoid the individual. When you do run into the person, conversations are kept brief and shallow. This strategy is very indirect and can affect the individuals' ability to maintain a friendship in the future.

withdrawal/avoidance tactics actively spending less time with the person.

Justification Messages

A fourth way to disengage from a relationship involves utilizing justification messages. This tactic has three important elements. The relationship partner:

1. States that he or she needs to stop seeing the other person.
2. Provides a reason for ending the relationship with the other person.

justification messages stating that he or she needs to stop seeing the other person; provides a reason for ending the relationship and recognizes that the relationship is not salvageable.

3. Recognizes that the relationship is not salvageable and may even become worse if the relationship continues.

For example, *"I cannot live with you anymore because all we do is fight and argue. I do not see things getting any better. I am worried that if we stay roommates, things will get even worse than they are now! Therefore, we can't be roommates next year because it is just not going to work."*

Negative Identity Management Messages

negative identity management a strategy used to hurry the disengagement process; has little consideration for the rejected partner.

The last category of messages, negative identity management, is typically used as a last resort to terminate a relationship, when partners do not want to remain friends after the breakup or when one relationship partner feels a need to facilitate the disengagement. This strategy that is used to speed up the disengagement process and has little consideration for the rejected partner. The leaver may employ manipulation as part of this tactic. For example, the leaver may spark a disagreement with the partner to create an unpleasant situation and then suggest, *"See, this isn't working . . . we should see other people."*

Now that we have an understanding of the tactics that are utilized to terminate relationships, it is important to remember there is no "one size fits all" solution. In this next section we will examine relationship termination in three types of relationships, including friendships, heterosexual romantic, and homosexual romantic. Each area will offer specific research findings that help to explain these relationship types and offer some insight into their unique characteristics.

TYPES OF RELATIONSHIPS: TERMINATING FRIENDSHIPS

Friendships are some of the most enduring relationships we have. Consider your own friendships you have had since youth with a shelf life of "forever." Then there are other friends who tend to drift in and out of our lives like last season's shoes. Why do some friendships tend to outlast others? Often, friendships are forged from things we share in common with others. For example, we meet classmates who live in the same dorm, have the same major, work at the same job, share the same religion or social group, or share the same enemy or mutual friend. Friendships may terminate because the very thing that brought the friends together no longer exists. People move away, change jobs, or move on to a different life stage (i.e., marriage, children, etc.) and no longer share the proximity and closeness that once protected the relationship.

There are a number of reasons individuals end friendships. For example, "Johnson and colleagues (2004) asked college students to identify why they ended a friendship. Reasons provided included the following (Johnson, Wittenberg, Haigh, Wigley, Becker, Brown, & Craig, 2004):

- Less affection (22.8 percent)
- Friend or self changed (21 percent)
- No longer participated in activities or spent time together (15.4 percent)
- Increase in distance (13 percent)

The way that someone ends a friendship depends on the intimacy, or close-ness, experienced in the relationship. One study compared the differences in dissolution between casual and best friends (Rose & Serafica, 1986). *Proximity* was a strong predictor of dissolution in casual friends. This makes sense when we think of our casual friends from high school. When high school is over and we are not seeing our friends regularly, we tend to lose touch. They also found that *decreased affection* between best friends was the most important predictor in ending the relationship. Individuals have higher relationship expectations for "best" friends when it comes to displays of affection and communication; therefore, when those expectations are not met, the relationship changes.

Another reason reported for best and close friendships dissolving was the interference from other relationships, such as romantic relationships. In other words, when new friendships and romantic partners enter the picture, it changes the dynamic of existing relationships. This plays a particularly det-rimental role in female friendships. When one individual begins to spend more time interacting with her romantic partner's friends than with her own friends, the neglected female friends are likely to become frustrated with her behavior.

Factors Prompting Friendship Termination

One study examined *why* and *how* close and lengthy friendships come to an end (McEwan, Babin, & Farinelli, 2008). Participants in the study responded to open-ended questions about why and how they ended their friendships. Next, the researchers placed the responses into four friendship dissolution categories:

1. **Disapproved behavior** friend engages in behavior that the other does not condone (example: drugs, alcohol).

2. **Competing relationships** friend spends time with family, romantic partner, or other friend(s) to the exclusion of the other partner and/or one friend does not get along with the other's family, romantic partner, or other friend(s).

3. **Betrayal** friend engaged in deception, infidelity, malicious talk, theft, and/ or exclusion that is disliked by or viewed as harmful to the other person.

4. **Increased distance** friends "grow apart" due to increased social or prox-emic distance.

Next, the researchers examined how the study participants terminated their friendships. Four common methods of friendship termination were identified (McEwan, Babin, & Farinelli, 2008):

1. **Faded away** non-intentional loss of communication. The communication between friends ceased.

2. **Purposeful avoidance** intentional reduction or stopping of communication, no direct communication between friends about the loss of contact

DO FEMALE SAME-SEX FRIENDSHIPS TERMINATE FOR DIFFERENT REASONS THAN MALE SAME-SEX FRIENDSHIPS?

Researchers say, YES! Females were more likely to ter-minate same-sex friendships due to a conflict situation, whereas males were more likely to terminate same-sex friendships as a result of fewer common interests (Swain, 1989; Johnson, et al., 2004).

> Friendships may terminate because the very thing that brought the friends together no longer exists.

> Rewards consist of behaviors or aspects of the relationship that are desirable, and that the recipient perceives as enjoyable or fulfilling.

3. **Direct request** non-hostile, specific request to stop communication and/or end the relationships

4. **Hostile interaction** physical or verbal aggression leading to the end of the relationship, which may include threats, heated arguments, or actual physical violence

As friendships start to deteriorate, individuals may neglect the responsibilities of the relationships by choosing to provide less time, energy, trust, understanding, and support to their friends. Individuals may start weighing the costs and rewards of the relationship in order to determine whether they should stay in the relationship. Recall our discussion of social exchange theory in Chapter 7. To review, social exchange theory refers to an assessment of costs and rewards in determining the value of pursuing or continuing a relationship (Thibault & Kelley, 1959). Rewards consist of behaviors or aspects of the relationship that are desirable, and that the recipient perceives as enjoyable or fulfilling. In friendships, rewards can include how much fun you have with the person, and the extent to which he or she is trustworthy, honest, sincere, helpful, and supportive. Relationship costs are perceived as undesirable behaviors or outcomes. Costs in friendships may be characterized as "toxic" behaviors: the extent to which a friend may be controlling, demanding, depressing, self-absorbed, deceitful, or unfair. Also, friendships take time and energy, which may be perceived as costly when we have less time and energy to devote to them. According to social exchange theory, when the costs of the relationship outweigh the rewards, we contemplate ending the friendship. In general, people use indirect or direct methods to end a friendship, and both strategies have benefits and drawbacks.

social exchange theory an assessment of costs and rewards in determining the value of pursuing or continuing a relationship.

Indirect Strategies for Ending Friendships

Indirect methods reflect your intention to gradually let go of the relationship by deviating away from a direct course of action. Baxter (1982, 1984) identified three indirect strategies used to terminate relationships:

1. Withdrawal of supportiveness and affection. Examples include, spending less time with the friend, sending fewer emails/texts, blocking the friend from your chat list, or defriending them from your social media.
2. Pseudo de-escalation or indicating the relationship will be "better off" by separating (verbally stating s/he wants to be less close). This is considered an indirect strategy because it is focused on being less close for the benefit of the relationship. For example, "Our relationship just needs a break for now so we can focus our families.
3. Cost-escalation: indirect attempts to make the relationship more unattractive (passive-aggressive behaviors)

indirect methods methods to decrease the intensity of the friendship by increasing the emotional and physical distance between you and your friend.

Pseudo de-Escalation indirect strategy to terminate a friendship in which the benefits of spending less time together are emphasized.

Cost Escalation indirect strategy to terminate a friendship in which attempts are made to make the relationship appear burdensome or unappealing due to the amount of effort the other person has to invest.

Indirect methods work best if your goal is to decrease the intensity of the friendship by increasing the emotional and physical distance between you and your friend. As stated earlier, sometimes relationship partners allow the communication that sustains the friendship to just fade away (McEwan et al., 2008). If you are trying to end a relationship using an indirect strategy, it is important NOT to share your personal problems, engage in deep conversations, and be available to this person, because this will send mixed messages about the status of your friendship. This may also mean declining invitations and avoiding hangouts or shared friends until you have reached your goal of ending the relationship.

There are drawbacks to using indirect methods to weaken relationship bonds. For example, giving excuses for not hanging out may backfire. Isaacs (1999) suggests that excuses allows the other person an opportunity to overcome your refusal; your excuse of "Oh, I can't afford the gas to get out there," may be met with "That's okay, I can pick you up."

In addition, because indirect methods of terminating friendships do not include any transparency about the relationship status, the friend is often left confused about your true feelings. Recipients of this tactic may keep trying to resurrect the friendship and inaccurately interpret your indirect attempts to slow down, or even end, the friendship. If this is the case, it may be time to adopt more direct approaches to ending the relationship.

Research has shown that the type of dissolution strategy used will influence the satisfaction levels of the "left" partner. For example, Collins and Gillath (2012) found that using open confrontation strategies such as "openly expressing" the reason were associated with greater levels of satisfaction for the "left" partner than engaging in avoidance and/or withdrawal strategies.

Therefore, if you are concerned about the satisfaction level of the individual you are leaving, it is best to be honest and open about your reasons for ending the friendship.

Direct Strategies for Ending Friendships

Direct methods involve specifically telling the friend how you feel about the status of your friendship. Direct strategies are more likely to be used in relationships when there is high intimacy/closeness and an overlap in social networks (Baxter, 1982). Direct approaches are used to end friendships when a recipient does not recognize the intent of indirect attempts or if individuals are interested in terminating the friendship abruptly due to some hurtful circumstance. If you choose to engage in this approach, be prepared to be assertive and to provide a valid reason for why you are ending the friendship. We recognize that this is not an easy task. However, understanding how to engage in assertive communication can help you navigate uncomfortable situations.

Direct methods refers to specific and straightforward strategies used in telling a friend how you honestly feel.

As discussed in Chapter 3, assertiveness involves defending your own rights and wishes while still respecting the rights and wishes of others. Booth-Butterfield (2006) feels individuals can maximize the effectiveness of their assertive communication by sending nonverbal messages that are consistent with the verbal. For example, you should strive to maintain eye contact, appear confident through your facial expressions, and use appropriately assertive gestures and a firm and confident tone of voice. Individuals can enhance their assertiveness and credibility by displaying confidence in their voice, gestures, posture, and facial expressions.

Booth-Butterfield offers a model of an appropriately assertive response that includes three components (ERA):

ERA model that outlines three components of appropriately assertive responses - empathy, rationale, and action.

1. Express *Empathy*
2. State *Rationale*
3. Provide *Action* Request

Read the textbox below for an example of how to use ERA to terminate a friendship.

ERA ASSERTIVE COMMUNICATION TOOL

First, express honest and sincere empathy for the situation:
   "I understand we have been friends for a long time."
Second, provide a rationale for your request:
   "However, we have both changed a lot over the last few years and we have different interests and goals. When we get together all we do is argue the entire time and get angry with each other."
Finally, provide the action statement:
   "I do not think we should be friends anymore."

TYPES OF RELATIONSHIPS: TERMINATING ROMANTIC RELATIONSHIPS

Typically, the decision to leave a romantic partner is a difficult and arduous task. For this reason, many people may recall staying in relationships much longer than they should have. In this section, we examine four common reasons individuals leave romantic relationships (adapted from Cupach & Metts, 1986). These include: (1) infidelity, (2) lack of commitment, (3) dissimilarity, and (4) outside pressures.

Infidelity

Infidelity behaving in a way that crosses the perceived boundary and expectation of an exclusive relationship.

Infidelity is defined as "a secret sexual, romantic, or emotional involvement that violates the commitment to an exclusive relationship" (Glass, 2002, p. 489). As suggested in the definition, infidelity can take many forms, including physical (holding hands), sexual (kissing and other activities), and emotional (sharing intimate conversation) (Spitzberg & Tafoya, 2005).

Researchers have examined various forms of infidelity and determined that males and females differ greatly in their responses to different types of infidelity. Men are more likely to be upset with a partner's sexual infidelity, while women tend to be more upset with a partner's emotional infidelity (Glass & Wright, 1985). In other words, males are more concerned with their partners' physical transgressions, while females are more hurt by their partners' emotional disclosures with another person.

Researchers have explored whether some marriages are more prone to infidelity than others. Infidelity is more likely to exist in marriages where there are frequent arguments about trust, narcissistic attitudes and behaviors exhibited by partners, and increased time spent apart (Atkins, Yi, Baucom, & Christensen, 2005).

While approximately 99 percent of married persons expect sexual fidelity from their spouse (Treas & Giesen, 2000), not many couples are

©conrado /Shutterstock.com

50–60 percent of married men and 45–55 percent of married women engage in some form of extramarital affair at some point in their marriage.

meeting those expectations. Although infidelity statistics are difficult to measure, some interesting findings that describe the pervasiveness of infidelity include the following:

- Atwood and Schwartz (2002) estimated that 50–60 percent of married men and 45–55 percent of married women engage in some form of extramarital affair at some point in their marriage.
- Infidelity is the most frequently cited cause of divorce (Amato & Rogers, 1997).
- 60 percent of dating relationships ended after infidelity was discovered (Feldman & Cauffman, 1999).
- Approximately 75 percent of male and 68 percent of female college students reported engaging in at least one form of infidelity, with 49 percent of men and 31 percent of women having ever engaged in a sexual infidelity (Wiederman & Hurd, 1999).
- 20–40 percent of married men and 20–25 percent of married women reported engaging in extramarital sexual infidelity during their lifetimes (Greeley, 1994; Tafoya & Spitzberg, 2007).

These alarming statistics imply that although not many condone infidelity, there are a significant proportion of people engaging in these types of behaviors.

So why are heterosexual married couples cheating? Fisher (2009) suggests that men are more likely to report *sexual motivations* for infidelity and are less likely to fall in love with an extramarital partner. Women tend to have an *emotional connection* with their extramarital partner and are more likely to have an affair because they are lonely. In fact, Fisher reports that 56 percent of men (and 34 percent of women) who have affairs claim to be happy in their marriages. While this may seem high, marital dissatisfaction still appears to be the single strongest predictor of infidelity (Whisman, Gordon, & Chatav, 2007).

Lack of Commitment

Another reason individuals provide for terminating romantic relationships is a lack of commitment. Commitment or one's "intent to persist in a relationship" (Rusbult, Martz, & Agnew, 1998, p. 359) can be expressed and reinforced in the everyday and often mundane tasks that couples endure (Weigel, 2008). For example, relationship partners might express commitment by providing affection and support, and working together to solve problems. Commitment is what sustains romantic couples "through the ups and downs and the good times and bad times" (Weigel & Ballard-Reisch, 2014, p. 331).

Although infidelity is one way to demonstrate an individual's lack of commitment, other ways include: not spending enough time together, not prioritizing the relationship, not valuing the other's opinion, experiencing power struggles, and not nurturing the maintenance and development of the relationship. Lack of commitment—or the omission of expressing one's intent to persist in a relationship—can foster feelings of abandonment and loneliness. Some relationship experts argue that partners' commitment to the relationship is a stronger predictor of relationship stability than feelings of love (Lund, 1985). This research was interested in studying heterosexual dating relationships in an attempt to determine whether love or commitment served as a stronger predictor of relationship stability. She found that couples with

Lack of Commitment neglecting to express one's intent to continue or persist in the current relationship.

higher levels of commitment were more likely to continue the relationship than those with high levels of love and low levels of commitment. In this study, couples' expectations of staying together proved to be more important to relationship stability than their feelings of love for each other. These findings are consistent with Fisher's (2009), who noted we may be lured outside of the relationship, even though we cite "loving" our partners.

It certainly makes sense that both our positive and negative experiences in our previous romantic relationships would affect our future relationships. Communication researchers sought to explore how closeness in previous relationships was related to current relationship commitment and satisfaction among college students in dating relationships (Merolla, Weber, Myers & Booth-Butterfield, 2004). Their results suggested the more close they felt in their past relationship, the less likely they were to report being satisfied and committed in their current dating relationship. These findings indicate how difficult it is sometimes for people to forget the past and fully embrace new relationships.

Dissimilarity

Scholars have identified similarity as one of two components that relationship dyads consider when deciding whether to stay together or to break up (Hill, Rubin, & Peplau, 1976). A longitudinal study suggested that couples who were most similar in educational plans, intelligence, and attractiveness were most likely to remain together, whereas couples that were different in the levels of these aspects were more likely to break up.

Some may say, "opposites attract," but the truth is that great amounts of dissimilarity in significant areas create more problems than solutions over the course of a relationship. Differences in backgrounds (religion, family values), intelligence (educational goals, IQ), attitudes concerning family roles, ethics, and communicating about conflicts and temperament (argumentativeness, assertiveness) may contribute to conflict situations and misinterpretations of behavior.

Interpersonal solidarity feelings of closeness between people that develop as a result of shared sentiments, similarities, and intimate behaviors.

Our similarity with romantic partners is often linked to our perception of solidarity with one another. Interpersonal solidarity refers to feelings of closeness between people that develop as a result of shared sentiments, similarities, and intimate behaviors (Wheeless, 1978). With that in mind, it makes sense that solidarity increases as relationships become more intimate, and it decreases as relationships turn toward termination (Wheeless, Wheeless, & Baus, 1984). As solidarity increases in romantic relationships, so do individuals' levels of trust, reciprocity, and self-disclosures (Wheeless, 1976). Also, the closer we feel to our partner, the more likely we are able to provide emotional support (Weber & Patterson, 1996). If individuals in romantic relationships perceive differences between themselves, there will be less trust, reciprocity, and emotional support, and fewer self-disclosures are likely to be shared.

outside pressure stress that stems from a relationship as a result of people external of the relationship such as friends, family, or coworkers.

Outside Pressures

External or outside pressure from friends, family, or occupations may negatively impact relationship satisfaction. Family members may put pressure on romantic relationships when they ask questions like "When are you two getting married?" or make comments such as, "You should save your money for a house!" and "I want to be a grandparent!" Friends may also exert pressure on romantic relationships by hinting that not enough time is spent with them. For couples in the public eye, the paparazzi acts as an external pressure peering over the hedge, demanding details and pushing expectations for the relationship on the couple. Additionally, work relationships or job stressors can impact the satisfaction in our romantic relationship. An increase in job demands, hours, and travel requirements are examples of significant occupational pressures that may affect relationship stability.

These outside pressures put a strain on our ability to make decisions. A theory that may help explain the link between outside pressures and relationship satisfaction is self-determination theory. According to self-determination theory, people have an innate psychological need to feel autonomous, or self-governing, in their behavior and relationships (Deci & Ryan, 1985; Deci, 2000, 2002). People want to feel free to choose their own paths in relationships, rather than be coerced or pressured into exhibiting certain behaviors. Ultimately, this self-initiated behavior will lead to better personal and social adjustment. Hence, those who report feeling responsible for, and in control of, their own decisions are also more secure and positive about their relationships with others.

> Some may say, "opposites attract," but the truth is that great amounts of dissimilarity in significant areas create more problems than solutions over the course of a relationship.

self-determination theory people have an innate psychological need to feel autonomous, or self-governing, in their behaviors.

HOMOSEXUAL RELATIONSHIPS: FACTORS INFLUENCING RELATIONSHIP QUALITY

Although scant research has addressed gay and lesbian relationship termination and whether this process differs from heterosexual relationships, one study found that cohabitating gay or lesbian partners are actually more similar when compared to married heterosexual partners (Kurdek, 1992, 1998). In a 1998 longitudinal study, he examined relationship satisfaction among partners from gay, lesbian, and heterosexual married couples over a five year period in which they completed a survey each year. Both gay and lesbian partners reported more frequent relationship dissolution compared to heterosexual spouses. Additionally, gay and lesbian partners reported more autonomy than married people. Furthermore, lesbian partners reported significantly more intimacy and equality than their married counterparts (Kurdek, 1998).

Another study examined factors that contributed to heterosexual and homosexual couples' *relationship quality* after a breakup (Lannutti & Cameron, 2002). For homosexual couples, factors that contributed to higher relationship quality included personal variables or those factors that emerged from the relationship. Some examples include the amount of liking for the ex-partner, the uniqueness of the relationship, and the hope for romantic renewal. In heterosexual couples the social environment (for example mutual friends or community) was instrumental in explaining relationship quality after a breakup, compared to homosexual couples.

Cohabitating gay or lesbian partners are more similar than different when compared to married heterosexual partners.

It makes sense that gay and lesbian relationships are influenced more by characteristics within the relationship and less by societal influences for relationship satisfaction due to their denial of legal and societal recognition over the years (Lannutti & Cameron, 2002). However, these trends may change now that homosexual marriages have become legalized.

Now that we have discussed factors related to satisfaction and dissolution in different relationship types, we turn our attention to what happens after the breakup. After a relationship ends it is normal to redefine the relationship and to determine whether or not to remain in contact with the former partner. In this section, we will review three popular areas that are addressed after a romantic breakup: (1) staying friends, (2) methods of coping, and (3) closure and forgiveness.

AFTER THE BREAKUP: REMAINING "JUST FRIENDS"

After a breakup, we sometimes want to remain friends with our "ex." This makes sense because we have self-disclosed personal information, relied on this person for emotional support and guidance, and often have a great deal in common. Think about the things that draw couples together in the first place. Research suggests that a couple is more likely to remain friends when the man has been the one who precipitated the breakup (or when the breakup was mutual) than when the woman initiated the breakup (Hill, Rubin, & Peplau, 1976).

Have you ever tried to remain friends after a breakup?

Other research suggests that if the couple was friends prior to the romantic involvement, their chances of returning to a friendship are significantly higher than those who never maintained a friendship (Metts, Cupach, & Bejlovec, 1989). Additionally, if the former partners were still receiving rewards or resources from the relationship, this could influence the impact of a partner's satisfaction with the post-breakup friendship (Busboom, Collins, & Givertz, 2002).

Certain relationship disengagement strategies are more effective in creating a positive post-breakup relationship. When we ask our students how they would prefer to end a romantic relationship, most agree that they prefer an honest and direct strategy such as justification. Negative disengagement strategies, such as withdrawal, avoidance, or negative identity management have been identified as inhibiting post-dating relationship quality (Metts et al., 1989; Banks et al., 1987; Busboom, Collins, & Givertz, 2002). If relationship partners would like to remain friends, then it is a good idea to use positive tone messages, justification, or other tactics that protect the other person's feelings.

While it is certainly possible to remain friends after a breakup, it is important that both parties agree with the new relational "rules." Discuss the boundaries of the relationship and be open about what is appropriate and inappropriate behavior in this newly defined relationship. It is not unusual for post-breakup friendships to cross friendship boundaries in times of distress due to the familiarity and security of the relationship.

Some relationships cycle through development and dissolution several times and are referred to as "on-again/off-again" relationships (Dailey, Pfiester, Jin, Beck & Clark, 2009). Research has found that these relationships do experience fewer positive behaviors such as validation and understanding (Daily et al., 2009) and less relational maintenance and greater relational uncertainty (Dailey, Hampel & Roberts, 2010). So, why do individuals go back to these relationships? Research suggests it may be they have lingering feelings, more effective conversations, negative experiences with others, and/or perceptions of positive changes in the partner (Dailey, Jin Pfiester, & Beck, 2011). Overall, communication scholars are interested in how these relationships are renegotiated and redefined. Duck (2006) reminds us that relationships are constantly changing and that some relationships do not just end because they did not work out. This makes sense for romantic relationships that involve children. Co-parenting after a breakup involves negotiating the relational status.

AFTER THE BREAKUP: METHODS OF COPING

Scholars also note that the dissolution of a romantic relationship can be one of the most painful and stressful experiences people endure in their personal lives (Feeney & Noller, 1992; Simpson, 1987). This section will discuss methods of coping with relationship dissolution and creating closure.

Because ending a relationship can be one of the most emotionally charged events we experience, often there is no easy or painless way to do it. No two relationships are identical in nature, and there are no scripts to terminate relationships. We are flooded with different emotions, including sadness, anger, fear, denial, guilt, and confusion. Sometimes we are relieved that the relationship is over and we are anticipating more rewarding relationships in the future. There are productive and unproductive ways to cope with the end of a relationship. Here are some of the most helpful methods of coping with relationship dissolution:

After a break-up, keep yourself busy with family or friends you many have neglected during the relationship.

1. *Give it time.* Recognize that relationship dissolution is a process and is not just a single event (Duck & Rollie, 2003). Allow yourself time to feel a range of emotions and recognize that this is normal and healthy. Do not reject your feelings or hide them behind negative coping strategies such as binge eating (or refusing to eat), binge drinking, or drug use.

2. *Rely on your social support network to stay busy.* Discuss your feelings with friends and family. Revisit the activities that you enjoy and invite friends to join you. Explore new hobbies or schedule a vacation with friends. Research has shown that women tend to have more people to confide in during difficult times, compared to men. Therefore it is not surprising that a man is significantly "more likely to enter rebound relationships than women" (Shimek & Bello, 2014, p. 38). Reaching out to friends and engaging in activities that were neglected during your romantic relationship are healthy coping strategies.

3. *Seek out professional help or a support group.* If you feel you are burdening your friends and family by talking about the breakup, or you continue to feel depressed or angry about the breakup, talk with a professional. Additionally, the sharing of emotional support in face-to-face and online support groups offers several psychological and physical health benefits (Campbell & Wright, 2002; Cawyer & Smith-Dupre, 1995; Lin & Peek, 1999; Wellman & Whortley, 1990). Personal counseling may be covered by health insurance, and most university counseling services are provided free of charge to students. You may be able to take advantage of resources that are included in your tuition. Discussing issues with a third party who has no personal involvement in your existing relationships can provide a fresh perspective.

4. Do not engage in social media surveillance. While it may be tempting to go on to social media to seek out information regarding an ex-partner, it is not healthy for your post break-up health. Perhaps, not surprisingly, communication scholars have found that young people who have engaged in higher levels of internet surveillance experience more breakup distress (Lukacs & QUan-Haase, 2015). Certainly, you may be able to recall a time you consoled a friend who found something disturbing online regarding an ex-partner. Perhaps an effective coping strategy would be to hide or avoid social media messages that may mention your ex-partner.

AFTER THE BREAKUP: CLOSURE AND FORGIVENESS

Closure refers to a level of understanding, or emotional conclusion, to a difficult life event, such as terminating a romantic relationship.

Closure refers to a level of understanding, or emotional conclusion, to a difficult life event, such as terminating a romantic relationship. In this situation, closure often includes the rationale for the breakup. Some research suggests that individuals need a certain level of closure in their breakup before they can effectively move on (Weber, 1998). The purpose of closure is to discuss things with your former partner that "worked" in the relationship as well as to discuss the challenges of the relationship in order to learn from them. Remember, the purpose of this discussion is to make future relationships more effective, and not to resurrect the terminated relationship. Therefore, blaming, accusations, and name-calling are counterproductive. If properly executed, this discussion is helpful in understanding what went wrong in the relationship, providing some direction for future relationships.

Granting forgiveness a powerful tool used to set yourself and your partner free from harboring negative feelings toward each other and perceptions of the relationship.

Granting forgiveness is one strategy used during closure. Forgiveness does not mean you forget, accept, understand, or excuse the behavior; it simply implies that you will not hold your partner in debt for his or her wrongdoing. Granting forgiveness is a powerful tool. When you forgive someone that you are terminating a relationship with, you set yourself free from harboring negative feelings. Negative feelings are detrimental to your ability to nurture future relationships. All in all, granting forgiveness is an investment in you!

Self-forgiveness refers to giving yourself permission and an opportunity to heal and move forward.

Self-forgiveness refers to giving yourself permission and an opportunity to heal and move forward. You give yourself permission to shed yourself of the burden, guilt, pain, and anger that is held inside of you. Once you grant yourself forgiveness you can focus on how to become a better person and make healthier choices in the future.

**RESEARCH IN REAL LIFE:
DO "REBOUND RELATIONSHIPS" ACTUALLY WORK?**

Could focusing on someone new or "rebounding" be helpful in letting go of an ex-partner? The following study was determined to answer this question.

Using attachment theory, researchers designed an experimental study that examined those individuals who were most likely to have the most emotional connection to ex-partners.

They found that their longing for their ex-partner was disrupted when they attempted to focus their attention on a new partner. In other words, they experienced less emotional pain from their previous relationship, when their attention was placed on someone new.

This research helps explain why individuals often turn to rebound relationships. Rebound relationships are described by the researchers as "an adaptive behavior" or a strategy that helps us adjust to another type of situation. The authors also add that "focusing on new relationship options—either a new relationship or an optimistic outlook on relationships—decreases attachment" to an ex-partner (Spielmann, MacDonald, & Wilson, 2009, p. 1391).

Creating closure optimally involves getting together with your "ex" face-to-face to discuss the good times and the bad. In most situations, this option is impossible because either it is too difficult to sit in the same room or a partner has physically moved away. Therefore, closure is often difficult and not easily attainable.

One way to create an emotional conclusion to a relationship is to reframe the event. Frequently, this is a way individuals can create a sense of closure without relying on the ex-partner. Reframing is a psychological process in which you change the way you look at the romantic termination in order to foster a more productive resolution. For example, if you are angry and hurt that your partner cheated on you, you may reframe the event by thinking about how dishonest the partner was. Instead of focusing on your hurt and anger, you psychologically emphasize that untruthfulness is not a characteristic of a person you want to share a romantic relationship with. You focus on recognizing signs of the cheating behavior and predictors of his or her behavior so you can be more aware in future relationships. By reframing the event, you are looking at the event in a different light, which enables you to move forward.

Reframing a psychological process in which you change the way you look at the romantic termination in order to foster a more productive resolution.

SUMMARY

This chapter reviewed how to assess relationship problems and factors that individuals consider when ending a relationship. In addition, we described the complex processes involved in ending our relationships by explaining Duck's four-phase process of decision making during relationship termination and Knapp's five stages of relationship deterioration. Research specific to different types of relationships such as friendships and romantic relationships was summarized. Finally, we discussed the processes involved in redefining the relationship, closure, and forgiveness after relationship termination. Ending a relationship with someone you cared about is often a difficult and challenging task. Understanding the key concepts and natural process of dissolution discussed in this chapter will help you determine when and how to end unhealthy relationships and accept termination as a natural progression.

DISCUSSION QUESTIONS

1. Were you able to remain friends with an ex-romantic partner? If so, what were some of the challenges as your relationship shifted from romantic to platonic?
2. What are some effective tactics that you have used to terminate friendships? Discuss the effectiveness (or ineffectiveness) of the strategies you selected.
3. Can you recall a time when you were able to reframe a difficult or challenging event in your life? Can you describe the event and how you applied reframing to understand it?

REFERENCES

Amato, P. R., & Rogers, S. J. (1997). A longitudinal study of marital problems and subsequent divorce. *Journal of Marriage and the Family, 59,* 612–624.

Atkins, D. C., Yi, J., Baucom, D. H., & Christensen, A. (2005). Infidelity in couples seeking marital therapy. *Journal of Family Psychology, 19,* 470–473.

Atwood, J. D., & Schwartz, L. (2002). Cyber-sex: The new affair treatment considerations. *Journal of Couple and Relationship Therapy, 1,* 37–56.

Banks, S. P., Altendorf, D. M., Green, J. O., & Cody, M. J. (1987). An examination of relationship disengagement: Perceptions, breakup strategies and outcomes. *The Western Journal of Speech Communication, 52,* 19–41.

Baxter, L. (1982). Strategies for ending relationships: Two studies. *Western Journal of Speech Communication, 46,* 233–242.

Booth-Butterfield, M. (2006). *Influential health communication.* Littleton, MA: Tapestry Press.

Busboom, A. L., Collins, D. M., & Givertz, M. D. (2002). Can we still be friends? Resources and barriers to friendship quality after romantic relationship dissolution. *Personal Relationships, 9,* 215–223.

Campbell, K. L., & Wright, K. B. (2002). Online support groups: An investigation of relationship among source credibility, dimensions of relational communication, and perceptions of emotional support. *Communication Research Reports, 19,* 183–193.

Cawyer, C. S., & Smith-Dupre, A. (1995). Communicating social support: Identifying supportive episodes in an HIV/aids support group. *Communication Quarterly, 43,* 243–259.

Cody, M. (1982). A typology of disengagement strategies and an examination of the role intimacy reactions to inequity and relational problems play in strategy selection. *Communication Monographs, 49,* 148–170.

Collins, T. J. & Gillath, O. (2012). Attachment, breakup strategies, and associated outcomes: The effects of security enhancement on the selection of breakup strategies. *Journal of Research in Psychology, 46,* 210–223.

Cupach, W. R., & Metts, S. (1986). Accounts of relational dissolution: A comparison of marital and non-marital relationships. *Communication Monographs, 53,* 311–334.

Dailey, R. M., Hampel, A. D., & Roberts, J. (2010). Relational maintenance in on-again/off-again relationships: An assessment of how relational maintenance, uncertainty, and relationship quality vary by relationship type and status. *Communication Monographs, 77,* 75-101.

Dailey, R. M., Jin, B., Pfiester, R. A., & Beck, G. (2011). On-again/off-again relationships: What keeps partners coming back? *Journal of Social Psychology, 151,* 417-440.

Dailey, R. M., Pfiester, A., Jin, B., Beck, G., & Clark, G. (2009). On-again/Off-again dating relationships: How are they different from other dating relationships. *Personal Relationships, 16,* 23-47.

Deci, E. L., & Ryan, R. M. (1985). *Intrinsic motivation and self determination in human behavior.* New York: Plenum Press.

Deci, E. L. (2000). The "what" and "why" of goal pursuits: Human needs and the self-determination of behavior. *Psychological Inquiry, 11,* 227–268.

Deci, E. L. (2002). Self-determination research: Reflections and future directions. In E. L. Deci & R. M. Ryan (Eds.), *Handbook of self-determination research* (pp. 431–441). Rochester, NY: University of Rochester Press.

Duck, S. W. (1982). A topography of relationship disengagement and dissolution. In S. W. Duck (Ed.), *Personal relationships 4: Dissolving personal relationships* (pp. 1–30). London: Academic Press.

Duck, S. & Rollie, S. (2003). Relationship Dissolution. In J. J. Ponzetti (Ed), *International encyclopedia of marriage and the family* (2nd ed.) (pp. 1297–1300). New York: Macmillan.

Feeney, J. A., & Noller, P. (1992). Attachment style and romantic love: Relationship dissolution. *Australian Journal of Psychology, 44,* 69–74.

Feldman, S. S., & Cauffman, E. (1999). Sexual betrayal among late adolescents: Perspectives of the perpetrator and the aggrieved. *Journal of Youth and Adolescence, 28,* 235–258.

Fincham, F. D. (1994). Cognition in marriage: Current status and future challenges. *Applied and Preventative Psychology: Current Scientific Perspectives, 3,* 185–198.

Fincham, F. D., & Bradbury, T. N. (1993). Marital satisfaction, depression and attributions: A longitudinal analysis. *Journal of Personality and Social Psychology, 64,* 442–452.

Fincham, F. D., Harold, G. T., & Gano-Phillips, S. (2000). The longitudinal association between attributions and marital satisfaction: Direction of effects and role of efficacy expectations. *Journal of Family Psychology, 14,* 267–285.

Fisher, H. (2009). *Why him? Why her?: Finding real love by understanding your personality type.* NY: Holt, Henry & Company, Inc.

Glass, S. P. (2002). Couple therapy after the trauma of infidelity. In A. S. Gurman & N. S. Jacobson (Eds.), *Clinical handbook of couple therapy* (3rd ed.) (pp. 489–507). New York: Guilford.

Glass, D. P., & Wright, T. L. (1985). Sex differences in type of extramarital involvement and marital dissatisfaction. *Sex Roles, 12,* 1101–1120.

Greeley, A. (1994). Marital infidelity. *Society, 31,* 9–13.

Hall, E. D., Travis, M., Anderson, S., & Henley, A. (2013). Complaining and Knapp's relationship stages: Gender differences in instrumental complaints. *Florida Communication Journal, 41,* 49–61.

Hill, C. T., Rubin, Z., & Peplau, L. A. (1976). Breakups before marriage: The end of 103 affairs. *Journal of Social Issues, 32,* 147–168.

Isaacs, F. (1999). *Toxic friends/true friends: How your friends can make or break your health, happiness, family and career.* Scranton: William Morrow & Co.

Johnson, A. J., Wittenberg, E., Haigh, M., Wigley, S., Becker, J., Brown, K., & Craig, E. (2004). The process of relationship development and deterioration: Turning points in friendships that have terminated. *Communication Quarterly, 52,* 54–67.

Knapp, M. L. (1978). *Social intercourse: From greeting to goodbye.* Boston: Allyn & Bacon.

Kurdek, L. A. (1998). Relationship outcomes and their predictors: Longitudinal evidence from heterosexual married, gay cohabiting, and lesbian cohabiting couples. *Journal of Marriage and the Family, 60,* 553–568.

Kurdek, L. A. (1992). Relationship stability and relationship satisfaction in cohabiting gay and lesbian couples: A prospective longitudinal test of the contextual and interdependence models. *Journal of Social and Personal Relationships, 9,* 125–142.

Lin, N., & Peek, M. K. (1999). Social networks and mental health. In A. V. Horwitz & T. L. Scheid (Eds.), *A handbook for the study of mental health: Social contexts, theories, and systems.* New York: Cambridge.

Lund, M. (1985). The development of investment and commitment scales for predicting continuity of personal relationships. *Journal of Social and Personal Relationships, 2,* 3–23.

Lannutti, P. J., & Cameron, K. A. (2002). Beyond the breakup: Heterosexual and homosexual post-dissolutional relationships. *Communication Quarterly, 50*(2), 153–170.

Lukacs, V. & Quan-Haase, A. (2015). Romantic breakups on Facebook: new scales for studying post-breakup behaviors, digital distress, and surveillance. *Information, Communication, and Society, 18,* 492, 508.

McEwan, B., Babin, G. B., & Farinelli, L. (2008). The end of a friendship: Friendship dissolution reasons and methods. Conference paper presented at the National Communication Association annual meeting. San Diego, CA.

Merolla, A. J., Weber, K. D., Myers, S. A., & Booth-Butterfield, M. B. (2004). The impact of past dating relationship solidarity on commitment, satisfaction, and investment in current relationships. *Communication Quarterly, 52,* 251–264.

Metts, S., Cupach, W. R., & Bejlovec, R. A. (1989). "I love you too much to ever start liking you": Redefining romantic relationships. *Journal of Social and Personal Relationships, 6,* 259–274.

Miller, G. E., & Bradbury, T. N. (1995). Refining the association between attributions and behavior in marital interaction. *Journal of Family Psychology, 9,* 196–208.

Rollie, S. S., & Duck, S. W. (2006). Divorce and dissolution of romantic relationships: Stage models and limitations. In J. H. Harvey & M. A. Fine (Eds.), *Handbook of divorce and relationship dissolution* (pp. 223-240). Mahwah, NJ: Lawrence Erlbaum Associates.

Rose, S., & Serafica, F. C. (1986). Keeping and ending casual, close, and best friendships. *Journal of Social and Personal Relationships, 3,* 275–288.

Rusbult, C. E., Martz, J. M., & Agnew, C. R. (1998). The Investment Model Scale: Measuring commitment level, satisfaction level, quality of alternatives, and investment size. *Personal Relationships, 5,* 357–391.

Shimek, C., & Bello, R. (2014). Coping with break-ups: Rebound relationships and gender socialization. *Social Sciences, 3,* 24–43.

Simpson, J. A. (1987). The dissolution of romantic relationships: Factors involved in relationship stability and distress. *Journal of Personality and Social Psychology, 53,* 683–692.

Spielmann, S. S., MacDonald, G., & Wilson, A. E. (2009). On the rebound: Focusing on someone new helps anxiously attached individuals let go of ex-partners. *Personality and Social Psychology Bulletin, 35,* 1382–1394.

Spitzberg, B., & Tafoya, M. (2005). Explorations in communicative infidelity: Jealousy, sociosexuality, and vengefulness. Paper presented at the International Communication Association annual meeting in New York, NY.

Swain, S. (1989). Covert intimacy: Closeness in men's friendships. In B. J. Risman & P. Schwartz (Eds.), *Gender in intimate relationships: A microstructural approach.* Belmont, CA: Wadsworth.

Tafoya, M. A., & Spitzberg, B. H. (2007). The dark side of infidelity: Its nature, prevalence, and communicative functions. In B. H. Spitzberg & W. R. Cupach (Eds.), *The dark side of interpersonal communication* (2nd ed.) (pp. 201-242). Mahwah, NJ: Lawrence Erlbaum Associates.

Thibault, J. W., & Kelley, H. H. (1959). *The social psychology of groups.* New York: Wiley.

Treas, J., & Giesen, D. (2000). Sexual infidelity among married and cohabiting Americans. *Journal of Marriage and the Family, 62,* 48–60.

Vangelisti, A. L. (2002). Interpersonal processes in romantic relationships. In M. L. Knappand & J. A. Daly. (Eds.), *Handbook of interpersonal communication* (pp. 643–679). Thousand Oaks, CA: Sage Publications.

Vangelisti, A. L. (1992). Communicative problems in committed relationships: An attributional analysis. In J. H. Harvery, T. L. Orbuch, & A. L. Weber (Eds.), *Attributions, accounts, and close relationships* (pp. 144–164). New York: Springer-Verlag.

Waldinger, R. J., & Schulz, M. S. (2006). Linking hearts and minds in couple interactions: Intentions, attributions, and overriding sentiments. *Journal of Family Psychology, 20,* 494–504.

Weber, A. L. (1998). Losing, leaving, and letting go: Coping with nonmarital breakups. In B. H. Spitzberg & W. R. Cupach (Eds.), *The dark side of close relationships* (pp. 267–306). Mahwah, NJ: Erlbaum.

Weber, K., & Patterson, B. R. (1996). Construction and validation of a communication based emotional support scale. *Communication Research Reports, 13*(1), 68–76.

Weigel, D. J. (2008) A dyadic assessment of how couples indicate their commitment to each other. *Personal Relationships, 15,* 17–39.

Weigel, D. J., & Ballard-Reisch, D. S. (2014). Constructing commitment in intimate relationships: Mapping interdependence in the every-day expressions of commitment. *Communication Research, 41,* 311–332.

Wellman, B., & Wortley, S. (1990). Different strokes for different folks: Community ties and social support. *American Journal of Sociology, 96,* 558–588.

Wheeless, L. (1976). Self-disclosure and interpersonal solidarity: Measurement, validation, and relationships. *Human Communication Research, 3*(1), 47–61.

Wheeless, L. (1978). A follow-up study of the relationships among trust, disclosure, and interpersonal solidarity. *Human Communication Research, 4*(2), 143–157.

Wheeless, L. R., Wheeless, V. E., & Baus, R. (1984). Sexual communication, communication satisfaction, and solidarity in the developmental stages of intimate relationships. *Western Journal of Speech Communication, 48,* 217–230.

Whisman, M. A., Gordon, K. C., & Chatav, Y. (2007). Predicting sexual infidelity in a population-based sample of married individuals. *Journal of Family Psychology, 21,* 320-324.

Wiederman, M. W., & Hurd, C. H. (1999). Extradyadic involvement during dating. *Journal of Social and Personal Relationships, 16,* 265–274.

The Dark Side of Relationships:
Deception, Embarrassment, Jealousy, Power, and Verbal Aggression

OBJECTIVES

- Define *deception* and explain interpersonal deception theory.
- Explain three reasons embarrassment occurs in social situations and identify three roles associated with embarrassment.
- Define *jealousy* and identify the six types of jealousy.
- Recall the five bases of power.
- Describe the three levels of influence.
- Explain how interpersonal conflicts turn dark by moving from argumentative messages to verbally aggressive messages.
- Recognize the impact of verbal aggression in romantic relationships, in the classroom, and in the workplace.

SCENARIO: SOUND FAMILIAR?

William was concerned his girlfriend, Katie, was cheating on him. One afternoon she left her cell phone on the table, and he grabbed it to see if he could find any information that would confirm his doubts. He noticed she had been texting a guy in her night class several times a day. He could tell by the messages they were more than friends. William also realized from reading the messages that Katie was not at the library the evening before as she had suggested. She had gone out to dinner. He contemplated how he should bring this issue up with Katie. Why would she lie?

KEY TERMS

Accounts	Concealment	Friend jealousy
Activity jealousy	Confessions	High aggression
Agape	Dark side of	Identification
Agent	communication	Integrative
Apologies	Deception	communication
Argumentativeness	Dominance	Internalization
Arousal relief theory	Embarrassment	Interpersonal
Clarity	Emotional infidelity	deception theory
Coercive power	Equivocation	(IDT)
Compensatory	Eros	Intimacy jealousy
restoration	Expert power	Jealousy
Completeness	Falsification	Jokes
Compliance	Family jealousy	Leakage cues

Legitimate power
Low aggression
Ludus
Mania
Moderate aggression
Negative affect
  aggression
Observer
Personalization
Physical evidence

Positive relational
  deceptive strategies
Power
Power jealousy
Pragma
Recipient
Referent power
Relevance/directness
Reward power
Romantic jealousy

Severe aggression
Sexual infidelity
Solicited confessions
Storge
Third-party
  information
Unsolicited
  confessions
Verbal aggression
Veridicality

OVERVIEW

This scenario reminds us that our interpersonal relationships can, and often do, experience a dark side. Friends and family members can deceive us, romantic partners may lie and cheat, and our colleagues and supervisors could attempt to abuse their power. As a result of these negative behaviors in our relationships, we can become angry, fearful, and perhaps even aggressive toward others. Although most of the research in communication is devoted to discussing appropriate and effective behavior to foster positive communicative outcomes, Cupach and Spitzberg challenged academic scholars to tackle problematic and disruptive communication patterns in their 1994 book, *The Dark Side of Interpersonal Communication*. The dark side of communication refers to negative communication exchanges that may contribute to dysfunctional interpersonal relationships. Some examples of dark communication that have been studied are: deception or lying, conflict, jealousy, relationship termination tactics, embarrassment, loneliness, co-dependency, and obsession or stalking (Spitzberg, 2006). This chapter recognizes that interpersonal relationships are not always filled with sunshine and smiles. People can, and do, lie, deceive, abuse power, and cheat in all types of relationships.

The goal of this chapter is to recognize the dark side of communication and to understand the motivation behind these behaviors. Although we cannot possibly attempt to discuss all of the communication behaviors that have been identified as potentially negative or dark, we have selected a few that most students in interpersonal communication are likely to encounter. Specifically, we will explore how and why individuals in romantic or platonic relationships deceive each other, become jealous, deal with social embarrassment, and engage in verbal aggression across a variety of contexts. To assist you in understanding how these concepts have been examined, we will discuss various studies that provide a clearer picture of these destructive forms of communicating. We will also provide suggestions on how to cope if you encounter these circumstances.

Dark side of communication an integrative metaphor for a certain perspective toward the study of human folly, frailty, and fallibility.

DECEPTION AND INTERPERSONAL RELATIONSHIPS

We do not typically enter into a relationship with the intent to be dishonest. However, engaging in deception in our interpersonal relationships is quite pervasive. Some researchers say it is just a common part of our daily lives. Feldman, Forrest, and Happ (2002) found that 60 percent of people lie at least once during a ten-minute conversation, and most told an average of two or three lies.

Results from this research also suggested:

- Men and women do not differ in the amount of lies told, but they do differ in content.
- Men typically lie to make themselves look better.
- Women lie most often to make the other person feel good.

Do you know what you look like when you are lying?

Their study concluded that most people lie in everyday conversations when they are trying to appear likable and competent.

Often times when we teach this class, we ask students to stop and think about how often they have already lied today. Students admit to telling lies about everything ranging from what they ate for breakfast to how they are actually feeling.

Deception is defined as "a message knowingly transmitted by a sender to foster a false belief or conclusion by a receiver" (Buller & Burgoon, 1996, p. 209). While we would like to believe that our relationships are built on truth and honesty, the reality is that friends, family members, and romantic partners deceive each other from time to time.

Consider this scenario:

> Jack had been infatuated with Kara since their freshman year of college. He was always extremely nervous about speaking with her and he came to terms with the fact that they would probably never be together. In the meantime, Jack started dating Kara's roommate, Laura. After three months, Jack actually started to fall for Laura, but his feelings for Kara remained unchanged. One evening, Kara asked Jack for a ride to the library. He agreed. In the car, Kara started expressing feelings for Jack. Jack was stunned. He just could not believe that this day had come. His heart raced as he tried to think of an appropriate reply. However, out of respect for his current relationship with Laura, he reluctantly told Kara that he would never have romantic feelings toward her.

Deception a message knowingly transmitted by a sender to foster a false belief or conclusion by a receiver.

In this example, Jack protects his current relationship with Laura by deceiving Kara about his true feelings. Of course, we know that not all deception is done with such honorable intentions.

> While a person may attempt to be strategic in creating a deceptive message, there are cues that alert the other person that the individual is being less than honest.

Buller and Burgoon (1996) proposed interpersonal deception theory (IDT) to explain the strategic choices made when engaging in deceptive communication (1996). While a person may attempt to be strategic in creating a deceptive message, there are cues that alert the other person that the individual is being less than honest. At the same time, the receiver of the message attempts to mask, or hide, his knowledge of the deception. Rather than directly accuse the person who is lying, the person may nod their head, offer verbal prompts ("I see!" or "So what else happened?"), and generally behave in ways designed to keep the source from seeing his suspicion. In essence, it is a back-and-forth

Interpersonal deception theory (IDT) explains the strategic choices made when engaging in deceptive communication; the source tries to mask the deception and the receiver tries to hide his suspicion of the deception.

game between relational partners. The source tries to mask the deception, and the receiver tries to hide his suspicion of the deception. Now, consider this example:

> Julie and Robbie have been dating for two years. During the fall semester of their junior year, Julie decided to study abroad in Scotland. Although Robbie was not happy that Julie was leaving, he was excited for her. At first, Julie was extremely homesick and spoke with Robbie every evening. As time passed, she met several new friends in Scotland and enjoyed going out dancing every night. Some evenings she had a little too much to drink and would end up kissing other men on the dance floor. Robbie continued to call Julie each night. He was becoming increasingly suspicious of Julie's behavior abroad. One evening he asked Julie, "Have you been with anyone since you've been there?"

There are three potentially deceptive responses that Julie can give.

Falsification a form of deception that requires telling an outright lie.

1. She can tell an outright lie or resort to falsification: "No, I have been completely faithful." Oftentimes this requires the source to create a fictional story to explain the lie.

Concealment a form of deception that involves partially telling the truth while leaving out important details.

2. Alternatively, Julie might partially tell the truth while leaving out important details. This refers to concealment: "Well, when I go out, I do dance with other guys." We typically do this when we want to hide a secret.

Equivocation a form of deception that involves being strategically vague.

3. Or Julie could engage in equivocation, or be strategically vague: "Just because I go out dancing does not necessarily mean I have to hook up with someone." This type of response is used to avoid the issue altogether.

In addition to managing the deceptive responses discussed previously (falsification, concealment, and equivocation), interpersonal deception theory also suggests that deceivers manipulate their verbal and nonverbal behavior to appear more credible (Burgoon et al., 1996).

This manipulation is accomplished by varying the message along five fundamental dimensions:

1. Completeness

2. Relevance/Directness

3. Clarity

4. Personalization

5. Veridicality

Completeness the extent of message details.

First, deceivers may vary on the completeness or extent of message details. The deceiver knows that an appropriate amount of information needs to be provided in order to be perceived as truthful by the receiver. The more practiced deceiver also realizes that specific details are probably best kept to a minimum; there is less for the receiver to challenge. When interpreting the completeness of a message, receivers may become suspicious if the information provided is too brief or vague.

A second fundamental dimension on which deceptive messages are manipulated is its relevance or directness. This refers to the extent to which the deceiver produces messages that are logical in flow and sequence, and are pertinent to the conversation. The more direct and relevant the message, the more it is perceived as truthful. Two indicators of potential deception are when a person goes off on a tangent in response to a question or is cautious in his or her response.

Relevance/directness the extent to which the deceiver produces messages that are logical in flow and sequence, and are pertinent to the conversation.

The extent to which the deceiver is clear, comprehensible, and concise is a third dimension of message manipulation. The clarity dimension varies along a continuum from very clear to completely ambiguous. The more evasive or vague a message is, the more cause there is for a receiver to probe for additional information and clarification.

Clarity a communication dimension that varies along a continuum from very clear to completely ambiguous.

A fourth dimension involves the personalization of the information. The extent to which the deceiver takes ownership of the information may vary. If the deceiver relies on verbal distancing or non-immediate communication, he will be perceived as less truthful. For example, the suggestions "everyone goes out during the week here" and "I just miss you so much that I am just trying to keep myself busy," are two examples that disassociate the deceiver with the behavior.

Personalization extent to which the deceiver takes ownership of the information.

The last dimension is the extent to which the deceiver appears to be truthful, or the veridicality of the message. This dimension is twofold: truthfulness (verbal) and believability (nonverbal). First, the message is constructed based on the objective truth value reported by the source. In other words, to what extent does the deceiver consider the message to be truthful? Next, the believability of the message is judged by the receiver. In evaluating the truthfulness of a message, receivers often rely on nonverbal cues that are the result of our body language.

Veridicality the extent to which the deceiver appears to be truthful.

Examples of behaviors believed to signal deception include increased blinking, speech errors, higher voice pitch, and enlarged pupils (Zuckerman & Driver, 1985). These unconscious behaviors are often referred to as leakage cues, and while deceptive individuals attempt to control these behaviors, others may be able to detect their dishonesty.

Leakage cues unconscious behaviors believed to signal deception.

WHY DO WE LIE?

Based on the high percentage of people who report engaging in deception, the question becomes, why are we so prone to lying? When asked, most people suggest that they lie to make themselves appear more admirable. As we stated earlier, research has found that we lie to appear competent and likable to others (Feldman, Forrest, & Happ, 2002). Therefore, it is not unusual for individuals to lie about their own personal attributes such as appearance, personality, income, career, grades, and past relational outcomes in an attempt to attract another person (Rowatt, Cunningham, & Druen, 1999).

According to the deception literature (Camden, Motley, & Wilson, 1984; DePaulo, Kashy, Kirkendale, Wyer, & Epstein, 1996), there are three types of lies that people tell:

1. Lying to harm others
2. Lying to protect self
3. Lying to spare others

© Uber Images/Shutterstock.com

People often tell lies to make themselves seem more attractive to someone new.

Understanding the ways in which messages are manipulated is one way to enhance your ability to detect deception.

Lying to Harm Others

The first type of deception, lying to harm others, is often the most damaging type of lie in interpersonal relationships. These types of lies are done to intentionally hurt others by distorting information, fabricating stories, or deliberately omitting important information. Perhaps the best example of lies designed to harm others are those seen during political campaign ads. Specific information about one's opponent is strategically distorted and manipulated in an attempt to damage his or her candidacy.

Lying to Protect Self

A more egotistical goal refers to lying to protect self. The goal of this type of lie is to make oneself look good. This can be accomplished by exaggerating praise and/or omitting weaknesses. In a study that examined sexual lies among college students, lying about the number of previous sexual partners emerged as the most frequently told lie (Knox et al. 1993). Regardless of whether the number of sexual partners was inflated to appear more experienced or reduced to appear more "pure," the goal of the lie was to enhance one's image.

Lying to Spare Others

The most common type of lie is to spare others. In the movie *A Few Good Men*, Jack Nicholson's character, Colonel Nathan R. Jessup, states, "You can't handle the truth." In this situation, Col. Jessup emphasizes that sometimes we lie in order to spare or protect others from the truth. Perhaps we want to avoid hurting the other person's feelings or damaging his self-esteem. At other times we may "stretch the truth" or omit details for the good of the relationship.

DETECTING DECEPTION

Understanding the ways in which messages are manipulated is one way to enhance your ability to detect deception. Let's discuss how we can utilize non-verbal and verbal strategies to detect deception. In a study on deceptive communication practices (Park et al., 2002), 202 college students were asked to recall a time when they had caught another person being deceptive. While a variety of discovery mechanisms were identified in the study, the three most prominent ones include the strategies labeled:

1. third-party information;
2. physical evidence; and
3. confessions.

Third-party information involves information being revealed by a person outside the relationship.

Third-party information involves information being revealed by a person outside the relationship. Suppose a teenager wants to go to a party while his parents are out of town, but he knows his parents would not approve. He lies to his parents and tells them that he is spending the night at his friend's house in case they call home while he is at the party. When his mother speaks with the friend's mother a few days later and thanks her for allowing him to stay at their house, the friend's mother reveals that he never spent the night. Thus the lie is revealed by an outside party.

Sometimes we are able to detect deception by doing our best Sherlock Holmes impression and looking for physical evidence or objects/artifacts that reveal one's deception. For instance, on an episode of *Grey's Anatomy*, Addison, Dr. Shepherd's wife, discovered a pair of black panties that clearly did not belong to her in her husband's tuxedo pocket. The physical evidence swiftly revealed Derek's betrayal and finally ended the fragile marriage. The classic lipstick-on-the-collar shtick is another familiar Hollywood portrayal of deception detection.

Another method by which deception is detected is via confessions or a verbal acknowledgement of the transgression made by the deceiver. Solicited confessions are often offered as the result of direct questioning or confrontation. Suppose you heard that your best friend went on a ski trip with a group of people the same weekend that the two of you had planned to go to a professional hockey game. Initially, he told you that he could not go to the game because he was swamped with homework. When you follow up and tell him that you heard he had gone skiing that same weekend, he feels guilty and confesses his lie. While some confessions are solicited, at other times these declarations come from out of the blue. Suppose your significant other spontaneously confesses that she has been reading your emails

> ## RESEARCH IN REAL LIFE: ARE THERE GOOD REASONS FOR LYING?
>
> While the definition of deception indicates that a source intentionally designs the message with the goal of instilling a false belief in the receiver, it is important to take a step back and consider the potential benefits of deception in relationships (Knapp & Vangelisti, 2006). Dan O'Hair and Michael Cody (1994) distinguish between positive and negative deceptive strategies. They suggest that strategies that enhance, escalate, repair, and improve relationships can be considered positive relational deceptive strategies. These include responses to the inevitable questions, "How do you like my new outfit?" or "What do you think of my new haircut?" In these situations we often respond with a white lie in order to foster liking, or positive affect. In other words, we are motivated to deceive:
>
> * to preserve the relationship;
> * to avoid hurting the other person's feelings;
> * to avoid a conflict; and
> * to protect a third party.
>
> If these are the motivations behind the deception, do you think it is acceptable? In other instances, we may decide that the deception is not worth the risk. How do you decide? What do you consider?

without your knowledge. Nothing caused you to suspect that she was engaging in this behavior, yet she decided to make an unsolicited confession. An important point to note is that we are often able to detect deception using a combination of cues—in fact, many people report a combination of verbal and nonverbal signals as tipping them off about dishonesty.

ANALYZING DECEPTIVE MESSAGES

Deception and lying are multidimensional constructs. Key components to consider when analyzing a deceptive message include: the importance of the relationship, the importance of the information to the relationship, and the costs and rewards associated with the lie. Not all lies are created equal. Consider the following three sets of questions posed by Knapp and Vangelisti (2006):

1. What is the potential outcome of the lie? Can it potentially benefit our relationship, or one of us, individually?
2. Based on the rules we have established for our relationship, is it reasonable and just for me to tell a lie? Or am I violating one of the spoken or unspoken expectancies that we have for our relationship? What lies would we agree upon that are acceptable versus unacceptable?

Positive relational deceptive strategies deceptive strategies that enhance, escalate, repair, and improve relationships.

Physical evidence objects/artifacts that reveal one's deception.

Confessions a verbal acknowledgement of the transgression or deception.

Solicited confessions often offered as the result of direct questioning or confrontation.

Unsolicited confessions declarations that are made unexpectedly or unprovoked.

3. Am I telling a lie in an attempt to protect my partner from being harmed? If I were to be caught telling the lie, would my partner understand my justification for telling the lie?

This research suggests that when we decide to lie, we must consider what will happen if my lie is detected. In other words, how will this effect the relationship? Often times, lying is a "deal breaker" for individuals in a relationship. Where is your lying threshold? Where is your partners lying threshold? What is the most important determinant in ending a relationship as a result of deception? Knapp and Vangelisti (2006) state that the more importance the receiver attaches to the information being lied about, the greater the chance that he or she will decide to end the relationship.

As you know, deception does not necessarily mean relationship termination. Interestingly, several scholars have found that despite partner deception, most romantic couples report staying together (see McCornack & Levine, 1990; Planap, Rutherford, & Honeycutt, 1988; and Bachman & Guerrero, 2006).

In all our relationships, we establish implicit and explicit rules. When these rules are violated it is considered a relational transgression. Partner deception is considered a transgression. Transgressions do not always mean there will be relationship termination. How we choose to verbally and nonverbally communicate after a transgression influences individuals' interpretation and response. For example, Horan (2012) found those individuals who receive high amounts of affection from their partners report being less hurt and ruminating less, compared to those relationships in which partners do not receive a lot of affection.

Now that you have a better understanding of the concept of deception, it is our hope that you will be strategic in your analysis of these messages and take time to understand why you and others choose to lie. Understanding these components can assist in developing healthy and effective interpersonal relationships. Now, we will turn our attention to another potential negative communication exchange, embarrassment.

EMBARRASSMENT: WHY DID I SAY THAT?

Can you remember a time when you had a huge crush on someone, and when you finally had the opportunity to talk to them and make that great first impression, something went horribly wrong and you ended up putting your foot in your mouth? Or have you ever told a joke at a party and nobody laughed? In these types of situations, we often experience social embarrassment. Recall our discussion regarding the role of self-presentation in relationships. When we perceive that our self-esteem has been threatened or if we have presented what we perceive to be a negative view of the self to others, embarrassment occurs. Our sense of identity is at stake if the response to our behavior is not what we expected.

Gross and Stone (1964) proposed that embarrassment emerges as the result of three factors that occur in social interaction. These can be summarized by a loss of or threat to our identity, confidence and/or poise.

Misrepresentations or cognitive shortcomings may cause us to feel embarrassment. Have you ever called someone by the wrong name or forgotten how you know someone? Losing confidence in our role or ability in a social situation can also cause

Embarrassment occurs when we perceive that our self-esteem has been threatened or we have presented what we perceive to be a negative view of the self to others.

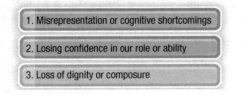

1. Misrepresentation or cognitive shortcomings

2. Losing confidence in our role or ability

3. Loss of dignity or composure

us to experience discomfort. Sometimes we script out an interaction, such as texting someone new, and the conversation does not turn out like we had anticipated. Finally, a loss of dignity, or composure, can cause us to become "red-faced." Examples of this may include tripping as you are making your way across the stage during commencement or discovering that your pants are unzipped after you have just had a conversation with your boss. More recent research by Sharkey and Stafford (1990) conceptualized six types of embarrassment. See Table 10.1 for types, examples and scenarios.

Our Role in Embarrassment

It is easy to see why we would be embarrassed in any of these situations, even if we were in control of our own behavior. We can just as easily become uncomfortable in those situations where we are the silent observer. Sattler (1965) identified three roles that exist in embarrassing social situations:

1. Agent
2. Recipient
3. Observer

As an **agent**, we are responsible for our own embarrassment, perhaps by accidentally swearing in front of our grandmother or unexpectedly burping during an important interview lunch.

In other situations, we are the **recipients**, or targets, of embarrassing communication. Examples of this type of embarrassment might include your best friend revealing to your secret crush that you are attracted to him and your mother telling your friend about the time you ran naked around the neighborhood when you were three years old.

Finally, it is likely that you can recall a situation where you were simply a bystander, or **observer**, of another's embarrassment and experienced feelings of discomfort yourself. In these situations, we often offer an awkward comment, express a reassuring remark, or simply attempt to ignore the situation.

Agent when we are responsible for our own embarrassment.

Recipient when we are targets of embarrassing communication.

Observer when we are bystanders to another's embarrassment and experience feelings of discomfort ourselves.

Table 10.1	**Sharkey and Stafford's Six Types of Embarrassment**	
Types of Embarrassment	**Example**	**Scenario**
Privacy Violations	Part of body is exposed accidentally; invasion of space; property;	Having a wardrobe malfunction
Lack of Knowledge or Skill	Forgetfulness; experiencing failure	Calling someone by the wrong name
Criticism and Rejection	Someone criticizes you in public and causes you to be the center of attention	Someone bullying a kid on the school bus by calling him/her names
Appropriate image	Body image, clothing or personal artifacts	Owning an outdated cell phone
Awkward Acts	Ungraceful actions; clumsiness	Falling on your way up to a stage to get an award
Environment	Being at the wrong place at the wrong time	Teenagers being seen with their parents

Responding to Embarrassment

How we respond to embarrassment can impact the overall impact on our interpersonal encounters. Edelmann (1985) identified three primary types of messages individuals use in response to embarrassing encounters:

1. accounts;
2. apologies; and
3. jokes.

Accounts provide a potential explanation for the cause of the embarrassing situation. Suppose you arrive at class only to discover that you forgot an important assignment that was due. You decide to speak with your instructor and explain that you have been overwhelmed with group projects in two other classes and with searching for a job. In some instances, we may feel the need to apologize for the embarrassing behavior.

Apologies are attempts to identify the source of blame for the incident. Suppose you accidentally revealed to your friend that she has not been included in the group's plans for the weekend. As you stumble over your words, you might comment, "I'm sorry. I didn't realize until now that you weren't invited," or "I didn't make the plans. They invited me along and I just assumed you were included, I'm so sorry". These responses are made with the hope that your friend will forgive you for the non-invitation.

Joking involves using humor to create a more light-hearted response to a situation. At the 2006 Academy Awards, Jennifer Garner tripped over her dress as she approached the podium. To cover her embarrassment, she joked, "I do all my own stunts." Similarly in 2013 Jennifer Lawrence tripped on her gown when she was making her way to the stage to accept her Best Actress Academy Award. The crowd gave her a standing ovation. When she arrived at the mic she stated, "You are standing up because you're feeling bad that I fell, and that's embarrassing".

According to **arousal relief theory** (Berylne, 1969), use of humor in embarrassing or difficult situations often evokes positive affective responses that can help individuals diffuse anxiety or stress. The next time that you find yourself becoming embarrassed in a social situation, remember—everyone experiences this discomfort at one time or another. While at the time it may appear to be a black cloud that hangs over your head, it is likely that these feelings will be temporary and short-lived. However, there are other dark aspects of interpersonal communication the impact of which may not be so minimal on our interactions and relationships. Next, let's consider another negative communication exchange, jealousy.

Accounts provide a potential explanation for the cause of the embarrassing situation.

Apologies attempts to identify the source of blame for the incident.

Jokes involves using humor to create a more lighthearted response to a situation.

Sometimes one embarrassing moment seems like it will last forever.

Arousal relief theory suggest that laughter can be used to release positive affective responses that can help individuals diffuse anxiety or stress.

© Axel Bueckert/Shutterstock.com

JEALOUSY IN INTERPERSONAL RELATIONSHIPS

Another aspect of interpersonal relationships that has received a lot of attention in the literature is jealousy. Jealousy causes us to experience a variety of emotions and sometimes causes us to communicate or react in ways that we normally would not. Consider some of the things that can cause us to experience jealousy:

- Your best friend recently went away to college. He sends you text messages describing all the fun he is having with his new roommate and other friends he has made in the dorm.
- A coworker talks about all the activities that she does with her young children. You wonder how she is able to find the time to finish her work and spend so much time with her kids, especially because you see yourself as a neglectful parent.
- Your relationship partner has been spending a great deal of time lately with a new friend and has expressed repeatedly how much he likes this friend.

In situations like those described in the scenarios above, it is normal to experience feelings of anger or sadness. Maybe we even feel a little bit envious or resentful.

> The next time that you find yourself becoming embarrassed in a social situation, remember—everyone experiences this discomfort at one time or another.

Jealousy has been defined as "a protective reaction to a perceived threat to a valued relationship, arising from a situation in which the partner's involvement with an activity and/or another person is contrary to the jealous person's definition of their relationship" (Hansen, 1985, p. 713). It is important to point out that this definition addresses the fact that jealousy can be experienced in various types of relationships, not just romantic, and can be induced by various issues or situations.

Types of Jealousy in Relationships

Bevan and Samter (2004) examined six different types of jealousy, three that are experienced as a result of the type of the relationship, and three that are based on the issues experienced between partners.

Types of Relationships

- Friend jealousy is typically the result of an individual's relationship with a friend. In this situation we often become frustrated and perceive them as being "taken" away from us.
- Family jealousy is the result of a partner's relationship with family members. An example of this may occur when we perceive our partner is spending too much time with their sibling or parent.
- Romantic jealousy is the result of a partner's relationship with another person and is associated with perceived intimacy between two people.

Issues in Relationships

- Power jealousy arises when we believe someone else has the ability to influence our partner. For example, if our partner had to make a difficult life decision about their job and was being influenced by their boss or colleague, we may experience power jealousy.
- Activity jealousy emerges when our relational partner dedicates time to various hobbies or interests. Have you ever become frustrated by the amount of attention that a friend dedicates to Xbox, fraternity or sorority

Jealousy a protective reaction to a perceived threat to a valued relationship, arising from a situation in which the partner's involvement with an activity and/or another person is contrary to the jealous person's definition of their relationship.

Friend jealousy result of an individual's relationship with another friend, whom we perceive as being taken away from us.

Family jealousy result of an individual's relationship with another family member, whom we perceive as being taken away from us.

Romantic jealousy the result of a partner's relationship with another person; associated with perceived intimacy between two people.

Power jealousy associated with perceptions that a partner's other relationships or obligations are viewed as more important than your relationship with the person.

Activity jealousy emerges when our relational partner dedicates time to various hobbies or interests.

Intimacy jealousy the result of the exchange of intimate or private information that a partner may share with a third party, someone not in the relationship.

activities, or sports? In these instances, the activities are perceived as a threat to your relationship.

- **Intimacy jealousy** is the result of the exchange of intimate or private information that a partner may share with a third party, someone not in the relationship. Suppose your significant other reveals to his best friend that he is undergoing a series of medical tests, but says nothing to you. When his best friend asks you how your spouse is feeling, you realize that he neglected to confide in you about his health problems. Your discovery of the "concealed" information results in feelings of intimacy jealousy. Later, you may discover that your partner simply did not want you to worry, and decided not to tell you until the results of the test were returned.

Have you ever found information on your partners phone that he/she has been concealing from you?

© Nicoleta Ionescu/Shutterstock.com

Why Does Jealousy Occur?

An extensive body of research on this topic has concluded that individuals evoke or suppress feelings of jealousy to obtain a variety of goals or objectives in their personal relationships. What causes us to experience feelings of jealousy? Guerrero and Anderson (1998) suggest that there are at least six jealousy-related goals.

1. **Maintain the Primary Relationship.** First, we become jealous in situations where we wish to maintain the primary relationship. Specifically, we are concerned with preserving the relationship. When individuals are interested in maintaining a current relationship, they will often compare themselves to a rival and try to appear more rewarding to their partner by compensating for any perceived shortcomings (Guerrero & Afifi, 1999). Making oneself appear more "attractive" than the competition (also referred to as compensatory restoration) may be an effective maintenance strategy—up to a point. Making incessant comparisons to rivals may cause your partner to perceive you as being desperate or insecure.

Compensatory restoration making oneself appear more "attractive" than the competition.

2. **Preserving One's Self-Esteem.** A second goal associated with jealousy is focused on preserving one's self-esteem. This jealousy goal is concerned with maintaining one's pride and with feeling good about oneself. Individuals who are concerned about protecting their self-esteem rarely seek out circumstances that may threaten how they view themselves (Kernis, 1995). Therefore, it comes as no surprise that the more an individual is focused on preserving his or her self-esteem, the more likely he or she is to avoid or deny jealous situations (Guerrero & Afifi, 1999). Since jealousy has a negative connotation in our culture and is related to perceptions of "weakness," it makes sense that these individuals are less likely to question or scrutinize their partners' behavior or to communicate jealous feelings.

3. **Reducing Uncertainty about the Relationship.** Another goal of jealousy is to reduce uncertainty about the relationship. The purpose of this type of jealousy is to help an individual learn where one stands in the relationship, predict the future of the relationship, and understand how the

other partner perceives the relationship. This was the only goal found to predict open and nonaggressive communication between partners (Guerrero & Afifi, 1999). If the purpose of jealousy is to reduce uncertainty and learn more about the partner, it makes sense that open and direct communication is essential to accomplishing this goal.

4. **Reducing Uncertainty about a Rival Relationship.**   A fourth goal involves reducing uncertainty about a rival relation-ship. This jealousy goal determines the threat of the competition, or how serious the rival relationship is. Individuals who focus on this goal often resort to indirect strategies, such as spying, checking up on the partner, or questioning the rival about the situation (Guerrero & Afifi, 1999). They may do this to save face with their partners so they are not perceived as "jealous" people.

5. **Re-assess the Relationship.**   When individuals are questioning the status of a relationship, they may use jealousy in an attempt to re-assess the relationship. This goal is concerned with comparing the cost with the benefits associated with the relationship. When analyzing this goal, Guerero and Afifi (1999) found that individuals typically engage in indirect strategies such as avoidance, distancing, or making the partner feel jealous. Essentially, individuals are seeking clarity on how their partners feel about them in the relationship. What does it mean when a partner responds to a jealous act? Perhaps you can use the reaction to a jealous event as a way to have further dialogue about the relationship. Certainly more direct communication is necessary to determine a partners status in a relationship.

6. **Restoring Equity through Retaliation.**   Do you know anyone who purposely evoked jealousy to get back at someone or to make his or her partner feel bad? The last goal of jealousy refers to this idea of restoring equity through retaliation. The purpose of evoking this type of jealousy response is to show the partner what it is like to experience negative emotions and to hurt the person as retribution for something the partner has done.

There are clearly a number of different reasons that relationship partners attempt to evoke jealousy responses from their partners. Are you curious to know how you may evoke jealousy? We have included a scale at the end of this chapter to measure the extent to which individuals evoke jealousy behaviors. Not surprisingly, experiencing heightened amounts of jealousy in relationships negatively affects relationship satisfaction (Guerrero & Eloy, 1992). Thus, it is important for you to understand the reasons why we evoke feelings of jealousy in others and, at the same time, to refrain from using tactics or strategies that cause others to feel jealous.

Characteristics Associated with Jealousy and Jealousy-evoking Behavior

Researchers have examined many questions associated with jealousy, including: How does someone become jealous? What types of relationships are more likely to evoke jealousy? What are the results of feeling jealous? Researchers have identified low levels of self-esteem and feelings of insecurity to be significant predictors of jealousy (McIntosh, 1989).

RESEARCH IN REAL LIFE: SEX DIFFERENCES IN JEALOUSY AT WORK

When a rival co-worker communicates with your supervisor, do you experience feelings of jealousy? More interestingly, would they be different for men and women? Researchers were interested in determining which attributes of a rival would induce the most jealousy (Buunk, Goor, & Solano, 2010). Following more of an evolutionary perspective, the authors assumed jealousy is more automatic and unconscious. The researchers assessed four specific attributes:

1. Social power and dominance or the extent to which one has more authority.
2. Physical attractiveness or beauty
3. Social-communal attributes, such as being a great listener
4. Physical dominance or strength

In same sex supervisors, results found that men experienced greater jealousy when their rivals had higher levels of perceived dominance or authority. For females, the level of perceived physical attractiveness of their rival resulted in higher levels of jealousy.

Another study found that jealousy is more likely to occur in relationships of shorter duration (for less than one year) than in those of longer duration (more than one year) (Knox, Zusman, Mabon, & Shriver, 1999). What conditions are most likely to elicit jealous reactions? A 1999 study (Knox et al.) found that talking to or about a previous partner is the action or topic that is most likely to evoke jealousy.

Are you guilty of attempting to make others feel jealous? Psychologists were concerned with what motivated individuals to engage in these jealousy-induction behaviors. They define romantic jealousy-induction as "a strategic behavioral process to elicit reactive, romantic jealousy from a partner in order to achieve a specific goal" (Mattingly, Whitson, & Mattingly, 2012, p. 276).

Their study revealed five motivations for romantic jealousy-induction:

1. To test the partner's love or strengthen the current relationship
2. To engage in revenge against the partner
3. To gain power or control over the partner
4. Because of a preoccupation with relationship security
5. Because of low self-esteem

Similarly, communication scholars have explored specific relationship types to predict these intentional jealousy-evoking behaviors. Do affection and love influence these behaviors? Goodboy, Horan, and Booth-Butterfield (2012) found that the amount of affection received from romantic partners is inversely related with jealousy-evoking behaviors. This affection was measured by Floyd and Morman's (1998) Affectionate Communication Index, which examines the extent to which partners believed their partners provided affection across three dimensions: *verbally* (e.g., "saying I love you"), *nonverbally*, (e.g., "holding hands"), and *supportive affection* (e.g., "praising his/her with compliments"). Therefore, these jealousy-evoking behaviors are related to the amount of affection in our relationships. So, what about love? The authors further explored Lee's (1973) typology of love styles. These six styles uniquely explain how individuals experience romantic love:

1. Eros lovers are described as passionate and intense; they have a strong commitment to the relationship sexually and value security, physical attraction, and beauty.
2. Ludus lovers want to "win" as many partners as possible and see love as a "game." They value having fun and tend to have shorter relationships as a result.
3. Storge lovers value love that is established through common interests and friendships. They tend to see love as developing over time with a strong commitment to the relationship.

Eros   a love style that is described as passionate and intense; these individuals have a strong commitment to the relationship sexually and value security, physical attraction, and beauty.

Ludus   a love style that values having fun; these individuals are interested in "winning" as many partners as possible; they see love as a "game."

Storge   a love style that involves individuals who value love that is established through common interests and friendships; they tend to see love as developing over time.

4. Pragma lovers are logical and realistic about their partners. They typically are looking for certain criteria that match their goals.

5. Mania lovers have a strong need to be loved and often develop obsessive and possessive tendencies. They value a strong attachment to their partners.

6. Agape lovers are described as selfless and committed to the relationship partner. They tend to put their partner's needs above their own and are described as altruistic and sacrificial.

Results from their study revealed that only the *ludus* and *mania* love styles were positive predictors of jealousy-evoking behavior.

Gender Differences and Jealousy

So, who is more jealous, males or females? Studies have found no significant differences between males and females with regard to one gender being more likely to emerge as a primary source of jealousy (Knox, Zusman, Mabon, & Shriver, 1999) or in the amount or duration of intensity of feeling jealousy (Pines & Friedman, 1998). However, research has shown that males and females do experience jealousy for different reasons.

For example:

- Males are more likely to become jealous as a result of sexual infidelity, whereas females become more jealous over emotional infidelity in heterosexual relationships (Buss et al., 1992; Frederick & Fales, 2014). Sexual infidelity refers to having sexual relations with someone outside of one's romantic relationship while emotional infidelity refers to engaging in an intense and deep emotional attachment to someone outside of the romantic relationship (Carpenter, 2012). Sexual infidelity may involve intercourse, oral sex, kissing, and sexual touch. Emotional infidelity typically involves the sharing of personal self-disclosures.

- Gay men, lesbian women, and bisexual men and women did not differ significantly on whether they were more upset over emotional or sexual infidelity (Frederick & Fales, 2014).

- Studies have found the reactions to different types of jealousy are similar for males and females (Dijkstar & Buunk, 2004). That is, emotional infidelity typically evoked responses of anxiety, worry, distrust, and suspicion, while responses to sexual infidelity were associated with feelings of sadness, rejection, anger, and betrayal.

- Women experience more jealousy in response to a physically attractive threat, while men become more jealous when the threat is perceived as being more socially dominant (Dijkstra & Buunk, 1998). Evolutionary psychologists argue the reason for this gender difference is due to the fact that our society typically rates a female's value in a relationship as determined by her physical attractiveness, whereas the relationship value of males is often evaluated by their status or dominance (Townsend & Levy, 1990).

Therefore, examining sexual and emotional infidelity can help us understand how males and females respond to jealousy.

Pragma a love style that involves lovers who are logical and realistic about their partners; they typically are looking for certain criteria that match their goals.

Mania a love style that involves a strong need to be loved; these individuals often develop obsessive and possessive tendencies; they value a strong attachment to their partners.

Agape a love style that is often described as selfless and altruistic; these individuals tend to put their partners' needs above their own

Sexual infidelity a type of infidelity that involves having sexual relations with someone outside of one's romantic relationship; this may include intercourse, oral sex, kissing, and sexual touch.

Emotional infidelity a type of infidelity that refers to engaging in an intense and deep emotional attachment to someone outside of the romantic relationship; it typically involves sharing personal self-disclosures.

Integrative communication this refers to a specific communicative response to jealousy; it involves direct and nonaggressive communication about jealousy with a partner.

Negative affect aggression this is a specific communication response to jealousy; it involves nonverbal expressions of jealousy-related affect that the partner can see.

Coping with Jealousy

The way people initially express feelings of jealousy to a partner will ultimately influence how the partner responds. Understanding positive emotional responses can help our interpersonal relationships when dealing with jealous interactions. Yoshimura (2004) found that responses such as integrative communication (e.g., directly talking about the jealousy issue) and negative affect expression (e.g., crying) were perceived as evoking positive emotional responses by the partner (see Table 10.2). In other words, expressing your feelings openly and directly with your partner and appearing hurt by the threat produces positive emotional and behavior outcomes. This same study also found that negative emotional outcomes were more likely to produce violent behavior and manipulation attempts by the other partner. See Table 10.2 for a complete list of the ways people respond to feelings of jealousy.

While we have explored the responses to jealousy, let us take a moment to consider the role that perceived influence and power can play in causing us to experience envy.

Table 10.2 Communicative Responses to Jealousy

Strategy	Definition/Examples
1. Negative affect expression	Nonverbal expressions of jealousy-related affect that the partner can see. *Examples:* acting anxious when with the partner, appearing hurt, wearing "displeasure" on face, crying in front of the partner
2. Integrative communication	Direct, nonaggressive communication about jealousy with the partner. *Examples:* disclosing jealous feelings to the partner, asking the partner probing questions, trying to reach an understanding with the partner, reassuring the partner that "we can work it out"
3. Distributive communication	Direct, aggressive communication about jealousy with the partner. *Examples:* accusing the partner of being unfaithful, being sarcastic or rude toward the partner, arguing with the partner, bringing up the issue over and over again to "bombard" the partner
4. Active distancing	Indirect, aggressive means of communicating jealousy to the partner. *Examples:* giving the partner the "silent treatment," storming out of the room, giving the partner cold or dirty looks, withdrawing affection and sexual favors
5. Avoidance/denial	Indirect, nonagressive communication that focuses on avoiding the jealousy-invoking issue, situation, or partner. *Examples:* denying jealous feelings when confronted by the partner, pretending to be unaffected by the situation, decreasing contact with the partner, avoiding jealousy-evoking situations
6. Violent communication/ threats	Threatening or actually engaging in physical violence against the partner. *Examples:* threatening to harm the partner if he/she continues to see the rival, scaring the partner by acting as if he/she were about to hit him/her, roughly pulling the partner away from the rival, pushing or slapping the partner

Strategy	Definition/Examples
7. Signs of possession	Publicly displaying the relationship to others so they know the partner is "taken." *Examples:* putting an arm around the partner and saying he or she is "taken," constantly introducing the partner as a "girl/boyfriend," telling potential rival of plans to be married, kissing the partner in front of potential rival
8. Derogating competitors	Making negative comments about potential rivals to the partner and to others. *Examples:* "badmouthing" the rival in front of the partner and his or her friends, expressing disbelief that anyone would be attracted to the rival
9. Relationship threats	Threatening to terminate or de-escalate the primary relationship or to be unfaithful. *Examples:* threatening to end the relationship if the partner continues to see the rival, threatening infidelity
10. Surveillance/ restriction	Behavioral strategies designed to find out about or interfere with the rival relationship. *Examples:* spying or checking up on the partner, looking through the partner's belongings for evidence of a rival relationship, pressing the redial button to see who the partner called last

Source: Adapted from Guerrero & Anderson, 1998; Guerrero, Anderson, Jorgensen, Spitzberg, & Eloy, 1995.

INTERPERSONAL POWER AND VERBAL AGGRESSION

A possible factor contributing to our tendency to encounter jealousy in relationships may be explained by the interpersonal power perceived by relational partners. In this section, we will take a closer look at the potential implications of power in relationships and explore power's relationship to verbal aggression and violence. Power can be defined as one's ability to influence others to behave in ways they normally might not. What types of power impact our relationships with others?

Types of Power

French and Raven (1960) identified five types of power that individuals typically use when they are attempting to influence others. The five classic power bases are:

1. Reward power is based on a person's perception that the source of power can provide rewards. Example: *I'll clean up the apartment and maybe my roommate will invite me to go with him on the ski trip with his family this weekend.*
2. Coercive power focuses on the perceived ability of the source to punish or to enact negative consequences. Example: *I have to finish this report today or I know my boss will make me come in this weekend.*
3. Legitimate power is centered on the perception that the source has authority because of a particular role that she plays in the relationship or a title that she holds. Example: *Because I'm the mommy, and I said so.*

Power one's ability to influence others to behave in ways they normally might not.

Reward power based on a person's perception that the source of power can provide rewards.

Coercive power focuses on the perceived ability of the source to punish or to enact negative consequences.

Legitimate power centered on the perception that the source has authority because of a particular role that she plays in the relationship or a title that she holds.

Referent power   based on a person's respect, identification, and attraction to the source.

Expert power   grounded in the perception that the source possesses knowledge, expertise, or skills in a particular area.

4. Referent power is based on a person's respect, identification, and attraction to the source. Example: *No matter how ridiculous I feel, I will dress up in a costume and go to this Halloween party because I am really attracted to you and want you to like me.*

5. Expert power is grounded in the perception that the source possesses knowledge, expertise, or skills in a particular area. Example: *I will listen to what she says about our household budget because she is the financial wizard in the family.*

French and Raven propose that it is the receivers' perception of the source of the message that is the key to analyzing power. We stated in earlier chapters that effective interpersonal communication is receiver-based. Thus, it is important to consider the receiver's perception of the source to predict future interactions. But do individuals have power if we do not give it to them? Based on the important role that receiver perception plays in the communication process, probably not.

Consider the following scenario:

> Alan had very little respect for his mother. At thirteen years old, he was completely out of control. He skipped school, ignored his mother's rules, and even hit his mother on several occasions when she attempted to discipline him. Finally, his mother had reached the breaking point. One night she caught Alan doing drugs with his friends in the basement. She reported Alan to the authorities and hoped that it would help him get back on track. But his misbehavior continued.

In this instance, Alan's mother should have legitimate power over him. However, his behavior is an obvious indicator that he does not perceive her to have any power in the relationship. Even when his mother attempts to utilize coercive power by calling the police, it does nothing to change Alan's perception. His inability to view his mother as having reward, coercive, or legitimate power even results in Alan's occasional use of physical violence. If you do not perceive your relational partner as having the power, then it is unlikely that you would comply with any requests he or she makes.

Understanding the relationship between attraction and power may help explain why some influence attempts are successful whereas others fail. Depending on the perceived power base, receivers will alter their perceptions of the source's attractiveness and determine the level of acceptance or resistance in response to the request. Suppose your best friend uses a threat, or coercive power, in an attempt to influence you. This will typically decrease your level of perceived attraction for your friend, and chances are that you will resist their request. On the other hand, if you perceive that the friend has the power to reward you as a result of the request, it is likely that you would find them more attractive and would have minimal resistance to the request. These same principles can be applied in a variety of relationships. What if your mother told you that if you cleaned your room she would reward you with $5.00 and a trip to the movies? You would be more willing to agree to her request and you would find her to be more interpersonally attractive than if she would have said, "If you don't clean your room, you will have to pay me $5.00 to do it for you, and you'll be grounded from the movies for the next week." Threats and coercive behavior typically breed resentment and result in higher levels of resistance.

Relationship between Power and Interpersonal Influence

To better understand the impact of power in our decisions of whether to comply with requests made in our interpersonal relationships, we look at the three levels of influence that can be achieved. These include compliance, identification, and internalization (Kelman, 1961).

1. Compliance occurs when an individual agrees to a request because he can see a potential reward or punishment for doing so. This level of influence is likely to persuade someone to do something, but his motivation is typically low and the change in the behavior is usually quite temporary. When you tell your roommate that she can have your car for the weekend if she drives you to the airport and she later complies with your request, you have influenced her at the compliance level. In this example, the only reason the roommate complies with the request is to obtain a reward.

2. If a person decides to agree to an influence attempt because she recognizes the potential benefits of doing so, or perhaps she wishes to establish a relationship with the source, then identification has occurred. A student agrees to his teacher's recommendation that he take honors level courses next semester to help prepare him for college instead of "cruising" in the regular classes with his friends. In this instance, individuals are typically more motivated to comply because they agree with the source's goals, interests, and values.

3. The last level of influence, internalization, is employed when an individual adopts a behavior because it is internally rewarding. In other words, it feels like the right thing to do. This type of influence is successful because the person sees the requested behavior as fitting within his or her existing value system. The individual agrees to the behavior because he intrinsically believes it should be done, not just because someone told him to do so. An example of this might be a spouse who takes on the responsibility of extra household or childcare duties in order to assist a partner who is experiencing a difficult time at work. In this instance, the person agrees to the request because of the value placed on family and the level of commitment made to the relationship. Table 10.3 summarizes the level of influence that can be achieved as a result of each of the five types of power.

Compliance occurs when an individual agrees to a request because he can see a potential reward or punishment for doing so.

Identification when a person decides to agree to an influence attempt because he recognizes the potential benefits of doing so, or if he wishes to establish a relationship with the source.

Internalization when an individual adopts a behavior because it is internally rewarding.

Table 10.3 **Types of Power and Their Impact on Levels of Influence**

Types of Power	Levels of Influence		
	Compliance	Identification	Internalization
Reward	X		
Coercive	X		
Legitimate	X		
Referent	X	X	X
Expert	X	X	X

Power versus Dominance in Relationships

What is the difference between power and dominance? Burgoon and Dillman (1995) argue, "Because power is broadly defined as the ability to exercise influence by possessing one or more power bases, dominance is but one means of many for expressing power" (p. 65). In other words, power is the potential to influence another's behavior, whereas dominance is a mechanism typically associated with attempts to express power and take control in a relationship. What is the relationship between talking and influence? One study found that the more an individual talks, the more opportunities he has to gain influence over others (Daly, McCroskey, & Richmond, 1977). A separate study suggests that managing what individuals talk about and "controlling the floor" are perceived as forms of interpersonal dominance or control (Palmer, 1989).

Dominance a mechanism typically associated with attempts to express power and take control in a relationship.

VERBAL AGGRESSION

There are two primary strategies that we use to gain influence over others. First, we can make rational arguments that present reasons for why their compliance is beneficial. A second strategy involves the use of negative communication behaviors such as attacks on another person's self esteem or character in an attempt to gain their compliance. As you can see, one of these strategies is positive, and the other is negative and potentially damaging to relationships. So why do some individuals choose to present rational arguments while others choose to attack? The explanation rests in the distinction between communication traits known as argumentativeness and verbal aggression.

How did you handle your aggression in your last argument?

Argumentativeness refers to the extent to which an individual challenges a position or issue (Infante & Rancer, 1982). A person can question or debate whether they should comply with a request without directly addressing the personal characteristics of the person making the request. When a request is addressed with a response that attacks the self-confidence, character, and/or intelligence of another person, verbal aggressiveness is being used (Infante & Wigley, 1986). Examples of verbally aggressive messages might include attacks on one's character or competence, teasing or ridiculing, or even making threats or jokes about another's appearance. It is not unusual to resort to verbally aggressive messages, when we run out of good arguments to make during a conflict situation. Just think about the last time you got into an argument. Did the conversation start calm with sound reasoning? Then what happened? Often times when we feel others are not listening or understanding we can escalate to more aggressive strategies. This is how productive conflict situations can eventually turn dark.

Argumentativeness refers to the extent to which an individual challenges a position or issue.

Verbal aggression when a request is addressed with a response that attacks the self-confidence, character, and/or intelligence of another person.

Low aggression characterized by yelling, crying, refusing to talk, or stomping out of the room.

Loreen Olson suggests that there are four levels of aggression that are experienced in our interpersonal encounters (2004).

1. Low aggression is characterized by yelling, crying, refusing to talk, or stomping out of the room.

© Stuart Jenner/Shutterstock.com

2. Moderate aggression involves more intense acts of verbal aggression such as verbal insults, swearing at the other, and indirect physical displays of anger such as kicking, hitting, throwing inanimate objects, or threatening to engage in these behaviors.

3. High aggression refers to intensive face threatening, verbal belittling, and direct physical contact with the other person in the form of slapping, shoving, or pushing.

4. The most serious level, severe aggression, includes intense verbal abuse and threats and involves physical attacks that include kicking, biting, punching, hitting with an object, raping, and using a weapon. Not only can verbally aggressive acts occur before relational conflicts, they can occur as a consequence to partner aggression and also serve to escalate the conflict. In relationships, struggles for power and control are often at the heart of reciprocated and escalating aggression between partners (Olson, 2004).

Now, we will explore the impact of verbal aggression across three distinct contexts, including in romantic relationships, in the classroom, and at work.

Verbal Aggression in Romantic Relationships

Does a history of verbal aggression in our families lead to verbally aggressive romantic relationships? Communication scholars found that individuals with a history of familiar verbal aggression in childhood are more desensitized in adulthood and are more tolerant of their own and their romantic partners' verbal aggression in romantic relationships (Aloia & Solomon, 2013). These results lend support to the idea that the more we are exposed to verbal aggressive messages in childhood, the more we engage and accept verbal aggression in our adult romantic relationships. However, what role does stress and anger have in the propensity to engage in verbal aggression in romantic relationships? One study suggests that, regardless of a relational partner's coping skills, verbal aggression is likely to occur once strong emotions, such as anger, have been evoked (Bodenmann, Meuwly, Bradbury, Gmelch, & Ledermann, 2010). The authors suggest that we should focus more on reducing stress in relationships to avoid such strong negative emotions, rather than directly trying to reduce verbal aggression in an angry partner.

While our first tendency is to assume that aggression and violence are often restricted to close relationships with romantic partners or family members, this is not the case. Researchers have examined their presence and impact in a variety of relational contexts, including in the classroom and at work.

Verbal Aggression in the Classroom

Since verbal aggression is perceived as a negative communication behavior, it should come as no surprise that researchers have identified several negative outcomes associated with teachers who use words to attack students in the classroom. Students who perceive their instructors as being verbally aggressive report

Moderate aggression involves more intense acts of verbal aggression such as verbal insults, swearing at the other, and indirect physical displays of anger such as kicking, hitting, throwing inanimate objects, or threatening to engage in these behaviors.

High aggression refers to intensive face threatening, verbal belittling, and direct physical contact with the other person in the form of slapping, shoving, or pushing.

Severe aggression includes intense verbal abuse and threats and involves physical attacks that include kicking, biting, punching, hitting with an object, raping, and using a weapon.

> One study suggests that, regardless of a relational partner's coping skills, verbal aggression is likely to occur once strong emotions, such as anger, have been evoked.

How would you handle a teacher bullying your child?

that they are less motivated in that class (Myers & Rocca, 2001). Also, they evaluate the teacher as being less competent and as behaving inappropriately (Martin, Weber, & Burant, 1997). In an environment where a student fears becoming the target of verbal abuse, less learning occurs (Myers, 2002) and the chances are greater that students will choose to avoid the situation by skipping class (Rocca, 2004). Outside the classroom, scholars have also explored the advisor-advisee relationship. One study concluded that as perceptions of the advisor's verbal aggressiveness with advisees increase, perceptions of advisor credibility decrease (Punyanunt-Carter & Wrench, 2008). When you consider that aggressiveness fosters a negative learning experience, the power of a teacher's communication becomes apparent.

Verbal Aggression in the Workplace

Another context that has been the target of research on verbal aggression is the workplace. It is important to understand the potential for verbal aggression and emotional abuse to occur in the organizational environment. Approximately 90 percent of adults report that they have been a victim of workplace bullying at some point during their professional career (Hornstein, 1996). A 2012 study found that verbal aggression by supervisors is related to employee dissatisfaction (Madlock & Dillow, 2012). The psychological impact of negative events, such as a supervisor's verbal aggression, has a lasting and more powerful impact than positive events, such as paying a compliment. These factors can impact employees' overall well-being. So why would employees stay in a position when their supervisor engages in verbal aggression? Study results suggest employees may choose to stay in a hostile work environment because of two reasons:

Approximately 90 percent of adults report that they have been a victim of workplace bullying at some point during their professional career.

1. Investment size is high
2. Quality of alternatives is low

Investment size may be considered high if an employee has a significant number of years of service, non-vested portions of retirement programs, and/or several rewarding work relationships. The quality of alternatives may be considered low if an employee does not perceive there is another job opportunity available to them.

It probably is no surprise that communication scholars (Madlock & Kennedy-Lightsey, 2010) found verbal aggression to be a negative predictor of:

- employees' communication satisfaction;
- organizational commitment; and
- job satisfaction.

However, it is interesting to note that this same study found supervisors' verbal aggression was a stronger predictor than supervisors' mentoring—suggesting once again that our negative experiences have more lasting impact than our positive experiences.

As we conclude this section on verbal aggression, we acknowledge that verbal aggression is not only enacted in face-to-face interactions.

RESEARCH IN REAL LIFE: EMPLOYEE ABUSE AND WORKPLACE BULLYING

Who is most likely to engage in bullying at work? The results may surprise you. According to the United States Hostile Workplace Survey in 2000:

* Women comprised 50 percent of the bullies.
* Female bullies target other women an overwhelming 84 percent of the time; male bullies target women in 69 percent of the cases; women are the majority (77 percent) of targets.
* The vast majority of bullies are bosses (81 percent); they have the power to terminate their targets at will.

In 2014, a Workplace Bullying Survey was conducted in the United States. Key findings taken directly from their homepage state:

* 27% have current or past direct experience with abusive conduct at work
* 72% of the American public are aware of workplace bullying
* Bosses are still the majority of bullies
* 72% of employers deny, discount, encourage, rationalize, or defend it
* 93% of respondents support enactment of the Health Workplace Bill

http://www.workplacebullying.org/wbiresearch/wbi-2014-us-survey/

SUMMARY

While the topics discussed in this chapter may not be particularly pleasant, it is important to address their role in our communication with others. Not all relationships are enjoyable. To use the analogy of a roller coaster, virtually all relationships experience ups and downs. In this chapter we have discussed the concept of interpersonal deception and explored the potential impact of telling lies. In addition, we discussed the potential embarrassment that pops up from time to time and causes us to become "red-faced" in our interactions. In keeping with color analogies, relationships often encounter the "green-eyed monster" when jealousy emerges and causes us to respond in ways that we might not otherwise. We identified power and influence as potential sources of jealousy and as something that can affect our interactions with others. The distinction between argumentativeness and aggressiveness was made, as we offered a glimpse into the ugly side of power, when it results in verbal attacks against others.

Oftentimes we hear the phrase, "Communication is the key to success." The purpose of this chapter was to introduce a few communication situations in which communication was *not part of the solution*, but was, in fact, *part of the problem*. It is important to remember that communication is a tool that can be used for good or evil purposes.

It is up to us to understand how to use communication effectively to accomplish our goals and to become more competent in our interactions with others. By offering you a glimpse into the "dark side" of communication, it is our hope that your relationships will encounter more "ups" than "downs."

DISCUSSION QUESTIONS

1. Most people would agree that there are times when it is okay to deceive a friend, family member, or romantic partner. Have you ever been in a particular situation where you felt it was justified or acceptable to deceive someone? What were the reasons for your deception?

2. What are some ways to make sure that your partner does not feel jealous in regard to your romantic relationship? What are some suggestions for dealing with someone who often reports jealous feelings?

3. How would you recommend training individuals to use less verbally aggressive messages to influence others? What factors would you consider in this training?

4. After you complete the Evoking-Jealousy Scale, give this scale to your partner. Discuss how the discrepancy in the two scores may impact your interpersonal communication. How can the information gained from these scores help your relationship to communicate more effectively?

REFERENCES

Aloia, L. S., & Solomon, D. H. (2013). Perceptions of verbal aggression in romantic relationships: The role of family history and motivational systems. *Western Journal of Communication, 77*(4), 411–423.

Bachman, G. F., & Guerrero, L. K. (2006). Forgiveness, apology, and communicative responses to hurtful events. *Communication Reports, 19*(1), 45–56.

Berlyne, D. E. (1969). Laughter, humor and play. In G. Lindzey and E. Aronson (Eds.), *Handbook of social psychology,* Vol. 3, (pp. 795–813). Reading, MA: Addison-Wesley.

Bevan, J. L., & Samter, W. (2004). Toward a broader conceptualization of jealousy in close relationships: Two exploratory studies. *Communication Studies, 55,* 14–28.

Bodenmann, G., Meuwly, N., Bradbury, T. N., Gmelch, S., & Ledermann, T. (2010). Stress, anger, and verbal aggression in intimate relationships: Moderating effects of individual and dyadic coping. *Journal of Social & Personal Relationships, 27*(3), 408–424.

Buller, D. B., & J. K. Burgoon. (1996). Interpersonal deception theory. *Communication Theory, 6,* 203–242.

Burgoon, J. K., Buller, D. B., Guerrero, L. K., Afifi, W., & Feldman, C. M. (1996). Interpersonal deception XII: Information management dimensions underlying types of deceptive messages. *Communication Monographs, 63,* 50–69.

Burgoon, J. K., & Dillman, L. (1995). Gender, immediacy and nonverbal communication. In P. J. Kalbfleisch and M. J. Cody (Eds.), *Gender, power, and communication in human relationships* (pp. 63–81). Hillsdale, NJ: Lawrence Erlbaum Associates.

Buss, D. M., Larsen, R. J., Westen, D., & Semmelroth, J. (1992). Sex differences in jealousy: Evolution, physiology, and psychology. *Psychological Science, 3,* 251–255.

Buunk, A. P., Goor, J. A., & Solano, A. C. (2010). Intrasexual competition at work: Sex differences in the jealousy-evoking effect of a rival characteristics in work settings. *Journal of Social and Personal Relationships, 27*(5), 671–684.

Camden, C., Motley, M. T., & Wilson, A. (1984). White lies in interpersonal communication: A taxonomy and preliminary investigation of social motives. *The Western Journal of Speech Communication, 48,* 309–325.

Carpenter, C. J. (2012). Meta-analysis of sex differences in responses to sexual versus emotional infidelity: Men and women are more similar than different. *Psychology of Women Quarterly, 36,* 25–37.

Cupach, W. R., & Spitzberg, B. H. (1994). *The dark side of interpersonal communication.* Hillsdale, NJ: Lawrence Erlbaum.

Daly, J. A., McCroskey, J. C., & Richmond, V. P. (1977). Relationship between vocal activity and perception of communicators in small group interaction. *Western Journal of Speech Communication, 41,* 175–187.

DePaulo, B. M., Kashy, D. A., Kirkendale, S. E., Wyer, M. M., & Epstein, J. A. (1996). Lying in everyday life. *Journal of Personality and Social Psychology, 70,* 979–995.

Dijkstar, P., & Buunk, B. P. (2004). Gender differences in rival characteristics that evoke jealousy in response to emotional versus sexual infidelity. *Personal Relationships, 11,* 395–408.

Dijkstra, P., & Buunk, B. P. (1998). Jealousy as a function of rival characteristics: An evolutionary perspective. *Personality and Social Psychology Bulletin, 24,* 1158–1166.

Edelmann, R. J. (1985). Social embarrassment: An analysis of the process. *Journal of Social and Personal Relationships, 2,* 195–213.

Feldman, R. S., Forrest, J. A., & Happ, B. R. (2002). Self-presentation and verbal deception: Do self-presenters lie more? *Basic and Applied Social Psychology, 24*(2), 163–170.

Floyd, K., & Morman, M. T. (1998). The measurement of affectionate communication. *Communication Quarterly, 46*(2), 144–162.

Frederick, D. A., & Fales, M. R. (2014). Upset over sexual versus emotional infidelity among gay, lesbian, bisexual and heterosexual adults. Archives of Sexual Behavior, 43, DOI: 0.1007/s10508-014-0409-9

French, J. P. R., & Raven, B. (1960). The bases of social power. In D. Cartwright and A. Zander (Eds.), *Group dynamics* (pp. 607–623). New York: Harper and Row.

Goodboy, A. K., Horan, S. M., & Booth-Butterfield, M. (2012). Intentional jealousy-evoking behavior in romantic relationships as a function of received partner affection and love styles. *Communication Quarterly, 60,* 3, 370–385.

Gross, E., & Stone, G.P. (1964). Embarrassment and the analysis of role requirements. *American Journal of Sociology, 70,* 1–15.

Guerrero, L. K., & Afifi, W.A. (1999). Toward a goal-oriented approach for understanding communicative responses to jealousy. *Western Journal of Communication, 63,* 216–248.

Guerrero, L. K., & Anderson, P. A. (1998). Jealousy experience and expression in romantic relationships. In P. A. Anderson & L. K. Guerrero (Eds.), *Handbook of communication and emotion* (pp. 155–188). San Diego, CA: Academic Press.

Guerrero, L. K., Anderson, P. A., Jorgensen, P. F., Spitzberg, B. H., & Eloy, S. V. (1995). Coping with the green-eyed monster: Conceptualizing and measuring communicative responses to romantic jealousy. *Western Journal of Communication, 59,* 270–304.

Guerrero, L. K., & Eloy, S.V. (1992). Relationship satisfaction and jealousy across marital types. *Communication Reports, 5,* 23–41.

Hansen, G. L. (1985). Dating jealousy among college students. *Sex Roles, 12,* 713–721.

Horan, S. M. (2012). Affection exchange theory and perceptions of relational transgressions. *Western Journal of Communication, 76,* 109–126.

Hornstein, H. A. (1996). *Brutal bosses and their prey. How to overcome and identify abuse in the workplace.* New York: Riverhead Books.

Infante, D. A., & Rancer, A. S. (1982). A conceptualization and measure of argumentativeness. *Journal of Personality Assessment, 46,* 72–80.

Infante, D. A., & Wigley, C. J. (1986). Verbal aggression: An interpersonal model and measure. *Communication Monographs, 53,* 61–69.

Kelman, H. C. (1961). Processes of opinion change. *Public Opinion Quarterly, 25,* 58–78.

Kernis, M. H. (1995). *Efficacy, agency and self-esteem.* New York: Plenum Press.

Knapp, M. L., & Vangelisti, A. L. (2006). Lying. In K. M. Galvin & P. J. Cooper (Eds.), *Making connections* (pp. 247–252). Los Angeles, CA: Roxbury.

Knox, D., Schact, C., Holt, J., & Turner, J. (1993). Sexual lies among university students. *College Student Journal, 27,* 269–272.

Knox, D., Zusman, M. E., Mabon, L., & Shriver, L. (1999). Jealousy in college student relationships. *College Student Journal, 33,* 328.

Lee, J. A. (1973). *The colors of love: An exploration of the ways of loving.* Don Mills, Ontario, Canada: New Press.

Madlock, P. E., & Dillow, M. R. (2012). The consequences of verbal aggression in the workplace: An application of the investment model. *Communication Studies, 63*(5), 593–607.

Madlock, P. E., & Kennedy-Lightsey, C. (2010). The effects of supervisors' verbal aggressiveness and mentoring on their subordinates. *Journal of Business Communication, 47*(1), 42–62.

Martin, M. M., Weber, K., & Burant, P. A. (1997). Students' perceptions of a teacher's use of slang and verbal aggressiveness in a lecture: An experiment. Paper presented at the Eastern Communication Association Convention, Baltimore, MD.

Mattingly, B. A., Whitson, D., & Mattingly, M. J. B. (2012). Development of the romantic jealousy-induction scale and the motives for inducing romantic jealousy scale. *Current Psychology, 31,* 263–281.

McCornack, S. A., & Levine, T. R. (1990). When loves become leery. The relationship between suspicion and accuracy in detecting deception. *Communication Monographs, 57,* 219–230.

McIntosh, E. G. (1989). An investigation of romantic jealousy among black undergraduates. *Social Behavior and Personality, 17,* 135–141.

Myers, S. A. (2002). Perceived aggressive instructor communication and student state motivation, learning and satisfaction. *Communication Reports, 15,* 113–121.

Myers, S. A., & Rocca, K.A. (2001). Perceived instructor argumentativeness and verbal aggressiveness in the college classroom: Effects on student perceptions of climate, apprehension, and state motivation. *Western Journal of Communication, 65,* 113–137.

O'Hair, H. D., & Cody, M. J. (1994). Everyday deception. In W. R. Cupach & B. Spitzberg (Ed.), *The dark side of interpersonal communication* (pp. 181–213). Hillsdale, NJ: Lawrence Erlbaum Associates.

Olson, L. N. (2004). Relational control-motivated aggression: A theoretically-based typology of intimate violence. *Journal of Family Communication, 4,* 209–233.

Palmer, M. T. (1989). Controlling conversations: Turns, topics and interpersonal control. *Communication Monographs, 56,* 1–18.

Park, H. S., Levine, T. R., McCornack, S. A., Morrison, K., & Ferrara, M. (2002). How people really detect lies. *Communication Monographs, 69,* 144–157.

Pines, A. M., & Friedman, A. (1998). Gender differences in romantic jealousy. *The Journal of Social Psychology, 138,* 54–71.

Planap, S., Rutherford, D., & Honeycutt, J. M. (1988). Events that increase uncertainty in personal relationships II: Replication and extension. *Human Communication Research, 14,* 516–547.

Punyanunt-Carter, N. M., & Wrench, J. S. (2008). Advisor-advisee communication two: The influence of verbal aggression and humor assessment on advisee perceptions of advisor credibility and affective learning. *Communication Research Reports, 22,* 303–313.

Rocca, K. A. (2004). College student attendance: Impact of instructor immediacy and verbal aggression. *Communication Education, 53,* 185–195.

Rowatt, W. C., Cunningham, M. R., & Druen, P. B. (1999). Lying to get a date: The effect of facial attractiveness on the willingness to deceive prospective dating partners. *Journal of Social and Personal Relationships, 16*(2), 209–223.

Sattler, J. M. (1965). A theoretical, developmental, and clinical investigation of embarrassment. *Clinical Psychology Monographs, 71,* 19–59.

Sharkey, W. F. & Stafford, L. (1990). Responses to Embarassment. *Human Communication Research, 17,* 315–342.

Spitzberg, B. H. (2006). A struggle in the dark. In K. M. Galvin & P. J. Cooper (Eds.), *Making connections* (pp. 240–246). Los Angeles, CA: Roxbury.

Townsend, J. M., & Levy, G. D. (1990). Effects of potential partners' costume and physical attractiveness on sexual and partner selection. *Journal of Psychology, 124,* 371–389.

Yoshimura, S. M. (2004). Emotional and behavioral responses to romantic jealousy expressions, *Communication Reports, 17,* 85–101.

Zuckerman, M., & Driver, R. (1985). Telling lies: verbal and nonverbal correlates of deception. In A. Siegman & S. Feldstein (Eds.), *Multichannel integrations of nonverbal behavior* (pp. 129–148). Hillsdale, NJ: Lawrence Erlbaum.

Intercultural Communication:
Variety Is the Spice of Life

OBJECTIVES

- Identify three reasons for studying the impact of diversity on interpersonal relationships.
- Distinguish between the concepts of culture and diversity.
- Explain three characteristics of culture.
- Explore factors that affect our perceptions of others: needs, beliefs, values, and attitudes.
- Recognize how stereotypes and prejudices influence interpersonal relationships.
- Describe the impact of Hofstede's four dimensions of cultural values on interpersonal communication.

SCENARIO: SOUND FAMILIAR?

Mariella and Tadashi had been dating since the beginning of fall semester. As their relationship grew more serious, they decided that Tadashi would go home with Mariella during spring break to meet her parents and siblings. Mariella was embarrassed by her family's behavior as she introduced Tadashi to them. Her brother and father raised their eyebrows as they opened the door to greet them, and Mari's little sister asked if he could show her some karate moves. To make matters worse, Mariella's mother apologized as they sat down to dinner, saying, "If Mari had told us you weren't American, I would have made something Chinese." Tad smiled and gently explained that while his parents were originally from Japan, he had been born and raised in Seattle.

KEY TERMS

Acceptance	Ethnocentrism	Love and belonging
Active strategies	Explicit learning	needs
Ageism	Feminine cultures	Low-context cultures
Attitudes	High-context cultures	Low power distance
Beliefs	High power distance	Masculine cultures
Collectivism	cultures	Needs
Culture	Homophily	Passive strategies
Discrimination	Implicit learning	Personal orientation
Diversity	Individualism	system
Esteem needs	Interactive strategies	Physiological needs
Ethnicity	knowledge	Power distance

Prejudice	Self-actualization	Uncertainty avoidance
Race	Self-disclosure	Uncertainty reduction
Racial profiling	Sexism	theory (urt)
Racism	Skills	Understanding
Regional differences	Social class	Values
Safety and security	Socialization	Verbal abuse
needs	Stereotyping	Violence

OVERVIEW

Throughout this text, we have discussed various aspects of interpersonal communication and the role that it plays in our relationships. As we approach the end of our journey of exploring the specifics of interpersonal communication, we would be remiss if we failed to discuss the one variable that *all* interpersonal relationships have in common: they are composed of diverse individuals. Typically, discussions of diversity focus on things that we can see: race, ethnicity, and gender are the most commonly identified elements when defining diversity.

Focusing our attention exclusively on obvious physical characteristics and differences may cause us to fail to recognize the important role that cultural attitudes, values, and norms play in our interpersonal relationships. These are only a few of the factors that create challenges for relational partners when trying to achieve shared meaning. Consider friends who argue with one another simply because they differ in their religious or political beliefs. Maybe you have had a difficult time with a teacher who doesn't seem to understand that your questions are not intended to "challenge authority," but are simply attempts to better understand the information being presented in class.

Our cultural attitudes can be hidden from the world if we carefully monitor our words and actions. However, there are numerous examples of celebrities whose prejudices were publicly expressed and recorded for the world to see:

- On July 28, 2006, actor Mel Gibson was pulled over while speeding on Pacific Coast Highway in Malibu, California. As officers were questioning Gibson, he began yelling at them, making anti-Semitic and sexist comments toward the arresting officers.
- Celebrity chef Paula Deen was fired by the Food Network in 2013 following charges of racial harassment that were filed by one of her employees. During television interviews regarding the case, Deen admitted to reporters that she had used racial slurs in the past.
- During the 2015 Academy Awards red carpet telecast, host Giuliana Rancic made a stereotypical and racist comment about singer Zendaya's dreadlocks as she arrived for the award show.

Our cultural attitudes can be hidden from the world if we carefully monitor our words and actions.

© Monkey Business Images /Shutterstock.com

What causes individuals to engage in such negative behavior? Why do people express such hurtful words and actions? One reason may be our inability to engage in effective interpersonal communication with those who are different. Understanding how our cultural background influences our communication preferences and our reactions to those who are different is an important first step to enhancing our interpersonal relationships.

Our decisions about how to communicate with others are typically grounded in our beliefs, values, and attitudes. If our beliefs or attitudes toward someone are negative, our communication may be negative as well. Our lack of knowledge about cultural differences results in uncertainty about what is considered appropriate or effective communication when we encounter cultural differences. In these situations, many people simply avoid communicating with diverse others. In this chapter we will explore a variety of concepts that help explain how culture and diversity influence our relationships with others.

CULTURE AND DIVERSITY DEFINED

Culture has been defined by scholars in a number of different ways. In fact, a 1952 book identified 156 different definitions of culture (Kroeber & Kluckhohn). In the 60+ years since these definitions were compiled, attention to the increasing diversity in our societies has prompted scholars to create even more descriptions to capture the changes in our world. Anthropologists have broadly defined culture as being composed

> Focusing our attention exclusively on obvious physical characteristics and differences may cause us to fail to recognize the important role that cultural attitudes, values, and norms play in our interpersonal relationships.

of perceptions, behaviors, and evaluations. Other researchers have adopted a descriptive approach to explaining culture. Their definitions include characteristics such as knowledge, morals, beliefs, customs, art, music, law, and values. In this text, we define culture as shared perceptions that shape the communication patterns and expectations of a group of people.

While the concept of culture focuses on aspects that are shared by groups, diversity refers to the unique qualities or characteristics that distinguish individuals or groups from one another. Awareness of the impact of diversity on communication can help you understand the challenges encountered in relationships. Consider the various levels of diversity that potentially impact our diverse views of relationships and communication (Figure 11.1).

culture shared perceptions that shape the communication patterns and expectations of a group of people.

diversity refers to the unique qualities or characteristics that distinguish individuals and groups from one another.

Figure 11.1 **Levels of diversity**

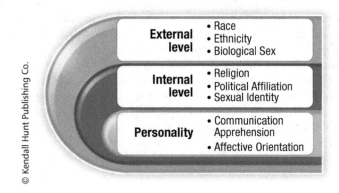

© Kendall Hunt Publishing Co.

© R. Gino Santa Maria/Shutterstock.com

Now more than ever, we have opportunities to form relationships with many different people.

THINK ABOUT IT...

In what ways do the following aspects of diversity impact communication in your relationships with others?

- Age
- Educational background
- Family status
- Geographical residence
- Military experience
- Physical and mental ability
- Sexual orientation
- Socioeconomic status
- Spiritual practice
- Work experience

External factors include those aspects of diversity that are readily visible, such as skin color or ethnic styles of dress. Since these are the things that we can see, we often use them to form our initial impressions about others. However, many of the differences that significantly impact on our communication with others are found at the internal level. These may include beliefs and attitudes associated with our religious or political affiliation. These attitudes and beliefs may be shared by cultures, or they may be more individualized. At the core of what makes each of us unique is our personality.

Unfortunately, many of our initial decisions to form relationships with others are based on assumptions and impressions formed by external-level factors. Upon closer analysis, you may find that you actually have *more* in common at the internal and personality levels with those who are different on the external level. Just because we may *look* different doesn't mean that we will *think* or *perceive* differently. Communication provides us with valuable information to determine how different we actually are from others.

Consider the characteristics that you share with your closest friend. You probably formed a friendship based on similarities in some of the factors listed above. Perhaps you are close in age and have similar educational backgrounds. Stop for a moment and consider the relationship implications as a result of differences in these factors. Consider how diversity impacts communication in the following relationship scenarios:

- A couple with different spiritual backgrounds needs to negotiate whose religious beliefs will be followed in raising their children.
- A son who is gay finds it difficult to communicate his feelings about his romantic partner to his heterosexual parents.
- A soldier tries to convey her beliefs about war and her value of freedom to her friends back home who have never served in the military.

When considering the many aspects of diversity, it is easy to see why many relationships encounter stumbling blocks as individuals attempt to navigate differences in knowledge, experiences, beliefs, and values. To evaluate how cultural differences impact your level of apprehension when communicating with others, complete the Personal Report of Intercultural Communication Apprehension (PRICA) scale at the end of this chapter.

Our culture shapes our perceptions and teaches us the preferred ways of behaving. For example, democracy is valued by many in the United States. Beginning in elementary school, students are taught the meaning of democracy. Later in life, they may witness people defending their rights to free speech via tweets or protests. Socialization refers to the process of learning about cultural norms and expectations. This is critical for an individual to become a functioning member of society. Keep in mind that our perceptions are highly

Socialization process of learning about one's cultural norms and expectations.

individualized, so much so that we may not consider that others see things differently. It may be easy to overlook the impact that diversity has on our communication patterns.

Communication behaviors are often unique to a culture, allowing us to easily identify members of various cultural groups. For example, an employee from Georgia assigned to work on a project with a team from Ohio may be easily identified by her accent. Culture is not only reflected in our behavior or language; it also influences our expectations. We form assumptions about how individuals should behave and what we should expect in our relationships with them. For example, Japan is considered to be a collectivistic culture that values and encourages group goals over individual achievement. A student from Japan who studies in the United States where individualism is valued may be uncomfortable in situations where he is "singled out" for his individual academic achievements and prefer to be acknowledged with his class.

While we each have diverse characteristics that make us unique, we also share some aspects in common with other members of our larger culture. These shared characteristics allow us to identify with various groups or co-cultures that help further define our identity.

CO-CULTURES WITHIN THE UNITED STATES

Within the larger cultural context, numerous co-cultures exist, each distinguishable by unique characteristics. It is important to note that you are a member of multiple co-cultures. Consider the man who identifies as a long-time employee of Quest Pharmaceuticals, in addition to being an adult, African-American Texan with Republican views, and of the Methodist faith. A total of seven co-cultures are claimed in this one example.

> It may be easy to overlook the impact that diversity has on our communication patterns.

Our multiple memberships may contribute to confusion and miscommunication in our relationships. Suppose you assume that because one of your soccer teammates likes sports, she would not be interested in classical music or the theatre. As you pass a poster announcing the upcoming cultural arts series on campus, you make some negative comments about "artsy geeks." What you do not know is that your teammate has studied classical music since a young age, and her mother is a trained opera singer. While this is an extremely simplified example, assuming that membership in one group precludes an individual from having interests in other groups can lead to embarrassing situations that can impact relationships. There are several examples of co-cultures that potentially shape our perceptions and our interactions.

Ethnicity

While the terms *race* and *ethnicity* have often been used synonymously, these two categories are unique. Ethnicity refers to the common heritage, or background, shared by a group of people. Categories may be established to identify the culture from which one's ancestors came. These include Irish-American, German-American, or Mexican-American. While there has been some debate over the connotations associated with the labeling of some of these groups, the intention of naming is simply for identification purposes.

Ethnicity the common heritage, or background, shared by a group of people.

Race

The diverse population of the United States continues to produce more interracial and interethnic relationships.

Race   genetically inherited biological characteristics such as hair texture and color, eye shape, skin color, and facial structure.

Race is the term used to refer to genetically inherited biological characteristics such as hair texture and color, eye shape, skin color, and facial structure. Terms used to describe different racial categories include Caucasian, African-American, and Asian.

An increase in the number of interracial and interethnic relationships prompted the U.S. government to update the categories one could choose to record their race on the U.S. Census. Prior to 2000, U.S. citizens were forced to choose one category to represent their racial or ethnic identity. Today, options have been added so people can more accurately report their identity. Figure 11.2 includes some of the categories included on the 2010 U.S. Census form to enable people to report those racial and ethnic groups with which they identify. Citizens can now identify as a member of multiple racial groups rather than being restricted to only one identity.

Figure 11.2 **Sample categories to identify racial and ethnic identity from the 2010 U.S. Census form**

→ **NOTE: Please answer BOTH Question 8 about Hispanic origin and Question 9 about race. For this census, Hispanic origins are not races.**

8. Is Person 1 of Hispanic, Latino, or Spanish origin?

☐ **No,** not of Hispanic, Latino, or Spanish origin
☐ Yes, Mexican, Mexican Am., Chicano
☐ Yes, Puerto Rican
☐ Yes, Cuban
☐ Yes, another Hispanic, Latino, or Spanish origin — *Print origin, for example, Argentinean, Colombian, Dominican, Nicaraguan, Salvadoran, Spaniard, and so on.* ↗

[_____]

9. What is Person 1's race? *Mark* ☒ *one or more boxes.*

☐ White
☐ Black, African Am., or Negro
☐ American Indian or Alaska Native — *Print name of enrolled or principal tribe.* ↗

[_____]

☐ Asian Indian   ☐ Japanese   ☐ Native Hawaiian
☐ Chinese   ☐ Korean   ☐ Guamanian or Chamorro
☐ Filipino   ☐ Vietnamese   ☐ Samoan
☐ Other Asian — *Print race, for example, Hmong, Laotian, Thai, Pakistani, Cambodian, and so on.* ↗   ☐ Other Pacific Islander — *Print race, for example, Fijian, Tongan, and so on.* ↗

[_____]

☐ Some other race — *Print race.* ↗

[_____]

Source: http://www.pewresearch.org/fact-tank/2014/05/05/millions-of-americans-changed-their-racial-or-ethnic-identity-from-one-census-to-the-next/

Regional Differences

Within a given culture, speech patterns, attitudes, and values may differ significantly depending on the geographic location that an individual calls home. Northern Germans express values that are quite different from those of southern Germans. Those who reside in northern Brazil communicate using nonverbal gestures that are unrecognizable to those from southern Brazil. Accents within a culture also vary depending on the geographic region. Japanese spoken in Okinawa takes on different tones when spoken in Tokyo. English spoken by those who live in the Amish region of Pennsylvania may be different from those living in Texas.

Dodd (1998) observed a variety of regional differences in communication styles within the boundaries of the United States. These include variety in the amount of animation, perceived openness, informal rapport, and rate of speech delivery. In 2003, the Harvard Dialect Survey identified a variety of regional differences in vocabulary and pronunciation within the United States (Vaux & Golder). While we may think we speak the same language, the potential for misunderstandings exists even within our nation's boundaries. Figure 11.3 highlights differences in regional dialects that are found as you travel across the United States.

regional differences variety in the communication styles within the larger culture. Examples may include the level of nonverbal animation, perceived openness, informal rapport, and rate of speech delivery.

Figure 11.3 **Sample questions from the 2003 Harvard Dialect Survey**

How would you address a group of two or more people?	You all Y'all Yinz Yous
What do you call a big road on which you drive fast?	Highway Freeway Expressway Parkway
What do you call the sweet spread that is put on a cake?	Frosting Icing
What do you call a large motor vehicle used to carry freight?	Semi Tractor-trailer 18-wheeler Rig/Big Rig
What do you call the long sandwich that contains deli meat, lettuce and so on?	Sub Grinder Hoagie Poor Boy Hero
What do you call the rubber-soled shoes worn in gym class or for athletic activities?	Sneakers Gym Shoes Jumpers Tennis Shoes Trainers
What do you call a sweetened carbonated beverage?	Soda Pop Coke Soft Drink

In addition to regional differences in language, distinctions in values also impact relationships. Consider distinctions between rural and urban co-cultures. Rural co-cultures tend to approach decisions more cautiously, while members of urban co-cultures are more willing to take risks and reach decisions more quickly.

Social Class

social class classifications used by members of a culture to group members on the basis of educational, occupational, or financial backgrounds, resulting in classifications and status differentials.

Communication challenges may be influenced by social class. Co-cultural categories are created on the basis of educational, occupational, or financial backgrounds, resulting in perceived status differentials. While many are hesitant to discuss their own social status or to address potential implications of class differentials on communication, research has identified some potential effects:

- Nearly 38 percent of patients indicated that they lacked confidence in understanding medical statistics. Many of these patients identified themselves as being low-income or low-education (Smith, Wolf, & Wagner, 2010).
- In a 2014 study examining socioeconomic status (SES) and parent-child communication regarding task completion, low-SES families tended to exhibit traditional gendered patterns. Mothers conveyed supportive messages and fathers focused on task completion. The opposite was true with high-SES families: mothers were more task-oriented and fathers were more focused on the relationship with the child (Grebelsky-Lichtman, 2014).

> Stratification in our relationships often occurs on the basis of homophily, the idea that we choose to be with people who are similar to us.

homophily stratification that occurs on the basis of similarity.

Stratification in our relationships often occurs on the basis of homophily, the idea that we choose to be with people who are similar to us. When initiating relationships, we seek out those in similar careers, with similar educational experiences, and of similar financial status. While social status may be considered a "taboo topic" for discussion, understanding its impact on our interactions is important.

CHARACTERISTICS OF CULTURE

Understanding what culture *is*, as well as the ways we identify with various co-cultures, is an important first step in exploring its impact on our relationships. In the next sections we explain the three primary characteristics of culture and *how* it becomes such an influential factor in our lives.

Culture Is Learned

The preferred ways of behaving as a member of a society are learned at a young age. Consider the learning experiences of children. Adults teach them how to say words, which foods can be eaten with the fingers and which should be eaten with utensils, and songs and rituals that are part of the culture. They may be taught that profanity is not acceptable and be rewarded for saying the Pledge of Allegiance. Children are even taught biases and prejudices. Expectations about the nature of relationships and communication are also learned at a young age.

For example, in the United States it is viewed as unacceptable for male friends to hold hands in public. In some Arab cultures it is not uncommon to see two men engage in this behavior. Society teaches us the behaviors that are accepted by most members of the culture, and, at the same time, instills within us a response mechanism for reacting to violations of cultural norms. Figure 11.4 highlights examples of learned cultural expectations for appropriate use of nonverbal communication.

Figure 11.4 Cultural norms for nonverbal behaviors that are learned

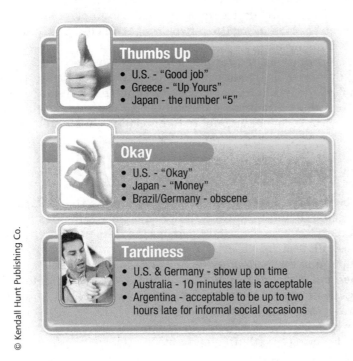

Thumbs Up
- U.S. - "Good job"
- Greece - "Up Yours"
- Japan - the number "5"

Okay
- U.S. - "Okay"
- Japan - "Money"
- Brazil/Germany - obscene

Tardiness
- U.S. & Germany - show up on time
- Australia - 10 minutes late is acceptable
- Argentina - acceptable to be up to two hours late for informal social occasions

© Kendall Hunt Publishing Co.

What is acceptable behavior in a culture is learned both explicitly and implicitly. Explicit learning involves actual instructions regarding the preferred way of behaving. A school may create a brochure that specifies the dress code required of all students, or a teacher may instruct students to raise their hand before speaking in class. Implicit learning occurs via observation. We are not directly told what behaviors are preferred; rather we learn by observing others. Our choices of what to wear for a first date or for the first day of work may be influenced by our observations of others or by scanning various media sources. We learn the preferred ways of a culture so as to be accepted.

Explicit learning involves direct instructions regarding a culture's preferred or expected ways of behaving.

Culture Is Dynamic

Over time, events occur that cause cultures to change. Consider how relationships were altered in the United States after the events of September 11th. In the days and months following the tragedy, people reported that they engaged in more frequent communication and open expressions of affection with family and friends.

Implicit learning learning about a culture's preferred or expected norms for behavior through indirect methods (e.g., observation).

Cultures and their members also change as a result of "borrowing" from other cultures. It is quite common to open a fashion magazine and see examples of trends being borrowed from other cultures. For example, U.S. stores and catalogues showcase Asian-inspired t-shirts and jewelry that include Chinese or Japanese writing.

Depending on a culture's approach to uncertainty, change may occur at different rates. Within the last decade, change has occurred at a rapid rate within the United States. Technological advances make some computers obsolete a year or two after purchase. Food, music styles, and exercise trends experience changes as each generation identifies new preferences. Not only do cultures change with regard to food and clothing styles, but popular culture also undergoes transitions. Reflect on how your own conversations are focused on or influenced by cultural trends. Figure 11.5 provides examples of trends for 2015 as identified by *The Washington Post*. After all, what we talk about one week may be "old news" the next.

Changes in our culture provide us with new topics for discussion and debate in our personal relationships. However, not all cultures embrace change. In fact, some cultures are reluctant to implement change and emphasize the importance of tradition and stability. This can create challenges when those who welcome change attempt to form relationships with those who are resistant to change.

Culture Is Pervasive

Culture is everywhere. Take a moment and look around you. Chances are that you see numerous examples of your culture's influence with one simple glance. Is there a smartphone on your desk? Perhaps there are posters, photos, or artwork on the walls. Is there a television turned on or music playing? Maybe you are on campus and there are other students nearby. Take a look at the style of their clothes and listen to the words they are saying to one another. Each of these things demonstrates the pervasive nature of culture. It surrounds us—in fact, we cannot escape the influence of our culture.

If one were to adopt a descriptive definition of culture, this prevalence could be seen as influencing everything: our expectations for relationships, the clothing

Figure 11.5 **Predictions for 2015 U.S. cultural trends**

The Washington Post's 2015 In/Out List

WHAT'S OUT	WHAT'S IN
Black Friday	Black November
Minimalist running shoes	Thick-cushioned soles
Binge watching	Binge listening
Hashtag activism	T-shirt advocacy
Zombie apocalypses	Climate change dystopias
Swiping right	Saying "hello"
"Yasss"	"On fleek"

Source: http://www.washingtonpost.com/wp-srv/artsandliving/features/2014/year-in-review/the-list.html we wear, the language we speak, the food we choose, and even our daily schedules. Culture is represented not only in our material possessions, but also in the values, beliefs, and attitudes that comprise our personal orientation system. It shapes virtually every aspect of our lives and influences our thoughts and actions.

By taking a moment to consider the impact that culture has on our lives, it becomes clear that culture and communication are inseparable. Our verbal and nonverbal messages are shaped by our culture's influence, and we learn about our culture through the messages we receive from others.

Becoming a competent communicator across cultures requires you to develop a game plan. Knowing that each person's communication is guided by his or her unique set of values, beliefs, and attitudes will prepare you for differences in your approaches to conversations. Just as a sports team needs to study plays, people need to study and understand the various elements that create confusion and miscommunication in cross-cultural encounters. If you discover that you offend or confuse someone, you may need to alter your verbal or nonverbal messages. This chapter will help you to develop a personal game plan for becoming a competent communicator in diverse interpersonal relationships.

CULTURAL INFLUENCE ON DATING EXPECTATIONS

Culture affects how we initiate and maintain our interpersonal relationships. In many European cultures, it is common for teenagers to go out on large "group" dates. Females in Australia may ask out males and offer to split the cost of a date. In China and Japan, dating is typically reserved for those who are older, usually in their twenties. Dating was discouraged in India until recently. Families were expected to introduce couples and help them get to know each other socially in preparation for marriage. While online dating has grown in popularity in the United States and many European countries, this method of initiating romantic relationships would be frowned upon in cultures that view dating as a time for getting to know one's potential future in-laws.

* In what ways does culture influence our expectations for other relationships (e.g., marital partners, sibling/parent relationships, co-workers)?

THE IMPACT OF CULTURAL DIVERSITY ON INTERPERSONAL RELATIONSHIPS

Recent changes in political and social policy, evolving demographics, and technological advances have provided us with countless opportunities for forming relationships with diverse others. Figure 11.6 highlights three of the many

Figure 11.6 **Reasons for exploring diversity and communication**

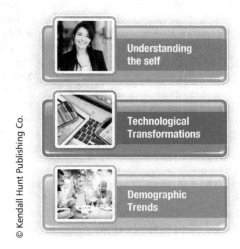

Understanding the self

Technological Transformations

Demographic Trends

reasons for exploring the impact of diversity on communication in interpersonal relationships, including: (1) increased awareness of self, (2) appreciation for technological transformations, and (3) understanding of demographic transitions.

Understanding the Self

Perhaps the simplest and most overlooked reason for studying the impact of diversity on our relationships is the opportunity it provides for exploring and understanding our own cultural background and identity. By delving into the cultural factors that influence communication patterns, we begin to gain an awareness of our own reasons for thinking and behaving as we do.

Technological Transformations

In the 1960s, McLuhan introduced the notion of a "global village" (McLuhan & Powers, 1989). He predicted that mass media and technology would bring the world closer together, a notion considered to be farfetched at that time. But a quick inventory of today's technologies, which provide opportunities for forming diverse relationships, reveals that McLuhan's vision was quite accurate. Airline travel, television, cell phones, and the Internet are just a few of the technologies that have changed the way we communicate. We now have the capability to travel around the world in a matter of hours, simultaneously view events as they occur in other cities and countries, and interact with persons from around the globe.

THINK ABOUT IT...

Janelle had grown up in a small town with a population of approximately 350. The population was entirely Caucasian, and the overwhelming majority of the residents were middle-class and Methodist. When she moved to a major metropolitan area, she encountered challenges associated with understanding cultural differences. Shortly after moving into her new apartment, she saw a neighbor in her building struggling to bring several bags of groceries from the parking garage. Janelle hurried to help her neighbor as she introduced herself and attempted to take a couple of bags from her neighbor's car. She was quickly told that her assistance was not needed. Later that evening, Janelle discussed the incident with her roommate, who pointed out, "You have to understand that people in large cities don't just walk up and help one another. Don't be offended. City folks need time to build the level of trust that you're accustomed to." As she reflected on why her first few weeks in the city were so frustrating, Janelle realized that she had been focusing on how "strange" other people were instead of considering how her *own* cultural background influenced her perceptions and expectations.

- Recall a time when you formed impressions based on your initial impressions of someone.
- How did your own cultural background influence your perceptions?

Opportunities provided by technology for forming relationships with diverse persons have increased exponentially over the past 20 years. The 2013 U.S. Census reported that nearly 84 percent of U.S. households owned a computer, and nearly 75 percent of homeowners reported that they had an Internet connection (File & Ryan, 2014). Figure 11.7 provides a summary by continent of the more than 3 billion Internet users worldwide (*http://www.internetworldstats.com/america.htm*). In the United States alone, nearly 310 million people use the Internet to find information and to form relationships with others. This is an increase of 187 percent from 2000–2014. Relationships can be initiated and maintained online with ease. Online assignments designed to connect students from diverse cultures, corporate meetings via Skype with colleagues from around the globe, and online video games that enable players to collaborate and compete from across the country are just a few examples of the ways in which the Internet has eliminated geographic boundaries for making connections.

©Andrey_Popov/Shutterstock.com

How has the Internet made it easier for us to know about world events as they occur?

Airline travel, television, cell phones, and the Internet are just a few of the technologies that have changed the way we communicate.

© Kendall Hunt Publishing Co.

Figure 11.7 **Global Internet usage statistics**

Internet Users in the World Distribution by World Regions - 2014

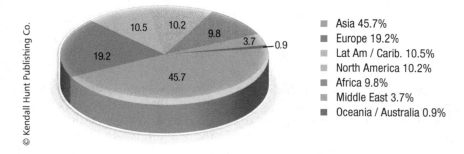

10.5 10.2 9.8 3.7 0.9
19.2
45.7

- Asia 45.7%
- Europe 19.2%
- Lat Am / Carib. 10.5%
- North America 10.2%
- Africa 9.8%
- Middle East 3.7%
- Oceania / Australia 0.9%

As corporate America expands its boundaries to include many overseas partners, work teams will be composed of members from diverse cultures. People come to the workplace with varied beliefs, experiences, and expectations about the role of communication in relationships at work. Technology provides us with opportunities to communicate with persons who come from backgrounds different from our own.

Due to increased opportunities for interactions with those from diverse backgrounds, relationship success depends on the ability to demonstrate communication competence across cultures.

Influence of Demographic Transitions

Over the past 30 years, the demographic composition of the United States has changed dramatically. Medical advancements have extended the life expectancy of Americans, so we have more generational differences to navigate. Immigration patterns have changed dramatically since the 1960s, when most immigrants came primarily from European countries. Today, nearly 90 percent of immigrants arrive from Latin American and Asian nations. Figure 11.8 highlights the predicted racial and ethnic composition of the United States.

Over the past decade, the number of interracial and interdenominational marriages has increased, and the U.S. workplace has seen a shift from the predominance of white male employees to a more diverse workforce that is also composed of women and racial and ethnic groups. Opportunities to expand our linguistic, political, and social knowledge abound.

Figure 11.8 Predicted U.S. demographic trends from 2015–2025

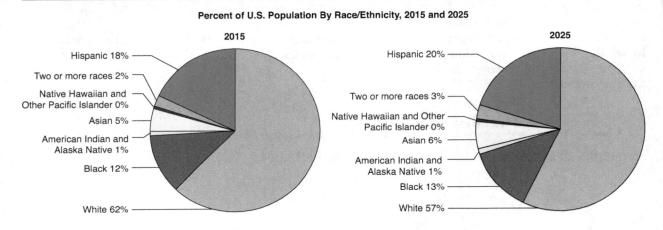

Percent of U.S. Population By Race/Ethnicity, 2015 and 2025

However, not all intercultural encounters are viewed as opportunities. While these demographic shifts create opportunities for diverse relationships, it is important to recognize that they present communication challenges as well. Uncertainty about other individuals creates tension, and the consequences of changing demographics are being felt in many social institutions. Consider the potential communication challenges faced in 2013 when students at Wilcox County High School in Georgia hosted the school's first racially integrated prom, despite protests and criticism from members of the local community. The debate over diverse beliefs about racial segregation resulted in heated debates and gained the attention of national media.

Due to increased opportunities for interactions with those from diverse backgrounds, relationship success depends on the ability to demonstrate communication competence across cultures. After all, achieving communication competence should be the ultimate goal in our interpersonal relationships. When the source and receiver are from diverse backgrounds and have unique expectations of communication, this goal may be a bit more difficult to achieve. Four core concepts that may assist us in enhancing cultural communication competence are: knowledge, understanding, skills, and acceptance. Let us examine each of these concepts more closely.

COMMUNICATION COMPETENCE: FOUR CORE CONCEPTS

Knowledge

Knowledge refers to the theoretical principles and concepts that explain behaviors occurring within a specific communication context. In other words, increasing your knowledge of communication theories and concepts will enhance your ability to understand and appreciate differences in intercultural relationships. You have already increased your knowledge base as a result of reading this textbook up to this point. Each of the concepts and theories that have been introduced has enhanced your understanding of the factors that impact communication in interpersonal relationships.

Consider how knowledge of communication theories can enhance our intercultural relationships. Berger and Calabrese's uncertainty reduction theory (URT) describes how we exchange information in an attempt to reduce ambiguity about others. Questions are asked to gain new knowledge about the other person and to assist us in forming effective interpersonal relationships. If we can predict the attitudes, behaviors, and emotions of others, we have reduced our uncertainty about the other person (Berger & Calabrese, 1975).

When crossing cultural lines, alleviating this ambiguity becomes a bit trickier. For example, the notion of what constitutes acceptable disclosures in interpersonal relationships in the United States might differ from what is considered proper in other cultures. Is it acceptable to ask about another person's occupation? About her family? How does the other person view status differentials, and what rules does he or she adopt for communicating with someone of different status? Berger (1979) identified three primary communication strategies used to reduce uncertainty in relationships (Figure 11.9). These are: passive strategies, active strategies, and interactive strategies.

Knowledge theoretical principles and concepts that explain behaviors occurring within a specific communication context.

uncertainty reduction theory tdescribes the process of exchanging information in an attempt to reduce ambiguity about others. Asking questions is a primary communication strategy used for reducing levels of uncertainty.

Figure 11.9 **Uncertainty reduction strategies**

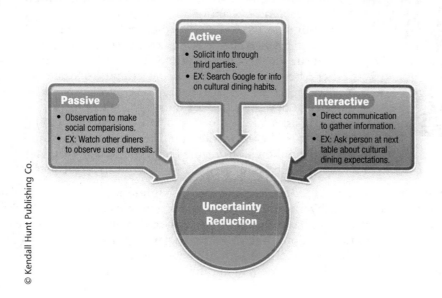

Passive strategies strategies used to reduce uncertainty about others. Typically involves observing and making social comparisons.

Active strategies strategies used to reduce uncertainty about others. Requires interacting with third parties to learn additional information about another person.

Interactive strategies strategies used to reduce uncertainty about others. Typically involves a face-to-face encounter between two individuals to directly exchange information.

self-disclosure sharing or revealing personal information about oneself with others.

Passive strategies typically involve observation and social comparison. We observe members of other cultures and make assessments as to the differences that exist. When one of your authors arrived in Hong Kong to teach summer classes, she did not speak Chinese. She spent many hours during her first weekend there sitting at the busy harbor, browsing through shopping areas and walking around campus to observe how people interacted with one another. Through her observations, she learned the cultural rules for personal space, noticed styles of dress and forms of nonverbal greetings, and became familiar with the protocol for communication between students and teachers on campus.

Active strategies require us to engage in interactions with others to learn additional information about the other person. Suppose your professor assigns you to have weekly conversations with an international partner during the semester. Prior to your first meeting, you may decide to ask other international students what they know about your conversation partner's culture, or you may go online and search for information about your conversation partner's culture.

Interactive strategies typically involve a face-to-face encounter between two individuals to reduce uncertainty. Typically, partners engage in self-disclosure as a means of sharing information about themselves with others. When examining cultural differences in disclosure, it was found that American college students disclose about a much wider range of topics—and to more people outside the family—whereas college students in Korea self-disclose mostly to immediate family members (Ishii, Thomas, & Klopf, 1993). Consider the following example:

Alicia was excited to learn that she had been selected to live with an international student in the dorm during her freshman year. She had been fortunate enough to travel with her parents on business trips to various countries for the past several years and found learning about other cultures to be fascinating. Her new roommate, Kyon, was from Korea. As they were unpacking their things, Alicia told Kyon about her hometown, her summer vacation to Hilton Head Island, and about all of her friends from high school who were attending their college. She shared how frightened she was about the first day of classes, and she laughed as she told Kyon how she had taken her schedule and walked around campus to locate her classrooms for the first day of class. Eventually, Alicia noticed that she had been doing all the talking, so she began asking Kyon questions. While Kyon was willing to discuss the classes she would be taking and the plane trip from Korea, she seemed reluctant to talk about her family, friends, or even her fears about starting college.

Schools teach children the cultural expectations for acceptable classroom behaviors.

©Monkey Business Images /Shutterstock.com

Without knowledge of cultural differences in communication styles, Alicia may have become easily frustrated by Kyon's lack of disclosure. After all, in the United States it is common to engage in question-asking and self-disclosure to reduce our uncertainty about others. But understanding that expectations for self-disclosure in Korea are different from those held by Americans will help alleviate the potential frustration and hurt feelings that could occur otherwise.

Knowledge of one's own culture is learned. Cultures teach their members preferred perceptual and communication patterns. Beginning at a very young age, this learning process instills knowledge about the culture's accepted behaviors. Communication is the channel for teaching these lessons.

Gaining cultural knowledge can remove some of the barriers that can create communication challenges in relationships with diverse people. But knowledge in and of itself is insufficient for achieving competence. We also need to gain an understanding of why others communicate the way they do.

Understanding

Understanding involves applying knowledge to specific situations in an attempt to explain the behaviors that are occurring. While you may know the definition of uncertainty reduction theory (URT), it is important to gain an understanding of *how* it impacts a particular interaction. Understanding involves exploring the roots, or sources, of communication, rather than simply explaining the behavior. Consider two coworkers who attempt to influence each other on a project on which they are collaborating. Joe is assertive and tries to persuade Maynae by directly disagreeing with her proposal. Maynae's cultural background is one that values saving face in front of others. Thus, she avoids directly disagreeing with Joe—rather, she nods her head and proceeds with the project as she originally planned. Both of them end up frustrated. Joe cannot understand why Maynae did not follow their game plan. Had she not nodded her head and agreed with him? Joe attributes Maynae's actions to her shyness. Maynae is frustrated by Joe's confusion. Did he not understand that she did not want to embarrass him in front of their colleagues?

©lightpoet/Shutterstock.com

A room full of students appearing to be similar on the surface could have many different cultural backgrounds.

Broadening our study of culture and diversity to understand the influence of elements such as race, ethnicity, language differences, and religious beliefs is essential for relationship success. But it is also important to understand that what works in one relationship may not work in another. Consider the example of the coach and her team. They know and understand multiple plays so they can choose the most effective one to enhance their chances of winning the game. Just as it would be ineffective to run the same play over and over again in a game, communicating with diverse persons in the same manner would not result in satisfying relationships. While this chapter will assist you in building knowledge and understanding of communication differences, acceptance of differences is also a key to interpersonal success.

Understanding involves applying knowledge to specific situations in an attempt to explain the behaviors that are occurring.

Acceptance refers to our cognizance of the feelings and emotions involved in our willingness to understand the behavior of diverse others.

Acceptance

Acceptance refers to our awareness of our feelings and emotions in response to diverse approaches to relationships and communication. It encompasses our willingness to understand the behavior of others. Accepting differences in behavior enables us to be less judgmental and to reject ethnocentric thinking. At times our intercultural apprehension inhibits us from seeing and perceiving things from the other person's point of view. Ethnocentrism refers to the tendency to perceive our own ways of behaving and thinking as being correct,

Ethnocentrism tendency to perceive our own ways of behaving and thinking as being correct or acceptable while evaluating the behaviors of others as incorrect or inferior.

Figure 11.10 Core elements of intercultural communication competence

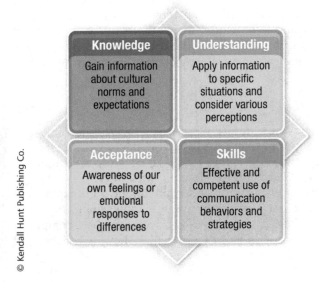

© Kendall Hunt Publishing Co.

or acceptable, and judging the behaviors of others as being "strange," incorrect, or inferior. You can assess your own level of ethnocentrism by completing the scale at the end of this chapter. A study of 107 college students found that ethnocentrism and intercultural apprehension prompted people to avoid intercultural conversations (Neuliep, 2012). By expanding our knowledge of other cultures and understanding the reasons for reactions to cultural differences, we will develop a more accepting attitude toward these unique tendencies. The only element remaining is to hone our communication and relational skills.

Skills

Skills specific communication behaviors that contribute to competent and effective interpersonal communication. Examples include effective listening, nonverbal sensitivity, and conflict management.

We have discussed many of the specific skills that are central to interpersonal communication throughout this text. Skills are the specific communication behaviors that contribute to competent and effective interpersonal relationships. Effective listening, assertiveness, responsiveness, nonverbal sensitivity, language comprehension, and conflict management are just a few of the many skills required in diverse relationships. It is important to note that there is a difference between knowing how to communicate effectively across cultures, and actually engaging in the appropriate behaviors. You might understand that the Chinese culture values silence, but because you are an extremely talkative person and are ineffective in practicing silence, you may be perceived as being rude when interacting with members of that culture.

Research points to the benefits of practicing intercultural communication skills through an examination of interactions that occur among college students. Those students who engage in frequent interactions with students of different racial backgrounds have positive discussions about race and ethnicity, tend to have a higher self-concept, and report that they are more satisfied with college (Smith & Associates, 1997).

PERSONAL ORIENTATION SYSTEM

Each individual has a set of predispositions that serves as a guide for thoughts, actions, and behaviors. These predispositions are composed of needs, beliefs, values, and attitudes and are commonly referred to as our personal orientation system. Communication plans and relationship expectations are developed and organized based on these characteristics.

Many of the components of the personal orientation system are learned within the cultural context. This learning begins at a young age. Messages are shared by parents, teachers, and friends who teach the younger members of society to perceive certain actions as good or bad, fair or unfair. For example, Chinese

> By expanding our knowledge of other cultures and understanding the reasons for reactions to cultural differences, we will develop a more accepting attitude toward these unique tendencies.

children are taught to value history and tradition, and stories of the past are viewed as lessons to guide their behavior. Children in the United States tend to view stories of the past as entertaining, but rather than focusing on tradition, they are encouraged to find new and innovative ways of doing things. When faced with decisions regarding the proper way to respond in situations, our needs, beliefs, values, and attitudes assist us in guiding our perception of a situation.

Needs

All individuals have needs that result in strong feelings of discomfort or desires. These needs motivate us to achieve satisfaction or comfort. A strong relationship exists between needs and interpersonal communication, with communication serving as the primary mechanism through which we satisfy needs. If a student needs to have an assignment explained more clearly, he or she must communicate that need to the instructor. If an employee needs assistance in obtaining a copy of a company report, communication with the human resources director or with a supervisor can satisfy the need.

Maslow's hierarchy of needs (1954) organizes the needs that humans must fulfill. A hierarchical structure helps us to understand the importance and priority of having some needs achieved before others.

At the most basic level are the physiological needs of humans. These include the need for food, clothing, and shelter. While most cultures are able to devote adequate attention to meeting these needs, others cannot. The next level includes safety and security needs. Individuals possess a motivation to feel safe and secure in their surroundings. However, cultures differ in their methods for satisfying this need.

At the middle of the hierarchy is the need for love and belonging. Schutz (1958) identified three basic needs across cultures: affection, control, and inclusion. We have a need to love and to be loved. Esteem needs are located at the next level of Maslow's hierarchy. Humans have a need to feel good about themselves. Interpersonal communication with others is one mechanism for meeting this need. Things that cultural members say and do impact the fulfillment of these needs. At the highest level of Maslow's hierarchy is self-actualization. This level is achieved when an individual feels that he or she has accomplished all that can be achieved in a lifetime. As the U.S. Army's motto

---

personal orientation system predispositions that serve as a guide for thoughts, actions, and behaviors; comprises one's needs, beliefs, values, and attitudes.

needs strong feelings of discomfort or desire that motivate individuals to achieve satisfaction or comfort.

physiological needs most basic needs identified in Maslow's Hierarchy of Needs. Includes food, clothing, and shelter.

safety and security needs second level of Maslow's Hierarchy. Addresses need to ensure feelings of safety and security and may include laws, freedom, order, and protection from those things that can cause harm.

love and belonging addresses our need to form interpersonal relationships to provide intimacy, love, and affection.

Esteem needs includes the need to accomplish goals and to attain prestige, respect, and status.

self-actualization the highest level of Maslow's hierarchy of needs. Involves the realization of achieving one's full potential in terms of personal growth and experiences.

Figure 11.11 Maslow's hierarchy of needs

Source: http://www.researchhistory.org/wp-content/uploads/2012/06/maslows-hierarchy-of-needs.gif

implies, self-actualization is fulfilled when an individual feels that the goal "be all that you can be" has been met.

When applying Maslow's hierarchy to our interpersonal relationships, it becomes apparent that communication is the means through which we fulfill most of our needs. It is also the key to understanding the needs of others. Considering the importance of the needs of others can help us alleviate some misunderstandings. Cultural differences may cause one person to have a need for power and status, while another may possess a strong need for friendship and affection. The intensity with which each of these needs is experienced may cause these two people to interact in very different ways.

Beliefs

Beliefs personal convictions regarding the truth or existence of things.

A second component of culture that guides our thoughts and behaviors is our belief system. Beliefs are an important part of understanding our interactions with diverse others because not only do they influence our conscious reactions to situations, but they dominate our subconscious thoughts as well. We are constantly influenced by our beliefs. They are our personal convictions regarding the truth or existence of things.

When crossing cultural borders, an examination of the beliefs possessed by a culture's members yields some fascinating differences. People from Malaysia believe that it is bad luck to touch someone on the top of the head as it is believed to be the location of the center of spiritual energy. Hawaiians possess a number of beliefs about the messages indicated by the appearance of a rainbow. Consider the superstitious beliefs held by members of the American culture. Walking under a ladder, having a black cat cross your path, and the groom seeing the bride on the wedding day prior to the ceremony are all believed to be signs of bad luck. These diverse beliefs impact our interpersonal communication.

Because most people do not question social institutions, many of the beliefs of a culture are perpetuated from generation to generation without any thought being given to the reasons for the existence of the beliefs. Some individuals have reported that reactions to their questioning of beliefs have been so negative that they feared rejection in their relationships and simply adopted the accepted beliefs into their own personal orientation system.

Values

Values serve as the guide for an individual's behavior. They dictate what we should and should not do. Kluckhohn (1951) describes values as a personal philosophy or set of standards that influences the choice of alternative actions that may be available. This definition highlights the relationship between values and communication in that values are communicated both explicitly and implicitly through our behaviors. The majority of our actions are reflective of the values that are firmly established in our personal orientation system.

values serve as guides for an individual's behavior and indicate what one views as being important or ethical.

Consider the values that are communicated in proverbs across cultures:

- "A stitch in time saves nine": communicates the value placed on addressing issues or problems when they are small rather than waiting until they grow bigger.
- "A bird in the hand is worth two in the bush": emphasizes the importance of practicality and being satisfied with what you have.
- "Friendship doubles our job and divides our grief": a Swedish proverb that highlights the value placed on friendships.

Nonverbal communication may be a more subtle means for communicating values. Many Asian cultures practice the custom of giving a gift to demonstrate the values of reciprocity and friendship. It is not unusual for students to offer their teachers gifts in exchange for the lessons that are learned. In the American culture, many teachers would be extremely uncomfortable accepting these gifts because they could be perceived as bribes. The rejection of gifts could potentially result in confusion in the student-teacher relationship, and make subsequent interactions uncomfortable. It is important to gain an understanding not only of the values held by a culture's members, but also the ways in which individuals communicate these values. By doing so, misunderstandings may be avoided.

Cultural Value Orientations

To understand the values shared by a culture's members, a number of scholars have developed models for studying value orientations. These models pose questions designed to measure the intensity with which a culture's members value specific characteristics.

How might this diverse group of college students differ in terms of their communication styles and preferences?

Kluckhohn and Strodbeck (1961) developed one of the first models of cultural value orientation, and it is still being used in research today. Questions are designed to gain insight into such perceptions regarding relationships between humans and humans and nature. Sample questions include:

- What is the basic nature of human beings? Are they inherently evil and incapable of being trusted, or do most humans have a good heart?
- How are social relationships organized? Are relationships viewed as being hierarchical with divisions of power? Or should equal rights be present in all social relationships?

As discussed earlier in the text, Hall's model of cultural values (1976) represents a continuum of characteristics associated with high-context and low-context cultures. These differences are characterized by distinct differences in communication styles. Cultures which fall at the low-context end of the continuum exhibit high verbal tendencies. This style is associated with a direct approach and verbal expressiveness. A philosophy of "say what you mean" is embraced. High-context cultures, on the other hand, prefer a more indirect style; cues about the intended message are interpreted through nonverbal channels. Whereas persons from a low-context culture expect messages to be direct, those from a high-context culture search the environment for cues. Rather than asking a person whether he or she is happy, high-context cultures would infer these feelings from other cues such as posture, facial expressions, and disposition. Consider the difficulties experienced by a couple who have different cultural backgrounds:

low-context cultures that emphasize the meanings conveyed via spoken words. Emphasis is on verbal communication.

High-context cultures cultures that place emphasis on the meanings that are conveyed via nonverbal cues.

> Alec was confused. He and Miki had been living together for the past year and were engaged to be married in a few months. One evening, Miki was silent as they ate dinner. He knew something was upsetting her, but she kept insisting that things were fine. Miki was extremely frustrated as well. Why did Alec always insist that she tell him what was wrong? Did she always have to put her feelings into words? Why couldn't Alec be more in tune with her nonverbal behaviors and understand that things were not quite right?

This example illustrates the difference between the influence of the low-context approach of the United States on Alec's behavior and the high-context approach of Miki's Japanese upbringing. Miki expects Alec to be more aware of the messages that are being communicated via nonverbal channels, while Alec expects Miki to say what is bothering her.

A final model of cultural values that was touched on earlier is presented by Hofstede (1980). Dimensions of values were identified by examining the attitudes of employees in more than 40 cultures. These dimensions include individualism/collectivism, power distance, masculinity/femininity, and uncertainty avoidance.

Individualism emphasizes individual accomplishments and achievements.

Collectivism emphasizes value and concern for the group.

Individualism/Collectivism. Individualism/collectivism describes the relationship between the individual and the groups to which he or she belongs. Individualistic cultures, such as in the United States, focus on individual accomplishments and achievements. Collectivism, or value and concern for the group, is the primary value of many Asian cultures. Consider the cultural differences portrayed in *Gung Ho*, a movie about an automobile manufacturing plant. In the film, Asian managers took great pride in their work. After all, their own performance ultimately reflected on the group. They would never dream of taking time off for personal reasons. American workers, whose behaviors reflected individualism, placed their individual needs over those of the company. Employees expected time off to be at the birth of a child or to keep a medical appointment. These differences in the values of the group versus the self had disastrous outcomes, with the company facing the risk of closing as a result of conflicting cultural values.

Power Distance.

Power distance refers to the distribution of power in personal relationships as well as within organizations. Low power distance cultures have a flat structure with most individuals being viewed as equals. The tendency to show favoritism to individuals based on their age, status, or gender is minimized. High power distance cultures are depicted by a tall hierarchical structure with distinct status differences.

Imagine the frustration experienced by a young intercultural couple who had been married for only a few months. The husband, who was Hispanic, was raised in a culture that places the man as the head of the household (high power distance). His wife, who was raised by a single working mother in New York City, valued her independence. The power differential in her family of origin was low, thus she anticipated that her husband would view her as an equal partner in their relationship. As a result of their differing values for status and power based on their roles as husband and wife, the couple experienced many arguments.

Masculine/Feminine.

Prevalence of masculine and feminine traits in a culture characterizes Hofstede's (1980) dimensions of masculinity and femininity. Masculine cultures demonstrate a preference for assertiveness, ambition, and achievement. Characteristics of responsiveness, nurturance, and cooperation are associated with cultures at the feminine end of this dimension. Gender roles in these cultures are perceived to be more equal. Cultures such as those found in Japan and Mexico exhibit more masculine tendencies, while those found in Brazil, Sweden, and Taiwan are more feminine.

Uncertainty Avoidance.

Uncertainty avoidance refers to the willingness of a culture to approach or to avoid change. Cultures high in uncertainty avoidance demonstrate a preference for avoiding change. They embrace tradition and order. China and Germany are examples of countries with cultures that

---

RESEARCH IN REAL LIFE

How does our uncertainty about relationships influence perceptions of the interactions we have with our romantic partners? A 2013 study by Theiss and Nagy of 294 college students from Korea (N=138) and the United States (N=156) examined cultural differences and the potential impact on relationship uncertainty. Participants in the study were asked to report their self-uncertainty about the relationship (their own commitment and liking in the relationship), partner uncertainty (the other's perceived commitment and liking), and relationship uncertainty (longevity of relationship and expectations for behaviors). Results of the study found that U.S. Americans indicated higher levels of all three types of certainty compared to Korean students. A possible explanation for these differences may be rooted in cultural tendencies toward collectivistic versus individualistic values. As a collectivistic culture, Koreans may not question or doubt their relationships as much as their individualistic U.S. counterparts. Americans are also more likely to use direct questioning (low-context) to inquire about the relationship status compared to Koreans (high-context).

In order to become more competent in our interactions with diverse others, it is important to realize that stereotypes can and do impact our perceptions and our communication.

Power distance refers to the distribution of power in personal relationships as well as within organizations.

Low power distance cultural orientation in which members of a culture are viewed as being equals with little differential in status.

High power distance cultures are depicted by tall hierarchical structures with distinct status differential. Strict adherence to rules and procedures.

Masculine demonstrate a preference for assertiveness, ambition, and achievement.

feminine demonstrate a preference for responsiveness, nurturance, and cooperation; gender roles are more equal.

Uncertainty avoidance willingness of a culture to approach or to avoid change.

avoid uncertainty and embrace tradition. Cultures low in uncertainty avoidance welcome the possibility of change and are more willing to take risks. The United States and Finland are more open to change and are more tolerant of taking risks and adopting new and innovative approaches.

Understanding these dimensions can provide cues as to which values are promoted among members of a culture. This information is useful for determining the appropriate methods to approach interpersonal communication and for providing valuable information that assists in checking the accuracy of one's perceptions.

Attitudes: Stereotyping and Prejudice

Throughout our lives, each of us develops learned predispositions to respond in favorable or unfavorable ways toward people or objects. These tendencies are known as attitudes. A primary goal of this chapter is to assist you in identifying your responses to differences as well as to help you to understand your internal orientations guiding these reactions. When we interpret another's cultural customs or actions as being "wrong" or "offensive," it is important to understand how our culture has influenced our own attitudes. Two types of attitudes to consider are stereotypes and prejudices.

attitudes learned predispositions to respond in favorable or unfavorable ways toward people or objects.

Stereotyping. Stereotyping results from our inability to see and appreciate the uniqueness of individuals. When generalizations about a group are made and are then attributed to any individuals who either associate with, or are members of, a specific group, the process of stereotyping evolves. Three steps have been identified in the process of stereotyping.

stereotyping generalizations about a group that are attributed to any individuals who either associate with, or are members of, the group.

The first step involves categorizing a group of people based on observable characteristics that they have in common. Consider the impressions of U.S. lifestyles that are conveyed on American movies and television shows. Many of these shows have gained global audiences, and members of other cultures use them as resources to increase their knowledge of the United States. In 2011, former U.S. Secretary of State Hillary Clinton cautioned about the stereotypes generated from our media as she shared, "I remember having an Afghan general tell me that the only thing he thought about Americans is that all the men wrestled and the women walked around in bikinis because the only TV he ever saw was *Baywatch* and *World Wide Wrestling*." (http://www.businessinsider.com/hillary-clinton-al-jazeera-2011-3)

The second step in stereotyping involves assigning characteristics to a group of people. An example of this would be a popular magazine characterizing mothers who are employed outside the home as being less dedicated to their children.

Finally, we apply those characteristics to any individual who is a member of that group. An example would be the teacher who assumes that a student-athlete is not serious about academic studies. Since the events of 9/11, some members of Arab cultures have reported that they have been subjected to racial profiling. Racial profiling occurs when law enforcement or other officials use race as a basis for investigating a person for criminal involvement. This is a result of applying the single characteristic of race in determining whether a person should be viewed as threatening.

Racial profiling occurs when race is used as a basis for investigating a person for criminal involvement.

While stereotyping can be irrational, it is actually quite normal. Because humans are uncomfortable with uncertainty, stereotyping enables us to make predictions about our potential interactions with others. In order to become more competent in our interactions with diverse others, it is important to realize that stereotypes *can* and *do* impact our perceptions and our communication.

Prejudice.   Another form of attitude that involves negative reactions toward a group of people based on inflexible and inaccurate assumptions is commonly known as prejudice. In essence, prejudice involves "pre-judging" individuals. Some of the most common forms of prejudice in the United States include racism, sexism, and ageism.

prejudice attitude or "pre-judgment" that involves negative reactions toward a group of people based on inflexible and inaccurate assumptions.

Racism.   Racism refers to prejudice against an individual or group based on racial composition. Recall from the first part of this chapter that race is a term used to refer to inherited biological characteristics such as skin color, eye color and shape, hair texture, and facial structure.

Racism prejudice against an individual or group based on racial composition.

Ageism.   Negative communication toward persons based on their age is referred to as ageism. In the United States, some people assume that senior citizens are incapable of making contributions to society and can be considered helpless. In 1967, Congress passed the ADEA (Age Discrimination in Employment Act) to protect older workers against age discrimination. According to the law, an employer cannot replace an employee over the age of forty with a younger person if the current employee is able to satisfactorily perform her or his job. Assumptions that shape faulty attitudes about older workers include:

ageism prejudice in which discrimination or negative communication is directed toward persons based on their age.

- They are "set in their ways" and resist change.
- Older people resist or have difficulty adjusting to new technology.
- They are slower than younger workers or can't perform demanding tasks.

Chances are you know many people over the age of 65 who debunk these myths. Prejudicial attitudes such as these can be damaging to workplace relationships if we fail to open our eyes to individual abilities.

RESEARCH IN REAL LIFE: COLLEGE STUDENTS' RACIAL ATTITUDES AND FRIENDSHIP DIVERSITY

Is there a relationship between college students' attitudes about racial diversity and their network of friends? A 2010 study of 480 college students asked the students to report the number of friends who were either racially or ethnically different from themselves. Participants in the study were asked to classify a list of racial and ethnic groups on the basis of "Whiteness." Next, they were asked to indicate what dimensions should be included in a definition of "race." Examples of elements included skin color, genetics, and nationality. Finally, students were asked to estimate the percentage of their friends who were from a different racial or ethnic group. Results of the study found that students who reported that fewer than 50 percent of their friends were racially/ethnically diverse were more likely to perceive race as primarily differences in skin color. Those with diverse friendships tended to view and define race by applying a variety of criteria. Results of this study point to the impact of diverse friendships on our conceptualization of race and ethnicity. The more diverse our friendships, the more broad we are in our perception of and descriptions of what constitutes diversity.

Sexism prejudice in which discrimination or negative communication is directed toward persons of a particular sex.

Sexism. Sexism refers to negative communication directed toward persons of a particular sex. In the United States, sexist attitudes have traditionally been directed toward females. As a result, females have experienced discrimination in the workplace and in other walks of life. While stories of sexism frequently focus on the prejudices against females, men also are subject to sexist behaviors. Consider the father who stays at home and raises the children. As he shops for groceries with the children in the cart or plays with them at the park on a sunny weekday afternoon, he may hear a comment such as, "It's so nice that he's babysitting the children!" Not surprisingly, he may become offended because it is assumed that he is not capable of being the primary caregiver for his children.

COMMUNICATING PREJUDICE

Verbal abuse process of engaging in comments or jokes that are insulting or demeaning to a targeted group.

There are three primary ways that we communicate prejudice. Verbal abuse refers to the process of engaging in comments or jokes that are insulting or demeaning to a targeted group. Consider the impressions that we form of people as a result of their negative verbal behaviors toward others. For example, the racist comments made by Paula Deen may have caused some of her fans to question their positive attitudes toward the celebrity chef.

Discrimination denying an individual or group of people their rights.

Discrimination involves denying an individual or group of people their rights. While prejudice involves negative cognitions, or thoughts, discrimination is displayed when behaviors are used to express one's negative cognitions. Typically, discrimination is expressed through negative verbal comments made toward a group or an individual, with physical avoidance being the ultimate goal.

violence most severe form of prejudice, which often results in physical harm or excessive force.

The most severe form of prejudice is violence which often results in physical harm or excessive force. On November 24, 2014, the jury in the trial involving a Ferguson, Missouri, police officer decided not to indict him for shooting an African American teen. As word of the verdict spread, riots erupted throughout the city. During the next week, the world watched as physical attacks, arson, protests, and looting occurred throughout the city. In the end, more than 25 businesses were burned, 80 arrests were made the first night of the riots, and the city suffered over $5 million in damages from the buildings that were destroyed. This violence demonstrates the potentially extreme outcome of prejudice.

Functions of Prejudice

While prejudice is often based on false, irrational, and inflexible generalizations, it is often considered "normal." Why do individuals form prejudices? Figure 11.12 highlights three of the primary reasons expressed by others for forming prejudices.

Acceptance refers to our cognizance of the feelings and emotions involved in our willingness to understand the behavior of diverse others.

Acceptance. Acceptance is when a person communicates negative feelings toward a particular group in order to fit in within a desired group. An example of this is when a fraternity member expresses hatred for another fraternity's members. When asked why he has these strong feelings, the only reason offered is "because all Alpha Betas dislike them."

Ego-defensive. Another reason for communicating prejudice is to defend the ego. By expressing negative feelings and attitudes toward a group of people, individuals create a scapegoat for their own misfortunes. An employee was

Figure 11.12 Functions of prejudice

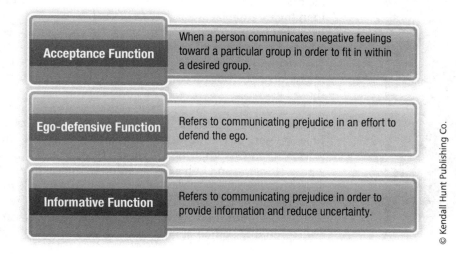

Acceptance Function — When a person communicates negative feelings toward a particular group in order to fit in within a desired group.

Ego-defensive Function — Refers to communicating prejudice in an effort to defend the ego.

Informative Function — Refers to communicating prejudice in order to provide information and reduce uncertainty.

© Kendall Hunt Publishing Co.

overheard expressing his prejudice against women being selected for administrative positions. Upon further questioning, he admitted that he did not actually harbor any ill feelings toward women supervisors. Rather, he was frustrated by the fact that a woman had been offered the position rather than him.

Informative.   A final reason for prejudice is to provide information. As was stated earlier, humans have a need to reduce uncertainty. Unfortunately, many individuals form prejudices as a means for forming knowledge about a group of people with whom little or no contact has been made. The information provided by our prejudices may serve the purpose of allowing us to make sense of the world. For example, you may form a bias against members of a culture that you've never met or visited in order to help you anticipate or predict how you should communicate in your initial interactions.

Our needs, values, beliefs, and attitudes are extremely influential in guiding our expectations for our own and for others' communication. Careful consideration of the impact of these variables is required in order to engage in effective intercultural relationships.

SUGGESTIONS FOR EFFECTIVE INTERPERSONAL RELATIONSHIPS WITH DIVERSE OTHERS

As shown throughout this chapter, culture causes us to perceive things in unique ways. But there are strategies that can assist us in avoiding misunderstandings. Each of the suggestions below requires us to dedicate effort to understanding and practicing better interpersonal communication.

- Engage in careful listening and clear communication. Focus on listening for what is really being said, not what you want to hear. Be clear and explicit in your communication.

Culture surrounds our lives and its influence is everywhere.

- Refrain from judging people based on observable differences such as race, ethnicity, or gender. Remember, internal factors contributing to diversity may be more influential than the external factors that we can readily see.
- Be patient with yourself. Remember that becoming an effective cross-cultural communicator requires skill and knowledge. It takes time to practice those skills. You may make mistakes, but there are lessons to be learned from those faux pas.
- Seek out opportunities to interact with those from diverse cultures. Be willing to take risks and to make mistakes.
- Practice patience with others. Cultural influences are powerful, and making the transition from one culture's way of thinking and behaving to another's takes time.
- Check for understanding. Do not be afraid to ask for clarification or to ensure that you understood what was being communicated. One simple question now can save offending someone later.

SUMMARY

Throughout this chapter we have discussed the prevalence of diversity in *all* of our interpersonal relationships. While diversity is most frequently identified based on observable characteristics such as race, ethnicity, or sex, it is important to consider additional variables that influence our communication choices as we interact with others. Individual beliefs, attitudes, and values have a significant impact on the messages we send as well as on our reactions to the messages that we receive. At this point we would like to reiterate the importance of studying and understanding the impact of cultural diversity on our interpersonal interactions—by taking a moment to enhance your own knowledge and skills, you are better equipped to understand the reasons underlying your own communication preferences as well as the communication choices of others.

DISCUSSION QUESTIONS

1. Reflect on your cultural background. Identify five ways that you are different from your friends and from your co-workers. Discuss how these differences may lead to miscommunication in your personal and professional relationships.

2. What are some ways that you explicitly and implicitly learned about your culture's expectations for communication and expected behaviors?

3. Identify strategies for enhancing your own intercultural communication competence in your personal relationships. What strategies could be used to enhance competence in your professional relationships?

REFERENCES

Berger, C. (1979). Beyond initial interactions. In H. Giles and R. St. Clair (Eds.), *Language and social psychology* (122–144). Oxford: Basil Blackwell.

Berger, C., & Calabrese, R. (1975). Some explorations in initial interaction and beyond: Toward a developmental theory of interpersonal communication. *Human Communication Research, 1,* 99–112.

Dodd, C. (1998). *Dynamics of intercultural communication* (5th ed.). San Francisco, CA: McGraw-Hill.

Grebelsky-Lichtman, T. (2014). Parental patterns of cooperation in parent-child interactions: The relationship between verbal and nonverbal communication. *Human Communication Research, 40*(1), 1–29.

File, T., & Ryan, C. (2014). Computer and Internet Use in the United States: 2013. Retrieved May 21, 2015, from http://www.census.gov/content/dam/Census/library/publications/2014/acs/acs-28.pdf

Hall, E. T. (1976). *Beyond culture.* Garden City, NY: Anchor.

Hofstede, G. (1980). Motivation, leadership, and organizations: Do American theories apply abroad? *Organizational Dynamics, Summer,* 42–63.

Ishii, S., Thomas, C., & Klopf, D. (1993). Self-disclosure among Japanese and Americans. *Otsuma Review, 26,* 51–57.

Kluckhohn, C. (1951). Values and value-orientation in the theory of action. In T. Parsons and E. Shils (Eds.), *Toward a general theory of action* (pp. 388–433). Cambridge, MA: Harvard University Press.

Kluckhohn, C., & Strodbeck, F. (1961). *Variations in value orientations.* Evanston, IL: Row, Peterson.

Kroeber, A. L., & Kluckhohn, C. (1952). *Culture: A critical review of concepts and definitions.* Cambridge, MA: Harvard University Press.

Martin, J. D., Trego, A. B., Nakayama, T. K. (2010). College students' racial attitudes and friendship diversity. *The Howard Journal of Communication, 21*(2), 97–118.

Maslow, A. (1954). *Motivation and personality.* New York, NY: Harper.

McLuhan, M., & Powers, B. (1989). *The global village: Transformations in world life and media in the 21st century.* New York: Oxford University Press.

Neuliep, J. W. (2012). The relationship among intercultural communication apprehension, ethnocentrism, uncertainty reduction, and communication satisfaction during initial intercultural interaction: An extension of Anxiety and Uncertainty (AUM) Theory. *Journal of Intercultural Communication Research, 41*(1), 1–16.

Schutz, W. (1958). *FIRO: A three dimensional theory of interpersonal behavior.* New York: Holt, Rinehart & Winston.

Smith, S. G., Wolf, M. S., & Wagner, C. (2010). Socioeconomic status, statistical confidence, and patient-provider communication: An analysis of the Health Information National Trends Survey (HINTS 2007). *Journal of Health Communication, 15,* 169–185.

Smith, D., & Associates. (1997). *Diversity works: The emerging picture of how students benefit.* Washington, DC: Association of American Colleges and Universities.

Theiss, J. A., & Nagy, M. E. (2013). A relational turbulence model of partner responsiveness and relationship talk across cultures. *Western Journal of Communication, 77*(2), 186–209.

Vaux, B., & Golder, S. (2003). *The Harvard Dialect Survey.* Cambridge, MA: Harvard University Linguistics Department.

Family Communication:
It's All Relative

OBJECTIVES

- Identify sibling relational maintenance strategies.
- Describe elements of systems theory and examine their impact on family interactions.
- Explain family communication patterns theory.
- Identify family types identified by Koerner and Fitzpatrick.
- Discuss ways in which families form their own identity (stories, myths, metaphors, themes).
- Explain the ABCX model of stress as it applies to family interactions.

SCENARIO: SOUND FAMILIAR?

As the end of the semester approached, Bailey felt more stress than he had ever experienced in his life. He knew that his parents were going to be less than pleased when he told them about his decision to change his major, and he was worried about how he would break the news to them that his roommate got him a summer job with his father's company and he wouldn't be coming home this summer. A few minutes after he tweeted, "Stressed to the max—parental units are NOT going to be happy!" his cell phone rang. As he glanced and saw his mother's Caller ID, he groaned and considered letting the phone go to voice mail. "That's what I get for accepting my parents' requests to follow me on Twitter," he thought to himself as he reluctantly answered the call.

KEY TERMS

ABCX model	Conformity orientation	Family communication
Acute stressor	Consensual families	patterns theory
Ambiguous	Content expectations	Family events
boundaries	Conversation	Family Metaphors
Birth stories	orientation	Family Myths
Boomerang children	Courtship stories	Family stories
Boundaries	Deidentification	Family systems theory
Calibration	Disconfirming	Family Themes
Chronic stressor	communication	Hierarchy
Confirmation	Equifinality	humor
Confirming	Escape	Independent couple
communication	External stressor	Interdependence

Internal stressor   Pluralistic families   Stories of survival
Involuntary stressor   Protective families   Symbolic interactionism
Laissez-faire families   Rejection   Traditional couples
Launching stage   Relational expectations   Verbal aggression
Non-normative stressor   Separate couples   Voluntary stressor
Normative stressor   Social support   Wholeness

OVERVIEW

Of all the relationships we form throughout our lifetime, our family relationships are the most enduring. We begin this chapter by advancing an important question about family communication: What makes family relationships unique from the other types of interpersonal relationships we experience in a lifetime? Vangelisti (2004) describes the significance of the family by labeling it "the crucible of society" (p. ix). These relationships are unique from other types of interpersonal relationships because they are described as both voluntary and involuntary and play a significant role in shaping self-perceptions. After all, our family relationships offer our first glimpse into what it means to form an intimate connection with another person.

"The family. We were a strange little band of characters trudging through life sharing diseases and toothpaste, coveting one another's desserts, hiding shampoo, borrowing money, locking each other out of our rooms, inflicting pain and kissing to heal it in the same instant, loving, laughing, defending, and trying to figure out the common thread that bound us all together" (p. 9).

Source: Bombeck, E. (1987). *Family: The ties that bind...and gag!* New York: McGraw-Hill.

Consider the fact that families have unique communicative features. After all, you have a frame of reference for understanding communication in families since these are the first and likely to be the longest-lasting relationships formed in your life. Perhaps the best way to understand family relationships is to take a look at the role of interpersonal communication in the family and how it shapes our sense of identity and serves as a model for communication choices. Even in situations where relationships with family members have become strained, the bonds shape an individual's sense of self, serve as a model for desirable or undesirable communication, and shape expectations for future relationships. In this chapter we examine classic and contemporary family communication research, theories, and concepts. We will also address interpersonal communication concepts as they apply across the family life span.

DEFINITION OF FAMILY

If you were asked to list the number of people you consider to be part of your family, who would you include? Would you list in-laws, close family friends, close personal friends, neighbors, siblings' spouses, stepfamilies, or even coworkers? Would you include only those relatives related by blood or marriage? When students are asked this question, they often include a wide range of individuals in their list of family members. Most family relationships are described as *involuntary* because we do not get to choose our parents, siblings, cousins, aunts, uncles, grandparents, and so on.

© Volt Collection/Shutterstock.com

Most family relationships are involuntary because we don't get to choose who to include.

Some family relationships may be formed of *voluntary* members. An example of this is the television series *Friends*, which showcases how non-biological relationships can fulfill family roles.

As we grow older, our choices of who we include in our "family" expand. Voluntary families are created as a result of conscious decisions made to include others in the familial relationship. For example, we select our spouse or life partner. We all have experience with family relationships, but have you considered the unique nature of these bonds? A scene from the 2005 film *The Family Stone* illustrates this sense of family obligation. Sarah Jessica Parker portrays a young woman struggling to be accepted by her fiancé's close-knit family. At one point she becomes frustrated and asks her future mother-in-law, "What's so great about you guys?" Diane Keaton replies, "Uh, nothing . . . it's just that we're all that we've got." Each family member recognizes other family members' idiosyncrasies, but also realizes that the strength of the family bond surpasses all other relationships.

TYPES OF FAMILY RELATIONSHIPS

It is difficult to describe a "typical" family in the twenty-first century. Over the years, the structure of the typical American family has changed. The *Handbook of Family Communication* explores several different family types such as intact families, divorced or single parent families, stepfamilies, and gay or lesbian families. But while the types may have changed, core family relationships continue to exist and have provided scholars with opportunities to take a glimpse into how communication develops in these relationships. While we do not have the space to discuss all family types, three specific interpersonal relationships that exist in the family structure will be discussed: marital relationships, parent-child relationships, and sibling relationships.

> Even in situations where relationships with family members have become strained, the bonds shape an individual's sense of self, serve as a model for desirable or undesirable communication, and shape expectations for future relationships.

Marital Relationships

According to family communication researchers Turner and West (2002), "marriage is often seen as the most important intimate relationship two people can share" (p. 232). Some research indicates that individuals in healthy marriages tend to be both healthier and happier than unmarried individuals or those in unhealthy relationships. The longstanding question posed by researchers from a variety of academic and professional fields has always been how to obtain and maintain an enduring marital relationship.

Each life partner brings his or her own set of expectations to the marital relationship. Tune into a television talk show and at some point you will likely see a couple asking the host to solve their marital problems. It is not unusual for the host to identify differing expectations as the root of the problem. Earlier in this text, we mentioned that messages have both content and relational dimensions. The same is true of our expectations for marital relationships—couples hold content expectations and relational expectations for their partners.

©bikeriderlondon /Shutterstock.com

Individuals in healthy marriages tend to be healthier and happier than others.

Content expectations focus on how the relationship is defined by the role each partner plays in the family.

Relational expectations refer to the similarity, or correspondence, of the emotional, or affective, expectations each partner has for defining the relationship.

traditional couples couples who exhibit a high level of interdependence and sharing in their relationships with one another.

ditional couples adopt conventional roles in their marriages.

Content Expectations.

Content expectations focus on how the relationship is defined by the role each partner plays. Roles are defined by the expectations held for a position in the family. The ABC television show *Wife Swap* focused on the role expectations established for wives in two different types of families. In each episode, the wives switched families for two weeks. Clashes ensued over differing content expectations for husbands' and wives' roles in housekeeping and child-rearing. It is important to note that one of the difficult tasks involved in the marital relationship is ensuring that the two sets of expectations are congruent.

Relational Expectations.

Relational expectations refer to the similarity, or correspondence, of the emotional, or affective, expectations each partner has for defining the relationship. In one episode of *Wife Swap*, the Kraut and Hardin wives exchange households. One wife spends considerable time shopping and focusing on current fashion trends while her husband tends to the household duties. She is perceived to focus on herself rather than on the emotional needs of family members. The other wife expects all family members to participate in household chores, and the couple has formed the expectation that the role of the wife will include being responsible for homeschooling the children. She is extremely involved in every aspect of the children's lives and is aware of any changes in their emotional states. When the two families swap wives for the two-week period, they discover that their relational expectations are incongruent in the new environment. This often causes the sparks to fly! When the wives are in their own homes, communication is more satisfying because their spouses and children have congruent expectations for the relationship. They have become comfortable with the communication expectations associated with the maternal roles. Marital satisfaction is greater in relationships where couples discuss their expectations for the relationship—failure to talk about expectancies is often equated to playing "guess what's inside my mind."

To explain the various expectations that couples have for communication and for the relationship, Fitzpatrick (1987) developed a model to distinguish each couple type and how they view role conventionality, interdependence, and their approach to conflict. Three couple types were identified: traditionals, separates, and independents (see also Figure 12.1). Characteristics that distinguish the various couple types from one another are their expectations for sex roles and their approach to conflict in the relationship.

Traditionals.

Those who exhibit a high level of interdependence and sharing are considered traditional couples. Conventional sex roles are adopted in traditional couples, with males performing tasks such as lawn care, automobile maintenance, and taking out the garbage. Women fulfill the role of nurturing caregiver and are responsible for housekeeping and childcare duties. In her research, Fitzpatrick (1987) found that traditionals tend to be the most satisfied of the three couple types. A 2009 study of 210 couples found that traditional couples reported the highest level of commitment to the relationship compared to other couple types (Givertz, Segrin, & Hanzal). Clear expectations for the roles partners will play and for their relationship result in dedication to the relationship.

Figure 12.1 Description of marital types

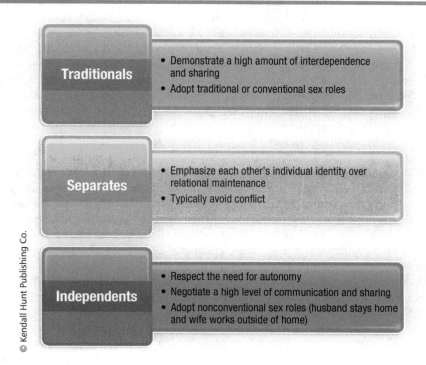

Traditionals
- Demonstrate a high amount of interdependence and sharing
- Adopt traditional or conventional sex roles

Separates
- Emphasize each other's individual identity over relational maintenance
- Typically avoid conflict

Independents
- Respect the need for autonomy
- Negotiate a high level of communication and sharing
- Adopt nonconventional sex roles (husband stays home and wife works outside of home)

© Kendall Hunt Publishing Co.

Separates. Separate couples tend to emphasize each individual's identity and independence over maintaining the relationship. In addition to maintaining conventional sex roles in the relationship, this couple is characterized by their avoidance of conflict. As is evident, this couple type typically reports a low level of marital satisfaction. Givertz, Segrin, and Hanzal (2009) found that separate couples experience the lowest levels of marital satisfaction and commitment of the three couple types.

> Marital satisfaction is greater in relationships where couples discuss their expectations for the relationship.

Separate couples tend to emphasize each individual's identity and independence over maintaining the relationship.

Independents. Independent couples simultaneously respect the need for autonomy and engage in a high level communication and sharing with one another. Sex roles in the independent relationship are unconventional. Individual freedom is a priority, and partners are willing to engage in conflict when they disagree on issues and tend to be assertive in expressing and defending their position on issues.

Independent couple describes a couple that simultaneously respects the need for autonomy and engages in a high level of communication and sharing with one another.

Parent-Child Relationships

Consider for a moment that the first family relationship formed is between a parent and a child. As well as having a legal responsibility to care for and protect their children, parents are responsible for the moral and character development of their children— not an easy task. In his book, *Family First*,

Young children assert their independence when they state they want to "do it all by myself."

©Oksana Kuzmina /Shutterstock.com

Dr. Phil McGraw (2004) discusses the role that parents play in preparing children for life's challenges, and points out that parents need to realize the influence they have as a result of the messages they communicate to their children.

A parent's role is complicated; biological and emotional attachments create a special bond that makes communication both rewarding and frustrating at times. Television shows such as *Nanny 911* and *Super Nanny* provide parents with advice for managing interactions with their children. They also provide a glimpse into the parenting challenges experienced by others, offering support to parents who can see that others are enduring the same, or worse, situations.

Over the course of the family life cycle, communication between parents and children evolves as new events occur. It is during this time that the dialectical tensions between autonomy and connection are perhaps the strongest. In the beginning of their lives children are totally dependent on the parents to provide for them and look out for their best interests. In the United States, many parents begin teaching children at a young age to become independent. Children are encouraged to learn to eat by themselves, pick out their own clothes, and to explore their individual interests in sports and other extracurricular activities. But even while encouraging independence, many parents simultaneously reinforce the message that they are still connected to their children. Providing children with cellular telephones is one strategy currently used by parents to stay connected as their children explore autonomy.

As children progress through adolescence, a new set of communication issues needs to be considered. Up to this point, children have been encouraged to become independent, but eventually the dialectical tension between autonomy and connection kicks in and parents may begin to feel that children are becoming too independent. Adolescence is often a difficult transition period for both children and parents alike, and it is not uncommon for conflicts to occur during this time in the family life cycle. A common communication issue during this period involves the negotiation of rules, with new guidelines for behavior being added on a regular basis as parents and children clash over preferences for clothes, manners, curfews, and activities. As the occurrence of parent-child conflict increases during adolescence, issues that once seemed unimportant now take on new relevance. Consider the issues you and your parents disagreed on during your adolescence. Why do you think communication surrounding these issues was so problematic?

As children grow up, identify their aspirations, and pursue their goals, families may find that their time is divided, and this provides yet another source of tension in the household. A 2015 study examining the impact of the time mothers spend with young children (ages 3–11) and teens (ages 12–18) found that the time spent directly engaged together during younger years does not have a significant impact on the child's behavior or academic success. However, there are important social and academic implications for increased mother-child time during the teen years. Teens who spend time with their mothers are less likely to engage in risky behaviors, and time spent with both parents together enhanced the teen's sense of well-being (Milkie, Nomaguchi, & Denny, 2015). Figure 12.2 highlights some of the trends in the amount of time parents spent with their children from 1965 to 2010.

While many adult privileges are granted to children when they reach the age of eighteen, parents and children view and negotiate the transition to

Figure 12.2 The average number of hours U.S. parents spent with their children each week, 1965–2010

Spending time with the kids

The average number of hours parents spent with their children each week rose since 1985.

MOTHERS 10.5 | 7.3 | 8.5 | 11.2 | 12 | 13.9 | 13.7

FATHERS 2.6 | 2.4 | 3 | 4.5 | 6.9 | 6.4 | 7.2

1965 | 1975 | 1985 | 1995 | 1999 | 2004 | 2010

Source: http://www.washingtonpost.com/local/making-time-for-kids-study-says-quality-trumps-quantity/2015/03/28/10813192-d378-11e4-8fce-3941fc548f1c_story.html

adulthood in different ways. The period when children begin the separation process from their parents is often referred to as the launching stage. However, this term is often misleading because many families continue to experience a sense of interdependence in their lives for a period of time after the child reaches legal age. For example, after returning to college after Christmas break, one student was overheard saying, "It was kind of nice being back home and knowing that my mom would stay up and wait for me to come in at night. I guess I have to admit that I missed that during my first semester at college." While some may find comfort in the old routines, others may find that new rules need to be negotiated during the launching stage. Statistics reported on forbes.com indicate that approximately 13 percent of adult children move back home with their parents after living on their own for a period of time. Researchers have coined the term boomerang children to refer to young adults who return home to live with their parents after living on their own for a period of time. Daily chores, financial contributions, and respect for household rules are only a few of the topics that require negotiation between boomerang children and their parents as they readjust to living under the same roof again.

©David Pereiras /Shutterstock.com

During adolescence, issues that once were insignificant can result in conflict.

launching stage the period when children begin the separation process from their parents.

boomerang children young adults who return home to live with their parents after living on their own for a period of time.

Divorce and remarriage create additional issues to consider in parent-child interactions. Stepfamilies face unique challenges that revolve around issues relating to discipline, resources, and ties to the biological family unit. According to a 2011 Pew Research Center report, almost 42% of American adults are part of a steprelationship, as a stepparent, a stepsibling, or a stepchild. Should stepfamilies and stepchildren expect communication and relationships to be similar to those between biological parents and children? Family communication scholars use the analogy of starting a novel halfway through the book to describe the experience of negotiating the stepfamily relationship (Coleman, Ganong, & Fine, 2004).

Images of stepfamilies portrayed in stories and the media often depict these relationships as filled with challenges and negative communication. In the 1998 film *Stepmom*, a conversation between a biological mother (Jackie) and her daughter (Anna) about her stepmother (Isabel) illustrates one of many potential communication issues associated with stepfamily relationships.

Anna: I think Isabel's pretty.

Jackie: Yeah, I think she's pretty too . . . if you like big teeth.

Anna: Mom?

Jackie: Yes, sweetie?

Anna: If you want me to hate her, I will.

(*Stepmom*, directed by Chris Columbus, 2hr. 4 min., 1492 Pictures, 1998.)

Anger or guilt can impact communication about the relationship, and both children and parents may find it difficult to be open about their true feelings. Not only are families required to negotiate nuances (such as children addressing stepparents as "Mom" or "Dad"), but the role of step grandparents in the blended family is also a consideration. Gold (2015) offers suggestions to assist stepgrandparents in adapting to the new family structure. These include:

- Respect the rules established by the new stepparent. Resist the temptation to "take sides" in situations involving the stepparent and stepchild.
- Be flexible and understand that the new family needs to create their own traditions. Have a conversation with the new spouse and their children about your traditions to see where they might "fit" into the new family's plans.
- Realize that stepgrandchildren have tremendous adjustments in their lives. Do not force affection (hugs, kisses) until they are ready. Learn about and support the stepgrandchildren's interests before expecting them to become interested in you. (Gold, 2015)

Relational Maintenance in Parent-Child Relationships.

Parents and children often find the need to increase efforts in maintaining their relationship as children grow older and gain more autonomy. Activities, new friends, and, eventually, the process of starting a new family can detract from the time and energy available for relationships with parents. In some instances, the onset of these maintenance challenges begins much earlier when parents decide to divorce. Non-custodial parents are faced with identifying new strategies to maintain their relationship with their children in the absence of the close physical proximity they once shared.

While many strategies used to maintain the relationship are similar to those found in other types of relationships, a 1999 study by Thomas-Maddox identified several strategies unique to this context:

- Non-custodial parents indicated that they depend on mediated communication (sending letters, emails, phone calls) and material/monetary offerings (sending gifts, taking children on "exciting" trips) to maintain their relationship.
- Children identified strategies for maintaining their relationship with non-custodial parents that include mediated communication, proximity (living with non-custodial parent during summer vacations and breaks by choice), and suggesting joint activities (proposing ideas such as going to the movies).

Parents and children often find the need to schedule special time together to maintain their relationship as children grow older.

©Jacek Chabraszewski /Shutterstock.com

While being physically separated as a result of this difficult decision may not be easy for parents and children, there are communication strategies that can be used to continue the relationship from a distance.

Parents and children often find the need to increase efforts in maintaining their relationship as children grow older and gain more autonomy.

Sibling Relationships

Relationships with siblings generally last the longest, given that our brothers and sisters are often still with us long after our parents are gone. Approximately 80 percent of individuals have siblings and, with the exception of firstborn children, sibling relationships are simultaneously formed with parent relationships. In their younger years, siblings often spend more time playing and interacting with one another than they do with their parents. But that does not necessarily mean these relationships are always positive. One minute siblings may be collaborating to "team up" against their parents, and the next minute they may be fighting like cats and dogs.

RESEARCH IN REAL LIFE: THE IMPACT OF OVERINVOLVED PARENTING

Is it possible for parents to become too controlling and involved in their children's lives? A 2014 study by Givertz and Segrin of 339 college students and their parents asked a series of questions to explore the role that parenting style plays in shaping family satisfaction and a child's sense of identity and entitlement. The study concluded that:

- Both parents and children report higher levels of family satisfaction when parents adopt an authoritative communication style that is open.
- Parents reported using authoritarian and permissive styles less frequently than their children perceived them using them.
- Families that exhibit high levels of adaptability and cohesion report greater levels of satisfaction.
- Children whose parents exhibited controlling (authoritarian) behaviors reported lower levels of self-efficacy and higher levels of perceived entitlement.

Overall, parents perceived their family as higher in cohesiveness and more effective in communicating with one another compared to the evaluations of their children.

- Do you think your evaluations of family satisfaction, cohesion, and parenting styles would be similar to your parents' evaluations? Why or why not?
- What factors do you think impact the different ways in which parents and children view the family relationship?

Communication in the sibling relationship often reflects both negative and positive characteristics. As family resources such as time, parents' attention, or physical objects are perceived to be scarce, siblings may engage in conflict or competition. Same-sex siblings tend to be more competitive than opposite-sex siblings. In some instances, siblings may be expected to fulfill the role of teacher or "co-parent." If you have siblings, chances are you have probably been instructed to "Watch out for your brother (or sister)" at some point in time. Often this occurs in single-parent families or in families where both parents are employed outside the home.

As siblings approach adolescence, their relationship experiences new transformations. Perhaps the competition for resources may become more intense, or siblings experience frustration when they are compared to one another. In these instances, a sibling may seek deidentification from other siblings. Deidentification is defined as an individual's attempt to create a distinct identity that is separate from that of their siblings. Have you ever had a teacher compare you to an older sibling? Or perhaps you have had friends at school who point out how similar or different you are compared to your brother or sister. When siblings are constantly evaluated against one another, they may experience a desire to create a unique identity and sense of self. Perhaps your ability to play soccer was often compared to one of your siblings who also played soccer. In an effort to distinguish yourself from your sibling, you quit playing soccer and played basketball instead.

Deidentification an individual's attempt to create a distinct identity that is separate from that of their siblings.

Maintenance in Sibling Relationships

Relational maintenance is of particular importance in the sibling relationship, since these typically last longer than any other family relationship. In a study designed to investigate unique maintenance strategies employed by siblings, six behaviors were identified (Myers & Weber, 2004). These include the following (see also Figure 12.3):

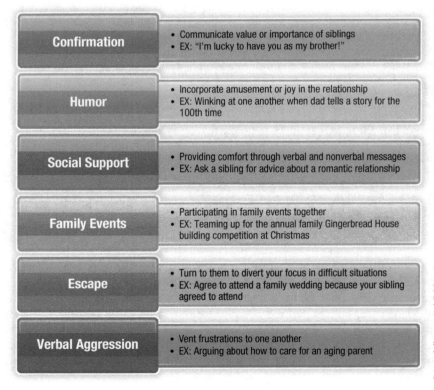

Figure 12.3 **Sibling relational maintenance strategies**

Confirmation	• Communicate value or importance of siblings • EX: "I'm lucky to have you as my brother!"
Humor	• Incorporate amusement or joy in the relationship • EX: Winking at one another when dad tells a story for the 100th time
Social Support	• Providing comfort through verbal and nonverbal messages • EX: Ask a sibling for advice about a romantic relationship
Family Events	• Participating in family events together • EX: Teaming up for the annual family Gingerbread House building competition at Christmas
Escape	• Turn to them to divert your focus in difficult situations • EX: Agree to attend a family wedding because your sibling agreed to attend
Verbal Aggression	• Vent frustrations to one another • EX: Arguing about how to care for an aging parent

- **Confirmation.** Confirmation consists of messages used to communicate the importance or value of siblings in one's life. Statements such as, "I'm lucky to have you as my brother" or "I really appreciate having you here to support me" are often viewed as validating the relationship.
- **Humor.** Often siblings use humor as a way to bring amusement or enjoyment to their relationship. Sharing private jokes about family members or making fun of their behaviors are ways siblings use humor to strengthen their bond.
- **Social support.** Siblings provide social support to one another by using comforting strategies to assist one another through difficult times. Asking a sibling for advice or sharing information about difficulties in other relationships illustrates the trust that is present in the relationship.
- **Family events.** Siblings often maintain and strengthen their relationships with each other and other family members through participation in family events. They may agree to visit their parents at the same time during the summer or holidays to spend time together.
- **Escape.** Siblings approach the time and communication spent with one another as an escape or diversion during difficult situations.
- **Verbal aggression.** While the final strategy, verbal aggression, may seem counterintuitive to maintaining a relationship, this maintenance mechanism allows siblings to vent their frustrations with one another. Yelling at one another may be the most effective method for having their concerns heard in a specific situation.

Additional research on adult sibling maintenance identified verbal statements, nonverbal gestures, and social support as additional options for strategies that are often used when siblings make purposeful or strategic attempts to maintain a relationship, as opposed to using messages and behaviors that are more habitual or routine (Myers, Byrnes, Frisby, & Mansson, 2011).

confirmation relational maintenance strategy in which messages are designed to communicate the importance or value of a family member in one's life.

humor relational maintenance strategy in which family members incorporate amusement or joy to sustain the relationship.

social support relational maintenance strategy in which family members provide comfort for one another via verbal and/or nonverbal messages.

©Volt Collection /Shutterstock.com

Often siblings use humor as a strategy to maintain their relationship with one another.

FAMILY COMMUNICATION THEORIES

Several theories can be applied to the study of communication in family relationships. Recall the definition of interpersonal communication: a process that occurs in a specific context and involves an exchange of verbal or nonverbal messages between two connected individuals with the intent to achieve shared meaning. The family is one context of connected individuals in which these interactions occur. Scholars of family communication have applied a variety of interpersonal theories to explain these interactions. In essence, virtually any theory of interpersonal communication could be applied to the study of families. Three theories that have specific implications for the family relationship include systems theory, family communication patterns theory, and symbolic interactionism.

family events relational maintenance strategy in which family members participate in events together as a means of sustaining their relationship.

escape relational maintenance strategy in which family members turn to one another to divert one's focus during difficult situations.

Family Systems Theory

Systems theory has been employed by family scholars to explore a variety of interactions, including children's attitudes about their single parent dating (Marrow-Ferguson & Dickson, 1995), family involvement in addressing

verbal aggression relational maintenance strategy in which family members vent or express their frustrations with one another.

children's problems at school (Walsh & Williams, 1997), and adolescent abuse of their parents (Eckstein, 2004).

In essence, virtually any theory of interpersonal communication could be applied to the study of families.

Family systems theory is one of the most frequently used theories in family communication scholarship (Stamp, 2004). The basic premise behind this theory is that family relationships can be treated as systems and can include the study of systemic qualities such as wholeness, interdependence, hierarchy, boundaries, calibration, and equifinality (Stamp, 2004). Each of the elements of systems theory is particularly relevant in explaining how and why family members relate to one another (See Figure 12.4).

Family systems theory proposes that family relationships can be treated as systems and includes the study of six elements to explain how and why family members relate to one another.

Figure 12.4 Elements of family systems

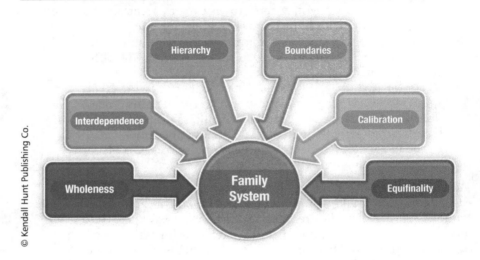

© Kendall Hunt Publishing Co.

Wholeness implies that a family creates its own personality or culture, and that this personality is unique from that of each family member.

Wholeness. Wholeness implies that a family creates its own personality or culture, and that this personality is unique from that of each family member. Many studies that have applied systems theory recognize that in order to understand the dynamics of families, the role of individual family members must be considered as well.

Interdependence proposes that the family system is composed of interrelated parts, or members, and a change experienced by one family member is likely to result in changes that impact all other family members.

Interdependence. Interdependence proposes that the family system comprises interrelated parts, or members. A change experienced by one family member is likely to result in changes that impact all other family members. Suppose a child catches the flu and cannot attend school for several days. If both parents work outside the home, one will have to make adjustments to his or her work schedule to stay at home with the child. To protect other family members from being exposed to the illness, family routines such as sharing dinner or watching television together may be altered.

hierarchy perceived levels of power or control associated with roles in the family.

Hierarchy. All systems have levels, or a hierarchy, present. Typically, parents take on the powerful roles in the family and are responsible for seeing that children's needs are fulfilled and that discipline and control are maintained in the system. It is important to note that power is often linked to respect among family members. We may differ in how we perceive power structures in the family. A 2008 study surveyed 133 African American, European American, and

Latina girls and their mothers to explore how culture influences the display of respect for power in families. Results indicated that:

- European American girls showed the lowest levels of respect for their mothers compared with the other two groups.
- In situations where conflict was present, African American and Latina mothers indicated that arguments were more intense than reported by European American mothers (Dixon, Graber, & Brooks-Gunn, 2008).

Boundaries. Families create boundaries that facilitate communication with members who are considered to be part of the system. These boundaries are often flexible as the family expands to include friends and pets. Ambiguous boundaries often create confusion about who family members perceive as being part of the system. Some families may view close friends as part of their family even in the absence of biological or legal connections. In these situations, even though the bonds are not biological, individuals may view one another as an important part of the family.

Parents often assume primary responsibility for childcare and discipline in the family.

boundaries created by families to indicate who is considered part of the family system. May be flexible to include the addition of new family members, friends, or even pets.

Calibration. The system element of calibration is the mechanism that allows the family to review communication in their relationships and decide if any adjustments need to be made to the system. For example, reality shows that feature families interacting with one another may provide examples of effective (or ineffective) family interactions that we can use as a reference or basis for comparison. Feedback communicated through messages received from others can also be taken into consideration. While waiting in line at the grocery store, a mother might receive a compliment about her well-behaved children. This provides her with feedback to gauge her performance as a parent.

Ambiguous boundaries vague or indistinguishable boundaries that may create confusion about who family members perceive as being part of the family system.

calibration a component of family systems theory that allows the family to review the communication in their relationships and decide if any adjustments need to be made to the system.

Equifinality. The final system element, equifinality, refers to a family's abilities to achieve the same goal by following different paths or using different communication behaviors. For example, one family may teach the children independence by communicating the expectation that the children are responsible for getting themselves up and getting ready for school in the morning. In another family, the mother might enter the bedroom and gently sing "Good Morning" to the children, lay out their school clothes, and have breakfast ready for them. Both families accomplish the same goal: working through the morning routine of getting to school on time. However, each family has a different method for accomplishing the goal.

equifinality a component of family systems theory that refers to a family's ability to achieve the same goal by following different paths or employing different communication behaviors.

Family Communication Patterns Theory

Perhaps one of the most complicated phenomena to factor into the family communication equation is the role that intrapersonal communication plays in the process. Family communication patterns theory is a comprehensive theory that focuses on the cognitive processes used to shape and guide our interpersonal interactions. Originally developed by McLeod and Chaffee (1972, 1973) as a way for explaining family members' interactions associated with television viewing, the goal of the theory was to explain how parents help children to understand messages received from multiple sources through mediated channels. But consider for a moment all of the different messages received from outside the family that are processed on a daily basis.

Family communication patterns theory focuses on how messages are processed and discussed within the family to create shared meaning. Includes the two primary orientations of conversation and conformity.

Ritchie and Fitzpatrick (1990) expanded the focus of this theory beyond mediated messages to focus on how a variety of messages are processed and discussed within the family to create shared meaning. This revised theory identified two primary orientations used by families: conversation and conformity

Conversation orientation refers to the level of openness and the frequency with which a variety of topics are discussed. Families who adopt a high conversation orientation encourage members to openly and frequently share their thoughts and feelings with one another on a wide variety of topics. It is rare that a topic is "off limits" for discussion in families who have a high conversation orientation. On the other hand, families with a low conversation orientation experience less frequent or less open interactions, and sometimes there are limits with regard to what topics can be discussed.

The second dimension of the communication pattern analysis focuses on the family's conformity orientation. **Conformity orientation** refers to the degree to which a family encourages autonomy in individual beliefs, values, and attitudes. Families who emphasize a high level of conformity in interactions encourage family members to adopt similar ways of thinking about topics, often with the goal of avoiding conflict and promoting harmony in the family. At the other end of the conformity continuum, family members are encouraged to form independent beliefs and attitudes, and these differing opinions are often perceived as having equal value in discussions and decision making.

To explain the interrelationship between conversation orientation and conformity orientation, Koerner and Fitzpatrick identified four different family types (2002). These include pluralistic, consensual, laissez-faire, and protective families. See Figure 12.5 for an integration of the family types into the two family orientations.

> **Conversation orientation** refers to the level of openness and the frequency with which a variety of topics are discussed.

> **Conformity orientation** focuses on the degree to which a family encourages autonomy in individual beliefs, values, and attitudes.

Figure 12.5 Family types as identified by family communication patterns theory

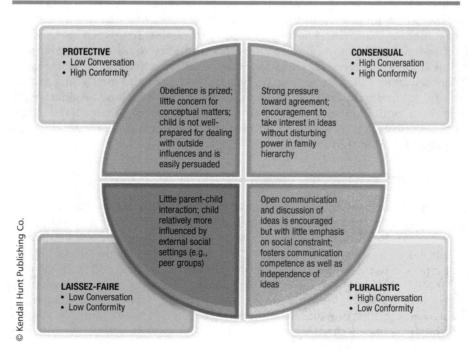

© Kendall Hunt Publishing Co.

Parents who encourage their children to form relationships outside the home and couples who believe that each partner should pursue his or her own network of friends typically do so in an effort to broaden the perspectives of individuals within the family. Complete the Family Communication Patterns scale located at the end of this chapter to find out what you perceive your family orientation to be.

Pluralistic. Pluralistic families adopt a high conversation orientation and a low conformity orientation. Almost anything goes in this family! A wide range of topics are discussed, and family members are encouraged to have their own opinions without feeling the pressure to agree with one another. Children in pluralistic families are often encouraged to participate in decision-making on topics ranging from where the family should go for vacation to the establishment of family rules.

Consensual. Consensual families adopt both a high conversation and a high conformity orientation. These families often encourage members to be open in their interactions with one another, but they expect that family members will adopt similar opinions and values. Parents in consensual families promote open conversations, but they still believe that they are the authority when it comes to decisions in the family.

Laissez-Faire. Laissez-faire families adopt both a low conversation and low conformity orientation. Rarely will family members talk with one another, and when conversations do occur, they are focused on a limited number of topics. Children are encouraged to make their own decisions, often with little or no guidance or feedback from their parents, in the laissez-faire family.

Protective. Protective families score low on conversation orientation and high on conformity. The phrase "Children should be seen but not heard" is characteristic of this family type. Parents are considered to be the authority, and children are expected to obey the family rules without questioning them.

Identifying and understanding the approaches used to communicate and to promote autonomy and independence is beneficial to understanding how these interactions shape both individual and family identities.

Symbolic Interaction Theory

Symbolic interactionism is perhaps one of the most widely applied theories in the study of family life. We discussed the role that messages play in assigning meaning to our experiences, and in how we perceive others and ourselves.

Mead's (1934) five concepts of symbolic interactionism (mind, self, I, me, and roles) are particularly useful in understanding the impact that family interactions have on shaping your identity. In his discussion of the concept of "mind," Mead explains the role that symbols play in creating shared meaning. Children interact with family members and learn language and social meanings associated with words. Similarly, Mead points out that our sense of "self" is developed through interactions with others. Families are influential in shaping this view of self through the messages and their reactions to one another.

Pluralistic families adopt a high conversation orientation and a low conformity orientation. Children are encouraged to participate in decision-making.

Consensual families promote open conversations while still maintaining control and authority when it comes to decisions in the family.

Laissez-faire families adopt both a low conversation and low conformity orientation. Family members rarely talk with one another, and when conversations occur they focus on a limited number of topics.

Protective families adopt a low conversation orientation and a high conformity orientation. Parents are considered to be the authority, and children are expected to obey the family rules without questioning them.

Symbolic interactionism proposes that one's sense of self is developed through interactions with others; families are influential in shaping this view of self through the messages and reactions to one another.

RESEARCH IN REAL LIFE: FAMILY COMMUNICATION PATTERNS AND STUDENTS' DECISIONS TO "FRIEND" PARENTS ON FACEBOOK

How likely would you be to "friend" your parent on Facebook? If you do provide them with access to your posts, would you change your privacy settings to limit what they could access or what others could post to your page? A 2013 study (Ball, Wanzer, & Servoss) asked 189 college students to report on their Facebook use and evaluate their family's communication patterns. Results found the following:

- A total of 154 students (82 percent) reported that they were Facebook friends with their parents.
- Females were 2.5 times more likely to friend their parents than males.
- Participants who perceive their families as having a higher conversation orientation were more likely to accept friend requests from their parents.
- Only 25 percent of the students who are Facebook friends with their parents adjusted their privacy settings to limit access to profile information.

Members gain a sense of how they are viewed by others from messages that are exchanged. Statements such as "You're such a good husband!" or "He's such a rotten kid" shape how individuals see themselves.

It is important to note that individual differences, such as personality traits or communication predispositions, may cause family members to view the same situation in very different ways. Consider the following scenario:

Kaija was quiet as Jay drove up the driveway. Jay smiled at her and said, "Trust me, they'll love you!" Kaija was meeting Jay's family for the first time since he had proposed. As they entered the front door, she was bombarded with hugs and kisses from various aunts, uncles, grandparents, and cousins. During dinner the talking never stopped! Kaija felt so left out—and nobody even seemed to care enough to ask her questions about herself. At one point, she slipped out to the back patio just to have a few moments of peace and quiet. As they drove back to campus, Jay commented, "Wasn't it a great evening! Everyone thought you were awesome!" Kaija couldn't believe what she had just heard. How could Jay have come to the conclusion that his family liked her? After all, they didn't take the time to find out anything about her. And the hugs and kisses were so intimidating. Kaija's family would have never shown such open displays of affection the first time they met Jay. She was confused—how could Jay have thought the evening went so great when she thought it had been horrible?

> Families are influential in shaping this view of self through the messages and their reactions to one another.

Who was correct in his or her assessment of the evening's events? Symbolic interactionism would indicate that both Jay and Kaija formed accurate perceptions. Each of them had formed his or her own meaning of the event based on their individual interpretations of the messages and behaviors. We learn in the scenario that Kaija's family would not have displayed affection so openly, while Jay's family background shaped his acceptance of effusive greetings. Our experiences in our family of origin shape the meanings we see in events, messages, and behaviors. The fact that Jay's family did not ask Kaija about herself caused her to perceive them as being uninterested. But suppose Jay had shared with his family that Kaija was an only child and tended to be shy around large groups. He may have asked them to refrain from bombarding her with questions that might cause her to feel uncomfortable. To better understand how symbolic interactionism applies to this scenario, it might be useful to examine the three underlying assumptions of the theory (LaRossa & Reitzes, 1993).

First, *our interactions with family members influence the meanings we assign to behaviors and messages.* Children determine if they should evaluate experiences as being positive or negative by watching the reactions of family members to various events and messages. A child whose parents avoid conflict may believe that conflict is a negative behavior that should be avoided at all costs. Coming from a family that shows caring through conversation, Kaija assigned a negative meaning to Jay's family's failure to ask her questions about herself.

Next, *individuals create a sense of self, which serves as a guide for selecting future behaviors.* We assess situations and take into consideration whether others will perceive behaviors and messages in a positive or negative way. This assumption goes beyond our own evaluation of events to include the perceptions of others. A child whose father has told him "You're a rotten kid" and "You'll never amount to anything" has learned to misbehave. As the negative messages are repeated, he comes to believe that others expect him to misbehave.

Finally, symbolic interactionism posits that the *behavior of family members is influenced by culture and society.* Perhaps this assumption sheds light on the reasons families are reluctant to admit that they experience conflict from time to time. Based on media portrayals of family life and from listening to the happy stories of other families, an expectation has been established that "normal" families do not fight.

CREATING A FAMILY IDENTITY

The family as a unit creates a collective identity. Communication is the primary mechanism for creating this family identity, with various messages and behaviors providing insight as to how the family views itself as a group. Four ways that families create and sustain an identity as a unit are through stories, myths, themes, and metaphors (see Figure 12.6). As we discuss each of these elements, reflect on your own family of origin and how these communicative acts shaped your sense of what it means to be a part of your family.

Family Stories

Family stories are narratives recounting significant events that have been shared by members. In essence, family life is composed of a series of stories. Because they are about shared experiences, these stories are often personal and emotional; they may evoke positive or negative feelings in family members. Individuals often use these stories to shape their own sense of identity. One of the authors of this textbook had a difficult time gaining confidence in her driving ability. Do you think it might be due in part to the fact that her family members enjoyed telling and retelling the story of how she was responsible for wrecking the family car when she was four years old?

Family stories narratives recounting significant events that have been shared by members.

Three types of family stories that have been studied by family scholars in an attempt to explain how families define their experiences are birth stories, courtship stories, and stories of survival.

Birth stories one type of family stories that describes how a person entered the family and defines how members "fit" into the system.

- Birth stories describe how each person entered the family and can define how members "fit" into the system. One woman shared a story of enduring a 42-hour labor prior to the birth of her son. She stated, "I guess I should have known then that he would always be challenging me because he gave me such a difficult time from the beginning!"

Courtship stories one type of family stories that provides a timeline for tracing romance in the family. Often used to describe how parents and grandparents met and how they decided that they were compatible.

- Courtship stories provide a timeline for tracing romance in the family. They are often used to describe how parents and grandparents met and how they decided that they were right for one another. When asked how he met his wife, a grandfather explained that she was working in the fields on her family farm and that it was love at first sight. He joked, "I knew she was a hard worker, so I asked her to marry me!" He then went on to explain that he knew she was devoted to helping her family and that she would be dedicated to her own family.

Stories of survival narratives used to explain how family members have overcome difficult times; often, they are told to help family members cope with challenges they face.

- Stories of survival are narratives used to explain how family members have overcome difficult times. They are often told to help family members cope with challenges. Three sisters who, at a young age, were physically abused by their father, discussed how they shared their stories with one another to assist in coping with their similar experiences. The sisters viewed the stories as therapeutic; they reinforced the notion that if they could survive the abuse of their father, they were strong enough to face any situation.

Family Myths

Family myths created to communicate the beliefs, values, and attitudes held by members to represent characteristics that are considered important to the family; are often fictional as they are based on an ideal image the family wishes to convey to others.

Family myths are created to communicate the beliefs, values, and attitudes held by members to represent characteristics that are considered important to the family. These myths are often fictional as they are based on an ideal image the family wishes to convey to others. Consider the following example:

"I couldn't believe what I was hearing! At my grandfather's funeral, my dad's family members were all talking about what a great man my grandfather was and how much they would miss him. My grandmother sobbed as she whispered, 'He was such a loving and caring man. I don't know what I'll do without him.' After the service, I asked my father why they were all referring to my grandfather that way. For years I had heard stories of the physical abuse that had taken place in the family during my dad's childhood, and I had heard my grandfather yell at my grandmother on numerous occasions. My dad responded, 'It's just easier on your grandmother if we all remember him in a positive way.'"

In this scenario, the family creates a myth that portrays the grandfather as a loving, caring man. Doing so enables them to protect the grandmother and to perpetuate the belief that he was a good father and husband. In the movie, *Doing Time on Maple Drive*, a family goes to great lengths to portray the image of the "perfect family" to their friends and neighbors. At one point, the son reveals to his parents that he attempted to commit suicide because he would rather be dead than admit to them that he is gay. This scene illustrates the power of family myths and the tremendous amount of pressure placed on family members to live up to the expectations communicated in these myths.

Family Metaphors

Sometimes families create family metaphors to assist in communicating how family life as a system is experienced by members. These metaphors make reference to specific objects, events, or images to represent the family experience and a collective identity. The metaphor of a "three-ring circus" may be used to describe the chaos and disorganization that exists within one family, while the "well-oiled machine" can depict the emphasis on control and organization that is the norm for another family. Metaphors can provide those within the family and outside of the family with an understanding of what behaviors are valued as well as how family members are expected to behave. A person from a "well-oiled machine" family can use the metaphor to understand the expectations associated with being a member of the family.

family metaphors references to specific objects, events, or images to represent the family experience and a collective identity.

Family Themes

Family themes represent important concerns regarding the expected relationship between family members and can assist family members in understanding how to direct their energy as a family unit. These themes often emerge from two primary sources—the background or experience of the parents, and the dialectical pulls experienced by the family. Suppose Joe and Marnie are having a difficult time managing the tensions of autonomy and connection as their children grow older, begin dating, and spend more time with friends than with family members. In an attempt to communicate their concern for the growing independence of family members, they remind the children that "Blood is thicker than water" and "Friends may come and go, but family is forever." These themes are intended to remind the children that, while they may form many relationships outside the unit, the strongest ties should be reserved for those in their family.

Family themes represent important concerns regarding the expected relationship between family members and can assist family members in understanding how to direct their energy as a family unit.

Figure 12.6 **Communication strategies used to shape and sustain family identity**

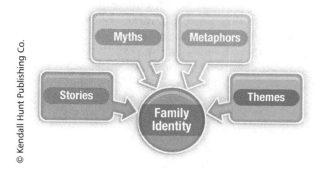

© Kendall Hunt Publishing Co.

CONSEQUENCES OF FAMILY RELATIONSHIPS

Throughout this text, various communication variables have been identified as being both beneficial and harmful to our interpersonal relationships. Because families play such a vital role in the development of our self-identity,

Offering encouragement fosters the development of intimacy in family relationships.

Confirming communication messages that indicate that we see family members in a way that is consistent with how they see themselves.

understanding how specific communication behaviors can enhance and damage our relationships and our sense of self is important.

Families can serve as the primary source of understanding and support for individuals. As we grow older, we receive messages that let us know that we are cared for and accepted. These perceptions are often shaped by the types of verbal and nonverbal cues we receive from others and are often linked to the formation of our sense of self. Three types of messages are often used to indicate whether family members view us in the same way we see ourselves:

- **Confirming communication** occurs when we treat and communicate with family members in a way that is consistent with how they see themselves. A child who perceives himself to be independent is confirmed when a parent gives him responsibility and allows him to make his own decisions.
- **Rejection** occurs when family members treat others in a manner that is inconsistent with how they see themselves. Can you recall a time when you felt like you were "grown up" but your parents treated you as though you were still a child?
- **Disconfirming communication** occurs when family members fail to offer any type of response. We often get caught up in our busy schedules and fail to communicate with family members. Even though our response is neither positive nor negative, it can cause others to feel dissatisfied with the relationship.

Understanding and supportive communication are related to family satisfaction. If we perceive family members as being there for us, we are more willing to exert energy toward developing a more intimate relationship.

Understanding and supportive communication are related to family satisfaction. If we perceive family members as being there for us, we are more willing to exert energy toward developing a more intimate relationship.

Rejection occurs when family members treat others in a manner that is inconsistent with how they see themselves.

Disconfirming communication occurs when family members fail to acknowledge or offer any type of feedback or response to another family member.

ABCX model includes various elements to examine the stress experienced by families and the various ways in which they cope with stress.

DIFFICULT COMMUNICATION

It is important to note that families are not immune to difficult communication. Just as romantic partners and friends experience highs and lows in relationships, so do families. Because families evolve as members grow and encounter new life experiences, additional communication challenges emerge. The key to managing these issues effectively and maintaining a positive relationship is to understand the role of communication in guiding us through the muddy waters.

Family Stress

Reuben Hill developed the **ABCX model** to study the stress experienced by families during war (1958). Each component of this model provides a glimpse into how different families cope with stress.

- "A" represents the stressor event and resulting hardship.
- "B" refers to the resources a family has available to manage the stress.
- Given that different families define stress in unique ways, "C" is used to explain how the family defines the stress.
- Depending on how a family defines "A," "B," and "C," the perception of an event as a crisis is represented by "X."

The model is useful for understanding how and why families label situations as stressful and cope with stressors. Consider the stress experienced by a military family when a mother is deployed and won't be home for months.

The mother has a young child who is left behind while she is stationed in Iraq. Her three-year-old son is confused and upset that his mother is away. His grandmother does her best to comfort him when he mistakes another woman for his mother and runs to her. His grandmother tries to explain that mommy is still far away, flying helicopters, soothing him until he falls asleep. Once he is tucked in bed, she must try to calm her own fears for her daughter's safety, knowing that she is in a hostile land. This is the life of a soldier's family.

"A" represents the stressor event of a young mother stationed with the U.S. military in Iraq. In this story, extended family members serve as resources to assist with the care of a three-year-old child in the absence of his mother, representing the "B" in the model. The confusion experienced by the grandmother as she tries to help her grandson cope with the separation causes her to define the stressor as emotionally draining (C). While the family knows that the daughter will return home eventually, they also understand that she chose to serve her country and realize the danger associated with this responsibility. This may keep the family from evaluating the stress as a crisis (X). Take a look at Figure 12.7 to review each step of the ABCX model.

Figure 12.7 The ABCX model of family stress

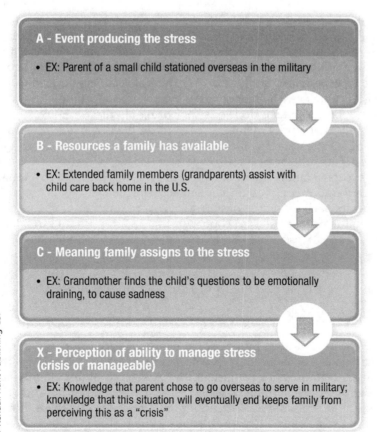

A - Event producing the stress

- EX: Parent of a small child stationed overseas in the military

B - Resources a family has available

- EX: Extended family members (grandparents) assist with child care back home in the U.S.

C - Meaning family assigns to the stress

- EX: Grandmother finds the child's questions to be emotionally draining, to cause sadness

X - Perception of ability to manage stress (crisis or manageable)

- EX: Knowledge that parent chose to go overseas to serve in military; knowledge that this situation will eventually end keeps family from perceiving this as a "crisis"

Stressor events can take many forms; Boss (1988) developed a typology of stressors that families face. Table 12.1 lists these various types of stressors.

Table 12.1 Types of Stressors

Types of Stressors

Internal • Originate with a family member	**External** • Originate outside the family
Normative • Expected; part of family life cycle	**Non-normative** • Unexpected
Voluntary • Stress that is sought out	**Involuntary** • Events that simply occur
Chronic • Long-term	**Acute** • Short-term

Internal stressor family stressors that result from within the family.

External stressor the result of an event that occurs outside the family.

Normative stressor stress-producing events that are expected to occur at some point during the course of the family life cycle.

Non-normative stressor unpredictable and often catches families "off guard."

voluntary stressor those events that family members seek out (such as changing careers or moving to a new home) that result in stress.

Involuntary stressor stress-producing events that unexpectedly occur within a family.

chronic stressor events that require families to cope with a stressful situation for an extended period of time.

Acute stressor relatively short-lived or temporary stress-producing events encountered by families.

Internal stressors are those that evolve from a family member. Examples might include a daughter's upcoming wedding or a teen who has tried to run away from home. External stressors, on the other hand, are often the result of an event that occurs outside the family, such as a hurricane destroying a family's home or even just an increase in the price of gasoline.

Normative stressors are those that are expected to occur at some point during the course of the family life cycle. The birth of a child or the death of an elderly parent are events that families anticipate dealing with at some point in time. Non-normative stressors are unpredictable and often catch families "off guard." While most people think that winning the lottery would be a great stressor to experience, families do not typically anticipate having difficulty dealing with the new challenges posed by their good fortune.

Some families make decisions that bring about voluntary stressors, or those events that family members seek out on their own accord. Examples of these types of stressors may include changing careers and moving to a new city or deciding to run for political office. Involuntary stressors are events that simply occur—a family member who is unexpectedly injured in a car accident or the announcement of an unplanned teen pregnancy.

Illnesses such as cancer or alcoholism are examples of chronic stressor events that require families to cope with the situation for an extended period of time. Acute stressors are relatively short-lived and include events such as a student getting suspended for misbehaving or losing the only set of keys to the family car.

SUMMARY

While we form countless interpersonal relationships throughout our lifetime, the relationships and interactions with family members are perhaps the most influential. Beginning at a young age, messages received from family members shape our identity and influence our own choice of communication behaviors. In addition to the individual identities that are shaped by these interactions, the family itself begins to create an identity that is shared by members.

Throughout this chapter we have discussed the importance of interpersonal communication throughout the family life cycle. Various interpersonal theories can be applied to the study of family communication to illustrate the dynamic nature of these relationships. While we often assume that "family is forever," it is important to recognize that just as other types of interpersonal relationships experience a "dark side," family relationships can experience challenging communication as well. By exploring the role that interpersonal communication plays in families, we are better able to understand our own family's communication tendencies, both when interacting with each other and when interacting with people from outside the family group.

RESEARCH IN REAL LIFE:
STRESS AND DECIDING HOW TO REVEAL FAMILY SECRETS

Identifying the right time and way to reveal a secret that has long been kept from family members can be stressful. In a 2009 study by Afifi and Steuber, 629 members from 171 different families were asked to describe a secret they were keeping from a family member and describe how they would reveal the secret if they were to share it. Six specific strategies for revealing secrets were identified in the study:

- **Directness:** tell the person face-to-face; reveal the secret if asked about it
- **Indirect mediums:** share the secret via email, letter, or text
- **Third-party revelation:** share the secret with someone else and let them reveal it
- **Incremental disclosure:** reveal small parts of the secret or share a similar secret from someone else to gauge reactions
- **Preparation and rehearsal:** plan a script or practice telling the secret to others
- **Entrapment:** leave clues or evidence about the secret and allow them to draw conclusions

---

DISCUSSION QUESTIONS

1. How would you define "family"? Who would you include in your family? Explain why these individuals are included. What individual differences affect how you define this term (e.g., sex, culture, age, your family of origin, relationship experiences) and who you include in your family?

2. Identify a family from one of your favorite television shows. Use systems theory to analyze the characters' communication patterns and relationships with one another (e.g., interdependence, wholeness, etc). Would you describe the family members' communication and relationships as healthy or unhealthy? Defend your response to this question and be sure to use specific examples to support your arguments.

3. Identify what you think are the "Top 5" issues facing families today. If you were to offer advice to families for communicating about these issues, what would you tell them?

REFERENCES

Afifi, T., & Steuber, K. (2009). The Revelation Risk Model (RRM): Factors that predict the revelation of secrets and the strategies used to reveal them. *Communication Monographs, 76*(2), 144¬–176.

Ball, H., Wanzer, M. B., & Servoss, T. J. (2013). Parent-child communication on Facebook: Family communication patterns and young adults' decision to "friend" parents. *Communication Quarterly, 61*(5), 615–629.

Boss, P. (1988). *Family stress management.* Newbury Park, CA: Sage.

Coleman, M., Ganong, L., & Fine, M. (2004). Communication in stepfamilies. In A. Vangelisti (Ed.), *Handbook of family communication.* (215–232). Mahwah, NJ: Lawrence Erlbaum Associates.

Dixon, S. V., Graber, J. A., & Brooks-Gunn, J. (2008). The roles of respect for parental authority and parenting practices in parent-child conflict among African American, Latino, and European American families. *Journal of Family Psychology, 22*(1), 1–10.

Dunn, A. (2015). Failure to launch: Adult children moving back home. Retrieved May 29, 2015, from http://www.forbes.com/sites/moneywisewomen/2012/06/06/failure-to-launch-adult-children-moving-back-home/

Eckstein, N. J. (2004). Emergent issues in families experiencing adolescent-to-parent abuse. *Western Journal of Communication, 68*(4), 365-388.

Fitzpatrick, M. A. (1987). Marital interaction. In C. Berger & S. Chaffee (Eds.), *Handbook of communication science* (564–618). Newbury Park, CA: Sage.

Givertz, M., Segrin, C., & Hanzal, A. (2009). The association between satisfaction and commitment differs across marital couple types. *Communication Research, 36*(4), 561–584.

Givertz, M., & Segrin, C. (2014). The association between overinvolved parenting and young adults' self-efficacy, psychological entitlement, and family communication. *Communication Research, 41*(8), 1111–1136.

Gold, J. M. (2015). Intergenerational attachments in stepfamilies: Facilitating the role of step-grandparents. *The Family Journal: Counseling and Therapy for Couples and Families, 23*(2), 194–200.

Hill, R. (1958). Generic features of families under stress. *Social Casework, 49,* 139–150.

Koerner, A. F., & Fitzpatrick, M. A. (2002). Toward a theory of family communication. *Communication Theory, 12,* 70–91.

LaRossa, R., & Reitzes, D. C. (1993). Symbolic interactionism and family studies. In P. G. Boss, W. J. Doherty, R. LaRossa, W. R. Schumm, & S. K. Steinmetz (Eds.), *Sourcebook of family theories and methods: A contextual approach* (135–163). New York, NY: Plenum Press.

Marrow-Ferguson, S., & Dickson, F. (1995). Children's expectations of their single-parent's dating behavior: A preliminary investigation of emergent themes relevant to single-parent dating. *Journal of Applied Communication Research, 23,* 1–17.

McGraw, P. (2004). *Family first: Your step-by-step plan for creating a phenomenal family.* New York: Free Press.

McLeod, J. M., & Chaffee, S. H. (1972). The construction of social reality. In J. Tedeschi (Ed.), *The social influence process* (pp. 50–59). Chicago, IL: Aldine-Atherton.

McLeod, J.M., & Chaffee, S.H. (1973). Interpersonal approaches to communication research. *American Behavior Scientist, 16,* 469–499.

Mead, G. H. (1934). *Mind, self and society.* Chicago: University of Chicago Press.

Milkie, M.A., Nomaguchi, K. M., & Denny, K. E. (2015). Does the amount of time mothers spend with their children or adolescents matter? *Journal of Marriage and Family, 77,* 355–372.

Myers, S. A., & Weber, K. D. (2004). Preliminary development of a measure of sibling relational maintenance behaviors: Scale development and initial findings. *Communication Quarterly, 52,* 334–346.

Myers, S. A., Byrnes, K. A., Frisby, B. N., & Mansson, D. H. (2011). Adult siblings' use of affectionate communication as a strategic and routine relational maintenance behavior. *Communication Research Reports, 28*(2), 151–158.

Ritchie, L. D. (1990). Family communication patterns: Measuring interpersonal perceptions of interpersonal relationships. *Communication Research, 17*(4), 523–544.

Ritchie, L. D., & Fitzpatrick, M. A. (1990). Family communication patterns: Measuring interpersonal perceptions of interpersonal relationships. *Communication Research, 17*, 523–544.

Stamp, G. H. (2004). Theories of family relationships and a family relationships theoretical model. In A. Vangelisti (Ed.), *Handbook of family communication.* (1–30). Mahwah, NJ: Lawrence Erlbaum Associates.

Thomas-Maddox, C. (1999). *Keeping the relationship alive: An analysis of relational maintenance strategies employed by non-custodial parents and their children following divorce.* Paper presented at the National Communication Association convention, Chicago, IL.

Turner, L. H., & West, R. (2002). *Perspectives on family communication.* McGraw-Hill: Boston, MA.

Ungricht, M. (2006, February 17). MSNBC Citizen Journalist Reports: Stories from front line families. Retrieved from http://msnbc.com/id/7012316/.

Vangelisti, A. (2004). *Handbook of family communication.* Mahwah, NJ: Lawrence Erlbaum Associates.

Walsh, W. M., & Williams, R. (1997). *School and family therapy: Using systems theory and family therapy in the resolution of school problems.* Springfield, IL: Charles C. Thomas.

Health Communication

chapter

13

OBJECTIVES

1. Understand the role communication plays in physical and mental health.

2. Explain the health communication cycle.

3. Distinguish health communication concerns between health contexts.

KEY TERMS

audience analysis
audience profile
channels
communication
  channels
communication
  objectives
communication
  strategies

communication
  vehicles
community
  development
health communication
health disparities
health equity
intended audiences
key groups

program outcomes
situation analysis
social determinants of
  health
stakeholders
underserved
  populations
vulnerable
  populations

Health communication is an evolving and increasingly prominent field in public health, health care, and the non-profit and private sectors. Therefore, many authors and organizations have been attempting to define or redefine it over time. Because of the multidisciplinary nature of health communication, many of the definitions may appear somewhat different from each other. Nevertheless, when they are analyzed, most point to the role that health communication can play in influencing, supporting, and empowering individuals, communities, health care professionals, policymakers, or special groups to adopt and sustain a behavior or a social, organizational, and policy change that will ultimately improve individual, community, and public health outcomes.

Understanding the true meaning of health communication and establishing the right context for its implementation may help communication managers and other public health, community development, and health care professionals identify early on the training needs of staff, the communities they serve, and others who are involved in the communication process. It will also help create the right organizational mind-set and capacity that should lead to a successful use of communication approaches to reach group-, stakeholder-, and community-specific goals.

CHAPTER OBJECTIVES

This chapter sets the stage to discuss current health communication contexts. It also positions the importance of health communication in public health, health care, and community development as well as the nonprofit and private sectors. Finally, it describes key elements, action areas, and limitations of health communication, and introduces readers to "the role societal, organizational, and individual factors" play in influencing and being influenced by public health communication (Association of Schools of Public Health, 2007, p. 5) and communication interventions in clinical (Hospitals and Health Networks, 2012) and other health-related settings.

DEFINING HEALTH COMMUNICATION

There are several definitions of health communication, which for the most part share common meanings and attributes. This section analyzes and aims to consolidate different definitions for health communication. This analysis starts from the literal and historical meaning of the word *communication*.

What Is Communication?

An understanding of health communication theory and practice requires reflection on the literal meaning of the word *communication*. *Communication* is defined in this way: "1. *Exchange of information*, between individuals, for example, by means of speaking, writing, or using a common system of signs and behaviors; 2. *Message*—a spoken or written message; 3. *Act of communicating*; 4. *Rapport*—a sense of mutual understanding and sympathy; 5. *Access*—a means of access or communication, for example, a connecting door" (*Encarta Dictionary*, January 2007).

In fact, all of these meanings can help define the modalities of well-designed health communication interventions. As with other forms of communication, health communication should be based on a two-way exchange of information that uses a "common system of signs and behaviors." It should be accessible and create "mutual feelings of understanding and sympathy" among members of the communication team and **intended audiences** or **key groups** (all groups the health communication program is seeking to engage in the communication process.) In this book, the terms *intended audience* and *key group* are used interchangeably. Yet, the term *key group* may be better suited to acknowledge the participatory nature of well-designed health communication interventions in which communities and other key groups are the lead architects of the change process communication can bring about. For those who always have worked within a participatory model of health communication interventions, this distinction is concerned primarily with terminology-related preferences in different models and organizational cultures. Yet, as *audience* may have a more passive connotation, using the term *key group* may indicate the importance of creating key groups' ownership of the communication process, and of truly understanding priorities, needs, and preferences as a key premise to all communication interventions.

Finally, going back to the literal meaning of the word *communication* as defined at the beginning of this section, **channels** or **communication channels** (the means or path, such as mass media or new media, used to reach out to and connect with key groups via health communication messages and materials) and messages are the "connecting doors" that allow health communication interventions to reach and engage intended groups.

Communication has its roots in people's need to share meanings and ideas. A review of the origin and interpretation of early forms of communication, such as writing, shows that many of the reasons for which people may have started developing graphic notations and other early forms of writing are similar to those we can list for health communication.

One of the most important questions about the origins of writing is, "Why did writing begin and for what specific reasons?" (Houston, 2004, p. 234). Although the answer is still being debated, many established theories suggest that writing developed because of state and ceremonial needs (Houston, 2004). More specifically, in ancient Mesoamerica, early forms of writing may have been introduced to help local rulers "control the underlings and impress rivals by means of propaganda" (Houston, 2004, p. 234; Marcus, 1992) or "capture the dominant and dominating message within self-interested declarations" (Houston, 2004, p. 234) with the intention of "advertising" (p. 235) such views. In other words, it is possible to speculate that the desire and need to influence and connect with others are among the most important reasons for the emergence of early forms of writing. This need is also evident in many other forms of communication that seek to create feelings of approval, recognition, empowerment, or friendliness, among others.

Health Communication Defined

One of the key objectives of **health communication** is to engage, empower, and influence individuals and communities. The goal is admirable because health communication aims to improve health outcomes by sharing health-related information. In fact, the Centers for Disease Control and Prevention (CDC) define *health communication* as "the study and use of communication strategies to inform and influence individual and community decisions that enhance health" (CDC, 2001; US Department of Health and Human Services, 2012a). The word *influence* is also included in the *Healthy People 2010* definition of health communication as "the art and technique of informing, influencing, and motivating individual, institutional, and public audiences about important health issues" (US Department of Health and Human Services, 2005, pp. 11–12).

Yet, the broader mandate of health communication is intrinsically related to its potential impact on vulnerable and underserved populations. **Vulnerable populations** include groups who have a higher risk for poor physical, psychological, or social health in the absence of adequate conditions that are supportive of positive outcomes (for example, children, the elderly, people living with disability, migrant populations, and special groups affected by stigma and social discrimination). **Underserved populations** include geographical, ethnic, social, or community-specific groups who do not have adequate access to health or community services and infrastructure or information. "Use health communication strategies … to improve population health outcomes and health care quality, and to achieve health equity," reads *Healthy People 2020* (US Department of Health and Human Services, 2012b). **Health equity** is providing every person with the same opportunity to stay healthy or to effectively cope with disease and crisis, regardless of race, gender, age, economic conditions, social status, environment, and other socially determined factors. This can be achieved only by creating a receptive and favorable environment in which information can be adequately shared, understood, absorbed, and discussed by different communities and sectors in a way that is inclusive and representative of vulnerable and underserved groups. This requires an in-depth understanding of the needs, beliefs, taboos, attitudes, lifestyle, socioeconomics, environment, and social norms of all key groups and sectors that are involved—or should be involved—in the communication process. It also demands that communication is based on messages that are easily understood. This is well characterized in the definition of *communication* by Pearson and Nelson (1991), who view it as "the process of understanding and sharing meanings" (p. 6).

A practical example that illustrates this definition is the difference between making an innocent joke about a friend's personality trait and doing the same about a colleague or recent acquaintance. The friend would likely laugh at the joke, whereas the colleague or recent acquaintance might be offended. In communication, understanding the context of the communication effort is interdependent with becoming familiar with intended audiences. This increases the likelihood that all meanings are shared and understood in the way communicators intended them. Therefore, communication, especially about life-and-death matters such as in public health and health care, is a long-term strategic process. It requires a true understanding of the key groups and communities we seek to engage as well as our willingness and ability to adapt and redefine the goals, strategies, and activities of communication interventions on the basis of audience participation and feedback.

Health communication interventions have been successfully used for many years by public health and nonprofit organizations, the commercial sector, and others to advance public, corporate, clinical, or product-related goals in relation to health. As many authors have noted, health communication draws from numerous disciplines and theoretical fields, including health education, social and behavioral sciences, community development, mass and speech communication, marketing, social marketing, psychology, anthropology, and sociology (Bernhardt, 2004; Kreps, Query, and Bonaguro, 2007; Institute of Medicine, 2003b; World Health Organization [WHO], 2003). It relies on different communication activities or action areas, including interpersonal communication, mass media and new media communication, strategic policy communication and public advocacy, community mobilization and citizen engagement, professional medical communications, and constituency relations and strategic partnerships (Bernhardt, 2004; Schiavo, 2008, 2011b; WHO, 2003).

Table 13.1 provides some of the most recent definitions of health communication and is organized by key words most commonly used to characterize health communication and its role. It is evident that "sharing meanings or information," "influencing individuals or communities," "informing," "motivating individuals and key groups," "exchanging information," "changing behaviors," "engaging," "empowering," and "achieving behavioral and social results" are among the most common attributes of health communication.

Another important attribute of health communication should be "to support and sustain change." In fact, key elements of successful health communication interventions always include long-term program sustainability as well as the development of communication tools and steps that make it easy for individuals, communities, and other key groups to adopt or sustain a recommended behavior, practice, or policy change. If we integrate this practice-based perspective with many of the definitions in Table 13.1, the new definition on page 327 emerges.

Table 13.1 Health Communication Definitions

Key Words	Definitions
To inform and influence (individual and community) decisions	"Health communication is a key strategy to *inform* [emphasis added throughout table] the public about decisions health concerns and to maintain important health issues on the public agenda" (New South Wales Department of Health, Australia, 2006).
	"The study or use of communication strategies *to inform and influence* individual and community decisions that enhance health" (CDC, 2001; US Department of Health and Human Services, 2005).
	Health communication is a "means to disease prevention through behavior modification" (Freimuth, Linnan, and Potter, 2000, p. 337). It has been defined as "the study and use of methods to *inform and influence* individual and community decisions that enhance health" (Freimuth, Linnan, and Potter, 2000, p. 338; Freimuth, Cole, and Kirby, 2000, p. 475).
	"Health communication is a process for the development and diffusion of messages to specific audiences in order to *influence* their knowledge, attitudes and beliefs in favor of healthy behavioral choices" (Exchange, 2006; Smith and Hornik, 1999).
	"Health communication is the use of communication techniques and technologies to (positively) *influence* individuals, populations, and organizations for the purpose of promoting conditions conducive to human and environmental health" (Maibach and Holtgrave, 1995, pp. 219–220; Health Communication Unit, 2006). "It may include diverse activities such as clinician-patient interactions, classes, self-help groups, mailings, hot lines, mass media campaigns, and events" (Health Communication Unit, 2006).
Motivating individuals and key groups	"The art and technique of informing, influencing and *motivating* individual, institutional, and public audiences about important health issues. Its scope includes disease prevention, health promotion, health care policy, and business, as well as enhancement of the quality of life and health of individuals within the community" (Ratzan and others, 1994, p. 361).
	"Effective health communication is the art and technique of *informing, influencing, and motivating* individuals, institutions, and large public audiences about important health issues based on sound scientific and ethical considerations" (Tufts University Student Services, 2006).
Change behavior, achieve social and behavioral results	"Health communication, like health education, is an approach which attempts to *change a set of behaviors* in a large-scale target audience regarding a specific problem in a predefined period of time" (Clift and Freimuth, 1995, p. 68),
	"There is good evidence that public health communication has affected health behavior ... In addition, ... many public agencies assume that public health communication is a powerful tool for *behavior change*" (Hornik, 2008a, pp. xi–xv).
	"... *behavior change* is credibly associated with public health communication ..." (Hornik, 2008b, p.1).
	"... health communication strategies that are collaboratively and strategically designed, implemented, and evaluated can help to improve health in a significant and lasting way. Positive results are achieved by empowering people *to change their behavior* and by facilitating *social change*" (Krenn and Limaye, 2009).

(continued)

Table 13.1	Health Communication Definitions (*continued*)

Key Words	Definitions
	Health communication and other disciplines "may have some differences, but they share a common goal: creating *social change* by changing people's attitudes, external structures, and/ or *modify or eliminate certain behaviors*" (CDC, 2011a).
Increase knowledge and understanding of health-related issues	"The goal of health communication is to *increase knowledge and understanding* of health-related issues and to improve the health status of the intended audience" (Muturi, 2005, p. 78).
	"Communication means a process of *creating understanding* as the basis for development. It places emphasis on people interaction" (Agunga, 1997, p. 225).
Empowers people	"Communication *empowers people* by providing them with knowledge and understanding about specific health problems and interventions" (Muturi, 2005, p. 81).
	"... transformative communication... seek[s] not only to educate people about health risks, but also to facilitate the types of social relationships most likely to *empower* them to resist the impacts of unhealthy social influences" (Campbell and Scott, 2012, pp. 179–180).
	"Communication processes are central to broader *empowerment* practices through which people are able to arrive at their own understanding of issues, to consider and discuss ideas, to negotiate, and to engage in public debates at community and national levels" (Food and Agriculture Organization of the United Nations and others, 2011, p. 1).
Exchange, interchange of information, two-way dialogue	"A process for partnership and participation that is based on *two-way dialogue*, where there is an interactive *interchange of information*, ideas, techniques and knowledge between senders and receivers of information on an equal footing, leading to improved understanding, shared knowledge, greater consensus, and identification of possible effective action" (Exchange, 2005).
	"Health communication is the scientific development, strategic dissemination, and critical evaluation of relevant, accurate, accessible, and understandable health *information communicated to and from intended audiences* to advance the health of the public" (Bernhardt, 2004, p. 2051).
Engaging	"One of the most important, and largely unrecognized, dimensions of effective health communication relates to how *engaging* the communication is" (Kreps, 2012a, p. 253).
	"To compete successfully for audience attention, health-related communications have to be polished and *engaging*" (Cassell, Jackson, and Cheuvront, 1998, p. 76).

Health communication is a multifaceted and multidisciplinary field of research, theory, and practice. It is concerned with reaching different populations and groups to exchange health-related information, ideas, and methods in order to influence, engage, empower, and support individuals, communities, health care professionals, patients, policymakers, organizations, special groups and the public, so that they will champion, introduce, adopt, or sustain a health or social behavior, practice, or policy that will ultimately improve individual, community, and public health outcomes.

HEALTH COMMUNICATION IN THE TWENTY-FIRST CENTURY: KEY CHARACTERISTICS AND DEFINING FEATURES

Health communication is about improving health outcomes by encouraging behavior modification and social change. It is increasingly considered an integral part of most public health interventions (US Department of Health and Human Services, 2012a; Bernhardt, 2004). It is a comprehensive approach that relies on the full understanding and participation of its intended audiences.

Health communication theory draws on a number of additional disciplines and models. In fact, both the health communication field and its theoretical basis have evolved and changed in the past fifty years (Piotrow, Kincaid, Rimon, and Rinehart, 1997; Piotrow, Rimon, Payne Merritt, and Saffitz, 2003; Bernhardt, 2004). With increasing frequency, it is considered "the avant-garde in suggesting and integrating new theoretical approaches and practices" (Drum Beat, 2005).

Most important, communicators are no longer viewed as those who write press releases and other media-related communications, but as fundamental members of the public health, health care, nonprofit, or health industry teams. Communication is no longer considered a skill (Bernhardt, 2004) but a science-based discipline that requires training and passion, and relies on the use of different **communication vehicles** (materials, activities, events, and other tools used to deliver a message through communication channels; Health Communication Unit, 2003b) and channels. According to Saba (2006):

> In the past, and this is probably the most prevalent trend even today, health communication practitioners were trained "on-the-job." People from different fields (sociology, demography, public health, psychology, communication with all its different specialties, such as filmmaking, journalism and advertising) entered or were brought into health communication programs to meet the need for professional human resources in this field. By performing their job and working in teams, they learned how to adapt their skills to the new field and were taught by other practitioners about the common practices and basic "lingo" of health communication. In the mid-90s, and in response to the increasing demand for health communication professionals, several schools in the United States started their own curricular programs and/or "concentrations" in Health Communication. This helped bring more attention from the academic world to this emerging field. The number of peer-reviewed articles and several other types of health communication publications increased. The field moved from in-service training to pre-service education.

As a result, there is an increasing understanding that "the level of technical competence of communication practitioners can affect outcomes." A structured approach to health communications planning, a spotless program execution, and a rigorous evaluation process are the result of adequate competencies and relevant training, which are supported by leading organizations and agendas in different fields (Association of Schools of public Health, 2007; US Department of Health and Human Services, 2012b; American Medical Association, 2006; Hospitals and Health Network, 2012; National Board of Public Health

Examiners, 2011). "In health communication, the learning process is a lifetime endeavor and should be facilitated by the continuous development of new training initiatives and tools" (Schiavo, 2006). Training may start in the academic setting but should always be influenced and complemented by practical experience and observations, and other learning opportunities, including in-service training, continuing professional education, and ongoing mentoring.

Health communication can reach its highest potential when it is discussed and applied within a team-oriented context that includes public health, health care, community development, and other professionals from different sectors and disciplines. Teamwork and mutual agreement, on both the intervention's ultimate objectives and expected results, are key to the successful design, implementation, and impact of any program.

Finally, it is important to remember that there is no magic fix that can address health issues. Health communication is an evolving discipline and should always incorporate lessons learned as well as use a multidisciplinary approach to all interventions. This is in line with one of the fundamental premises of this book that recognizes the experience of practitioners as a key factor in developing theories, models, and approaches that should guide and inform health communication planning, implementation, and assessment.

Table 13.2 lists the key elements of health communication, which are further analyzed in the following sections.

People-Centered

Health communication is a long-term process that begins and ends with people's needs and preferences. In health communication, intended audiences should not be merely a *target* (even if this terminology is used by many practitioners from around the world primarily to indicate that a communication intervention will focus on, benefit, and engage a specific group of people that shares similar characteristics—such as age, socioeconomics, and ethnicity. It does not necessarily imply lack of audience participation) but an active participant in the process of analyzing and prioritizing the health issue, finding culturally appropriate and cost-effective solutions, and becoming effectively engaged as the lead change designer in the planning, implementation, and assessment of all interventions. This is why the term *key group* may better

Table 13.2	Key Characteristics of Health Communication

- People-centered
- Evidence-based
- Multidisciplinary
- Strategic
- Process-oriented
- Cost-effective
- Creative in support of strategy
- Audience- and media-specific
- Relationship building
- Aimed at behavioral and social results
- Inclusive of vulnerable and underserved groups

represent the role communities, teachers, parents, health care professionals, religious and community leaders, women, and many other key groups and stakeholders from a variety of segments of society and professional sectors should assume in the communication process. Yet, different organizations may have different cultural preferences for specific terminology even within the context of their participatory models and planning frameworks.

In implementing a people-centered approach to communication, researching communities and other key groups is a necessary but often not sufficient step because the effectiveness and sustainability of most interventions is often linked to the level of engagement of their key beneficiaries and those who influence them. Engaging communities and different sectors is often accomplished in health communication practice by working together with organizations and leaders who represent them or by directly involving members of a specific community at the outset of program design. For example, if a health communication intervention aims to reach and benefit breast cancer survivors, all strategies and key program elements should be designed, discussed, prioritized, tested, implemented, and evaluated together with membership organizations, patient groups, leaders, and patients who can speak for survivors and represent their needs and preferences. Most important, these groups need to feel invested and well represented. They should be the key protagonists of the action-oriented process that will lead to behavioral or social change.

Evidence-Based

Health communication is grounded in research. Successful health communication interventions are based on a true understanding not only of key groups but also of situations and sociopolitical environments. This includes existing programs and lessons learned, policies, social norms, key issues, work and living environments, and obstacles in addressing the specific health problem. The overall premise of health communication is that behavioral and social change is conditioned by the environment in which people live and work, as well as by those who influence them. Several socially determined factors (also referred to as **social determinants of health**)—including socioeconomic conditions, race, ethnicity, culture, as well as having access to health care services, a built environment that supports physical activity, neighborhoods with accessible and affordable nutritious food, health information that's culturally appropriate and accurately reflects literacy levels, and caring and friendly clinical settings—influence and are influenced by health communication (Association of Schools of Public Health, 2007). This requires a comprehensive research approach that relies on traditional, online, and new media-based research techniques for the formal development of a **situation analysis** (a planning term that describes the analysis of individual, social, political, environmental, community-specific, and behavior-related factors that can affect attitudes, behaviors, social norms, and policies about a health issue and its potential solutions) and **audience analysis** (a comprehensive, research-based, participatory, and strategic analysis of all key groups' characteristics, demographics, needs, preferences, values, social norms, attitudes, and behavior). The **audience profile**, a report on all findings, is the culminating step of a process of effective engagement and participation that involve all key groups and stakeholders in the overall analysis). Situation and audience analyses are fundamental and interrelated steps of health communication planning (the audience analysis is described in this book as a component of the situation analysis), which should be participatory and empowering in their nature.

Multidisciplinary

Health communication is "transdisciplinary in nature" (Bernhardt, 2004, p. 2051; Institute of Medicine, 2003b) and draws on multiple disciplines (Bernhardt, 2004; WHO, 2003). Health communication recognizes the complexity of attaining behavioral and social change and uses a multifaceted approach that is grounded in the application of several theoretical frameworks and disciplines, including health education, social marketing, behavioral and social change theories, and medical and clinical models. It draws on principles successfully used in the nonprofit and corporate sectors and also on the people-centered approach of other disciplines, such as psychology, sociology, and anthropology (WHO, 2003). It is not anchored to a single specific theory or model. With people always at the core of each intervention, it uses a case-by-case approach in selecting those models, theories, and strategies that are best suited to reach their hearts; secure their involvement in the health issue and, most important, its solutions; and support and facilitate their journey on a path to better health.

Piotrow, Rimon, Payne Merritt, and Saffitz (2003) identify four different "eras" of health communication:

> (1) The *clinic era*, based on a medical care model and the notion that if people knew where services were located they would find their way to the clinics; (2) the *field era*, a more proactive approach emphasizing outreach workers, community-based distribution, and a variety of information, education, and communication (IEC) products; (3) the *social marketing era*, developed from the commercial concepts that consumers will buy the products they want at subsidized prices; and, (4) … the era of *strategic behavior communications*, founded on behavioral science models that emphasize the need to influence social norms and policy environments to facilitate and empower the iterative and dynamic process of both individual and social change, (pp. 1–2)

More recently, health communication has evolved toward a fifth "era" of strategic communication for behavioral and social change that rightly emphasizes and combines behavioral and social science models and disciplines along with marketing, medical, and social norms-based models, and aims at achieving long-lasting behavioral and social results. However, even in the context of each different health communication era, many of the theoretical approaches of other periods still find use in program planning or execution. For example, the situation analysis of a health communication program still uses commercial and social marketing tools and models—even if combined with community dialogue and other participatory or new media-based methods—to analyze the environment in which change should occur. Instead, in the early stages of approaching key opinion leaders and other key **stakeholders** (all individuals and groups who have an interest or share responsibilities in a given issue, such as policymakers, community leaders, and community members), keeping in mind McGuire's steps about communication for persuasion (1984; see Chapter Two), may help communicators gain stakeholder support for the importance or the urgency of adequately addressing a health issue. This theoretical flexibility should keep communicators focused on key groups and stakeholders and always on the lookout for the best approach and planning framework to achieve behavioral and social results by engaging and empowering people. In concert with the other features previously discussed, it also enables the overall communication process to be truly fluid and suited to respond to people's needs.

The importance of a somewhat flexible theoretical basis, which should be selected on a case-by-case basis (National Cancer Institute, 2005a), is already supported by reputable organizations and authors. For example, publications by the US Department of Health and Human Services (2002), and the National Cancer Institute at the National Institutes of Health (2002) points to the importance of selecting planning frameworks that "can help [communicators] identify the social science theories most appropriate for understanding the problem and the situation" (National Cancer Institute at the National Institutes of Health, 2002, p. 218). These theories, models, and constructs include several theoretical concepts and frameworks that are also used in motivating change at individual and interpersonal levels or organizational, community, and societal levels (National Cancer Institute at the National Institutes of Health, 2002) by related or complementary disciplines.

The goal here is not to advocate for a lack of theoretical structure in communication planning and execution. On the contrary, planning frameworks, models, and theories should be consistent at least until preliminary steps of the evaluation phase of a program are completed. This allows communicators to take advantage of lessons learned and redefine theoretical constructs and **communication objectives** (the intermediate steps that need to be achieved in order to meet program goals and outcome objectives; National Cancer Institute, 2002) by comparing **program outcomes,** which measure changes in knowledge, attitudes, skills, behavior, and other parameters, with those that were anticipated in the planning phase. However, the ability to draw on multiple disciplines and theoretical constructs is a definitive advantage of the health communication field and one of the keys to the success of well-planned and well-executed communication programs.

Strategic

Health communication programs need to display a sound strategy and plan of action. All activities need to be well planned and respond to a specific audience-related need. Consider the example of Bonnie, a twenty-five-year-old mother who is not sure about whether to immunize her newborn child. Activities in support of a strategy that focuses on facilitating communication between Bonnie and her health care provider make sense only if evidence shows all or any of the following points: (1) Bonnie is likely to be influenced primarily, or at least significantly, by her health care provider and not by family or other new mothers; (2) there are several gaps in the understanding of patients' needs that prevent health care providers from communicating effectively; (3) providers lack adequate tools to talk about this topic with patients in a time-effective and efficient manner; (4) research data have been validated by community dialogue and other participatory methods that are inclusive of Bonnie and her peers; and (5) Bonnie and her peers and organizations that represent them have participated in designing all interventions.

Communication strategies (the overall approach used to accomplish the communication objectives) need to be research-based, and all activities should serve such strategies. Therefore, we should not rely on any workshop, press release, brochure, video, or anything else to provide effective communication without making sure that its content and format reflect the selected approach (the strategy), and that this is a priority to reach people's hearts. For this purpose, health communication strategies need to respond to an actual need that has been identified by preliminary research and confirmed by the intended audience.

Process-Oriented

Communication is a long-term process. Influencing people and their behaviors requires an ongoing commitment to the health issue and its solutions. This is rooted in a deep understanding of key groups, communities, and their environments, and aims at building consensus among affected groups, community members, and key stakeholders about the potential plan of action.

Most, if not all, health communication programs change or evolve from what communication experts may have originally envisioned due to the input and participation of communities, key opinion leaders, patient groups, professional associations, policymakers, community members, and other key stakeholders.

In health communication, engaging key groups on relevant health issues as well as exploring suitable ways to address them is only the first step of a long-term, people-centered process. This process often requires theoretical flexibility to accommodate people's needs, preferences, and priorities.

While in the midst of many process-oriented projects, many practitioners may have noticed that health communication is often misunderstood. Health communication uses multiple channels and approaches, which, despite what some people may think, include but are not limited to the use of the mass media or new media. Moreover, health communication aims at improving health outcomes and in the process help advance public health and community development goals or create market share (depending on whether health communication strategies are used for nonprofit or for-profit goals) or encourages compliance to clinical recommendations and healthy lifestyles. Finally, health communication cannot focus only on channels, messages, and media. It also should attempt to involve and create consensus and feelings of ownership among intended audiences.

Exchange, a networking and learning program on health communication for development that is based in the United Kingdom and has multiple partners, views health communication as "a process for partnership and participation that is based on two-way dialogue, where there is an interactive interchange of information, ideas, techniques, and knowledge between senders and receivers of information on an equal footing, leading to improved understanding, shared knowledge, greater consensus, and identification of possible effective action" (2005). This definition makes sense in all settings and situations, but it assumes a greater relevance for health communication programs that aim to improve health outcomes in developing countries. Communication for development often needs to rely on creative solutions that compensate for the lack of local capabilities and infrastructure. These solutions usually emerge after months of discussion with local community leaders and organizations, government officials, and representatives of public and community groups. Word of mouth and the ability of community leaders to engage members of their own communities is often all that communicators have at hand.

Consider the case of Maria, a mother of four children who lives in a small village in sub-Saharan Africa together with her seventy-five-year-old father. Her village is almost completely isolated from major metropolitan areas, and very few people in town have a radio or know how to read. Maria is unaware that malaria, which is endemic in that region, poses a higher risk to children than to the elderly. Because elderly people benefit from a high hierarchical status in that region, if Maria is able to find money to purchase mosquito nets to protect someone in her family from mosquito bites and the consequent threat of malaria, she would probably choose that her father sleep under them, leaving her children unprotected. This is despite the high mortality rate from malaria among children in her village. If her village's community leaders told her to do otherwise, she would likely change her practice and protect her children. This may be the first building block toward the development and adoption of new social norms not only by Maria but also her peers and other community members.

Involving Maria's community leaders and peers in the communication process that would lead to a potential change in her habits requires long-term commitment. Such effort demands the involvement of local organizations and authorities who are respected and trusted by community leaders, as well as an open mind in listening to suggestions and seeking solutions with the help of all key stakeholders. Because of the lack of local capabilities and limited access to adequate communication channels, this process is likely to take longer than any similar initiative in the developed world. Therefore, communicators should view this as an ongoing process and applaud every small step forward.

Cost-Effective

Cost-effectiveness is a concept that health communication borrows from commercial and social marketing. It is particularly important in the competitive working environment of public health and nonprofit organizations, where the lack of sufficient funds or adequate economic planning can often undermine important initiatives. It implies the need to seek solutions that allow communicators to advance their goals with minimal use of human and economic resources. Yet, communicators should use their funds as long as they are well spent and advance their evidence-based strategy. They should also seek creative solutions that minimize the use of internal funds and human resources by seeking partnerships, using existing materials or programs as a starting point, and maximizing synergies with the work of other departments in their organization or external groups and stakeholders in the same field.

Creative in Support of Strategy

Creativity is a significant attribute of communicators because it allows them to consider multiple options, formats, and media channels to reach and engage different groups. It also helps them devise solutions that preserve the sustainability and cost-effectiveness of specific health communication interventions. However, even the greatest ideas or the best-designed and best-executed communication tools may fail to achieve behavioral or social results if they do not respond to a strategic need identified by research data and validated by key stakeholders from intended groups. Too often communication programs and resources fail to make an impact because of this common mistake.

For example, developing and distributing a brochure on how to use insecticide-treated nets (ITNs) makes sense only if the intended community is already aware of the cycle of malaria transmission as well as the need for protection from mosquito bites. If this is not the case and most community members still believe that malaria is contracted by bathing in the river or is a complication of some other fevers (Pinto, 1998; Schiavo, 1998, 2000), the first strategic imperative is disease awareness, with a specific focus on the cycle of transmission and subsequent protective measures. All communication materials and activities need to address this basic information need before talking about the use of ITNs and reasons to use them as an alternative to other potential protection methods. Creativity should come into play in devising culturally friendly tools to start sharing information about malaria and to engage community members in designing a community-specific communication intervention that would encourage protective behaviors and would benefit the overall community. In a nutshell, we should refrain from using creativity to develop and implement great, sensational, or innovative ideas when these do not respond to people's needs and key strategic priorities of the health communication intervention.

Audience- and Media-Specific

The importance of audience-specific messages and channels became one of the most important lessons learned after the anthrax-by-mail bioterrorist attacks that rocked the United States in October 2001. At the time, several letters containing the lethal agent *Bacillus anthracis* were mailed to senators and representatives of the media (Jernigan and others, 2002; Blanchard and others, 2005). The attack also exposed government staff workers, including US postal workers in the US Postal Service facility in Washington, DC, and other parts of the country, to anthrax. Two workers in the Washington facility died as a result of anthrax inhalation (Blanchard and others, 2005).

Communication during this emergency was perceived by several members of the medical, patient, and worker communities as well as public figures and the media to be often inconsistent and disorganized (Blanchard and others, 2005; Vanderford, 2003). Equally important, postal workers and US Senate staff have reported erosion of their trust in public health agencies (Blanchard and others, 2005). Several analyses point to the possibility that the *one message-one behavior approach* to communication (UCLA Department of Epidemiology, 2002)—in other words, using the same message and strategic approach for all audiences, which is likely to result in the same unspecific behavior that may not be relevant to specific communities or groups—led to feelings of being left out among postal workers, who in the Brentwood facility in Washington, DC, were primarily African Americans or individuals with a severe hearing impairment (Blanchard and others, 2005). They also point to the need for public health officials to develop the relationships that are needed to communicate with groups of different racial and socioeconomic backgrounds as well as "those with physical limitations that could hinder communication, such as those with hearing impairments" (Blanchard and others, 2005, p. 494; McEwen and Anton-Culver, 1988).

The lessons learned from the anthrax scare support some of the fundamental principles of good health communication practices. Messages need to be key group-specific and tailored to channels allowing the most effective reach, including among vulnerable and underserved groups. Because it is very likely that communication efforts may aim at producing multiple key group-appropriate behaviors, the one message-one behavior approach should be avoided (UCLA Department of Epidemiology, 2002) even when time and resources are lacking. As highlighted by the anthrax case study, in developing audience-specific messages and activities, the contribution of local advocates and community representatives is fundamental to increase the likelihood that messages will be heard, understood, and trusted by intended audiences.

Relationship Building

Communication is a relationship business. Establishing and preserving good relationships is critical to the success of health communication interventions, and, among other things, can help build long-term and successful partnerships and coalitions, secure credible stakeholder endorsement of the health issue, and expand the pool of ambassadors on behalf of the health cause.

Most important, good relationships help create the environment of "shared meanings and understanding" (Pearson and Nelson, 1991, p. 6) that is central to achieving social or behavioral results at the individual, community, and population levels. Good relationships should be established with key stakeholders and representatives of key groups, health organizations, community-based organizations, governments, and many other. critical members of the extended health communication team.

Aimed at Behavioral and Social Results

Nowadays, we are transitioning from the "era of strategic behavior communications" (Piotrow, Rimon, Payne Merritt, and Saffitz, 2003, p. 2) to the *era of behavioral and social impact communication*. Several US and international models and agenda (for example, *Healthy People 2020*, COMBI, Communication for Development; see Chapter Two) support the importance of a behavioral and social change-driven mind-set in developing health communication interventions. Although the ultimate goal of health communication has always been influencing behaviors, social norms, and policies (with the latter often being instrumental in institutionalizing social change and norms), there is a renewed emphasis on the importance of establishing behavioral and social objectives early on in the design of health communication interventions.

"What do you want people to do?" is the first question that should be asked in communication planning meetings. Do you want them to immunize their children before age two? Become aware of their risk for heart disease and behave accordingly to prevent it? Ask their dentists about oral cancer screening? Do you want local legislators to support a stricter law on the use of infant car seats? Or communities and special groups to create an environment of peer-to-peer support designed to discourage adolescents from initiating smoking? Or encourage people from different sectors (for example, employers, clinicians, etc.) to provide social support and tools to members of underserved communities so they are more likely to adopt and sustain a healthy lifestyle? Answering these kinds of questions is the first step in identifying suitable and research-based objectives of a communication program.

Although different theories may specifically support the importance of either behavioral or social results as key outcome indicators, these two parameters are actually interconnected. In fact, social change typically takes place as the result of a series of behavioral results at the individual, group, community, social, and political levels.

Inclusive of Vulnerable and Underserved Groups

With a precise mandate from *Healthy People 2020* and the fact that several international organizations, such as UNICEF, have been investing overtime in rolling out an equity-based approach to programming, health communication is increasingly considered a key field that can contribute to a reduction of **health disparities** ("diseases or health conditions that discriminate and tend to be more common and more severe among vulnerable and underserved populations" [Health Equity Initiative, 2012b]; or overall differences in health outcomes) and an advancement of health equity. Therefore, health communication programs need to be mindful and inclusive of vulnerable and underserved populations. Such inclusiveness is not only limited to making sure that programs intended for the general population or specific communities also have a measurable impact on disadvantaged groups but it also entails that such groups are involved in the planning, implementation, and evaluation of all interventions so that their voices are heard and considered as part of the overall communication process. This is also important to build leadership capacity among vulnerable and underserved groups so they can adequately address current and future health and community development topics and find their own solutions to pressing issues.

THE HEALTH COMMUNICATION ENVIRONMENT

When looking at the health communication environment where change should occur and be sustained (Figure 13.1), it becomes clear that effective communication can be a powerful tool in seeking to influence all of the factors that are highlighted in the figure. It is also clear that regardless of whether these factors are related to the audience, health behavior, product, service, social, or political environment, all of them are interconnected and can mutually affect each other. At the same time, health communication interventions can tip the existing balance among these factors, and change the weight they may have in defining a specific health issue and its solutions as well as within the living, working, and aging environment of the people we seek to reach and engage in the health communication process.

Figure 13.1 also reflects some of the key principles of marketing models as well as the socioecological model (Morris, 1975), behavioral and social sciences constructs, and other theoretical models (VanLeeuwen, Waltner-Toews, Abernathy, and Smit, 1999) that are used in public health, health care, global health, and other fields to show the connection and influence of different factors (individual, interpersonal, community, sociopolitical, organizational, and public policy) on individual, group, and community behavior as well as to understand the process that may lead to behavioral and social results.

Figure 13.1 | The Health Communication Environment

Communicatioin and Other Key Groups
Healthy beliefs, attitudes, and behaviour
Gender-related factors
Literacy levels
Risk factors
lifestyle issues
Socioeconomic factors
Living and working environments
Access to service and information

Political Environment
Policies, laws
Political willingness
and commitment
Levels of priority in
Political agenda

HEALTHA COMMUNICATION

Recommended Health or social Behaviour, Service, or Product
Benefits
Risks
Disadvantages
Price or lifestyle trade-off
Availability and access
Cultural and social acceptance

Social Environment
Stakesholders'beliefs, attitudes, and practices
Social norms and practies
Social structure
Social support
Existing initiatives and programs

HEALTH COMMUNICATION IN PUBLIC HEALTH, HEALTH CARE, AND COMMUNITY DEVELOPMENT

Prior to the recent call to action by many federal and multilateral organizations, which encouraged a strategic and more frequent use of communication, health communication was used only marginally in a variety of sectors. It was perceived more as a skill than a discipline and confined to the mere dissemination of scientific and medical findings by public health and other professionals (Bernhardt, 2004). This section reviews current thinking on the role of health communication in public health, health care settings, and community development, and also serves as a reminder of the need for increased collaboration among these important sectors.

Health Communication in Public Health

Health communication is a well-recognized discipline in public health. Many public health organizations and leaders (Bernhardt, 2004; Freimuth, Cole, and Kirby, 2000; Institute of Medicine, 2002, 2003b; National Cancer Institute at the National Institutes of Health, 2002; Piotrow, Kincaid, Rimon, and Rinehart, 1997; Rimal and Lapinski, 2009; US Department of Health and Human Services, 2005,2012b) understand and recognize the role that health communication can play in advancing health outcomes and the general health status of interested populations and special groups. Most important, there is a new awareness of the reach of health communication as well as its many strategic action areas (for example, interpersonal communication, professional medical communications, community mobilization and citizen engagement, and mass media and new media communication).

As defined by *Healthy People 2010* (US Department of Health and Human Services, 2005), in the US public health agenda, the scope of health communication in public health "includes disease prevention, health promotion, health care policy, and the business of health care as well as enhancement of the quality of life and health of individuals within the community" (p. 11–20; Ratzan and others, 1994). Health communication "links the domains of communication and health" (p. 11–13) and is regarded as a science (Freimuth and Quinn, 2004; Bernhardt, 2004) of great importance in public health, especially in the era of epidemics and emerging diseases, the increasing toll of chronic diseases, the aging of large segments and percentages of the population of many countries, urbanization, increased disparities and socioeconomic divides, global threats, bioterrorism, and a new emphasis on a preventive and patient-centered approach to health. Finally, *Healthy People 2020* establishes health communication as a key discipline in contributing to advance health equity (US Department of Health and Human Resources, 2012b).

Health Communication in Health Care Settings

Health communication has an invaluable role within health care settings. Although provider-patient communications—which is perhaps the best known and most important use of communication within health care settings—it is worth mentioning here that communication is also used to coordinate the activities of interdependent health care providers, encourage the widespread use of best clinical practices, promote the application of scientific advancements, and overall to administer complex and multisectoral health care delivery systems.

As *Healthy People 2020* suggests, by combining effective health communication processes and integrating them with new technology and tools, there is the potential to

- Improve health care quality and safety.
- Increase the efficiency of health care and public health service delivery.
- Improve the public health information infrastructure.
- Support care in the community and at home.
- Facilitate clinical and consumer decision-making.
- Build health skills and knowledge (US Department of Health and Human Services, 2012b).

Among other things, *Healthy People 2020's* recommendations reflect the support many reputable voices and organizations—in the United States and globally—have lent to the need for effective integration of the work and strategies from our public health and health care systems.

Health Communication in Community Development

As previously mentioned, health is influenced by many different factors and is not only the mere absence of illness. Health is a state of well-being that includes the physical, psychological, and social aspects of life, which in turn are influenced by the environment in which we live, work, grow, and age.

Community development refers to a field of research and practice that involves community members, average citizens, professionals, grant-makers, and others in improving various aspects of local communities. More traditionally, community development interventions have been dealing with providing and increasing access to adequate transportation, jobs, and other socioeconomic opportunities, education, and different kinds of infrastructure (for example, parks, community centers, etc.) within a given community or population. Yet, because all of these interventions or factors are greatly connected to people's ability to stay healthy or effectively cope with disease and emergency, many organizations have been calling for increased collaboration among the community development, health care, and public health fields (Braunstein and Lavizzo-Mourey, 2011).

Health communication can play a key role in moving forward such a collaborative agenda. It can help bridge organizational cultures and showcase relevant synergies among the works of public health, health care, and community development organizations and professionals; increase awareness on how key social determinants of health influence health outcomes; establish "good health," and more in general health equity, as key determinants of socioeconomic development; and engage and mobilize professionals from different sectors to take action. Health communication can be instrumental in empowering community members and professionals from different sectors to implement such cross-sectoral collaborative agenda, which would benefit different communities and populations in the United States and globally. We will continue to explore this important theme throughout the book.

THE ROLE OF HEALTH COMMUNICATION IN THE MARKETING MIX

As mentioned, health communication strategies are integral to a variety of interventions in different contexts. In the private sector, health communication strategies are primarily used in a marketing context. Still, many of the other behavioral and social constructs of health communication—and definitely the models that position people at the center of any communication intervention—are considered and used at least at an empirical level. As in other settings (for example, public health), health communication functions tend to be similar to those described in the "What Health Communication Can and Cannot Do" section of this chapter.

Many in the private sector regard health communication as a critical component of the marketing mix, which is traditionally defined by the key four Ps of social marketing product, price, place, and promotion—in other words, "developing, delivering, and promoting a superior offer" (Maibach, 2003).

OVERVIEW OF KEY COMMUNICATION AREAS

Global health communication is a term increasingly used to include different communication approaches and action areas, such as interpersonal communication, social and community mobilization, and advocacy (Haider, 2005; Waisbord and Larson, 2005). Well-planned health communication programs rely on an integrated blend of different action areas that should be selected in consideration of expected behavioral and social outcomes (WHO, 2003; O'Sullivan, Yonlder, Morgan, and Merritt, 2003; Health Communication Partnership, 2005a). Long-term results can be achieved only through an engagement process that involves key groups and stakeholders, implements participatory approaches to research, and uses culturally appropriate action areas and communication channels. Remember that there is no magic fix in health communication.

Message repetitiveness and frequency are also important factors in health communication. Often the resonance effect, which can be defined as the ability to create a snowball effect for message delivery by using multiple vehicles, sources, and messengers, can help motivate people to change by reminding them of the desired behavior (for example, complying with childhood immunization requirements, using mosquito nets for protection against malaria, attempting to quit smoking) and its benefits. To this end, several action areas are usually used in health communication and are described in detail in the topic-specific chapters in Part Two:

- *Interpersonal communication*, which uses interpersonal channels (for example, one-on-one or group meetings), and is based on active listening, social and behavioral theories, as well as the ability to relate to, and identify with, the audience's needs and cultural preferences and efficiently address them. This includes "personal selling and counseling" (WHO, 2003, p. 2), which takes place during one-on-one encounters with members of key groups and other key stakeholders, as well as during group events and in locations where materials and services are available. It also includes provider-patient communications—which has been identified as one of the most important areas of health communication (US Department of Health and Human Services, 2005) and should aim at improving health outcomes by optimizing the relationships between providers and their patients, and community dialogue, which is an example of interpersonal communication at scale and is used in research and practice to solicit community input and engage and empower participants throughout the communication process.
- *Mass media and new media communication*, which relies on the skillful use of culturally competent and audience-appropriate mass media, new media, and social media, as well as other communication channels to place a health issue on the public agenda, raise awareness of its root causes and risk factors, advocate for its solutions, or highlight its importance so that key stakeholders, groups, communities, or the public at large take action.
- *Community mobilization and citizen engagement*, a bottom-up and participatory process that at times more formally includes methods for public

consultations and citizen engagement. By using multiple communication channels, community mobilization seeks to involve community leaders and the community at large in addressing a health issue, participating in determining key steps to behavioral or social change, or practicing a desired behavior.

- *Professional medical communications,* a peer-to-peer approach intended to reach and engage health care professionals that aims to (1) promote the adoption of best medical and health practices; (2) establish new concepts and standards of care; (3) publicize recent medical discoveries, beliefs, parameters, and policies; (4) change or establish new medical priorities; and (5) advance health policy changes, among other goals.

- *Constituency relations and strategic partnerships in health communication,* a critical component of all other areas of health communication as well as a communication area of its own. Constituency relations refers to the process of (1) creating consensus among key stakeholders about health issues and their potential solutions, (2) expanding program reach by involving key constituencies, (3) developing alliances, (4) managing and anticipating criticisms and opponents, and (5) maintaining key relationships with other health organizations or stakeholders. Effective constituency relations often lead to strategic and multisectoral partnerships.

- *Policy communication and public advocacy,* which include government relations, policy briefing and communication, public advocacy, and media advocacy, and use multiple communication channels, venues, and media to influence the beliefs, attitudes, and behavior of policymakers, and consequently the adoption, implementation, and sustainability of different policies and funding streams for specific issues.

THE HEALTH COMMUNICATION CYCLE

The importance of a rigorous, theory-driven, and systematic approach to the design, implementation, and evaluation of health communication interventions has been established by several reputable organizations in the United States and globally (Association of Schools of Public Health, 2007; US Department of Health and Human Services, 2012b; WHO, 2003).

As previously mentioned in the book's introduction, Part Three provides detailed step-by-step guidance on health communication planning, implementation, and evaluation and at the same time also highlights the cyclical and interdependent nature of different phases of health communication interventions. Figure 13.2 briefly describes key phases of health communication planning and introduces the basic planning framework that is discussed in detail in Part Three. Figure 13.2 also shows how strategic Banning is directly connected to the other two stages of the health communication cycle (program implementation and monitoring, and evaluation, feedback, and refinement).

Figure 13.2 The Health Communication Cycle

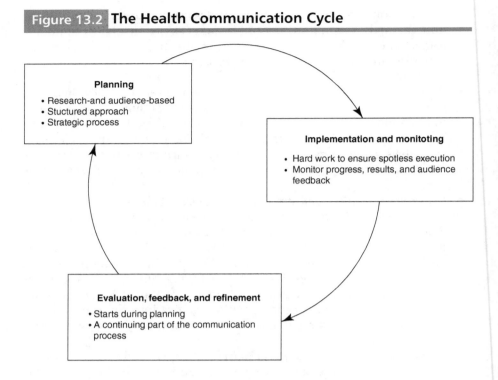

Planning
- Research-and audience-based
- Stuctured approach
- Strategic process

Implementation and monitoting
- Hard work to ensure spotless execution
- Monitor progress, results, and audience feedback

Evaluation, feedback, and refinement
- Starts during planning
- A continuing part of the communication process

WHAT HEALTH COMMUNICATION CAN AND CANNOT DO

Health communication cannot work in a vacuum and is usually a critical component of larger public health or community development interventions or corporate efforts. Because of the complexity of health issues, it may "not be equally effective in addressing all issues or relaying all messages" (National Cancer Institute at the National Institutes of Health, 2002, p. 3), at least in a given time frame.

Health communication cannot replace the lack of local infrastructure (such as the absence of appropriate health services or hospitals or other essential services that would provide communities with enhanced opportunities to stay healthy, as, for example, parks, adequate transportation systems, recreational facilities, bike-sharing programs, and stores that sell nutritious food) or capability (such as an inadequate number of health care providers in relation to the size of the population being attended). It cannot compensate for inadequate medical solutions to treat, diagnose, or prevent any disease. But it can help advocate for change and create a receptive environment to support the development of new health services or the allocation of additional funds for medical and scientific discovery, or access to existing treatments or community services, or the recruitment of health care professionals in new medical fields or underserved geographical areas. In doing so, it helps secure political commitment, stakeholder endorsement, and community involvement to encourage change, devise community-specific solutions, and improve health outcomes.

Because of the evolving role of health communication, other authors and organizations have been defining the potential contribution of health communication to the health care and public health fields. For example, the US National Cancer Institute at the National Institutes of Health (2002) has a homonymous section, which partly inspired the need for this section, in one of its publications on the topic.

Understanding the role and the potential impact of health communication is important to take full advantage of the contribution of this field to health and related social outcomes as well as to set realistic expectations on what can be accomplished among team members, program partners, key groups, and stakeholders. Table 13.3 provides examples of what health communication can and cannot do.

Table 13.3 **What Health Communication Can and Cannot Do**

Health Communication Can Help...	Health Communication Cannot...
Raise awareness of health issues and their root causes to drive policy or practice changes	Work in a vacuum, independent from other public health, health care, marketing, and community development interventions
Engage and empower communities and key groups	
Influence research agendas and priorities and support the need for additional funds for medical and scientific discovery	Replace the lack of local infrastructure, services, or capability
Increase understanding of the many socially determined factors that influence health and illness so they can be adequately addressed at the population and community levels	Compensate for the absence of adequate treat ment or diagnostic or preventive options or services
Encourage collaboration among different sectors, such as public health, community development, and health care	"Be equally effective in addressing all issues or relaying all messages," atleast in the same time frame (National Cancer Institute at the National Institutes of Health, 2002, p. 3)
Secure stakeholder endorsement of health and related social issues	
"Influence perceptions, beliefs and attitudes that may change social norms" (National Cancer Institute at the National Institutes of Health, 2002, p. 3)	
Promote data and emerging issues to establish new standards of care	
"Increase demand for health services" (National Cancer Institute at the National Institutes of Health, 2002, p. 3) and products	
Show benefits of and encourage behavior change	
"Demonstrate healthy skills" (National Cancer Institute at the National Institutes of Health, 2002, p. 3)	
Provoke public discussion to drive disease diagnosis, treatment, or prevention	
Suggest and "prompt action" (National Cancer Institute at the National Institutes of Health, 2002, p. 3)	

(continued)

| Table 13.3 | **What Health Communication Can and Cannot Do** (*continued*) |

Health Communication Can Help...	Health Communication Cannot...
Build constituencies to support health and social change across different sectors and communities	
Advocate for equal access to existing health products and services	
Strengthen third-party relationships	
Improve patient compliance and outcomes	

KEY CONCEPTS

- Health communication is a multifaceted and multidisciplinary field of research, theory, and practice. It is concerned with reaching different populations and groups to exchange health-related information, ideas, and methods in order to influence, engage, empower, and support different groups so that they will champion, introduce, adopt, or sustain a health or social behavior, practice, or policy that will ultimately improve individual, community, and public health outcomes.
- Health communication should be inclusive and representative also of vulnerable and underserved groups.
- Health communication is an increasingly prominent field in public health, health care, community development, and the private sector (both nonprofit and corporate).
- Health communication can play a key role in advancing health equity.
- Several socially determined factors (also referred to as *social determinants of health*) influence and are influenced by health communication.
- One of the key characteristics of health communication is its multidisciplinary nature, which allows the theoretical flexibility that is needed to consider and approach each situation and key group for their unique characteristics and needs.
- We are now in the era of behavioral and social impact communication. In fact, several US and international models and agendas support the importance of a behavioral and social change-driven mind-set in developing health communication interventions.
- Health communication is an evolving discipline that should always incorporate lessons learned and practical experiences. Practitioners should take an important role in defining theories and models to inform new directions in health communication.
- It is important to be aware of key features and limitations of health communication (and more specifically what communication can and cannot do).
- Health communication relies on several action areas.
- Well-designed programs are the result of an integrated blend of different areas that should be selected in light of expected behavioral and social outcomes.

FOR DISCUSSION AND PRACTICE

1. Did you have any preliminary idea about the definition and role of health communication prior to reading this chapter? If yes, how does it compare to what you have learned in this chapter?

2. In your opinion, what are the two most important defining features of health communication and why? How do they relate to the other key characteristics of health communication that are discussed in this chapter?

3. Can you recall a personal experience in which a health communication program, message, or health-related encounter (for example, a physician visit) has influenced your decisions or perceptions about a specific health issue? Describe the experience and emphasize key factors that affected your decision and health behavior.

4. Did you ever participate in the development or implementation of a health communication intervention? If yes, what were some of the key learnings and how do they relate to the attributes of health communication as described in this chapter?

5. Can you think of examples of health communication interventions that seek to benefit and address the needs of vulnerable and underserved groups in your neighborhood, community, city, and country? If yes, did you observe any results or impact among these groups?

CPSIA information can be obtained
at www.ICGtesting.com
Printed in the USA
LVHW060205140619
621128LV00001B/1/P

9 781524 992090